BEASTS *of* BURDEN™

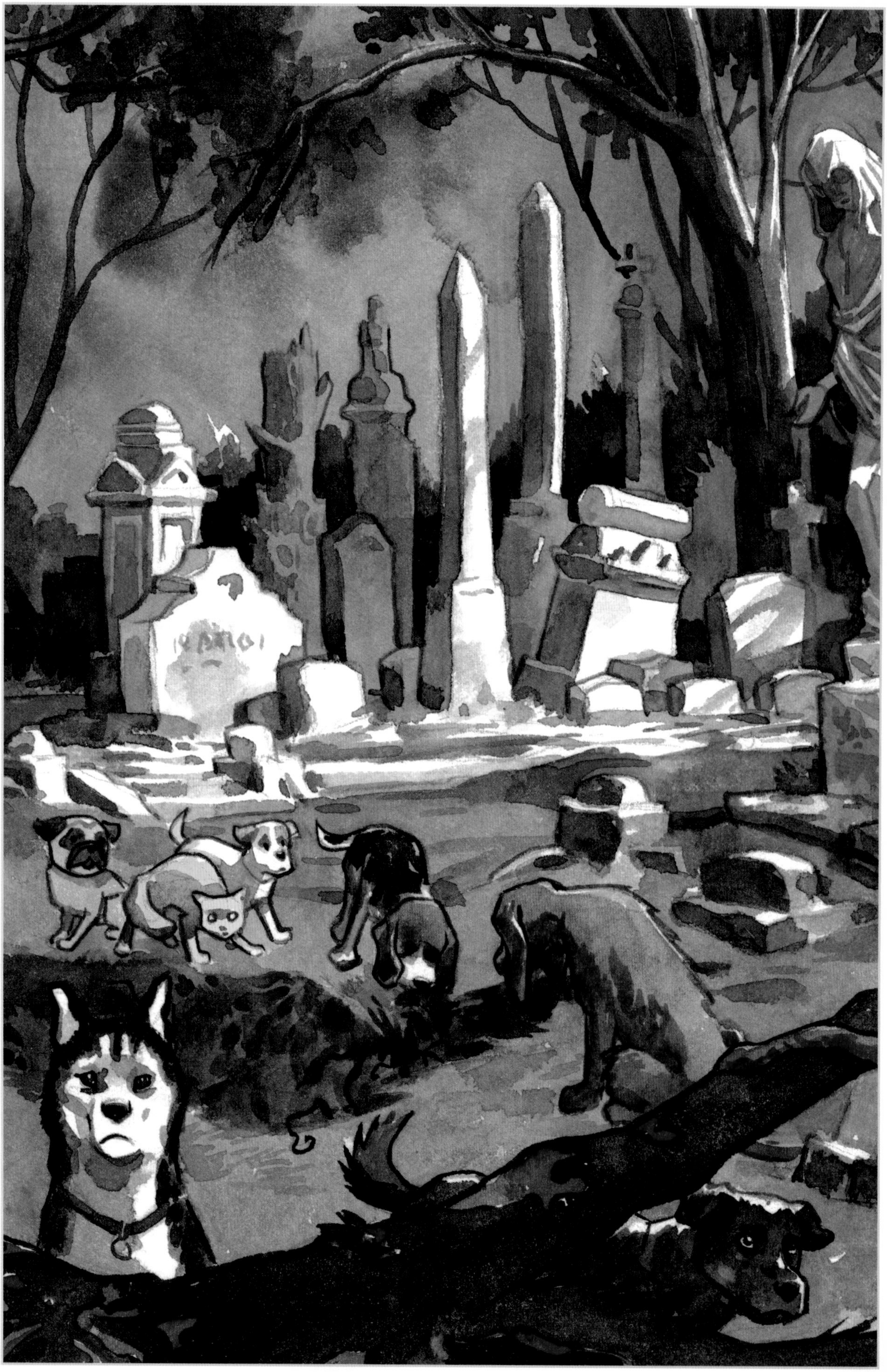

BEASTS *of* BURDEN™

ANIMAL RITES

Written by
EVAN DORKIN

✛

Art by
JILL THOMPSON

✛

Lettering by
JASON ARTHUR AND JILL THOMPSON

"A DOG AND HIS BOY" COWRITTEN BY SARAH DYER

DARK HORSE BOOKS®
MILWAUKIE, OREGON

TO **ARCHIE**, **SWEET** AS **SUGAR** AND **TOUGH** AS **NAILS**,
WHO ONCE SLEPT ON **EVAN'S FEET** ...
—J. T.

FOR **SARAH** AND **EMILY**. AND OF COURSE, **THE CATS**—
CRUSHY, **MIMSY**, AND THE MUCH-MISSED **MR. JINX** AND **PIXIE**.
—E. D.

President and Publisher **MIKE RICHARDSON**   Editor **SCOTT ALLIE**   Associate Editor **SIERRA HAHN**   Assistant Editors **DANIEL CHABON** AND **FREDDYE LINS**   Collection Designer **TINA ALESSI**

BEASTS OF BURDEN VOLUME 1: ANIMAL RITES

This volume reprints the comic-book series *Beasts of Burden* #1–#4 and "Stray" from *The Dark Horse Book of Hauntings*, "The Unfamiliar" from *The Dark Horse Book of Witchcraft*, "Let Sleeping Dogs Lie" from *The Dark Horse Book of the Dead*, and "A Dog and His Boy" from *The Dark Horse Book of Monsters*, all published by Dark Horse Comics.

Published by Dark Horse Books, a division of Dark Horse Comics, Inc.
10956 SE Main Street | Milwaukie, OR 97222 | darkhorse.com

To find a comics shop in your area, call the Comic Shop Locator Service toll-free at (888) 266-4226.

First edition: June 2010
ISBN 978-1-59582-513-1

3 5 7 9 10 8 6 4 2
Printed at Midas Printing International, Ltd., Huizhou, China

STRAY

No one remembers how many nights the summoning took.

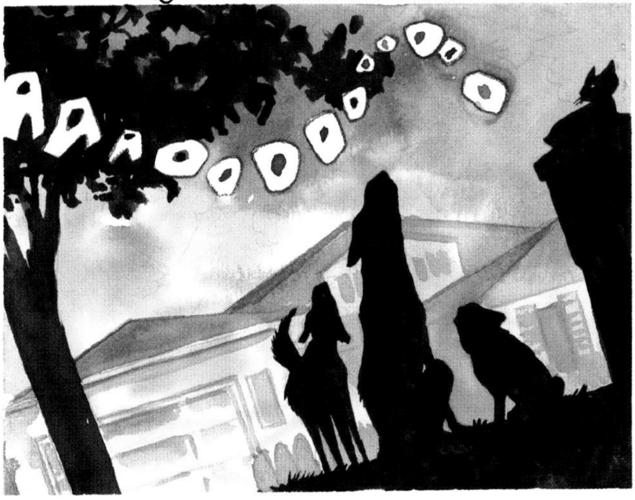

Some say as many as five, while others insist he arrived after the very first appeal.

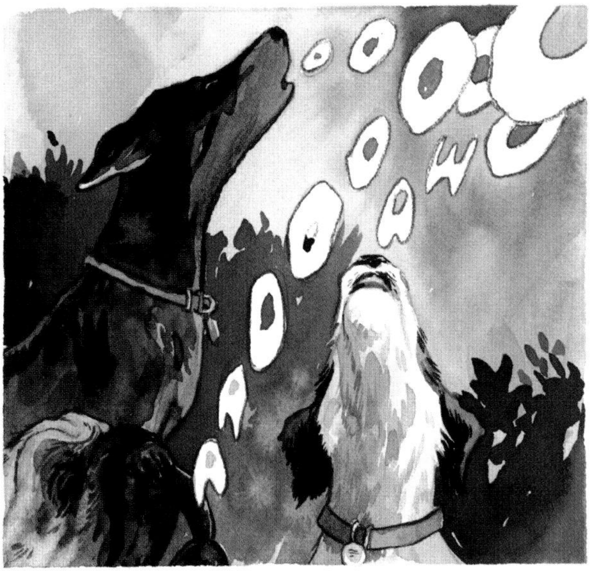

This is understandable, given the fact that dogs aren't exactly known for their keen sense of time.

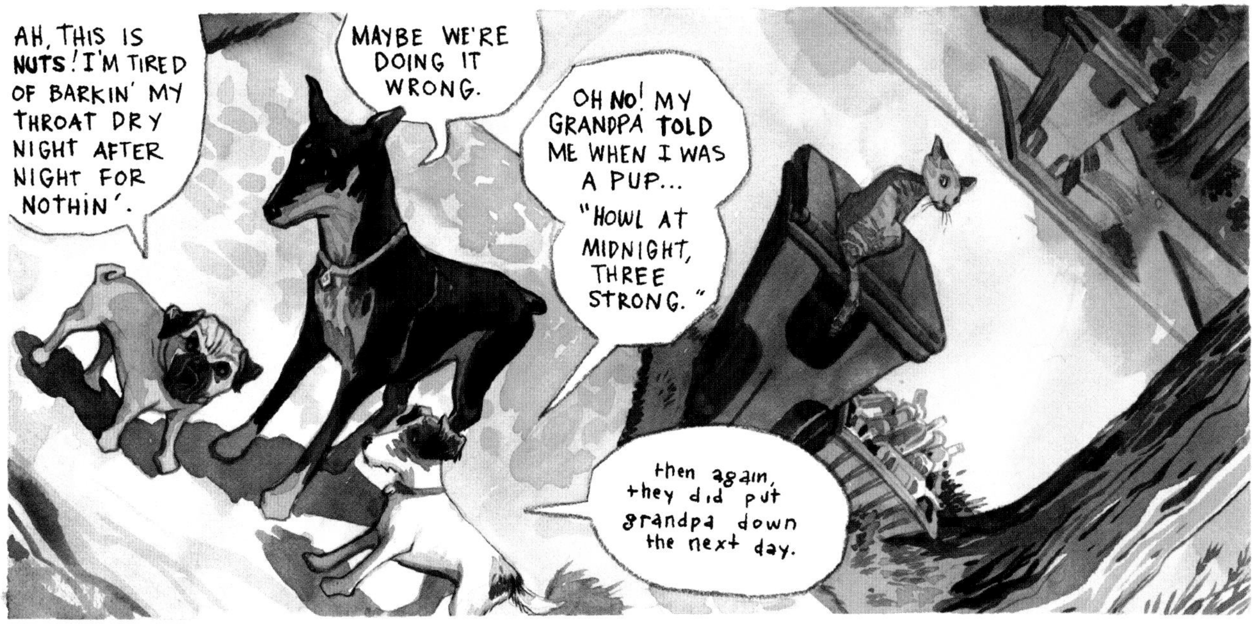

AH, THIS IS **NUTS**! I'M TIRED OF BARKIN' MY THROAT DRY NIGHT AFTER NIGHT FOR NOTHIN'.
MAYBE WE'RE DOING IT WRONG.
OH **NO**! MY GRANDPA **TOLD** ME WHEN I WAS A PUP... "HOWL AT MIDNIGHT, THREE STRONG."
then again, they did put grandpa down the next day.

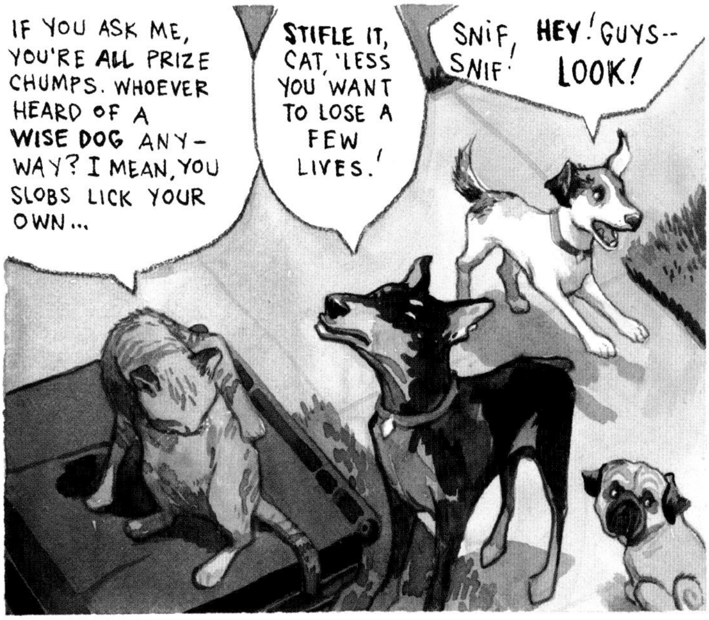

IF YOU ASK ME, YOU'RE **ALL** PRIZE CHUMPS. WHOEVER HEARD OF A **WISE DOG** ANY-WAY? I MEAN, YOU SLOBS LICK YOUR OWN...
STIFLE IT, CAT, 'LESS YOU WANT TO LOSE A FEW LIVES.
SNIF, SNIF!
HEY! GUYS-- **LOOK**!

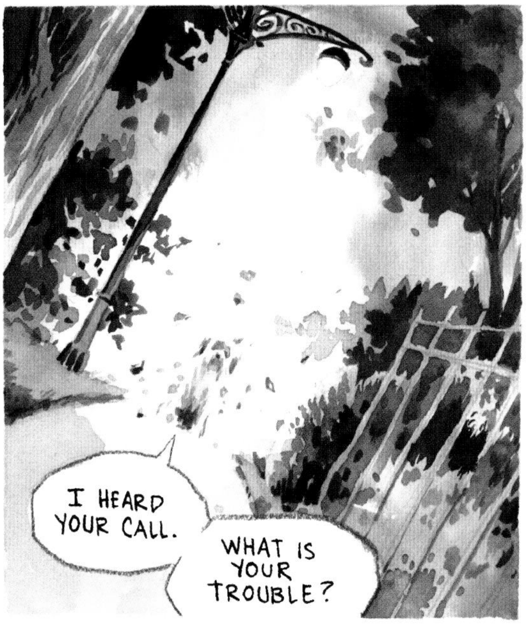

I HEARD YOUR CALL.
WHAT IS YOUR TROUBLE?

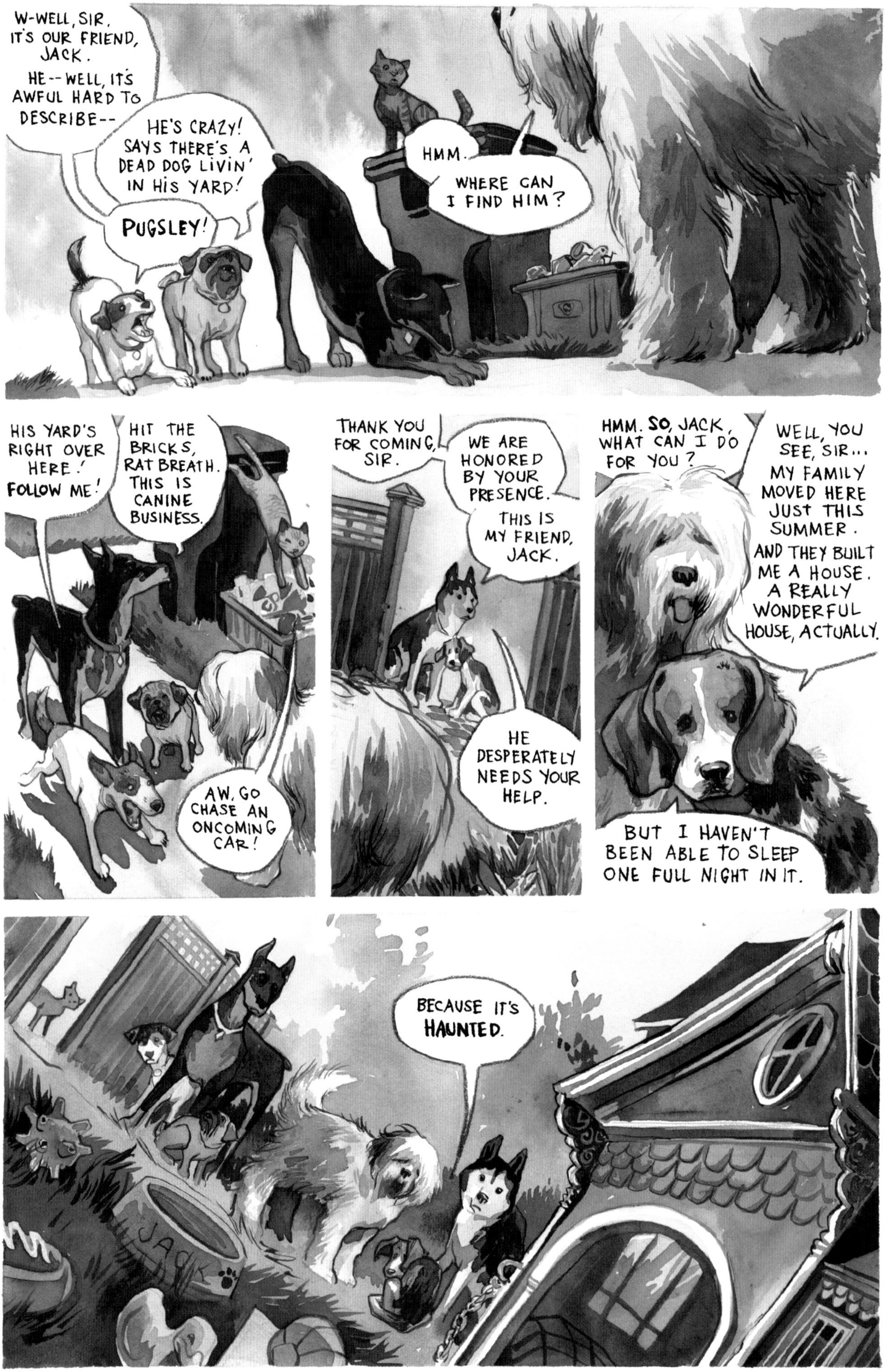
W-WELL, SIR, IT'S OUR FRIEND, JACK.
HE--WELL, IT'S AWFUL HARD TO DESCRIBE--
HE'S CRAZY! SAYS THERE'S A DEAD DOG LIVIN' IN HIS YARD!
PUGSLEY!
HMM.
WHERE CAN I FIND HIM?
HIS YARD'S RIGHT OVER HERE! FOLLOW ME!
HIT THE BRICKS, RAT BREATH. THIS IS CANINE BUSINESS.
AW, GO CHASE AN ONCOMING CAR!
THANK YOU FOR COMING, SIR.
WE ARE HONORED BY YOUR PRESENCE.
THIS IS MY FRIEND, JACK.
HE DESPERATELY NEEDS YOUR HELP.
HMM. SO, JACK, WHAT CAN I DO FOR YOU?
WELL, YOU SEE, SIR... MY FAMILY MOVED HERE JUST THIS SUMMER.
AND THEY BUILT ME A HOUSE. A REALLY WONDERFUL HOUSE, ACTUALLY.
BUT I HAVEN'T BEEN ABLE TO SLEEP ONE FULL NIGHT IN IT.
BECAUSE IT'S HAUNTED.
JACK

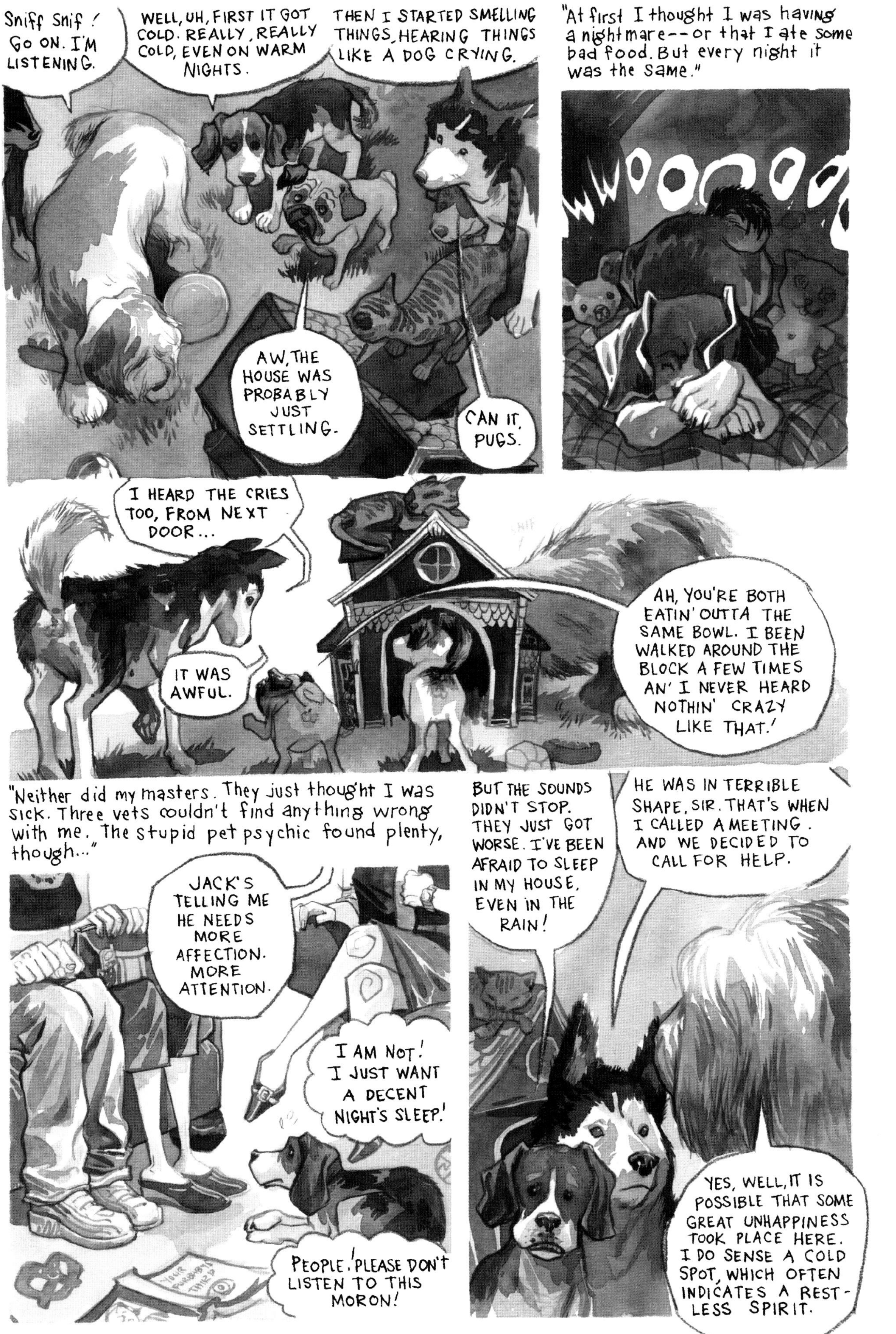
Sniff Snif! Go on. I'm listening.
Well, uh, first it got cold. Really, really cold, even on warm nights.
Then I started smelling things, hearing things like a dog crying.
Aw, the house was probably just settling.
Can it, Pugs.
"At first I thought I was having a nightmare--or that I ate some bad food. But every night it was the same."
WWOOOOOOO
I heard the cries too, from next door...
It was awful.
SNIF
Ah, you're both eatin' outta the same bowl. I been walked around the block a few times an' I never heard nothin' crazy like that.
"Neither did my masters. They just thought I was sick. Three vets couldn't find anything wrong with me. The stupid pet psychic found plenty, though..."
Jack's telling me he needs more affection. More attention.
I am not! I just want a decent night's sleep!
People! Please don't listen to this moron!
But the sounds didn't stop. They just got worse. I've been afraid to sleep in my house, even in the rain!
He was in terrible shape, sir. That's when I called a meeting. And we decided to call for help.
Yes, well, it is possible that some great unhappiness took place here. I do sense a cold spot, which often indicates a restless spirit.

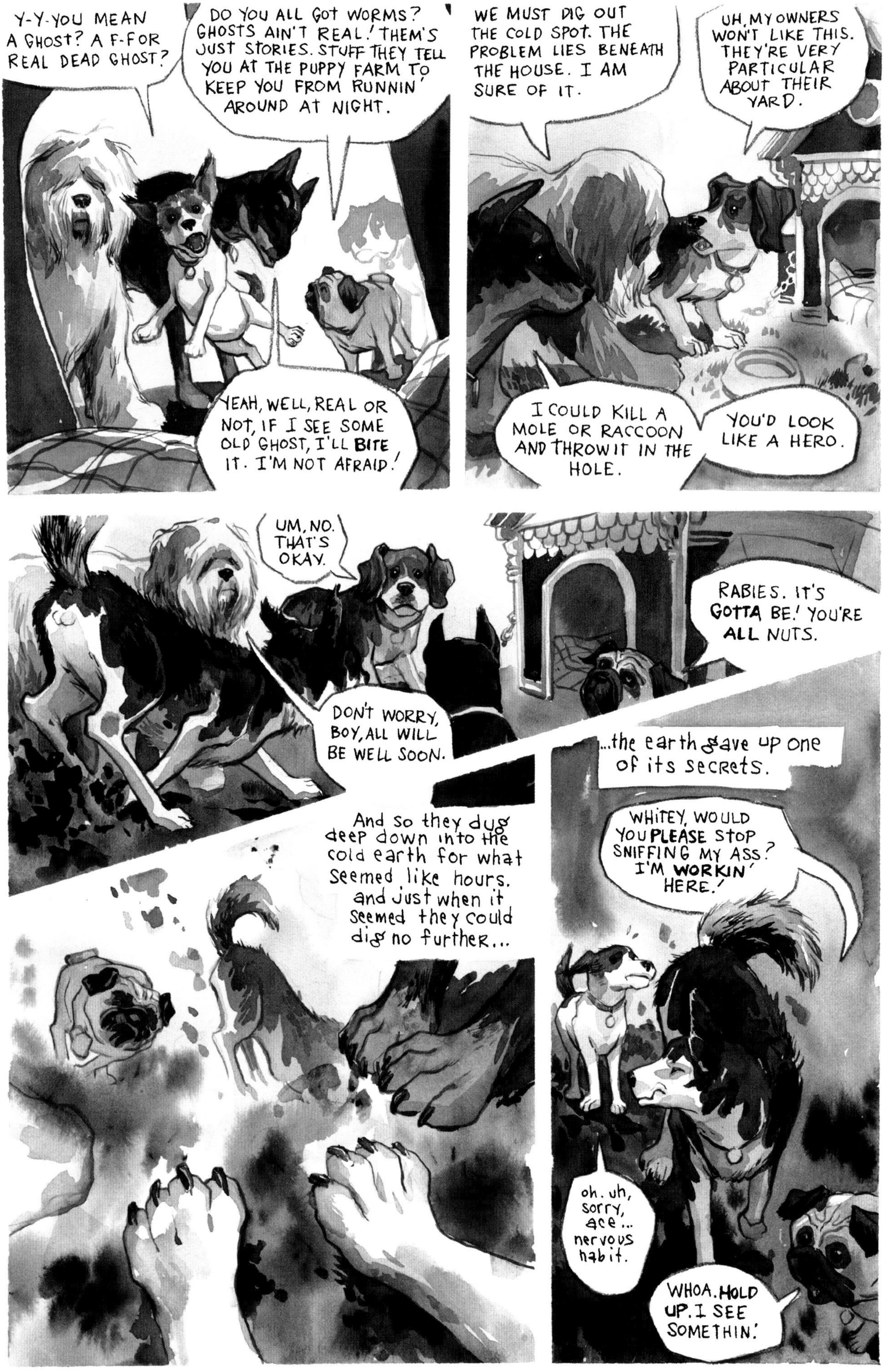

Y-Y-YOU MEAN A GHOST? A F-FOR REAL DEAD GHOST?
DO YOU ALL GOT WORMS? GHOSTS AIN'T REAL! THEM'S JUST STORIES. STUFF THEY TELL YOU AT THE PUPPY FARM TO KEEP YOU FROM RUNNIN' AROUND AT NIGHT.
YEAH, WELL, REAL OR NOT, IF I SEE SOME OLD GHOST, I'LL **BITE** IT. I'M NOT AFRAID!
WE MUST DIG OUT THE COLD SPOT. THE PROBLEM LIES BENEATH THE HOUSE. I AM SURE OF IT.
UH, MY OWNERS WON'T LIKE THIS. THEY'RE VERY PARTICULAR ABOUT THEIR YARD.
I COULD KILL A MOLE OR RACCOON AND THROW IT IN THE HOLE.
YOU'D LOOK LIKE A HERO.
UM, NO. THAT'S OKAY.
RABIES. IT'S **GOTTA** BE! YOU'RE **ALL** NUTS.
DON'T WORRY, BOY, ALL WILL BE WELL SOON.
And so they dug deep down into the cold earth for what seemed like hours. and just when it seemed they could dig no further...
...the earth gave up one of its secrets.
WHITEY, WOULD YOU **PLEASE** STOP SNIFFING MY ASS? I'M **WORKIN'** HERE!
oh. uh, sorry, ace... nervous habit.
WHOA. **HOLD UP**. I SEE SOMETHIN'.

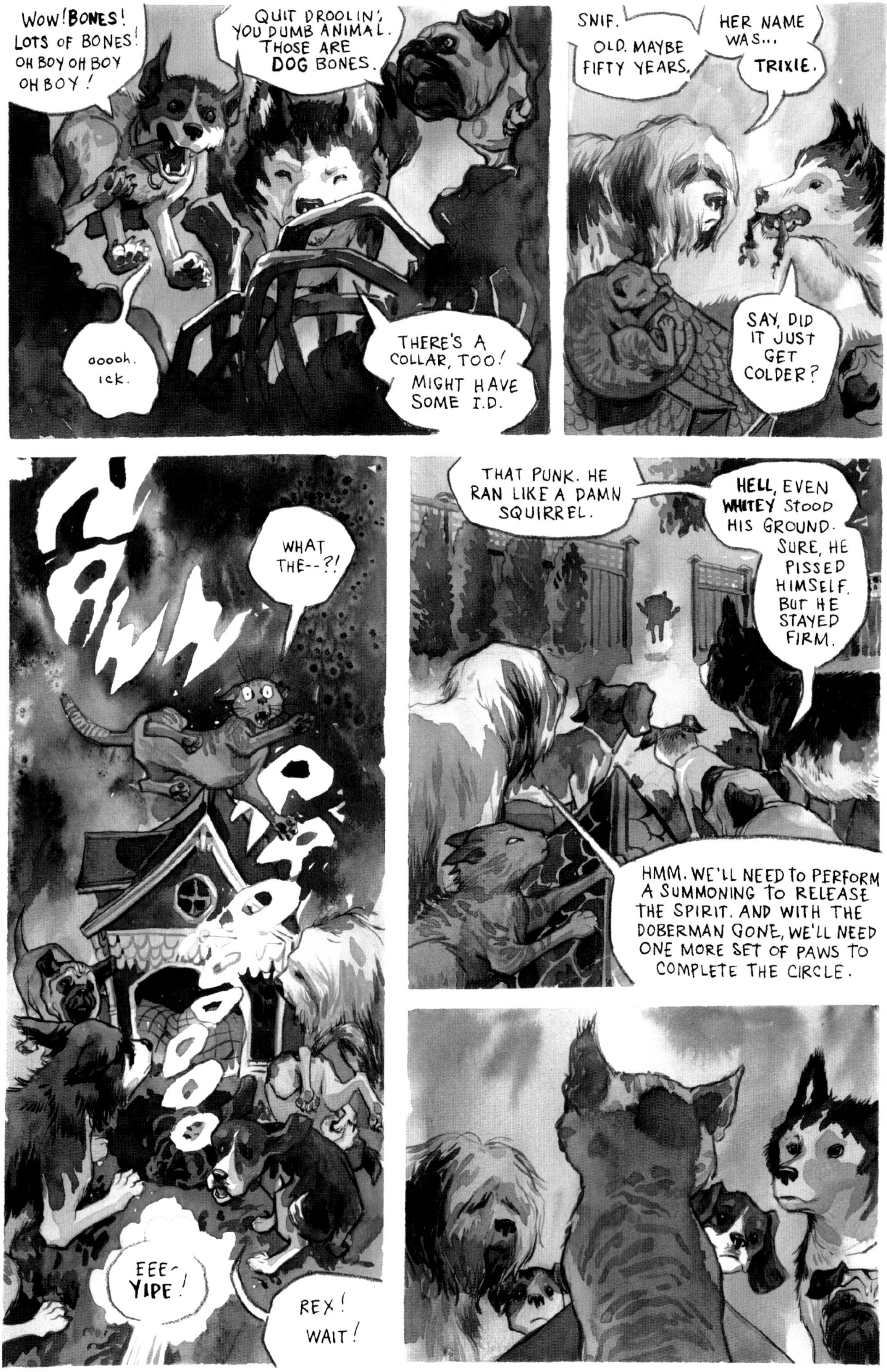

WOW! BONES! LOTS OF BONES! OH BOY OH BOY OH BOY!
QUIT DROOLIN', YOU DUMB ANIMAL. THOSE ARE DOG BONES.
oooh. ick.
THERE'S A COLLAR, TOO!
MIGHT HAVE SOME I.D.
SNIF.
OLD. MAYBE FIFTY YEARS.
HER NAME WAS... TRIXIE.
SAY, DID IT JUST GET COLDER?
WHAT THE--?!
EEE-YIPE!
REX! WAIT!
THAT PUNK. HE RAN LIKE A DAMN SQUIRREL.
HELL, EVEN WHITEY STOOD HIS GROUND.
SURE, HE PISSED HIMSELF. BUT HE STAYED FIRM.
HMM. WE'LL NEED TO PERFORM A SUMMONING TO RELEASE THE SPIRIT. AND WITH THE DOBERMAN GONE, WE'LL NEED ONE MORE SET OF PAWS TO COMPLETE THE CIRCLE.

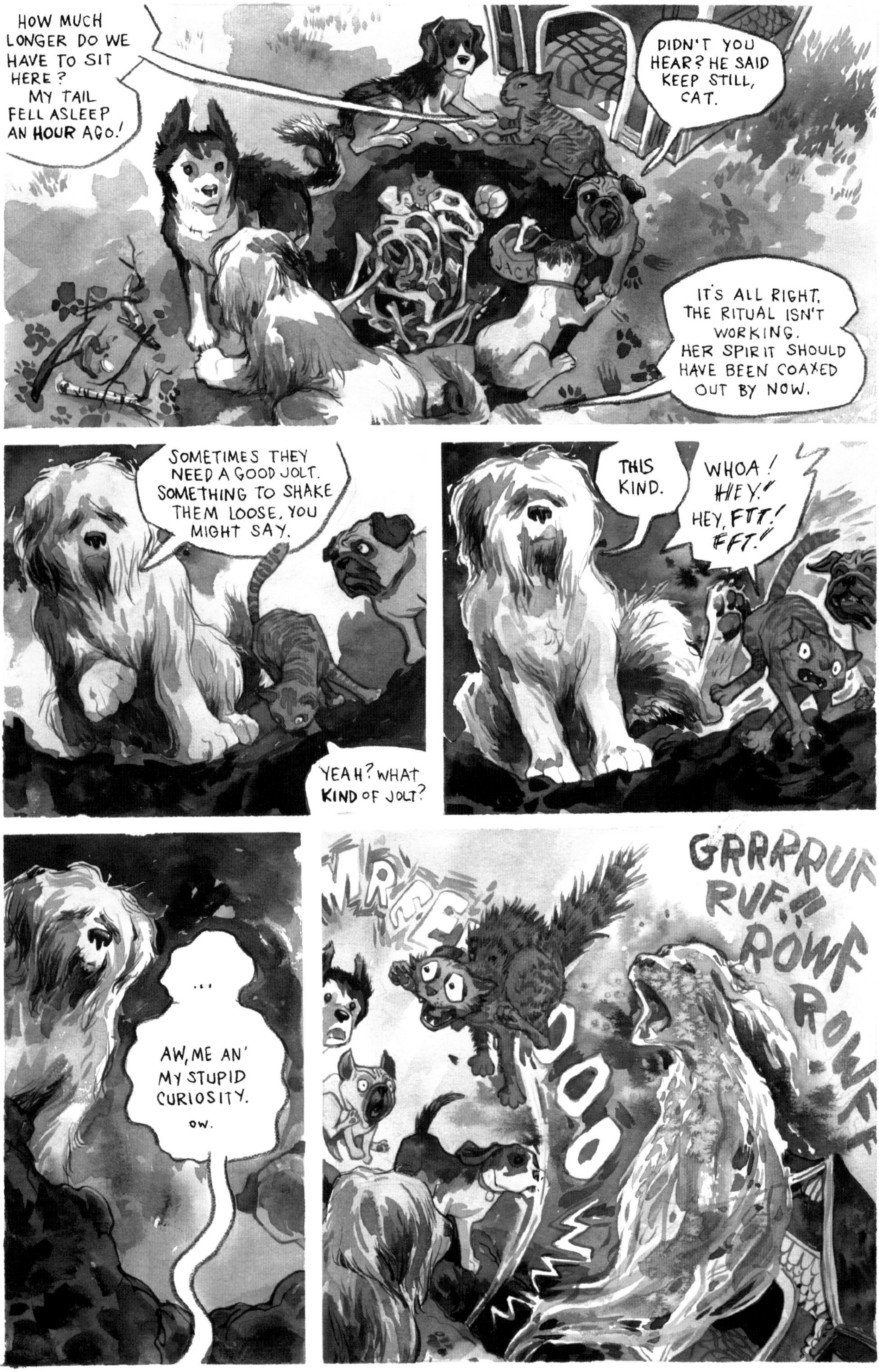
HOW MUCH LONGER DO WE HAVE TO SIT HERE? MY TAIL FELL ASLEEP AN HOUR AGO!
DIDN'T YOU HEAR? HE SAID KEEP STILL, CAT.
JACK
IT'S ALL RIGHT. THE RITUAL ISN'T WORKING. HER SPIRIT SHOULD HAVE BEEN COAXED OUT BY NOW.
SOMETIMES THEY NEED A GOOD JOLT. SOMETHING TO SHAKE THEM LOOSE, YOU MIGHT SAY.
YEAH? WHAT KIND OF JOLT?
THIS KIND.
WHOA! HEY! HEY, FTT! FFT!
...
AW, ME AN' MY STUPID CURIOSITY.
OW.
GRRRRUF RUF!! ROWF ROWF ROWF
OOOO

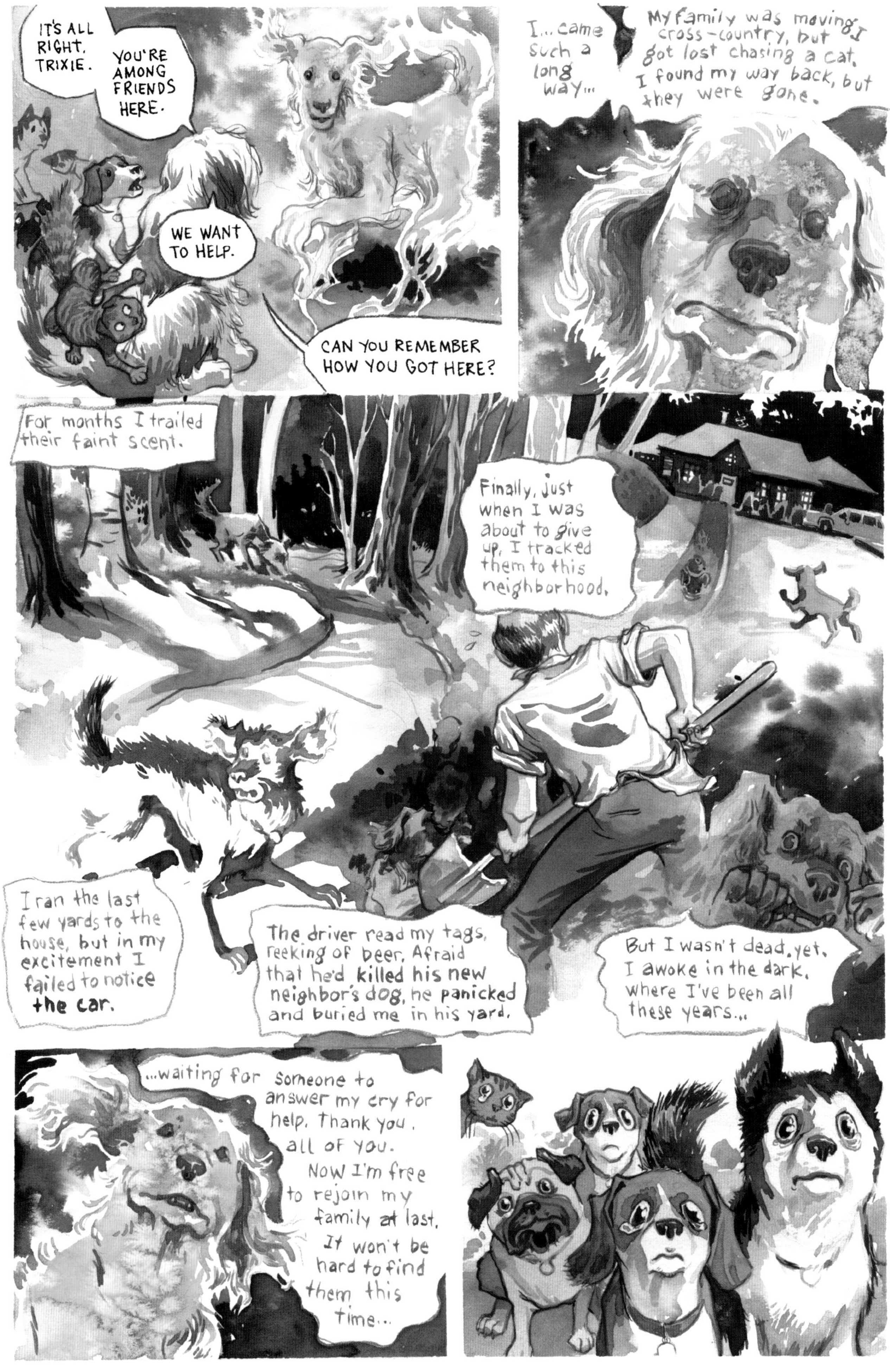
IT'S ALL RIGHT, TRIXIE.
YOU'RE AMONG FRIENDS HERE.
WE WANT TO HELP.
CAN YOU REMEMBER HOW YOU GOT HERE?
I... came such a long way...
My family was moving cross-country, but I got lost chasing a cat. I found my way back, but they were gone.
For months I trailed their faint scent.
Finally, just when I was about to give up, I tracked them to this neighborhood.
I ran the last few yards to the house, but in my excitement I failed to notice **the car.**
The driver read my tags, reeking of beer. Afraid that he'd **killed his new neighbor's dog**, he **panicked** and buried me in his yard.
But I wasn't dead yet. I awoke in the dark, where I've been all these years...
...waiting for someone to answer my cry for help. Thank you, all of you. Now I'm free to rejoin my family at last. It won't be hard to find them this time...

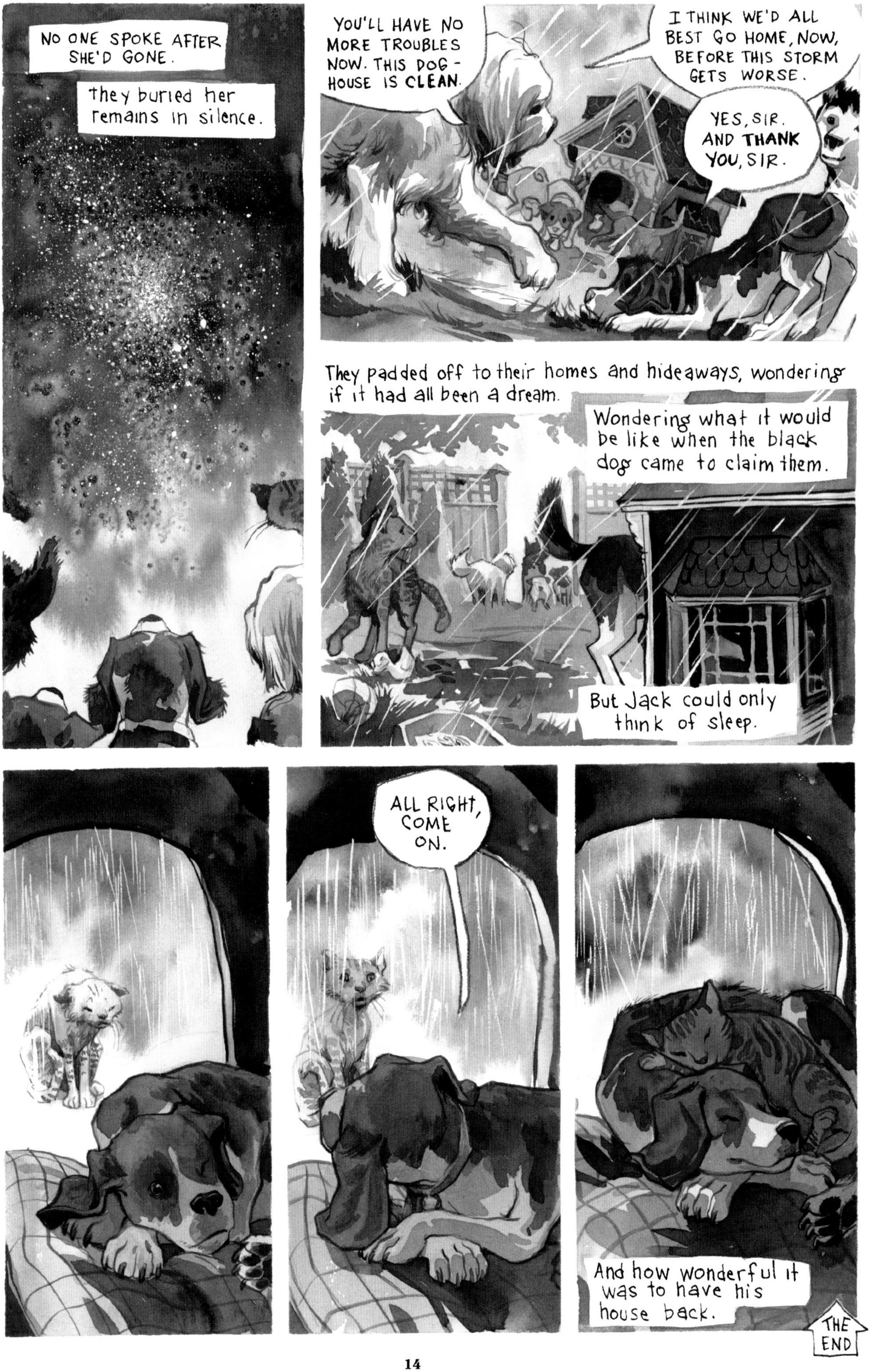

NO ONE SPOKE AFTER SHE'D GONE.
they buried her remains in silence.
YOU'LL HAVE NO MORE TROUBLES NOW. THIS DOG-HOUSE IS CLEAN.
I THINK WE'D ALL BEST GO HOME, NOW, BEFORE THIS STORM GETS WORSE.
YES, SIR. AND THANK YOU, SIR.
They padded off to their homes and hideaways, wondering if it had all been a dream.
Wondering what it would be like when the black dog came to claim them.
But Jack could only think of sleep.
ALL RIGHT, COME ON.
And how wonderful it was to have his house back.
THE END

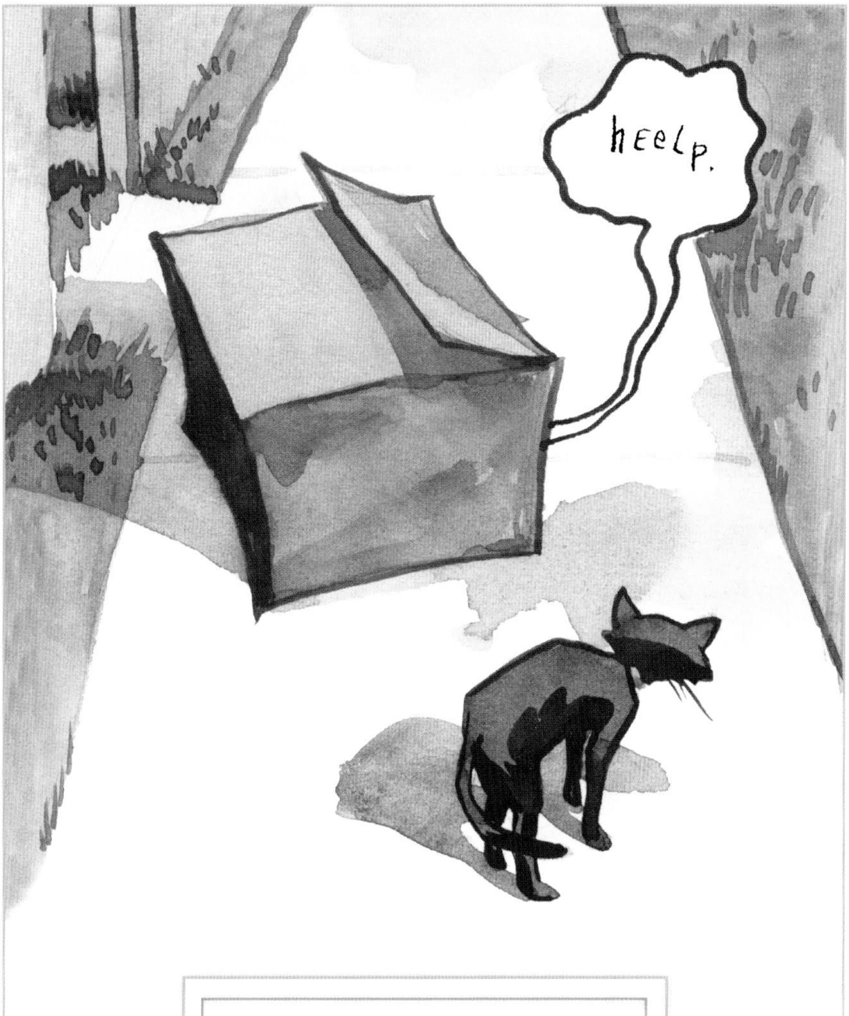
heelp.

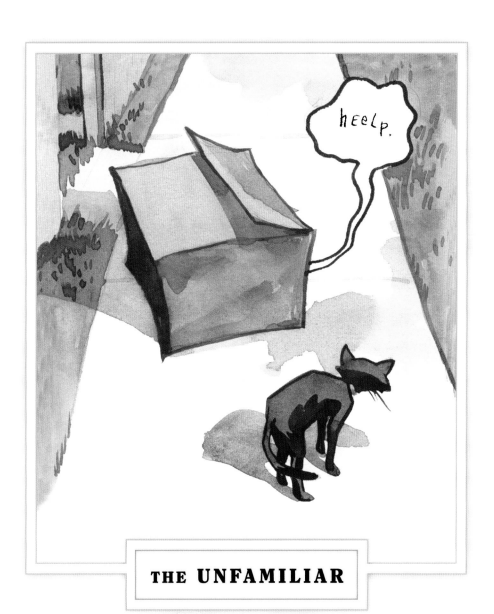

THE UNFAMILIAR

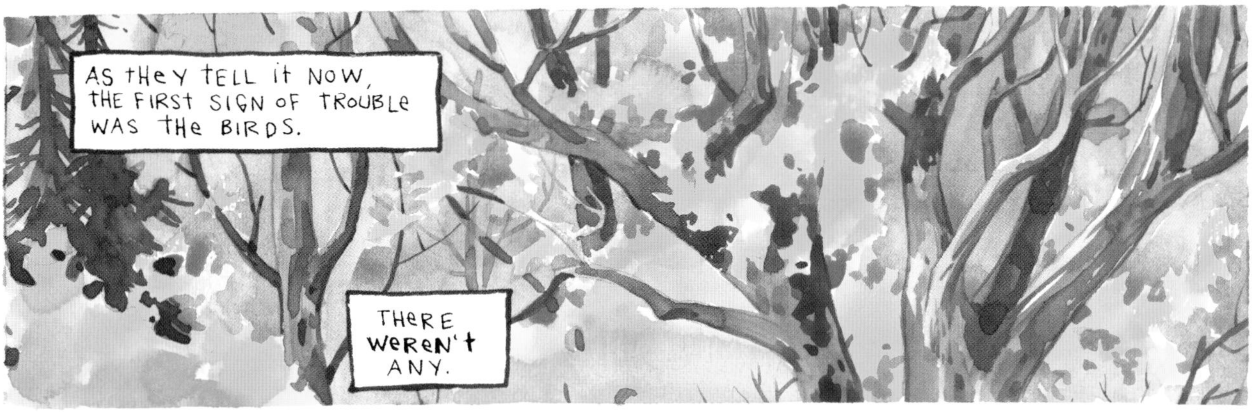
AS THEY TELL IT NOW, THE FIRST SIGN OF TROUBLE WAS THE BIRDS.
THERE WEREN'T ANY.

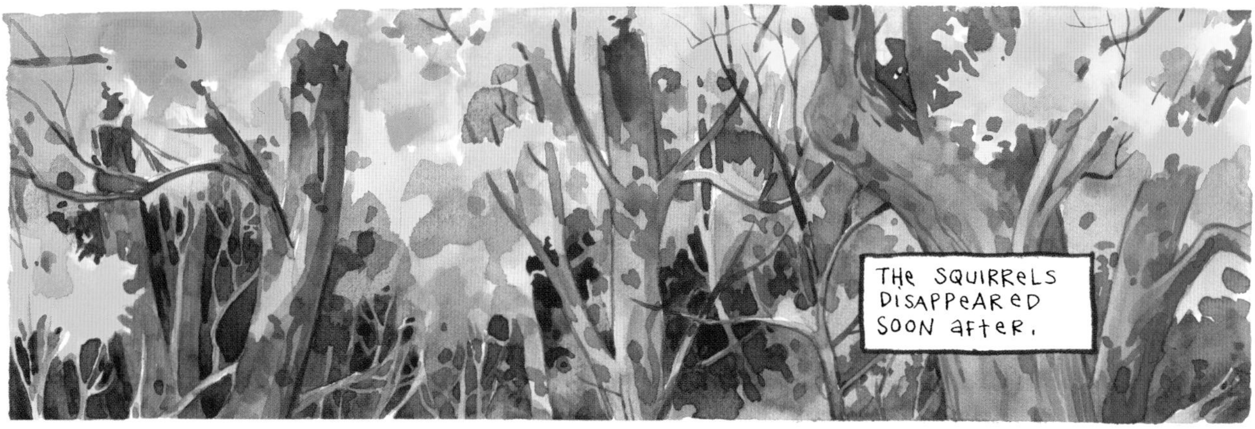
THE SQUIRRELS DISAPPEARED SOON AFTER.

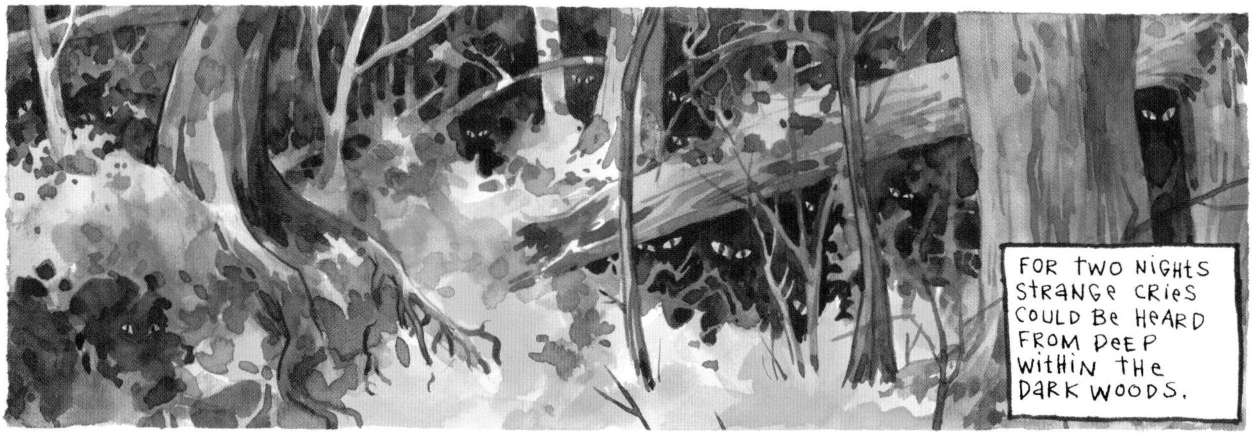
FOR TWO NIGHTS STRANGE CRIES COULD BE HEARD FROM DEEP WITHIN THE DARK WOODS.

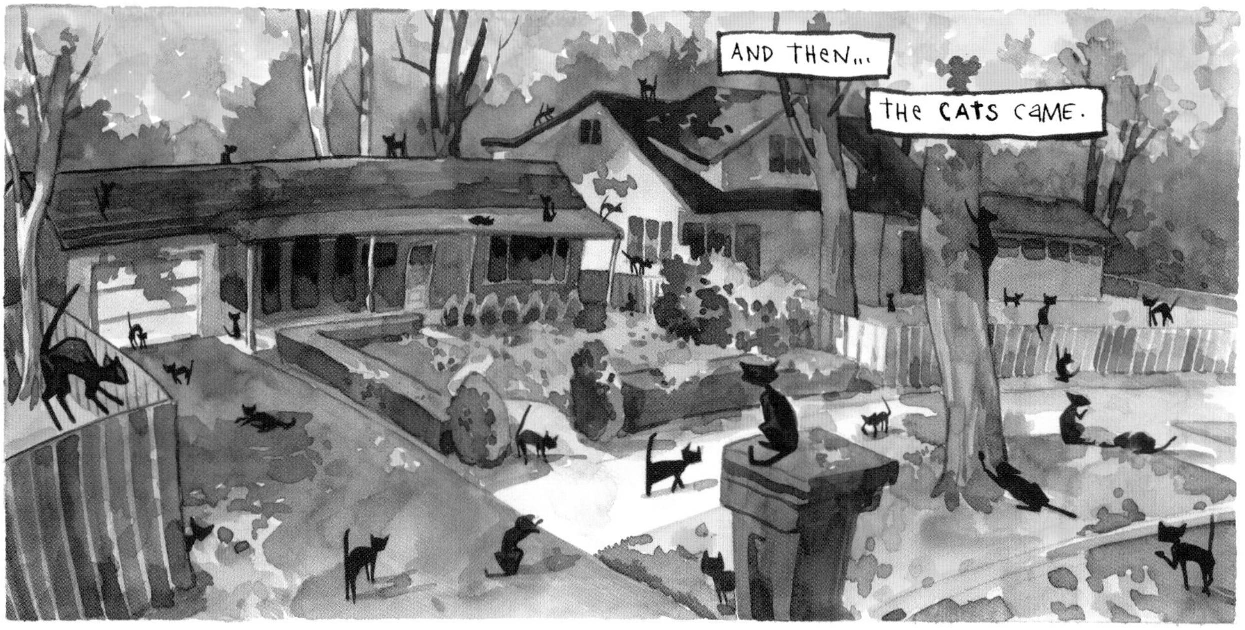
AND THEN...
THE CATS CAME.

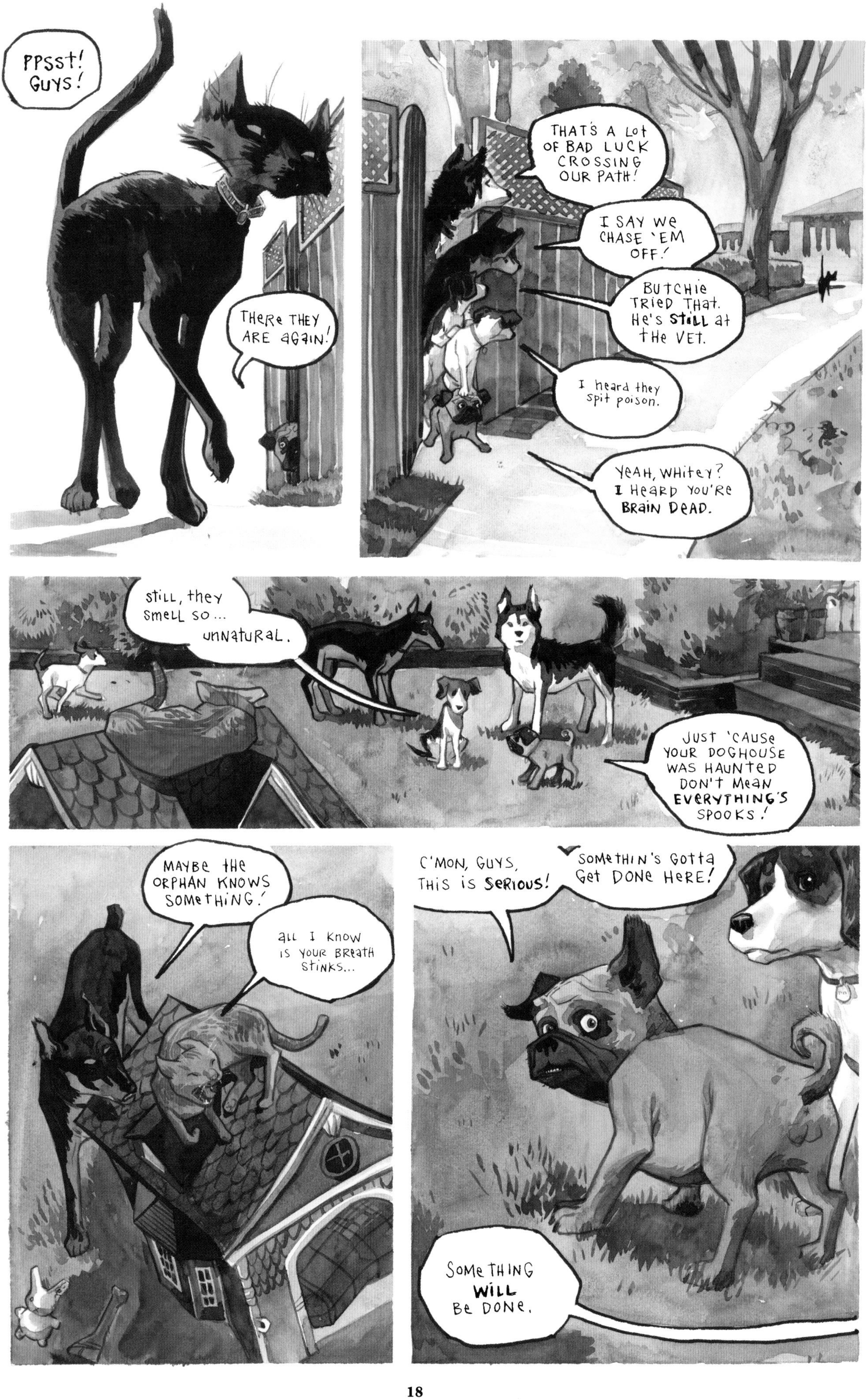
PPSST! GUYS!
THERE THEY ARE AGAIN!
THAT'S A LOT OF BAD LUCK CROSSING OUR PATH!
I SAY WE CHASE 'EM OFF!
BUTCHIE TRIED THAT. HE'S STILL AT THE VET.
I heard they spit poison.
YEAH, WHITEY? I HEARD YOU'RE BRAIN DEAD.
still, they smell so... unnatural.
JUST 'CAUSE YOUR DOGHOUSE WAS HAUNTED DON'T MEAN EVERYTHING'S SPOOKS!
MAYBE THE ORPHAN KNOWS SOMETHING!
all I know is your breath stinks...
C'MON, GUYS, THIS IS SERIOUS!
SOMETHIN'S GOTTA GET DONE HERE!
SOMETHING WILL BE DONE.

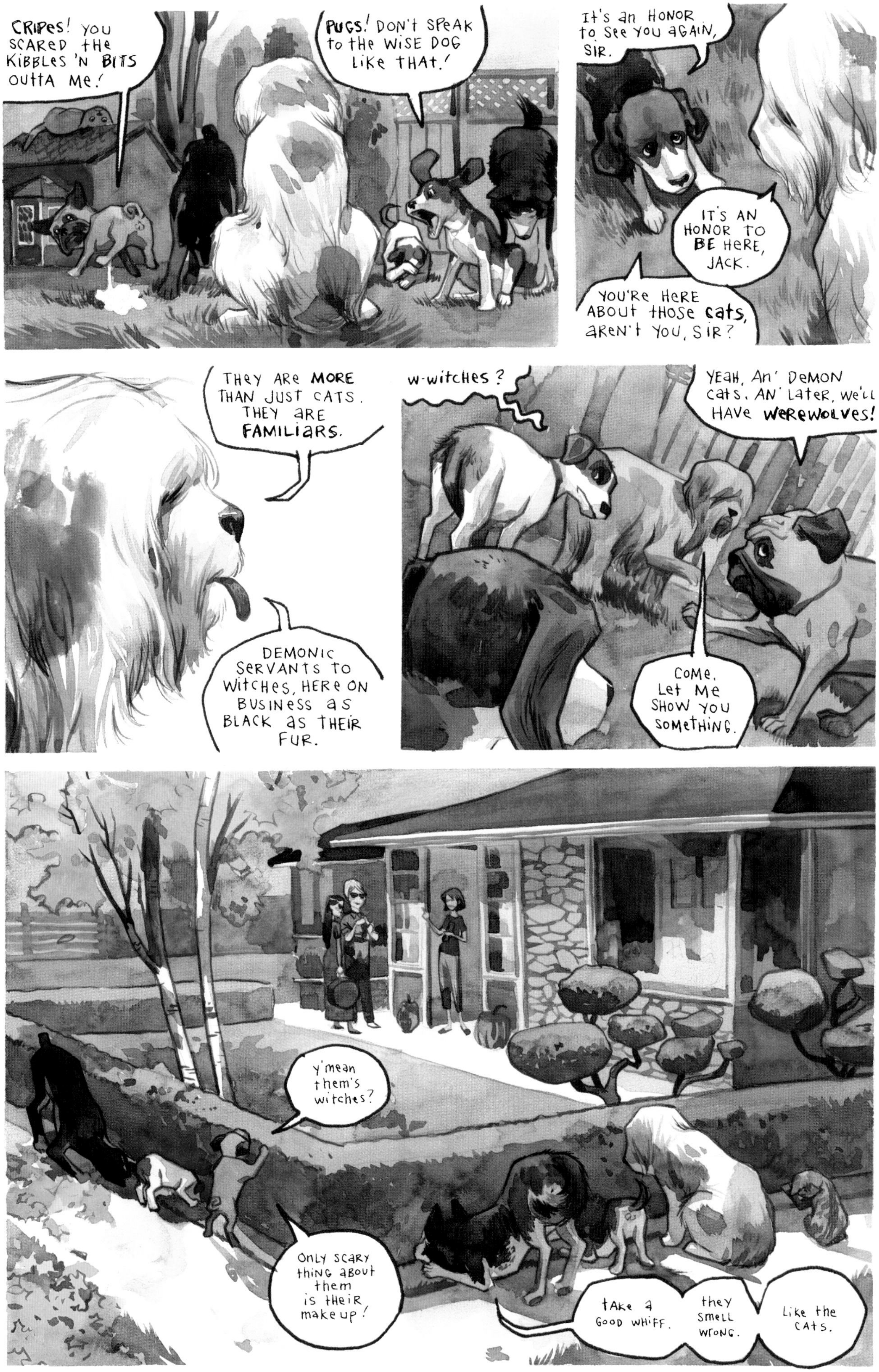
CRIPES! YOU SCARED THE KIBBLES 'N BITS OUTTA ME!
PUGS! DON'T SPEAK TO THE WISE DOG LIKE THAT!
IT'S AN HONOR TO SEE YOU AGAIN, SIR.
IT'S AN HONOR TO BE HERE, JACK.
YOU'RE HERE ABOUT THOSE CATS, AREN'T YOU, SIR?
THEY ARE MORE THAN JUST CATS. THEY ARE FAMILIARS.
DEMONIC SERVANTS TO WITCHES, HERE ON BUSINESS AS BLACK AS THEIR FUR.
W-WITCHES?
YEAH, AN' DEMON CATS. AN' LATER, WE'LL HAVE WEREWOLVES!
COME. LET ME SHOW YOU SOMETHING.
Y'MEAN THEM'S WITCHES?
ONLY SCARY THING ABOUT THEM IS THEIR MAKEUP!
TAKE A GOOD WHIFF.
THEY SMELL WRONG.
LIKE THE CATS.

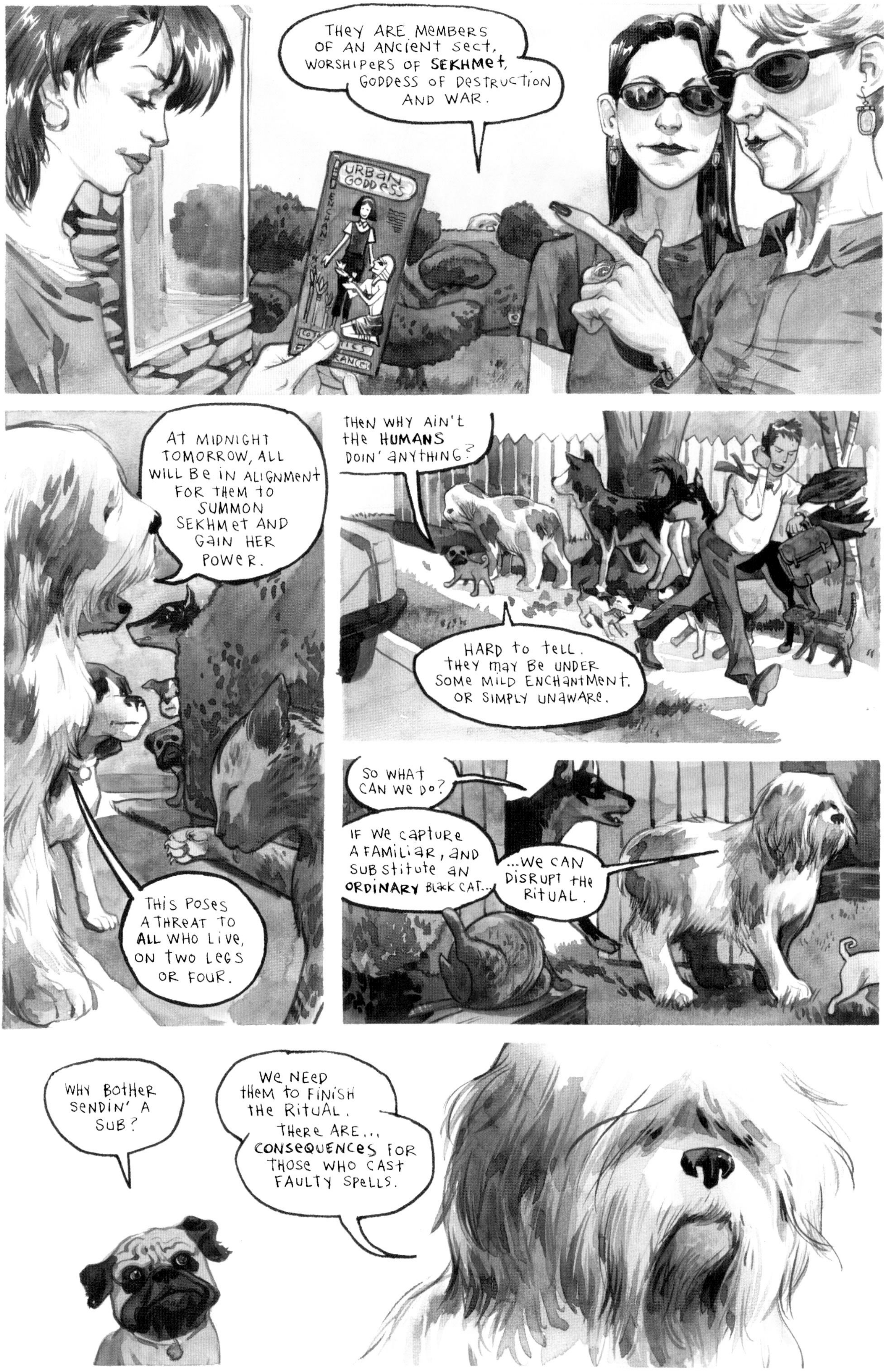

THEY ARE MEMBERS OF AN ANCIENT SECT, WORSHIPERS OF SEKHMET, GODDESS OF DESTRUCTION AND WAR.
URBAN GODDESS
AT MIDNIGHT TOMORROW, ALL WILL BE IN ALIGNMENT FOR THEM TO SUMMON SEKHMET AND GAIN HER POWER.
THIS POSES A THREAT TO ALL WHO LIVE, ON TWO LEGS OR FOUR.
THEN WHY AIN'T THE HUMANS DOIN' ANYTHING?
HARD TO TELL. THEY MAY BE UNDER SOME MILD ENCHANTMENT. OR SIMPLY UNAWARE.
SO WHAT CAN WE DO?
IF WE CAPTURE A FAMILIAR, AND SUBSTITUTE AN ORDINARY BLACK CAT...
...WE CAN DISRUPT THE RITUAL.
WHY BOTHER SENDIN' A SUB?
WE NEED THEM TO FINISH THE RITUAL. THERE ARE... CONSEQUENCES FOR THOSE WHO CAST FAULTY SPELLS.

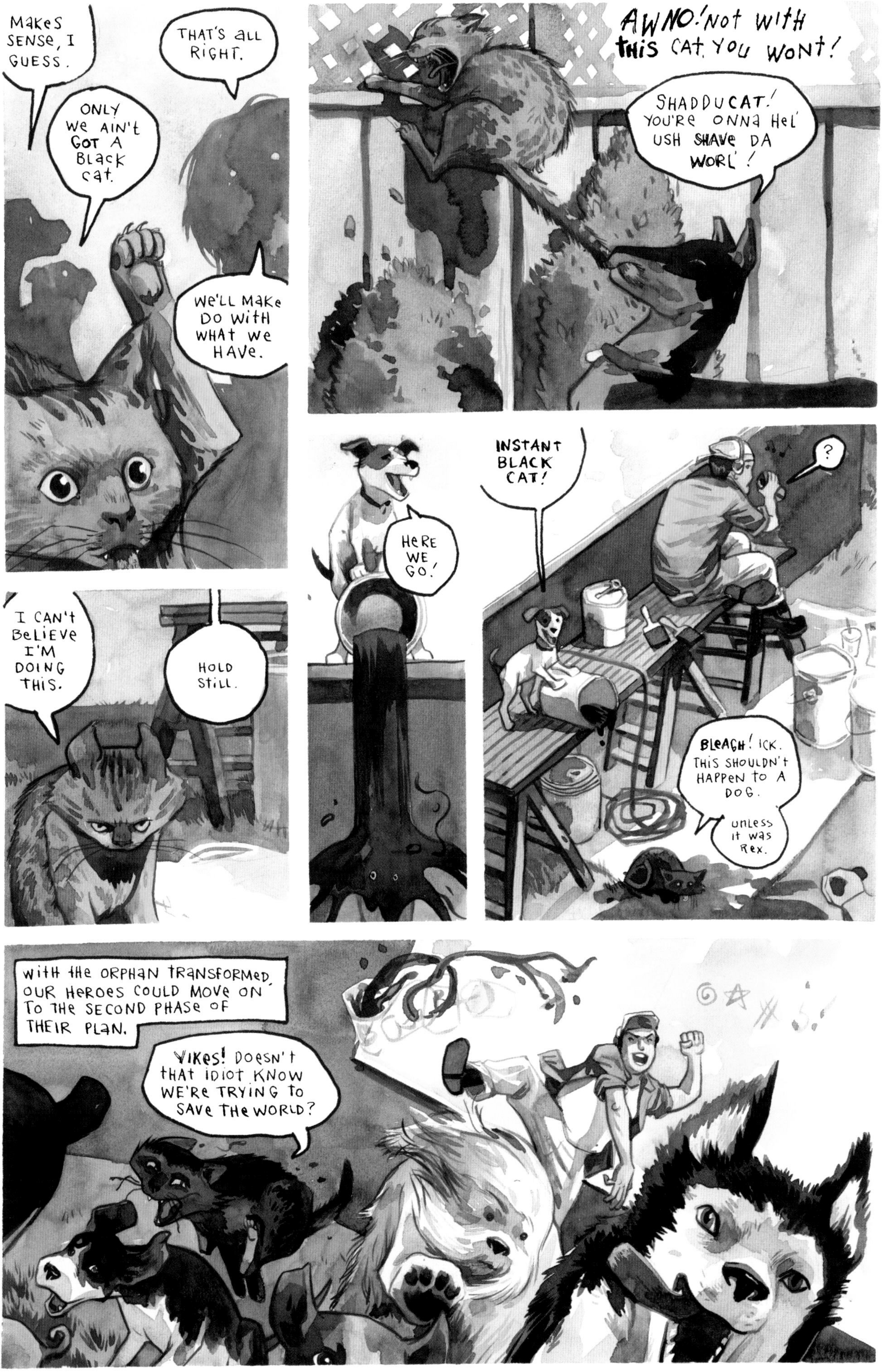
Makes sense, I guess.
That's all right.
Only we ain't got a black cat.
We'll make do with what we have.
AWNO! Not with this cat you wont!
SHADDUCAT! You're onna hel' ush shave da worl'!
I can't believe I'm doing this.
Hold still.
Here we go!
Instant black cat!
?
Bleagh! Ick. This shouldn't happen to a dog.
Unless it was Rex.
With the orphan transformed, our heroes could move on to the second phase of their plan.
Yikes! Doesn't that idiot know we're trying to save the world?

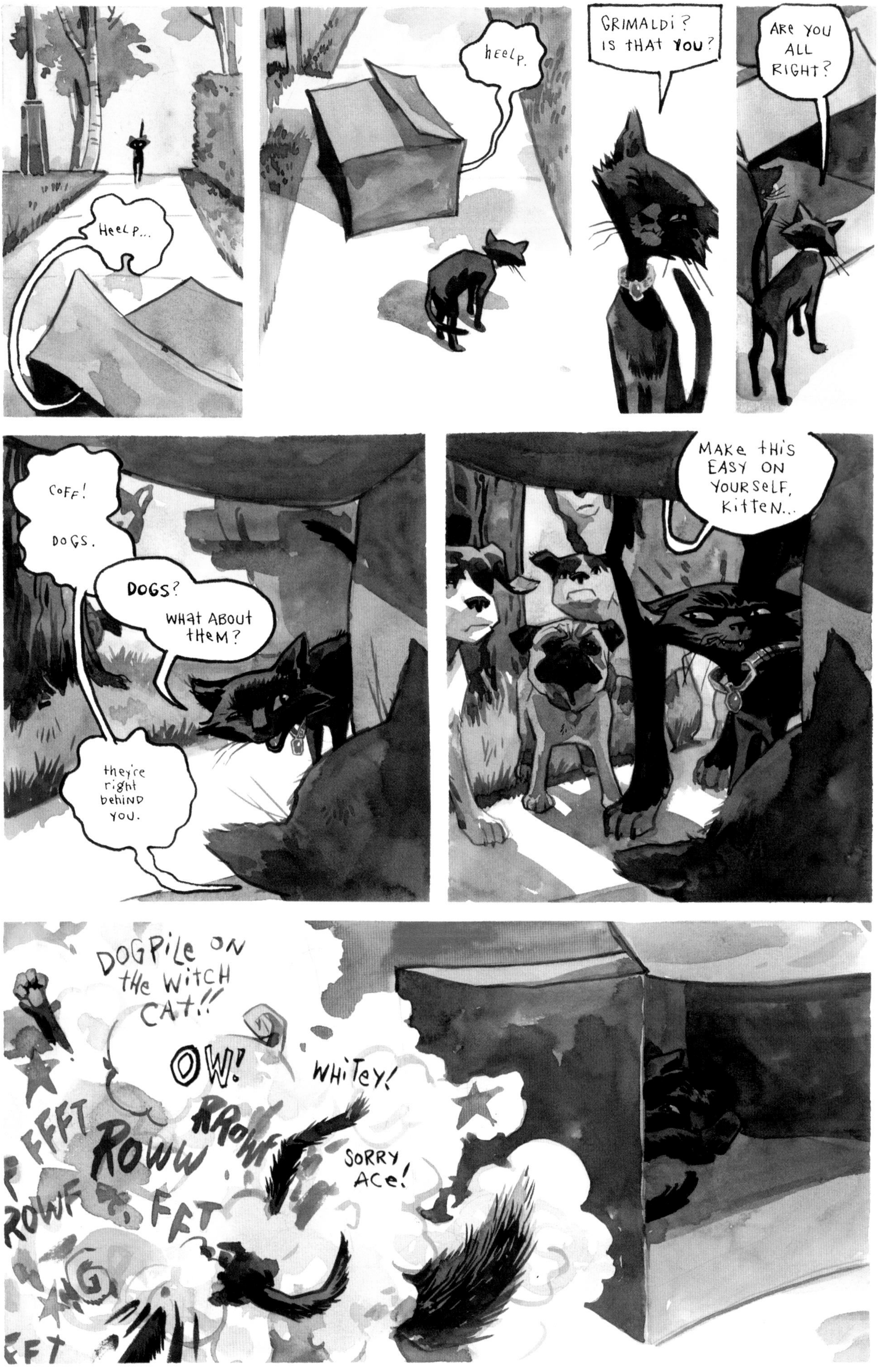
Heelp...
heelp.
GRIMALDI? IS THAT YOU?
ARE YOU ALL RIGHT?
COFF!
DOGS.
DOGS? WHAT ABOUT THEM?
they're right behind you.
MAKE THIS EASY ON YOURSELF, KITTEN...
DOGPILE ON THE WITCH CAT!!
OW!
WHITEY!
FFFT
ROWW
RROWF
SORRY ACE!
ROWF
FFT
FFT

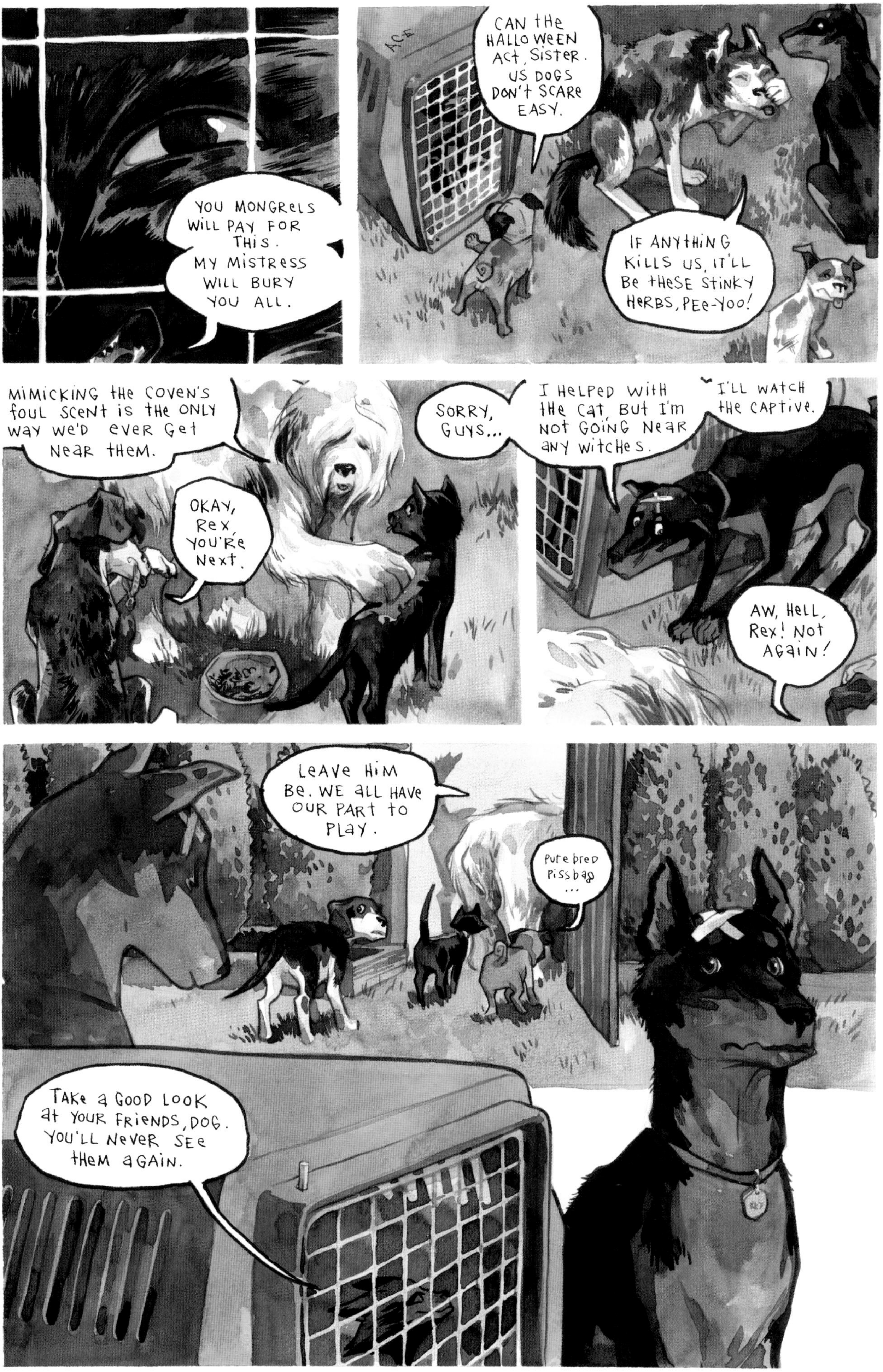

YOU MONGRELS WILL PAY FOR THIS. MY MISTRESS WILL BURY YOU ALL.
ACE
CAN THE HALLOWEEN ACT, SISTER. US DOGS DON'T SCARE EASY.
IF ANYTHING KILLS US, IT'LL BE THESE STINKY HERBS, PEE-YOO!
MIMICKING THE COVEN'S FOUL SCENT IS THE ONLY WAY WE'D EVER GET NEAR THEM.
SORRY, GUYS...
OKAY, REX, YOU'RE NEXT.
I HELPED WITH THE CAT, BUT I'M NOT GOING NEAR ANY WITCHES.
I'LL WATCH THE CAPTIVE.
AW, HELL, REX! NOT AGAIN!
LEAVE HIM BE. WE ALL HAVE OUR PART TO PLAY.
Purebred Pissbag...
TAKE A GOOD LOOK AT YOUR FRIENDS, DOG. YOU'LL NEVER SEE THEM AGAIN.

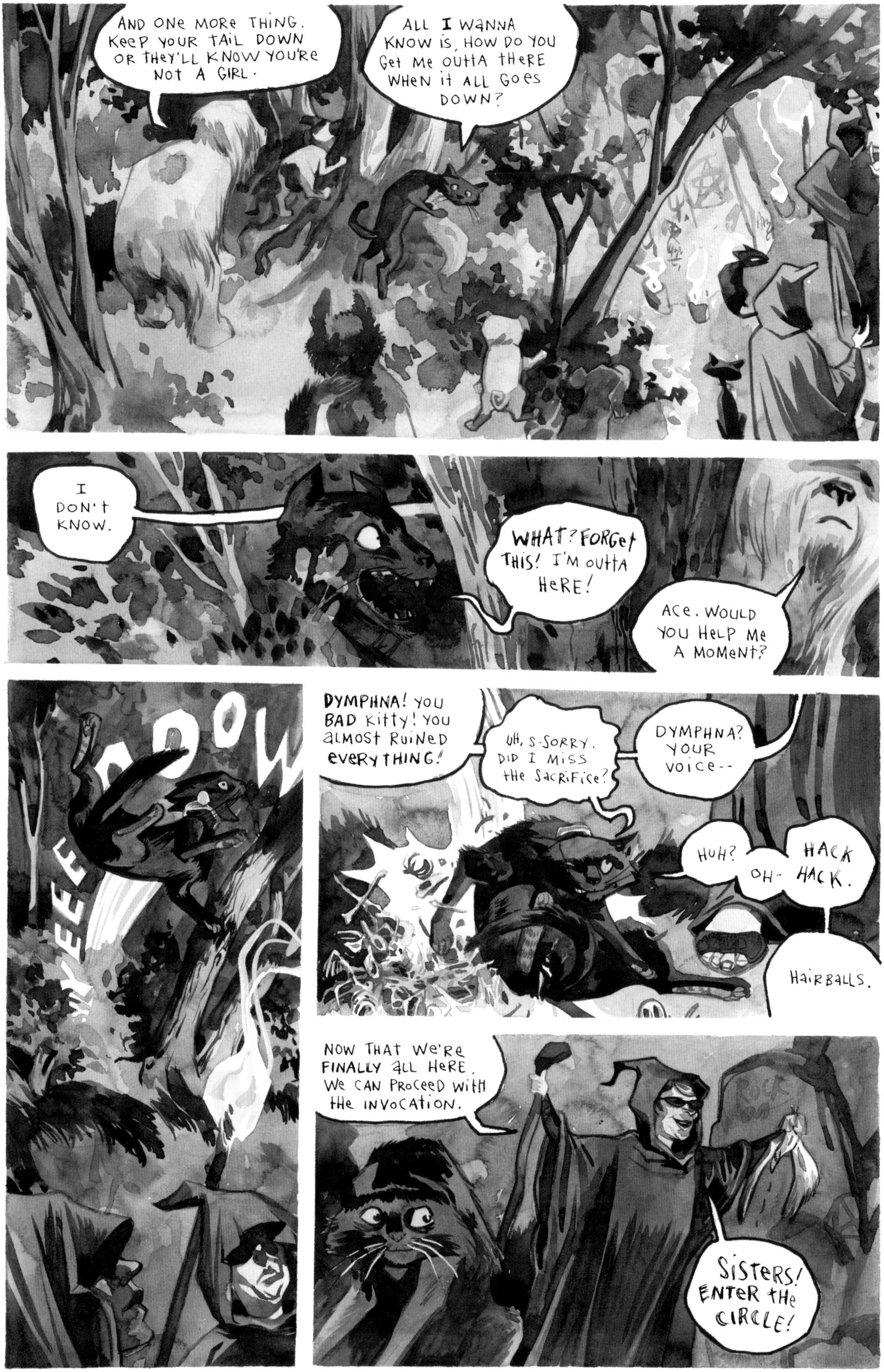
AND ONE MORE THING. KEEP YOUR TAIL DOWN OR THEY'LL KNOW YOU'RE NOT A GIRL.
ALL I WANNA KNOW IS, HOW DO YOU GET ME OUTTA THERE WHEN IT ALL GOES DOWN?
I DON'T KNOW.
WHAT? FORGET THIS! I'M OUTTA HERE!
ACE. WOULD YOU HELP ME A MOMENT?
DYMPHNA! YOU BAD KITTY! YOU ALMOST RUINED EVERYTHING!
UH, S-SORRY. DID I MISS THE SACRIFICE?
DYMPHNA? YOUR VOICE--
HUH?
OH-
HACK HACK.
HAIRBALLS.
NOW THAT WE'RE FINALLY ALL HERE, WE CAN PROCEED WITH THE INVOCATION.
SISTERS! ENTER THE CIRCLE!

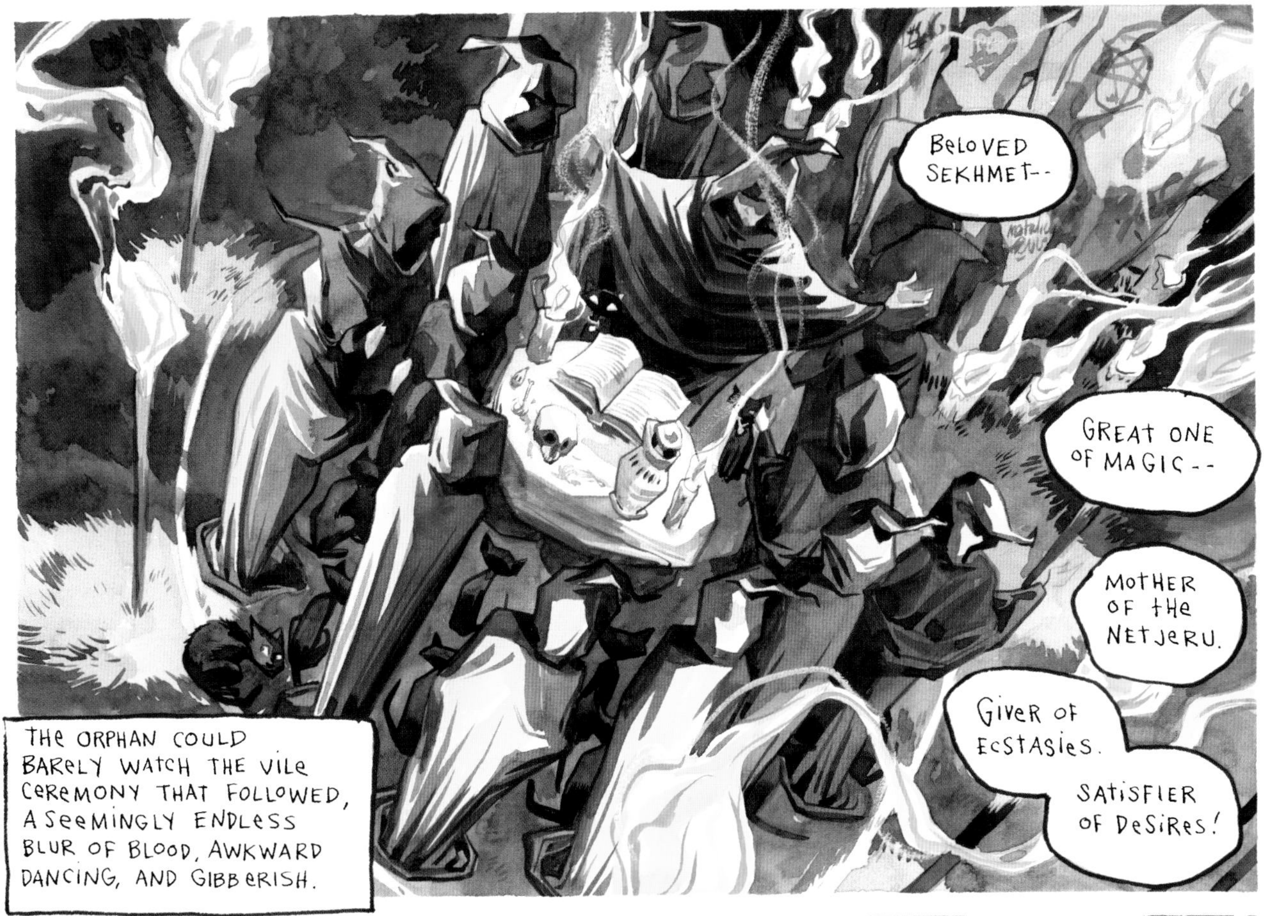
BeLOVED SEKHMET--
GREAT ONE OF MAGIC--
MOTHER OF THE NETJERU.
Giver OF EcSTASies.
SATISFIER OF DeSiRes!
THE ORPHAN COULD BARELY WATCH THE VILE CEREMONY THAT FOLLOWED, A SEEMINGLY ENDLESS BLUR OF BLOOD, AWKWARD DANCING, AND GIBBERISH.

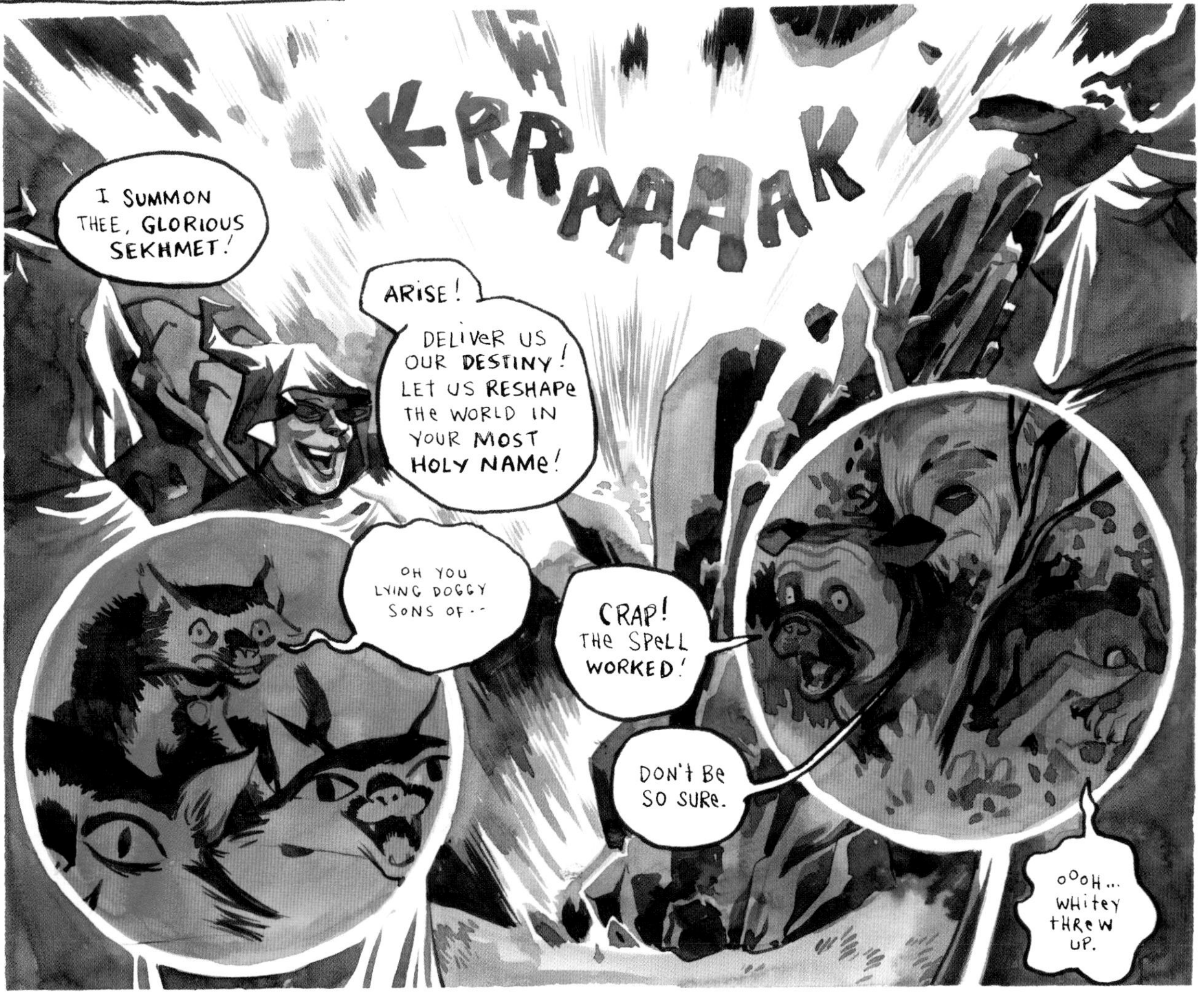
KRRAAAAK
I SUMMON THEE, GLORIOUS SEKHMET!
ARISE!
DELIVER US OUR DESTINY! LET US RESHAPE THE WORLD IN YOUR MOST HOLY NAME!
OH YOU LYING DOGGY SONS OF--
CRAP! THE SPELL WORKED!
DON'T BE SO SURE.
OOOH... WHITEY THREW UP.

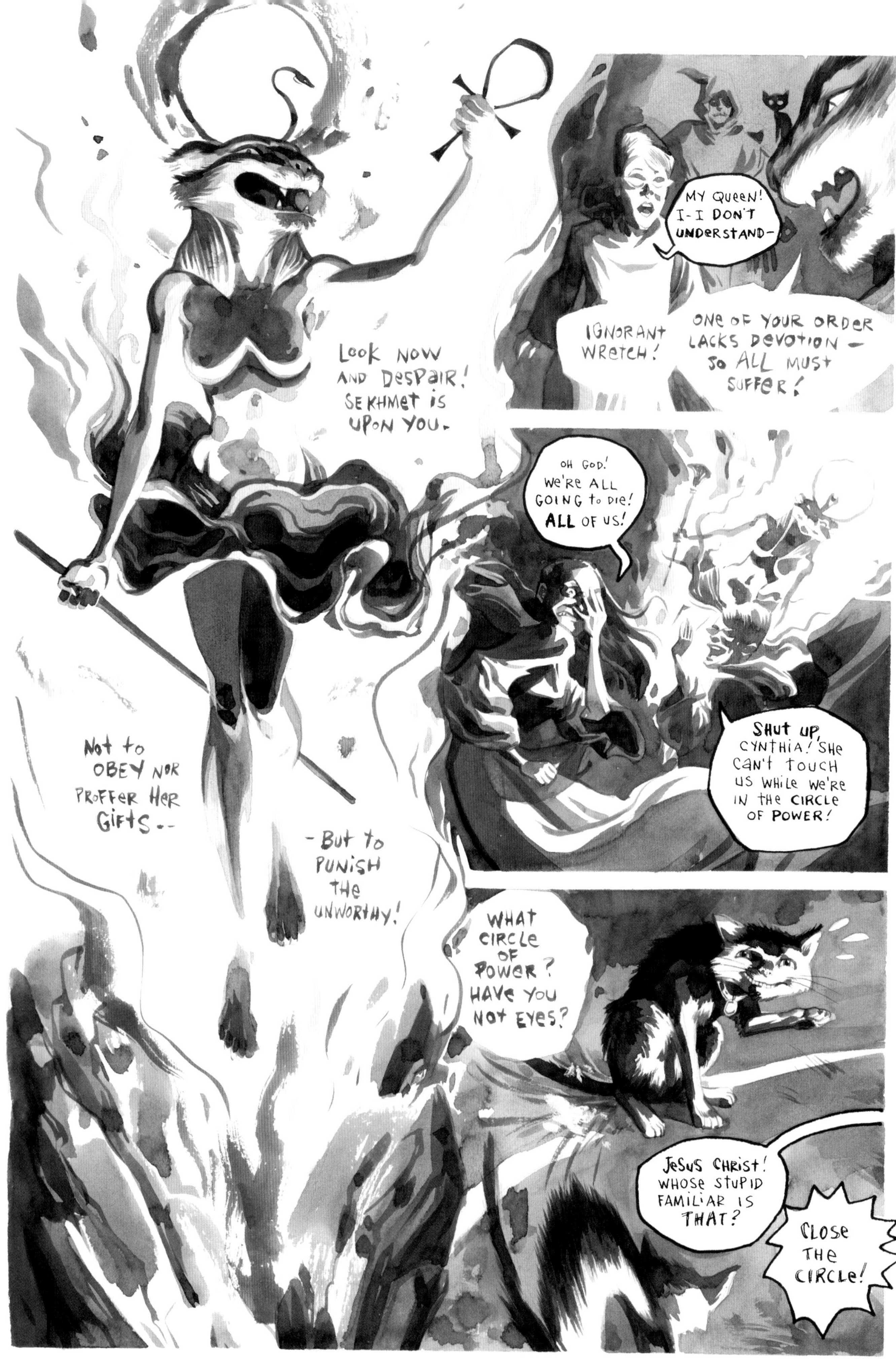

Look now and Despair! Sekhmet is upon you.
My Queen! I-I don't understand-
Ignorant wretch!
One of your order lacks devotion - so all must suffer!
Oh God! We're all going to die! ALL of us!
Shut up, Cynthia! She can't touch us while we're in the circle of power!
Not to obey nor proffer her gifts--
-But to punish the unworthy!
What circle of power? Have you not eyes?
Jesus Christ! Whose stupid familiar is that?
Close the circle!

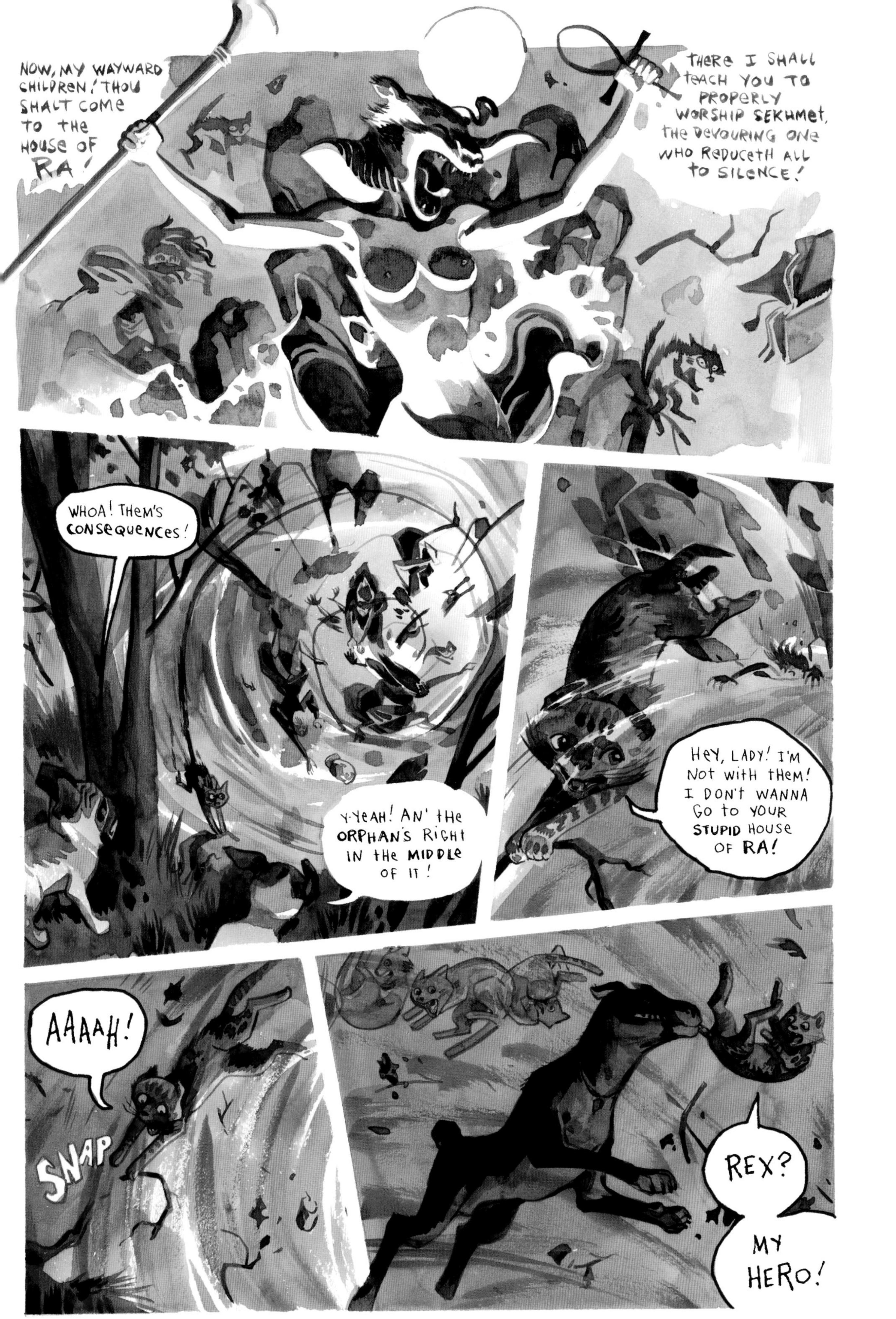
NOW, MY WAYWARD CHILDREN! THOU SHALT COME TO THE HOUSE OF RA!
THERE I SHALL TEACH YOU TO PROPERLY WORSHIP SEKHMET, THE DEVOURING ONE WHO REDUCETH ALL TO SILENCE!
WHOA! THEM'S CONSEQUENCES!
Y-YEAH! AN' THE ORPHAN'S RIGHT IN THE MIDDLE OF IT!
HEY, LADY! I'M NOT WITH THEM! I DON'T WANNA GO TO YOUR STUPID HOUSE OF RA!
AAAAH!
SNAP
REX?
MY HERO!

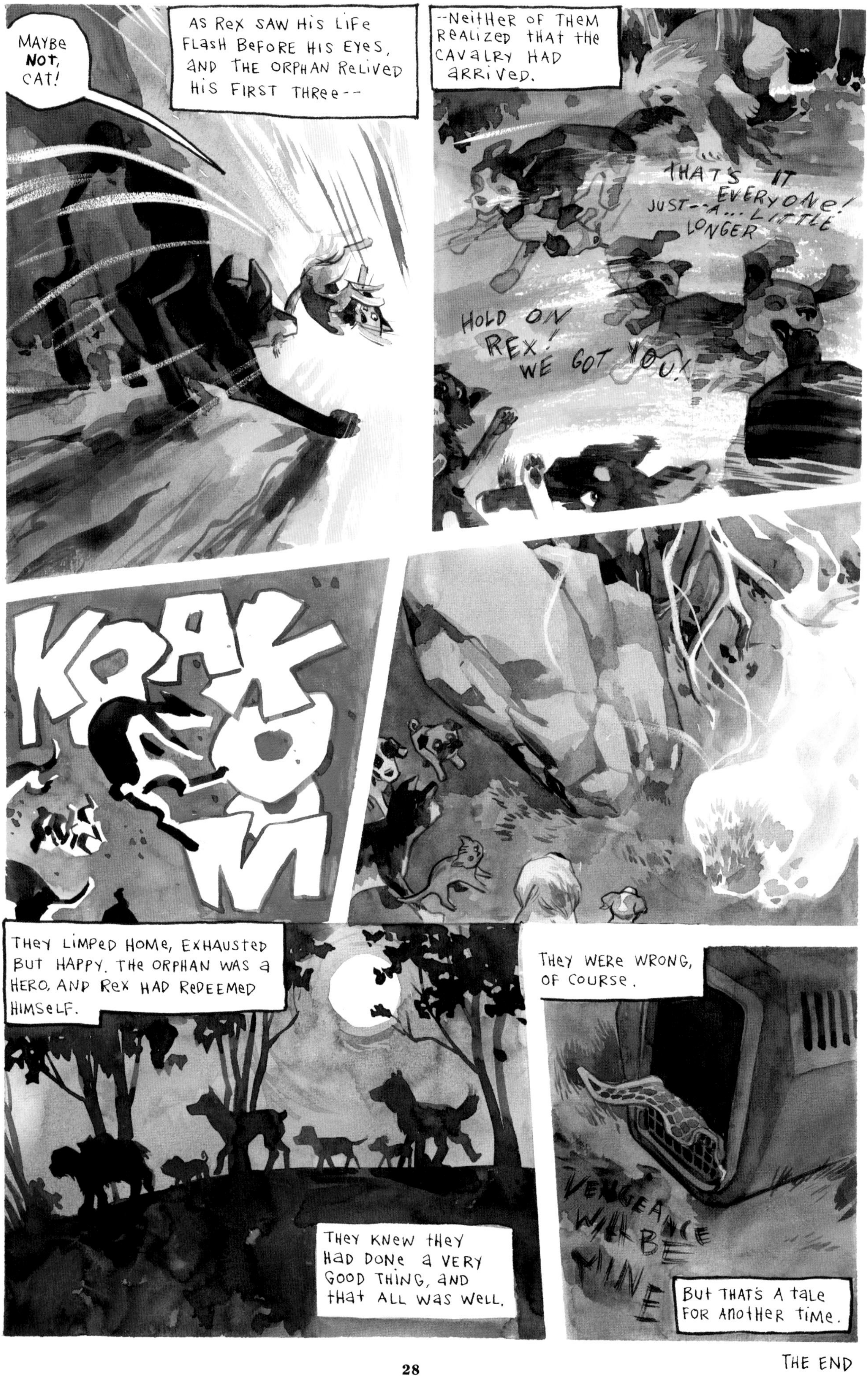
MAYBE NOT, CAT!
AS REX SAW HIS LIFE FLASH BEFORE HIS EYES, AND THE ORPHAN RELIVED HIS FIRST THREE--
--NEITHER OF THEM REALIZED THAT THE CAVALRY HAD ARRIVED.
THAT'S IT EVERYONE! JUST--A...LITTLE LONGER
HOLD ON REX! WE GOT YOU!
THEY LIMPED HOME, EXHAUSTED BUT HAPPY. THE ORPHAN WAS A HERO, AND REX HAD REDEEMED HIMSELF.
THEY KNEW THEY HAD DONE A VERY GOOD THING, AND THAT ALL WAS WELL.
THEY WERE WRONG, OF COURSE.
VENGEANCE WILL BE MINE
BUT THAT'S A TALE FOR ANOTHER TIME.

THE END

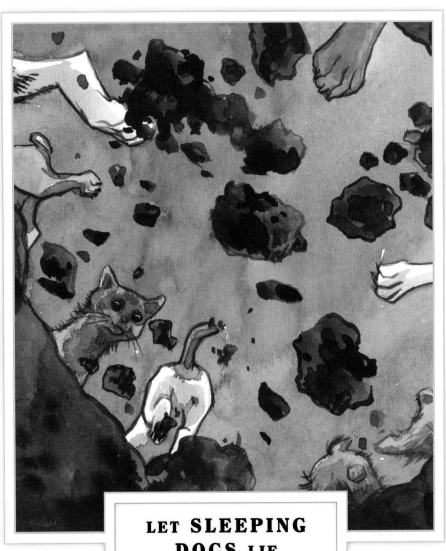

LET **SLEEPING**
DOGS LIE

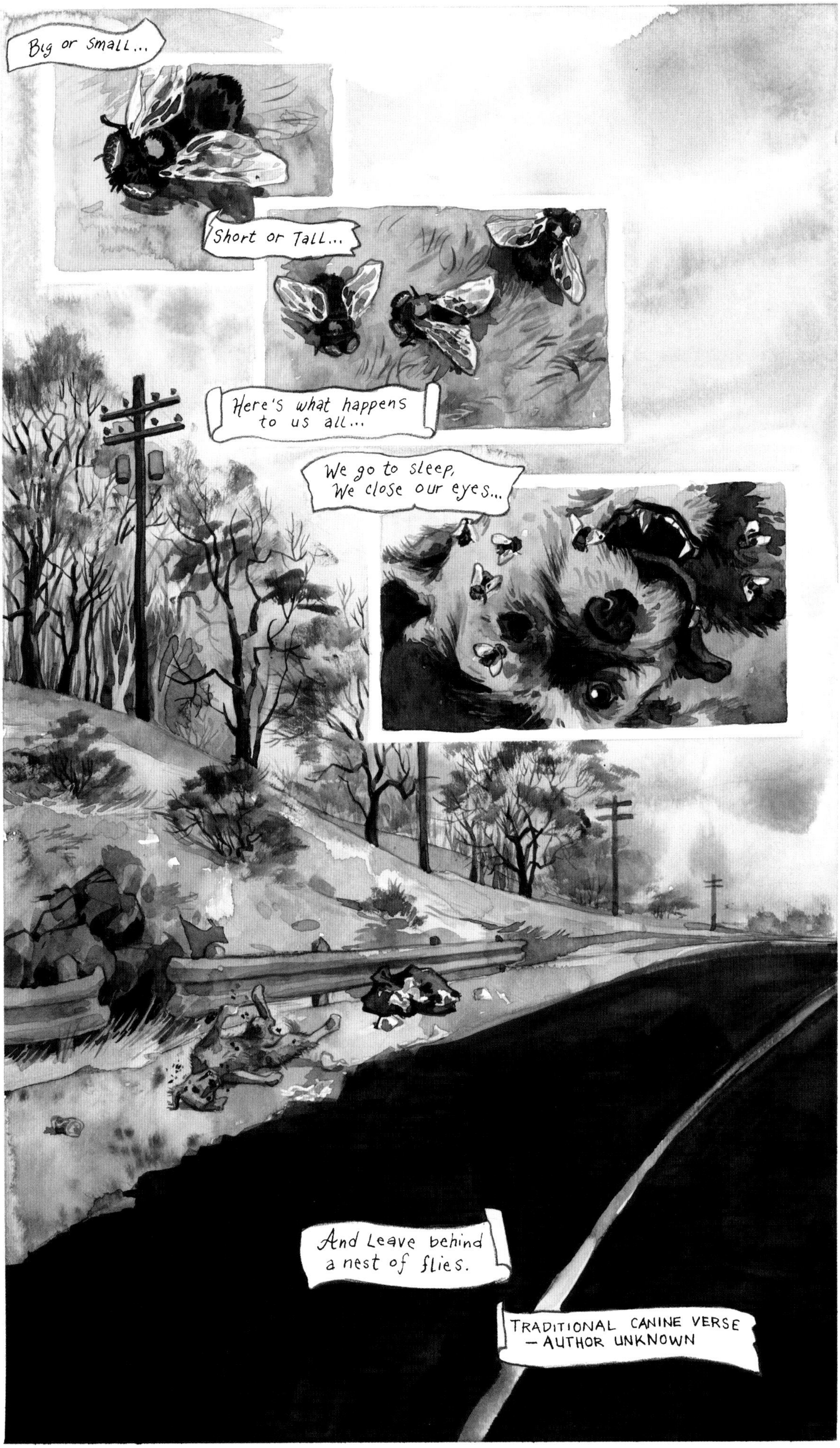
Big or small...
Short or Tall...
Here's what happens to us all...
We go to sleep, We close our eyes...
And Leave behind a nest of flies.
TRADITIONAL CANINE VERSE —AUTHOR UNKNOWN

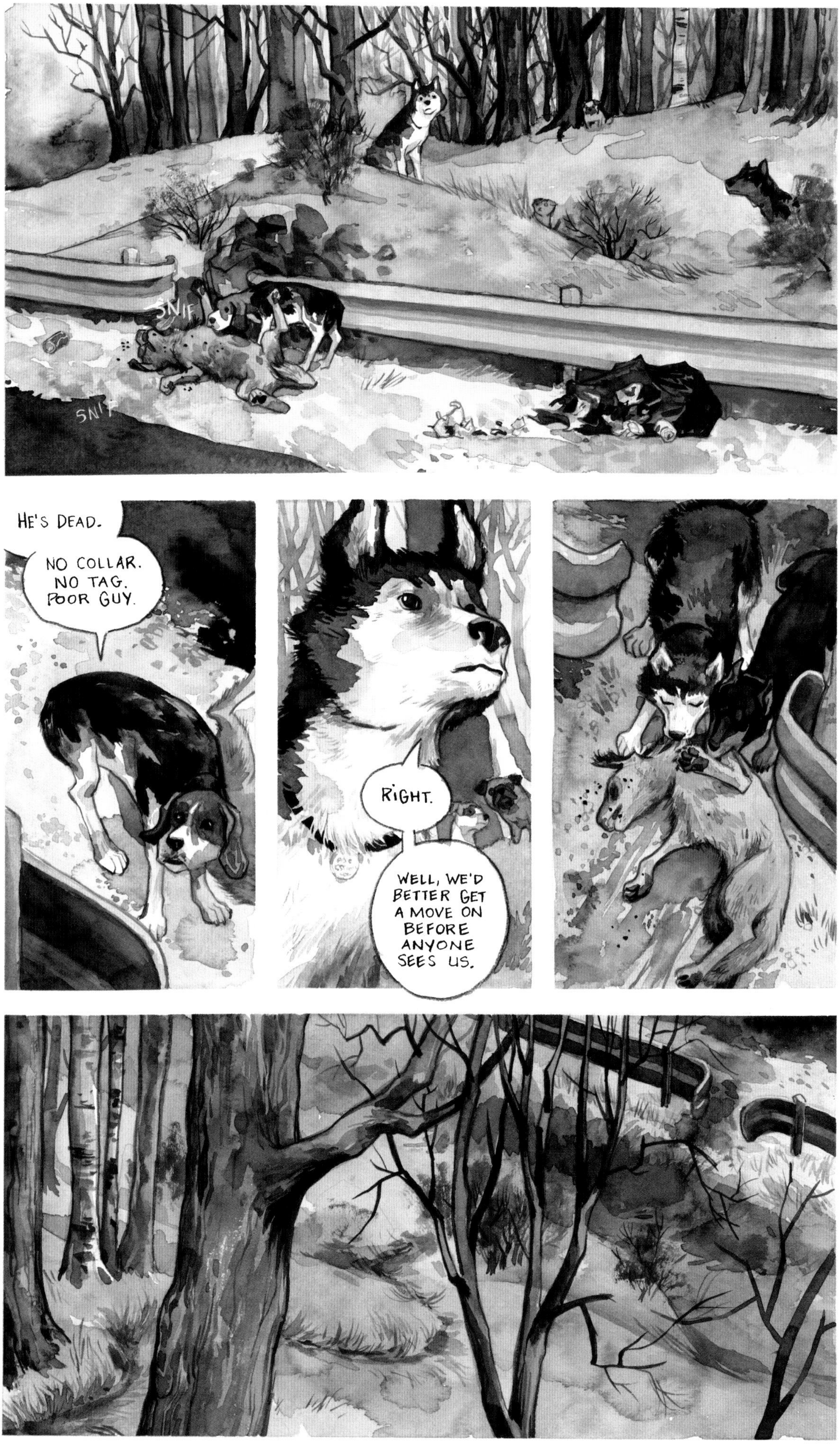
SNIF
SNIF
HE'S DEAD.
NO COLLAR. NO TAG. POOR GUY.
RIGHT.
WELL, WE'D BETTER GET A MOVE ON BEFORE ANYONE SEES US.

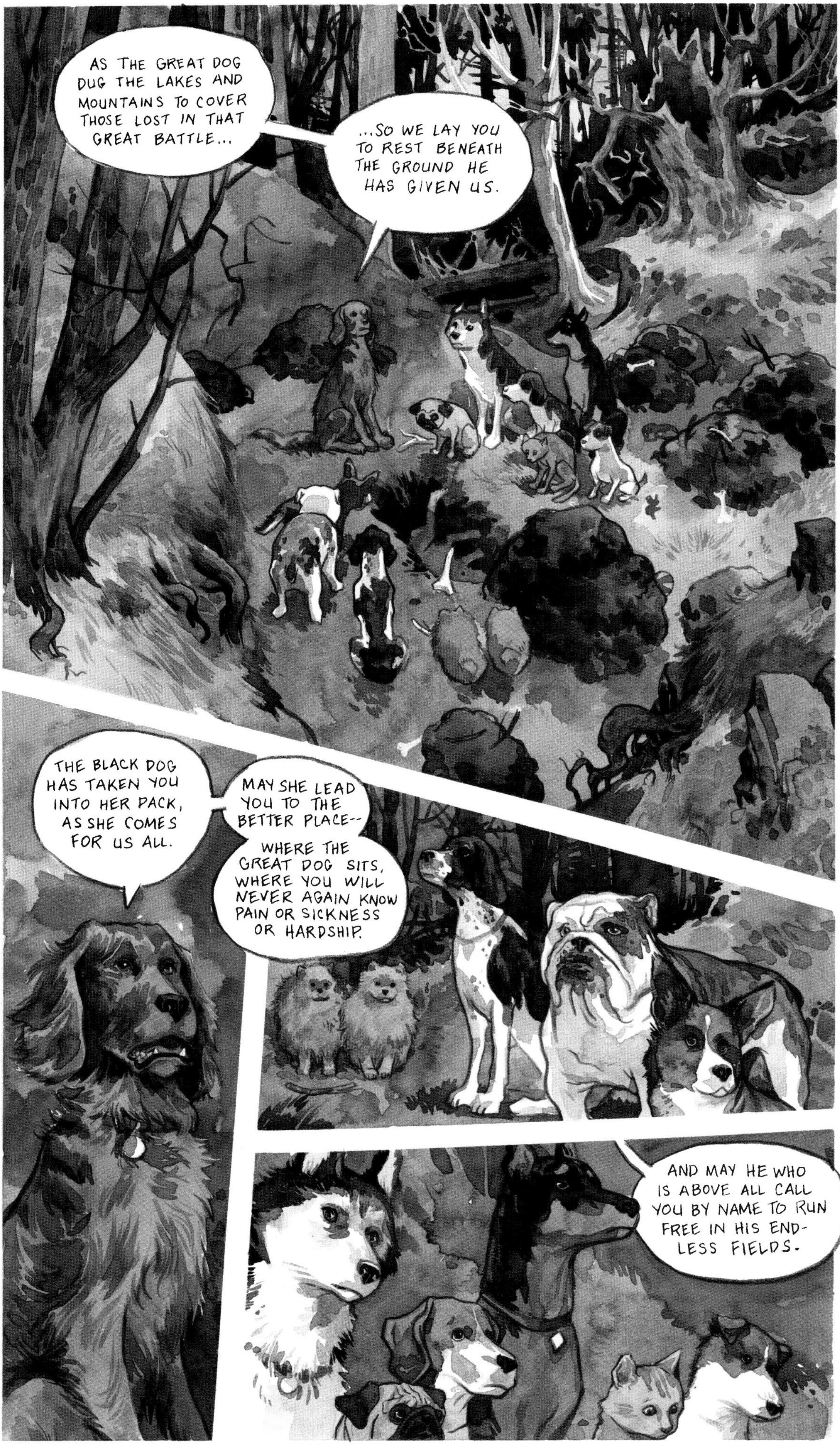
AS THE GREAT DOG DUG THE LAKES AND MOUNTAINS TO COVER THOSE LOST IN THAT GREAT BATTLE...
...SO WE LAY YOU TO REST BENEATH THE GROUND HE HAS GIVEN US.
THE BLACK DOG HAS TAKEN YOU INTO HER PACK, AS SHE COMES FOR US ALL.
MAY SHE LEAD YOU TO THE BETTER PLACE--
WHERE THE GREAT DOG SITS, WHERE YOU WILL NEVER AGAIN KNOW PAIN OR SICKNESS OR HARDSHIP.
AND MAY HE WHO IS ABOVE ALL CALL YOU BY NAME TO RUN FREE IN HIS ENDLESS FIELDS.

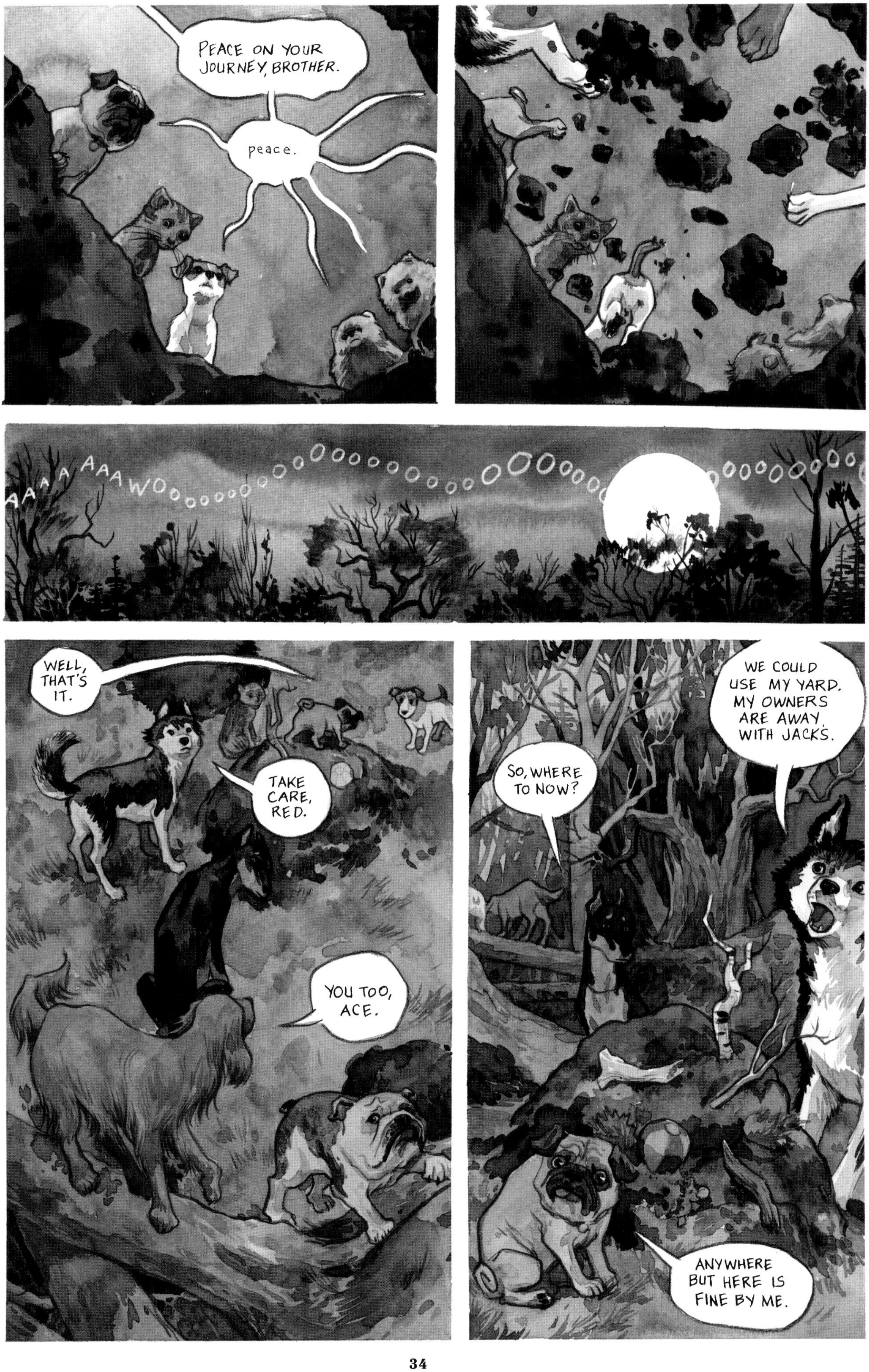
PEACE ON YOUR JOURNEY, BROTHER.
peace.
AAAAAAAWOoooooooOOOOOOOOOOOOoooOOOOOOOOooooooOOOO
WELL, THAT'S IT.
TAKE CARE, RED.
YOU TOO, ACE.
SO, WHERE TO NOW?
WE COULD USE MY YARD. MY OWNERS ARE AWAY WITH JACK'S.
ANYWHERE BUT HERE IS FINE BY ME.

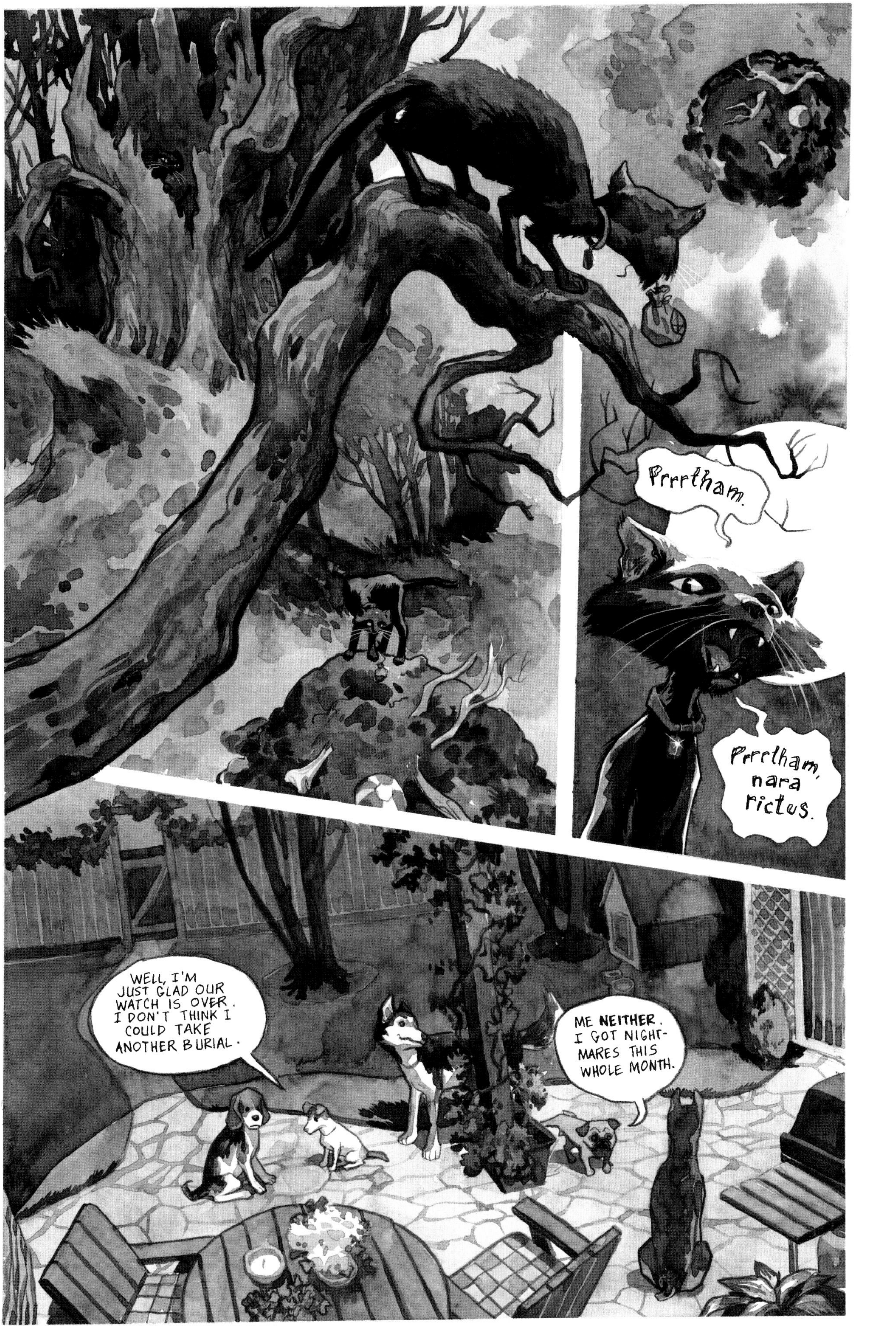
Prrrtham.
Prrrtham, nara rictus.
WELL, I'M JUST GLAD OUR WATCH IS OVER. I DON'T THINK I COULD TAKE ANOTHER BURIAL.
ME NEITHER. I GOT NIGHT-MARES THIS WHOLE MONTH.

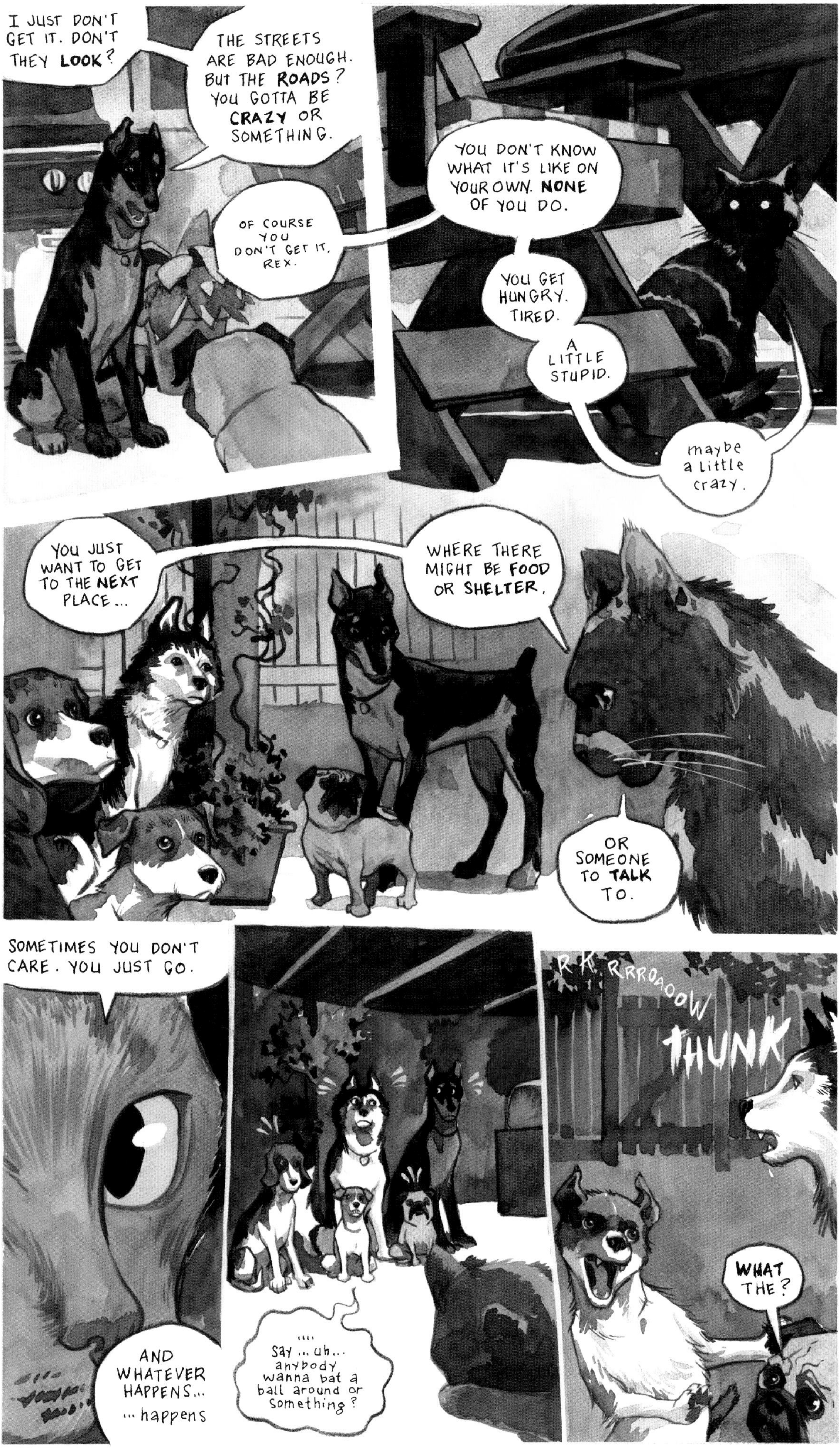
I JUST DON'T GET IT. DON'T THEY LOOK?
THE STREETS ARE BAD ENOUGH. BUT THE ROADS? YOU GOTTA BE CRAZY OR SOMETHING.
OF COURSE YOU DON'T GET IT, REX.
YOU DON'T KNOW WHAT IT'S LIKE ON YOUR OWN. NONE OF YOU DO.
YOU GET HUNGRY. TIRED.
A LITTLE STUPID.
maybe a little crazy.
YOU JUST WANT TO GET TO THE NEXT PLACE...
WHERE THERE MIGHT BE FOOD OR SHELTER.
OR SOMEONE TO TALK TO.
SOMETIMES YOU DON'T CARE. YOU JUST GO.
AND WHATEVER HAPPENS...
...happens
.... say ... uh... anybody wanna bat a ball around or something?
RR RRROAOOW
THUNK
WHAT THE?

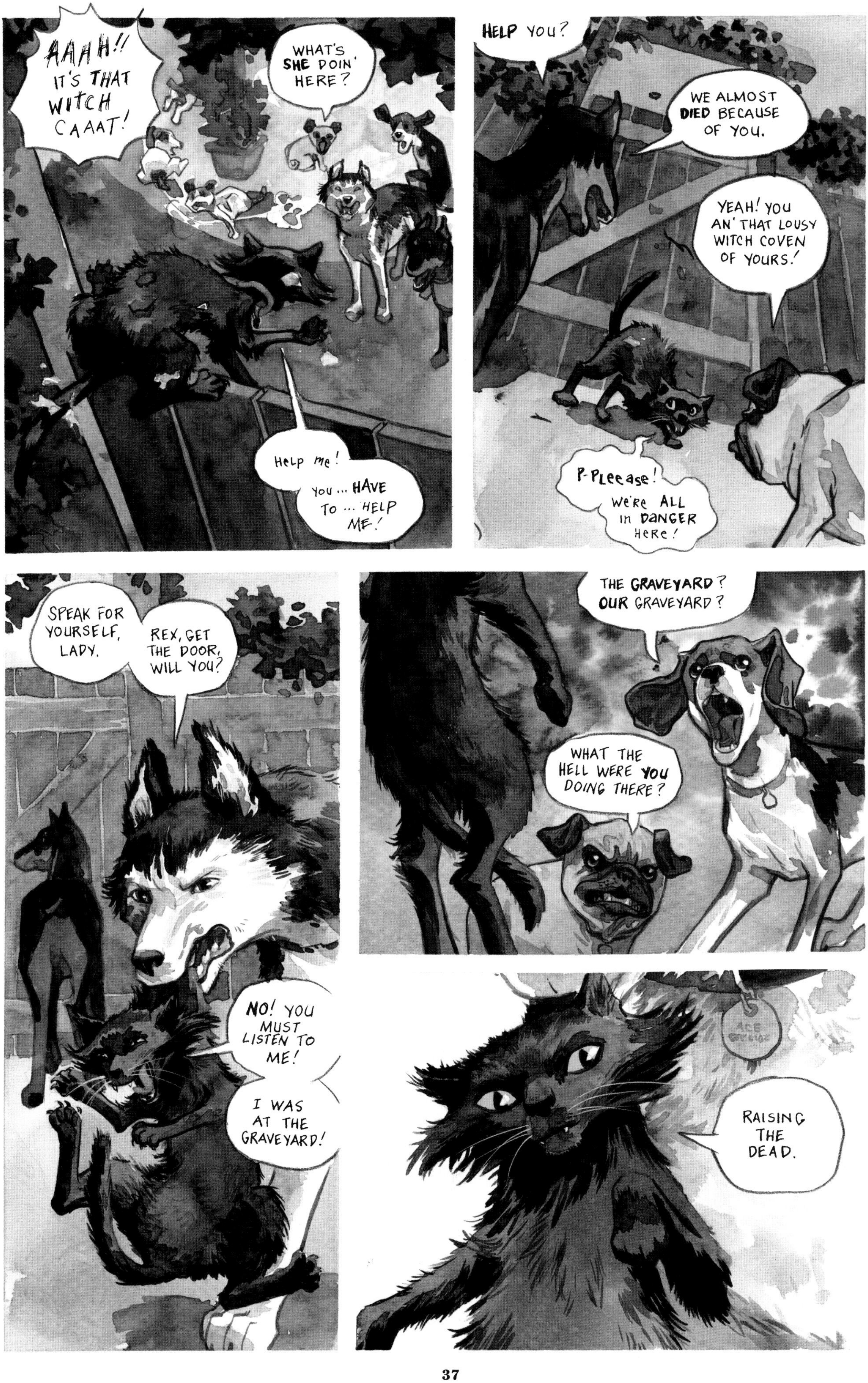
AAAH!! IT'S THAT WITCH CAAAT!
WHAT'S SHE DOIN' HERE?
Help me! You... HAVE to... HELP ME!
HELP you?
WE ALMOST DIED BECAUSE OF YOU.
YEAH! YOU AN' THAT LOUSY WITCH COVEN OF YOURS!
P-Pleease! We're ALL in DANGER here!
SPEAK FOR YOURSELF, LADY.
REX, GET THE DOOR, WILL YOU?
NO! YOU MUST LISTEN TO ME!
I WAS AT THE GRAVEYARD!
THE GRAVEYARD? OUR GRAVEYARD?
WHAT THE HELL WERE YOU DOING THERE?
RAISING THE DEAD.

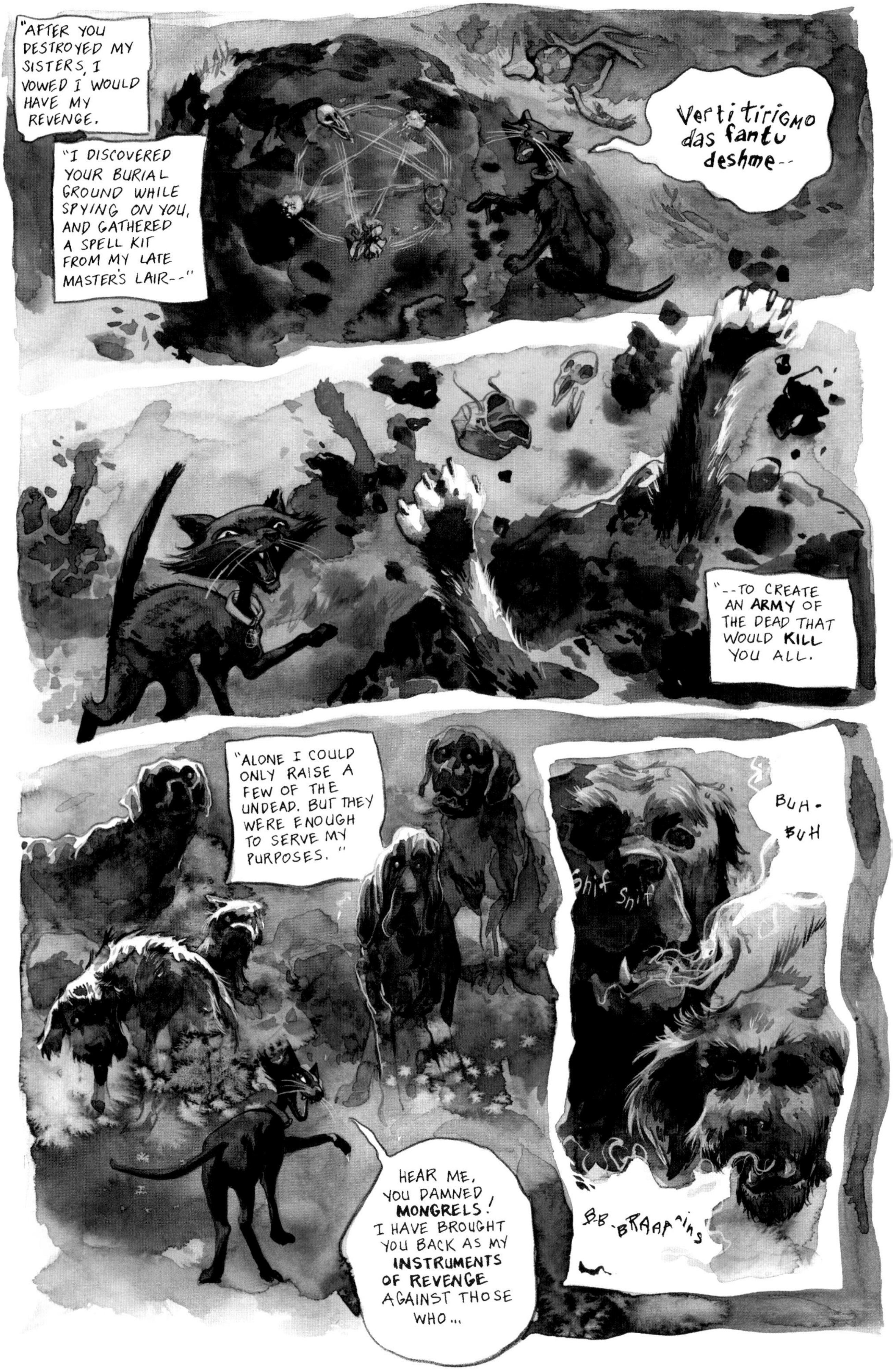
"AFTER YOU DESTROYED MY SISTERS, I VOWED I WOULD HAVE MY REVENGE.
"I DISCOVERED YOUR BURIAL GROUND WHILE SPYING ON YOU, AND GATHERED A SPELL KIT FROM MY LATE MASTER'S LAIR--"
Verti tirigmo das fantu deshme--
"--TO CREATE AN **ARMY** OF THE DEAD THAT WOULD **KILL** YOU ALL.
"ALONE I COULD ONLY RAISE A FEW OF THE UNDEAD. BUT THEY WERE ENOUGH TO SERVE MY PURPOSES."
HEAR ME, YOU DAMNED **MONGRELS**! I HAVE BROUGHT YOU BACK AS MY **INSTRUMENTS OF REVENGE** AGAINST THOSE WHO...
BUH-BUH
Shif Shif
B-B-BRAAAains

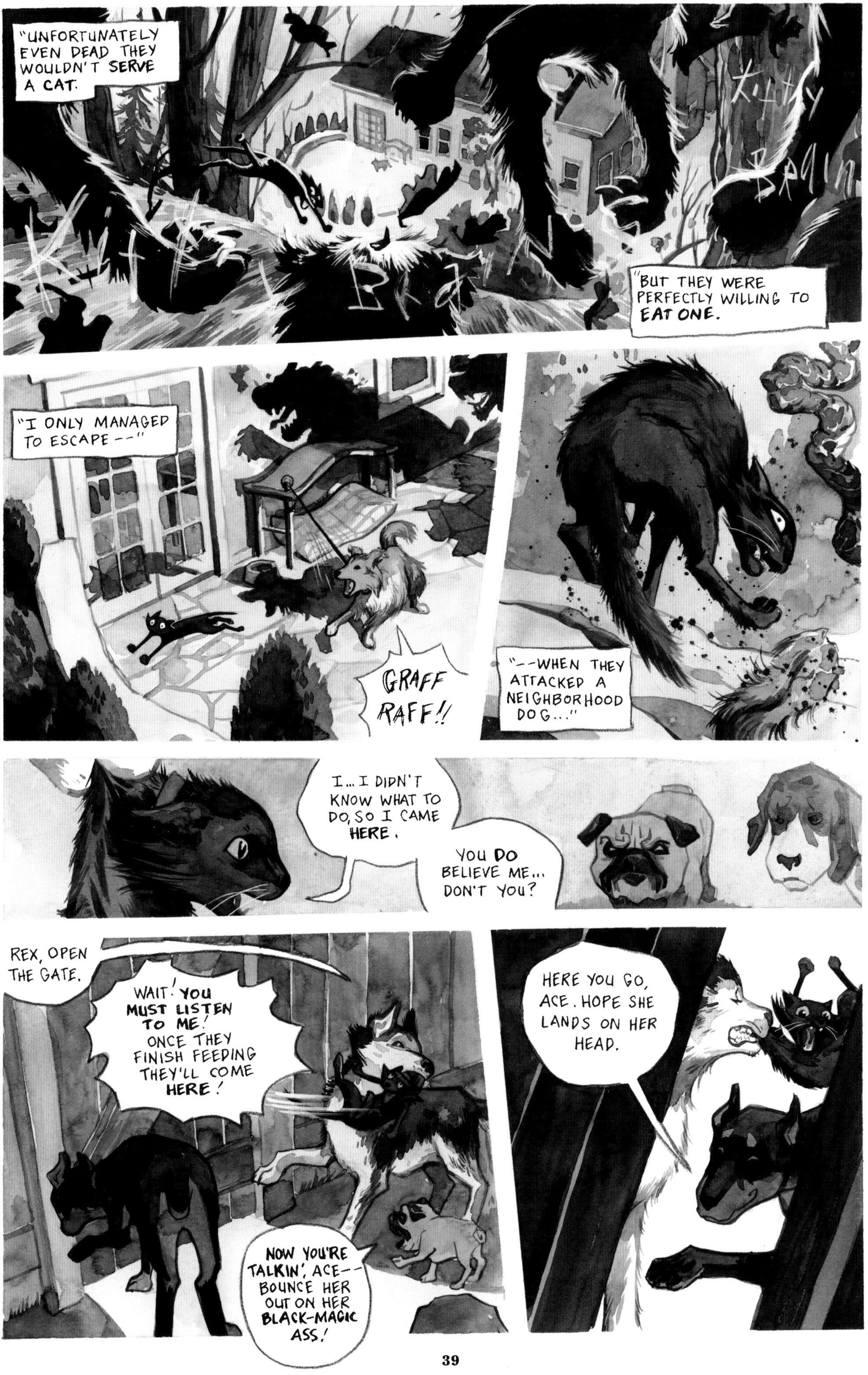
"UNFORTUNATELY EVEN DEAD THEY WOULDN'T SERVE A CAT.
"BUT THEY WERE PERFECTLY WILLING TO EAT ONE.
"I ONLY MANAGED TO ESCAPE --"
GRAFF RAFF!!
"--WHEN THEY ATTACKED A NEIGHBORHOOD DOG..."
I... I DIDN'T KNOW WHAT TO DO, SO I CAME HERE.
YOU DO BELIEVE ME... DON'T YOU?
REX, OPEN THE GATE.
WAIT! YOU MUST LISTEN TO ME! ONCE THEY FINISH FEEDING THEY'LL COME HERE!
NOW YOU'RE TALKIN', ACE-- BOUNCE HER OUT ON HER BLACK-MAGIC ASS!
HERE YOU GO, ACE. HOPE SHE LANDS ON HER HEAD.

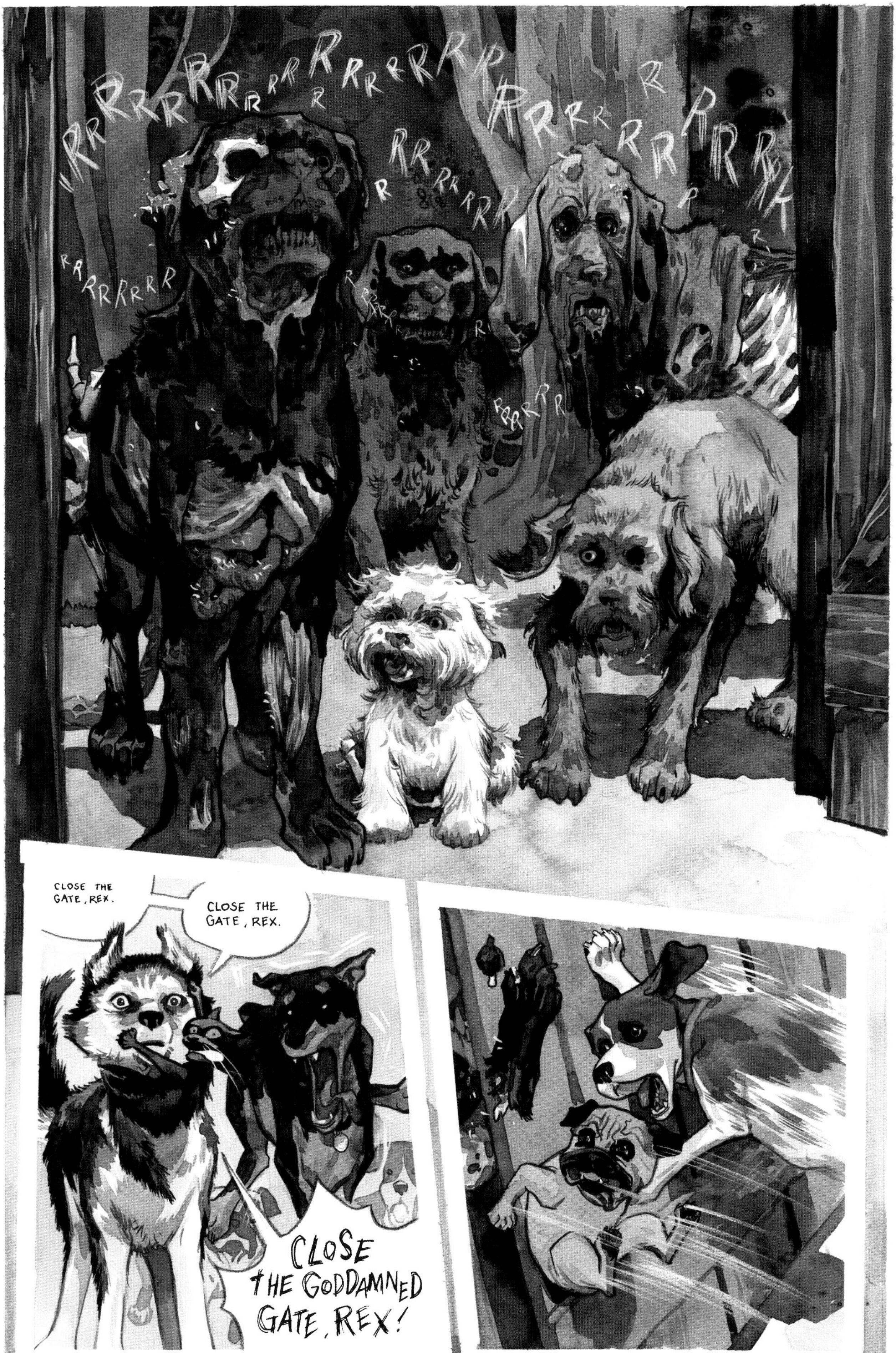

CLOSE THE GATE, REX.
CLOSE THE GATE, REX.
CLOSE THE GODDAMNED GATE, REX!

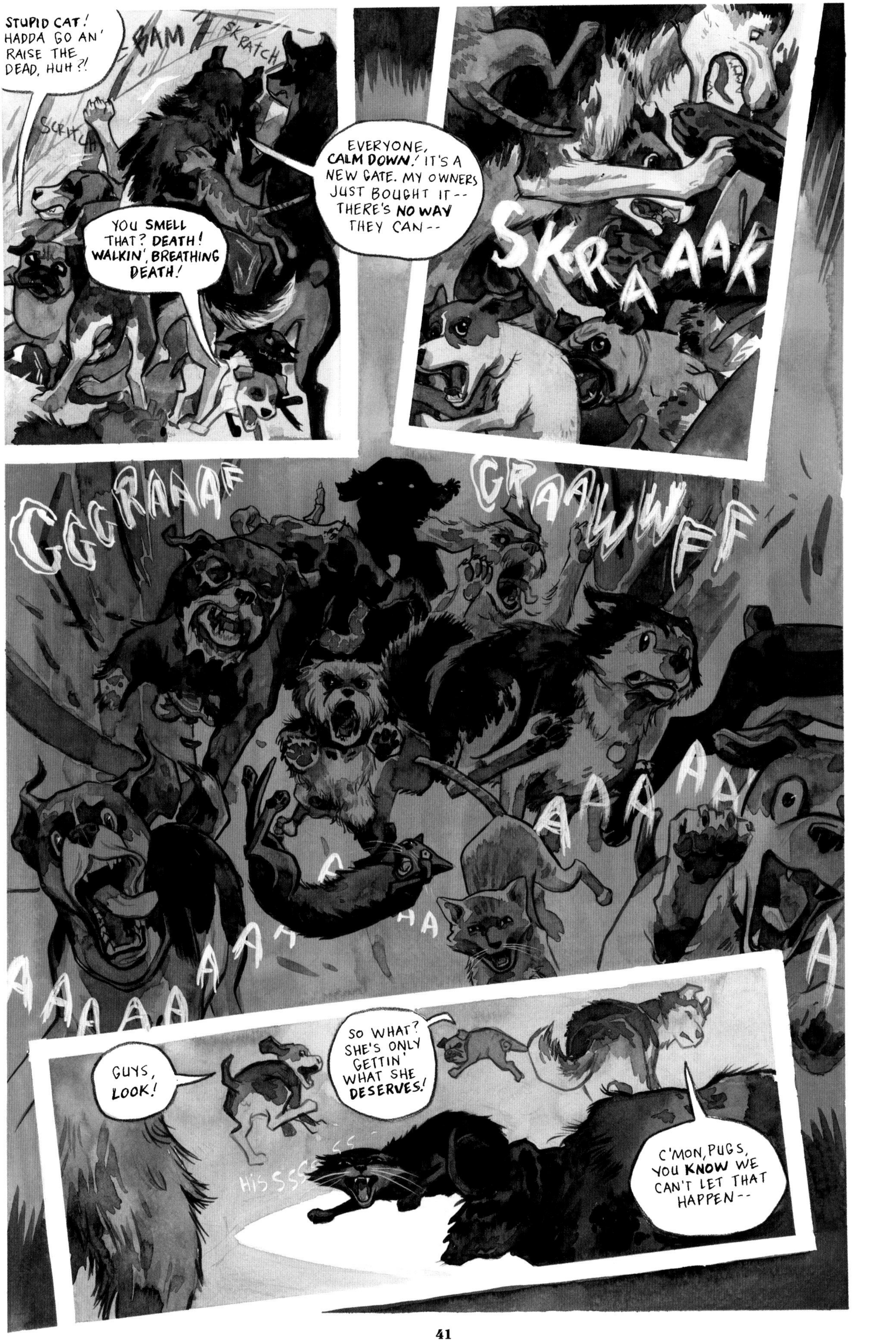
STUPID CAT! HADDA GO AN' RAISE THE DEAD, HUH?!
BAM
SKRATCH
SCRITCH
YOU SMELL THAT? DEATH! WALKIN', BREATHING DEATH!
EVERYONE, CALM DOWN! IT'S A NEW GATE. MY OWNERS JUST BOUGHT IT -- THERE'S NO WAY THEY CAN --
SKRAAAK
GGGRAAAF
GRAAWWFF
AAAAAAAAA
GUYS, LOOK!
SO WHAT? SHE'S ONLY GETTIN' WHAT SHE DESERVES!
HISSSS
C'MON, PUGS, YOU KNOW WE CAN'T LET THAT HAPPEN --

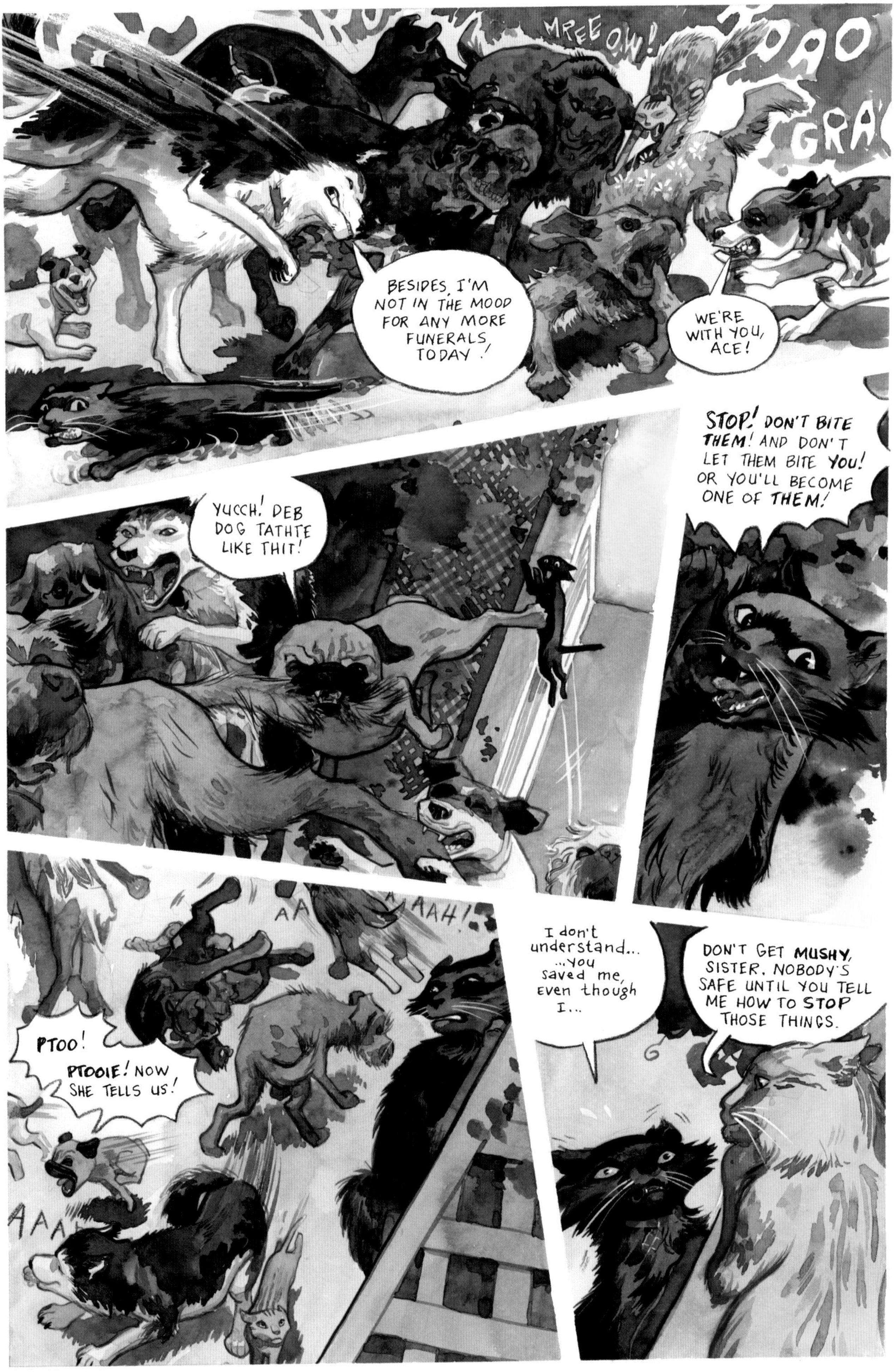
MREEOW!
BESIDES, I'M NOT IN THE MOOD FOR ANY MORE FUNERALS TODAY!
WE'RE WITH YOU, ACE!
STOP! DON'T BITE THEM! AND DON'T LET THEM BITE YOU! OR YOU'LL BECOME ONE OF THEM!
YUCCH! DEB DOG TATHTE LIKE THIT!
AAAH!
PTOO!
PTOOIE! NOW SHE TELLS US!
I don't understand... ...you saved me, even though I...
DON'T GET MUSHY, SISTER. NOBODY'S SAFE UNTIL YOU TELL ME HOW TO STOP THOSE THINGS.

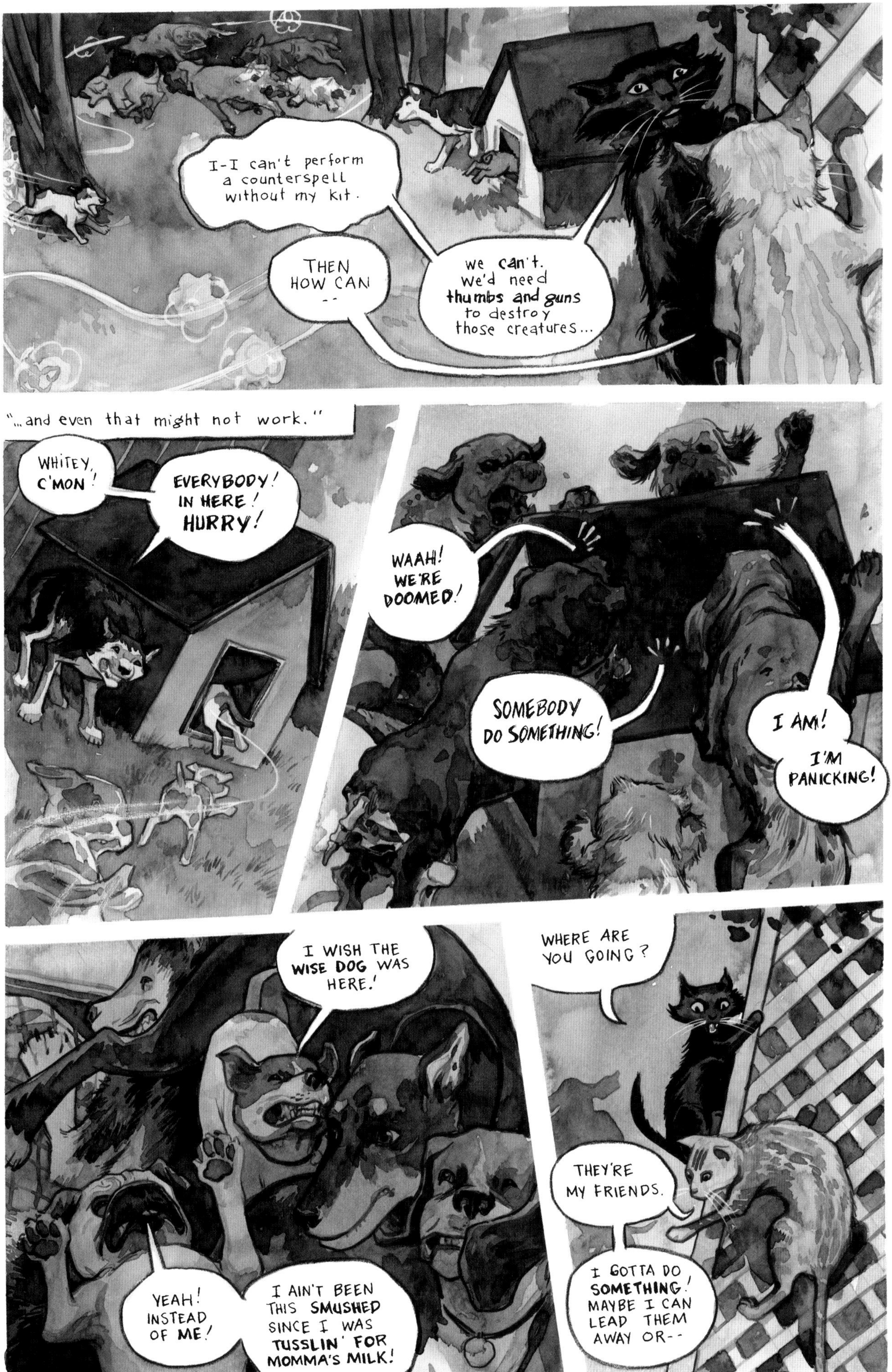

I-I can't perform a counterspell without my kit.
THEN HOW CAN --
we can't. we'd need thumbs and guns to destroy those creatures...
"...and even that might not work."
WHITEY, C'MON!
EVERYBODY! IN HERE! HURRY!
WAAH! WE'RE DOOMED!
SOMEBODY DO SOMETHING!
I AM!
I'M PANICKING!
I WISH THE WISE DOG WAS HERE!
YEAH! INSTEAD OF ME!
I AIN'T BEEN THIS SMUSHED SINCE I WAS TUSSLIN' FOR MOMMA'S MILK!
WHERE ARE YOU GOING?
THEY'RE MY FRIENDS.
I GOTTA DO SOMETHING! MAYBE I CAN LEAD THEM AWAY OR--

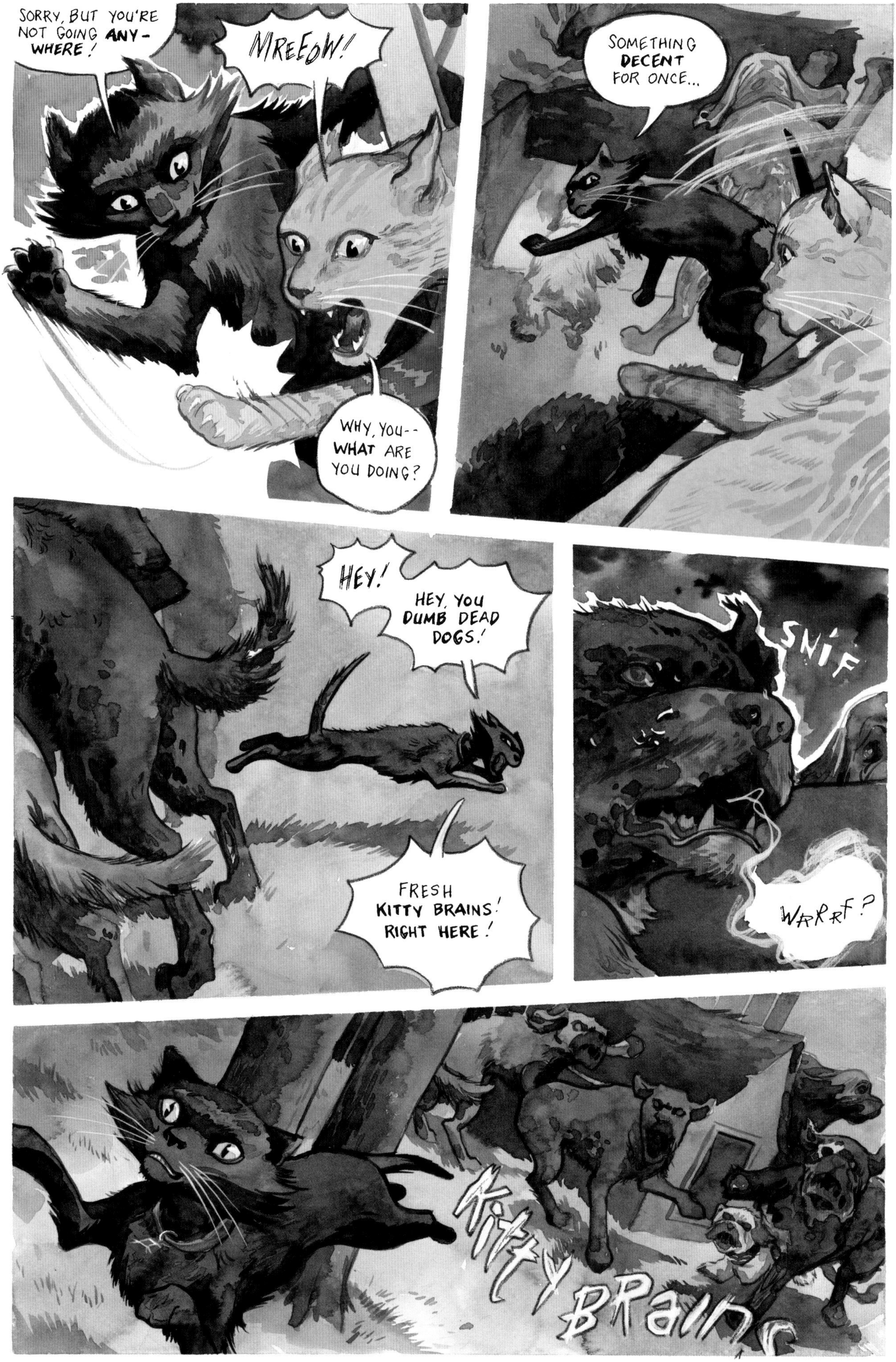
SORRY, BUT YOU'RE NOT GOING ANY-WHERE!
MREEOW!
WHY, YOU-- WHAT ARE YOU DOING?
SOMETHING DECENT FOR ONCE...
HEY!
HEY, YOU DUMB DEAD DOGS!
FRESH KITTY BRAINS! RIGHT HERE!
SNIF
WARRF?
KITTY BRAINS

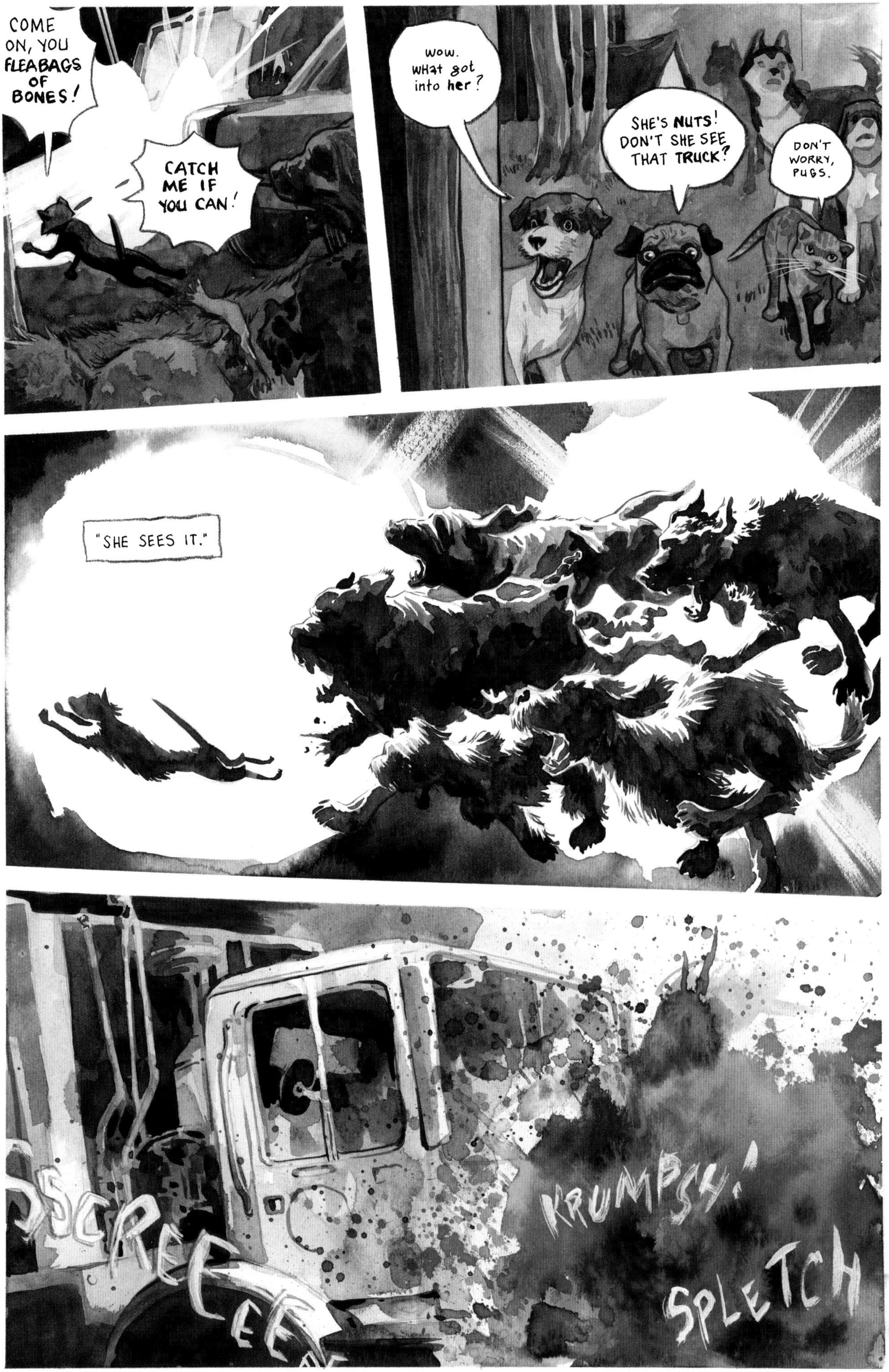
COME ON, YOU FLEABAGS OF BONES!
CATCH ME IF YOU CAN!
WOW. WHAT GOT INTO HER?
SHE'S NUTS! DON'T SHE SEE THAT TRUCK?
DON'T WORRY, PUGS.
"SHE SEES IT."
SSCREEEEE
KRUMPSH!
SPLETCH

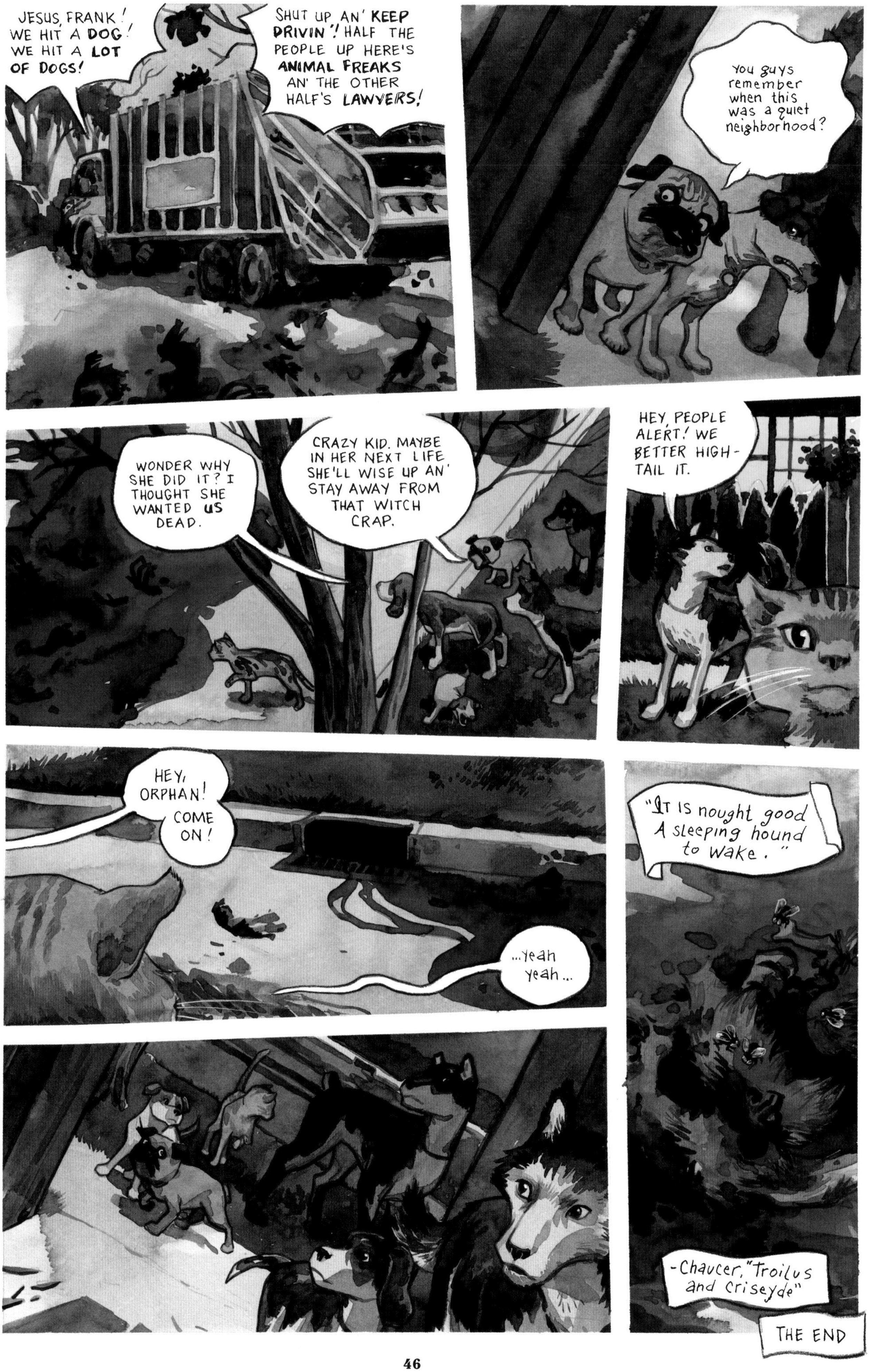
JESUS, FRANK! WE HIT A DOG! WE HIT A LOT OF DOGS!
SHUT UP AN' KEEP DRIVIN'! HALF THE PEOPLE UP HERE'S ANIMAL FREAKS AN' THE OTHER HALF'S LAWYERS!
You guys remember when this was a quiet neighborhood?
WONDER WHY SHE DID IT? I THOUGHT SHE WANTED US DEAD.
CRAZY KID. MAYBE IN HER NEXT LIFE SHE'LL WISE UP AN' STAY AWAY FROM THAT WITCH CRAP.
HEY, PEOPLE ALERT! WE BETTER HIGH-TAIL IT.
HEY, ORPHAN!
COME ON!
...yeah yeah...
"It is nought good A sleeping hound to wake."
-Chaucer, "Troilus and Criseyde"
THE END

A **DOG** AND HIS **BOY**

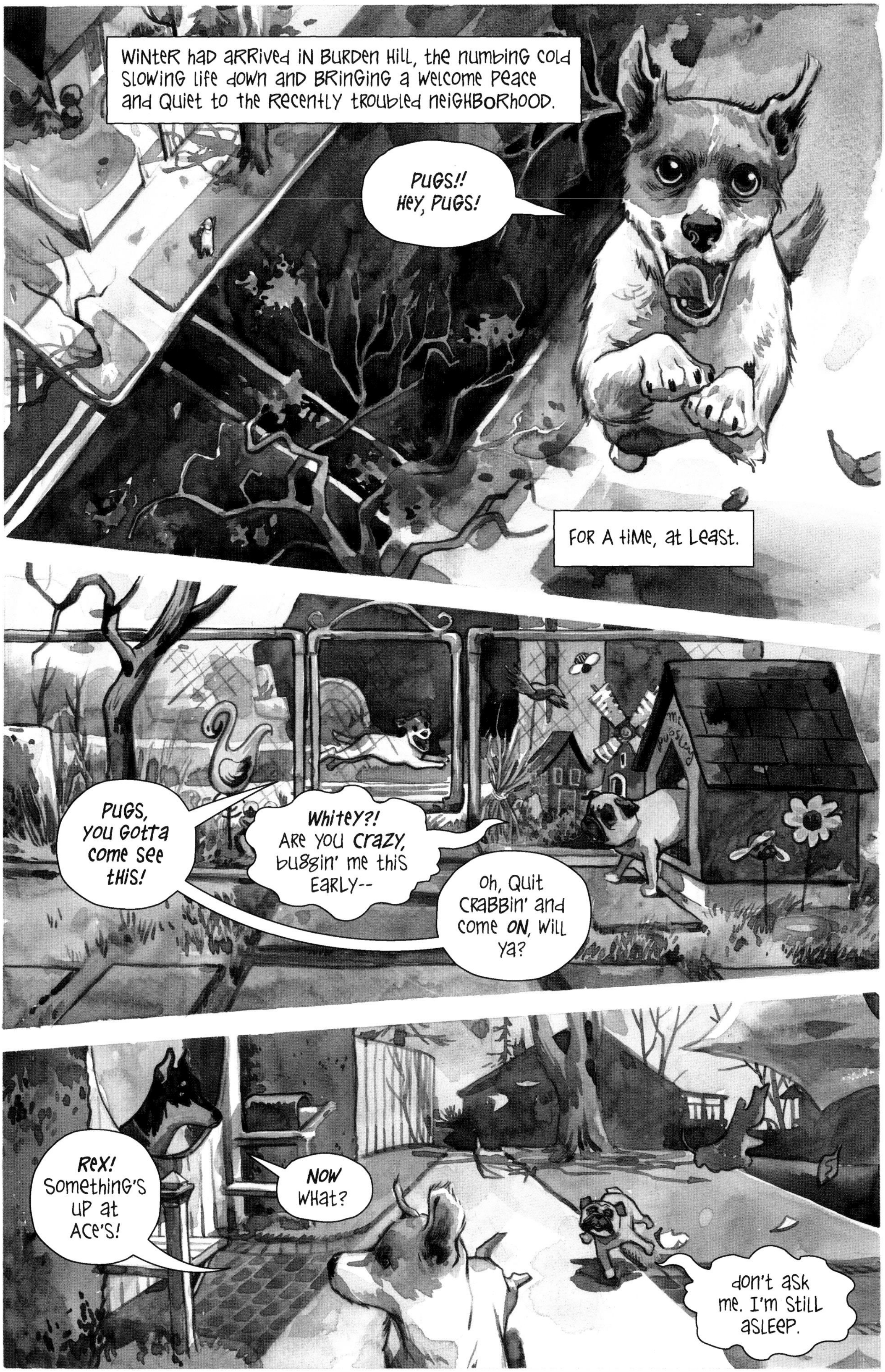
Winter had arrived in Burden Hill, the numbing cold slowing life down and bringing a welcome peace and quiet to the recently troubled neighborhood.
Pugs!! Hey, Pugs!
For a time, at least.
Pugs, you gotta come see this!
Whitey?! Are you crazy, buggin' me this early--
Oh, quit crabbin' and come on, will ya?
Rex! Something's up at Ace's!
Now what?
don't ask me. I'm still asleep.

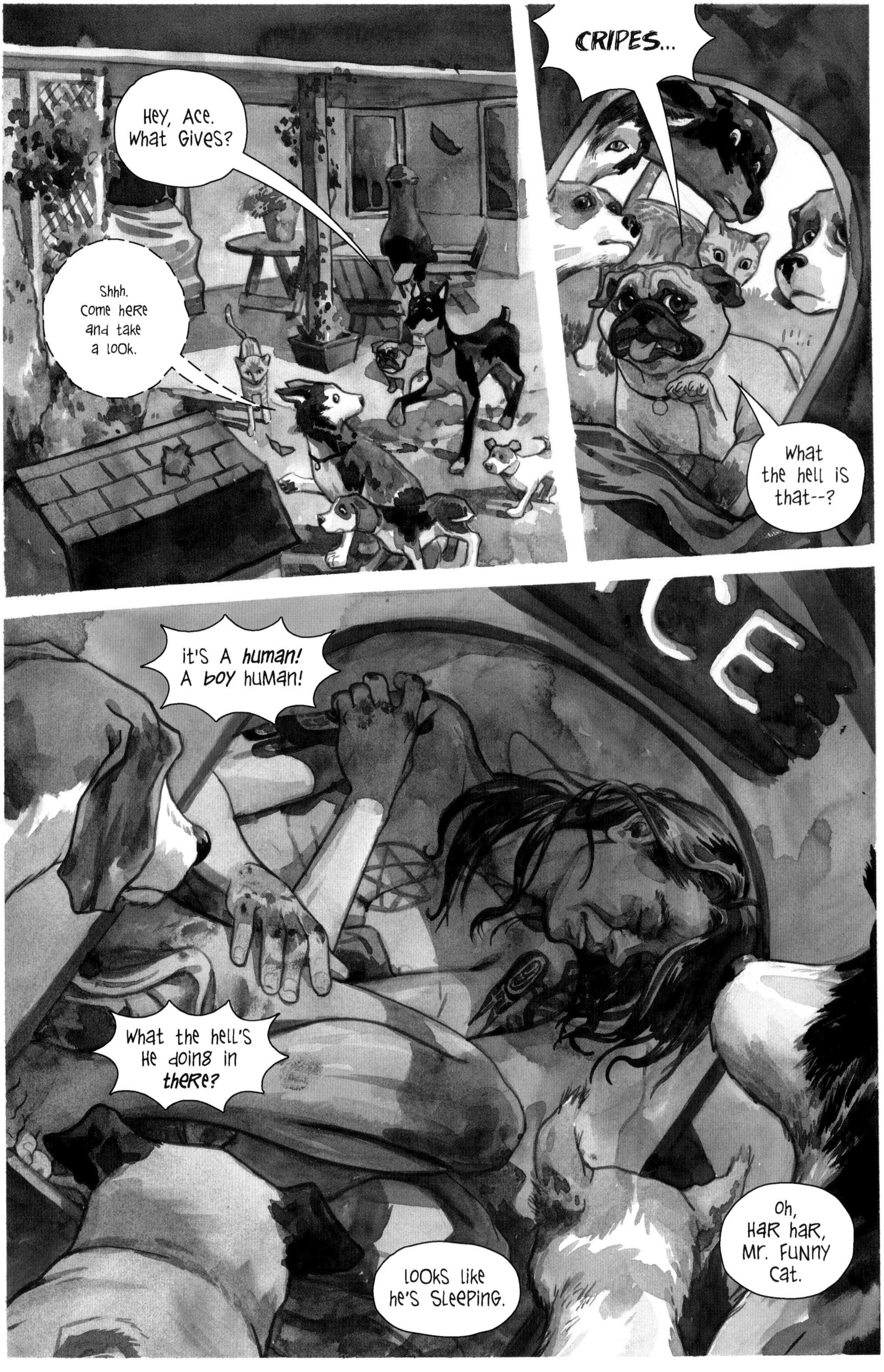
Hey, Ace.
What Gives?
Shhh.
Come here
and take
a look.
CRIPES...
What
the hell is
that--?
it's A *human!*
A *boy* human!
What the hell's
He doing in
there?
looks like
he's sleeping.
Oh,
Har har,
Mr. Funny
Cat.

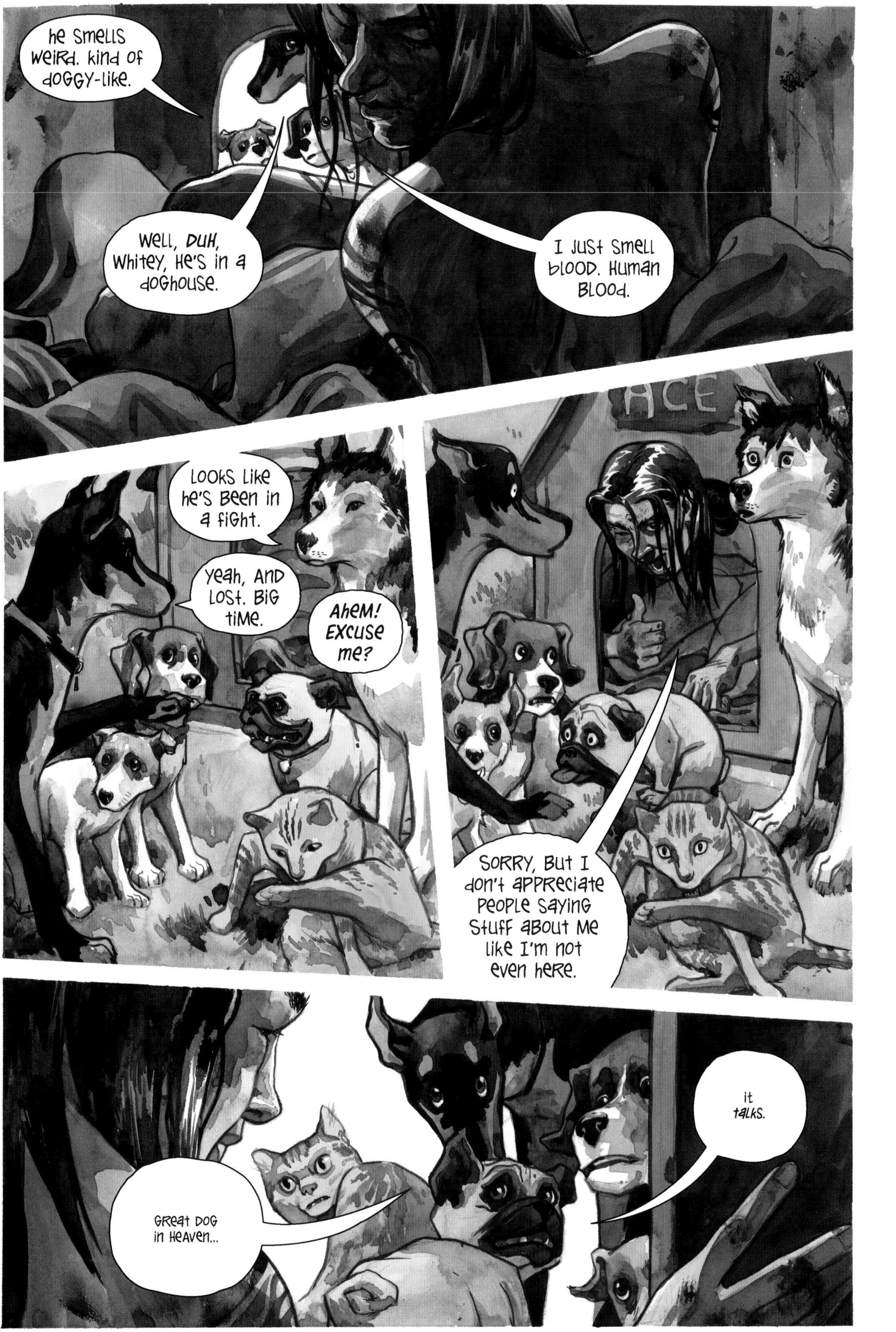
he smells weird. kind of doggy-like.
Well, *duh*, Whitey, he's in a doghouse.
I just smell blood. Human blood.
Looks like he's been in a fight.
Yeah, and lost. Big time.
Ahem! Excuse me?
Sorry, but I don't appreciate people saying stuff about me like I'm not even here.
it talks.
Great dog in heaven...

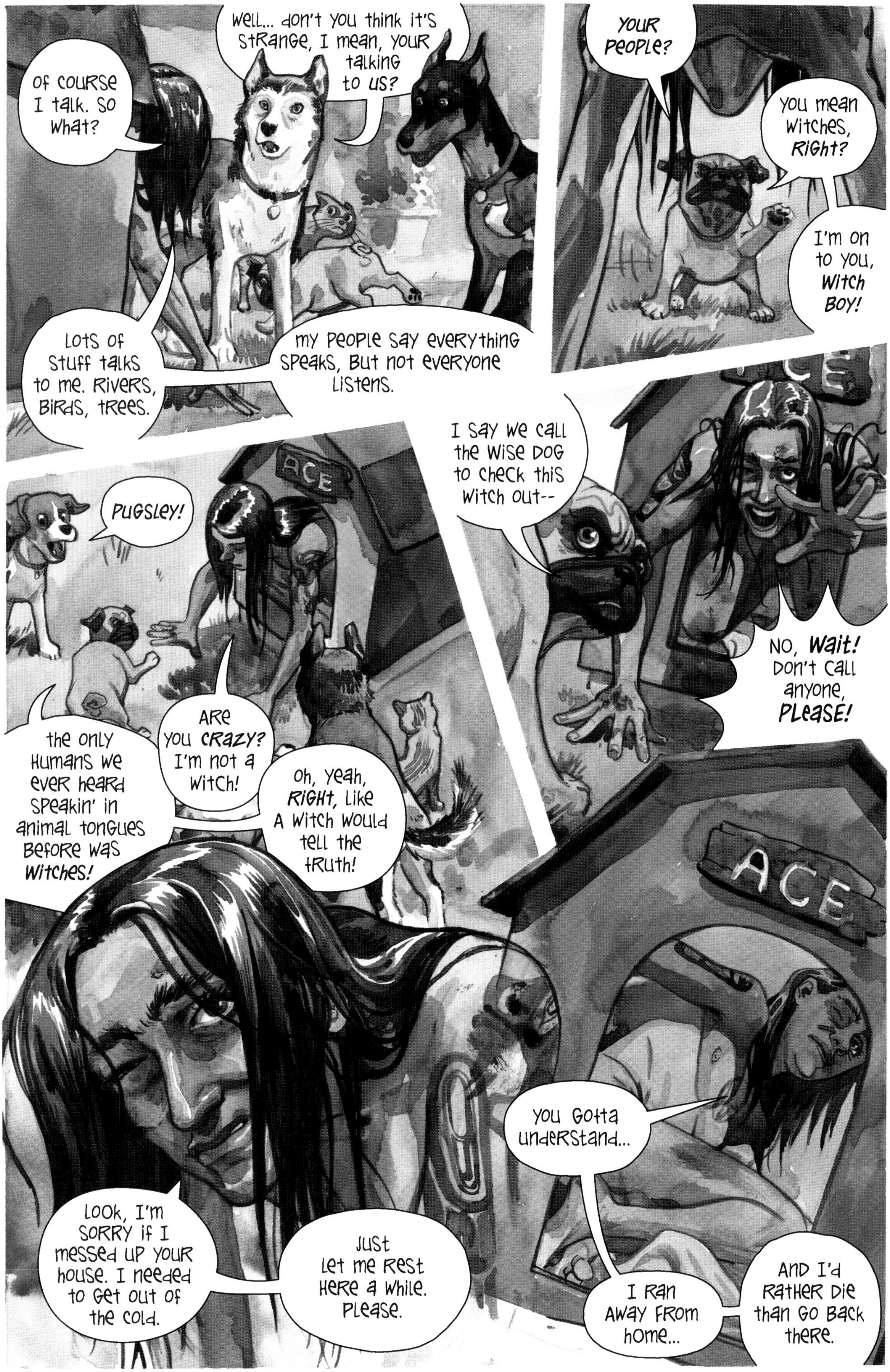
Of course I talk. So what?
Well... don't you think it's strange, I mean, your talking to us?
Lots of stuff talks to me. Rivers, birds, trees.
My people say everything speaks, but not everyone listens.
Your people?
You mean witches, right?
I'm on to you, witch boy!
Pugsley!
The only humans we ever heard speakin' in animal tongues before was witches!
Are you crazy? I'm not a witch!
Oh, yeah, right, like a witch would tell the truth!
ACE
I say we call the wise dog to check this witch out--
No, wait! Don't call anyone, please!
ACE
Look, I'm sorry if I messed up your house. I needed to get out of the cold.
Just let me rest here a while. Please.
You gotta understand...
I ran away from home...
And I'd rather die than go back there.

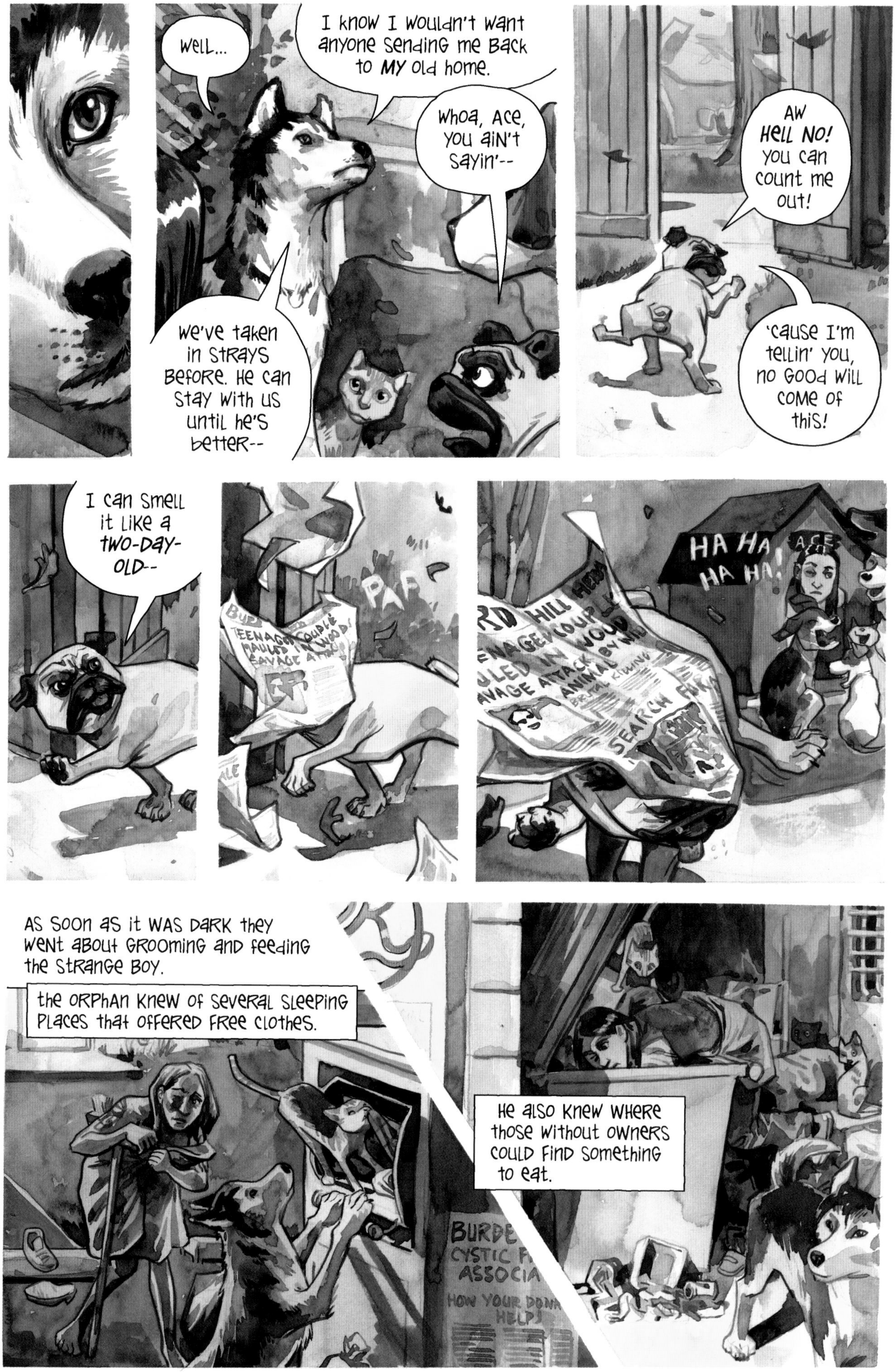
Well...
I know I wouldn't want anyone sending me back to MY old home.
Whoa, Ace, you ain't sayin'--
We've taken in strays before. He can stay with us until he's better--
AW HELL NO! You can count me out!
'cause I'm tellin' you, no good will come of this!
I can smell it like a two-day-old--
HA HA HA HA!
As soon as it was dark they went about grooming and feeding the strange boy.
the orphan knew of several sleeping places that offered free clothes.
He also knew where those without owners could find something to eat.

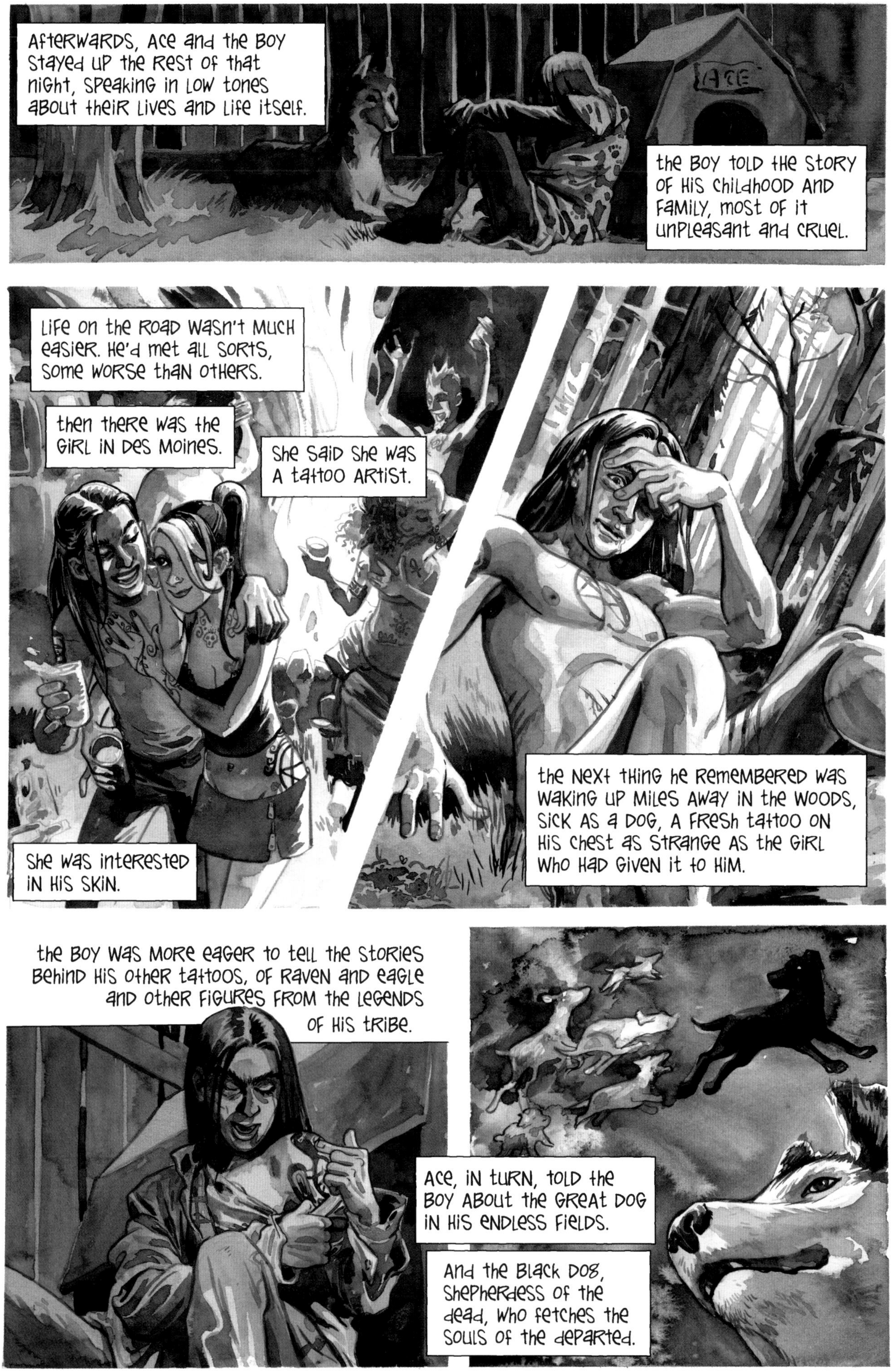
Afterwards, Ace and the Boy stayed up the rest of that night, speaking in low tones about their lives and life itself.
ACE
the Boy told the story of his childhood and family, most of it unpleasant and cruel.
Life on the road wasn't much easier. He'd met all sorts, some worse than others.
then there was the girl in Des Moines.
She said she was a tattoo artist.
She was interested in his skin.
the next thing he remembered was waking up miles away in the woods, sick as a dog, a fresh tattoo on his chest as strange as the girl who had given it to him.
the Boy was more eager to tell the stories behind his other tattoos, of Raven and Eagle and other figures from the legends of his tribe.
Ace, in turn, told the Boy about the Great Dog in his endless fields.
And the Black Dog, shepherdess of the dead, who fetches the souls of the departed.

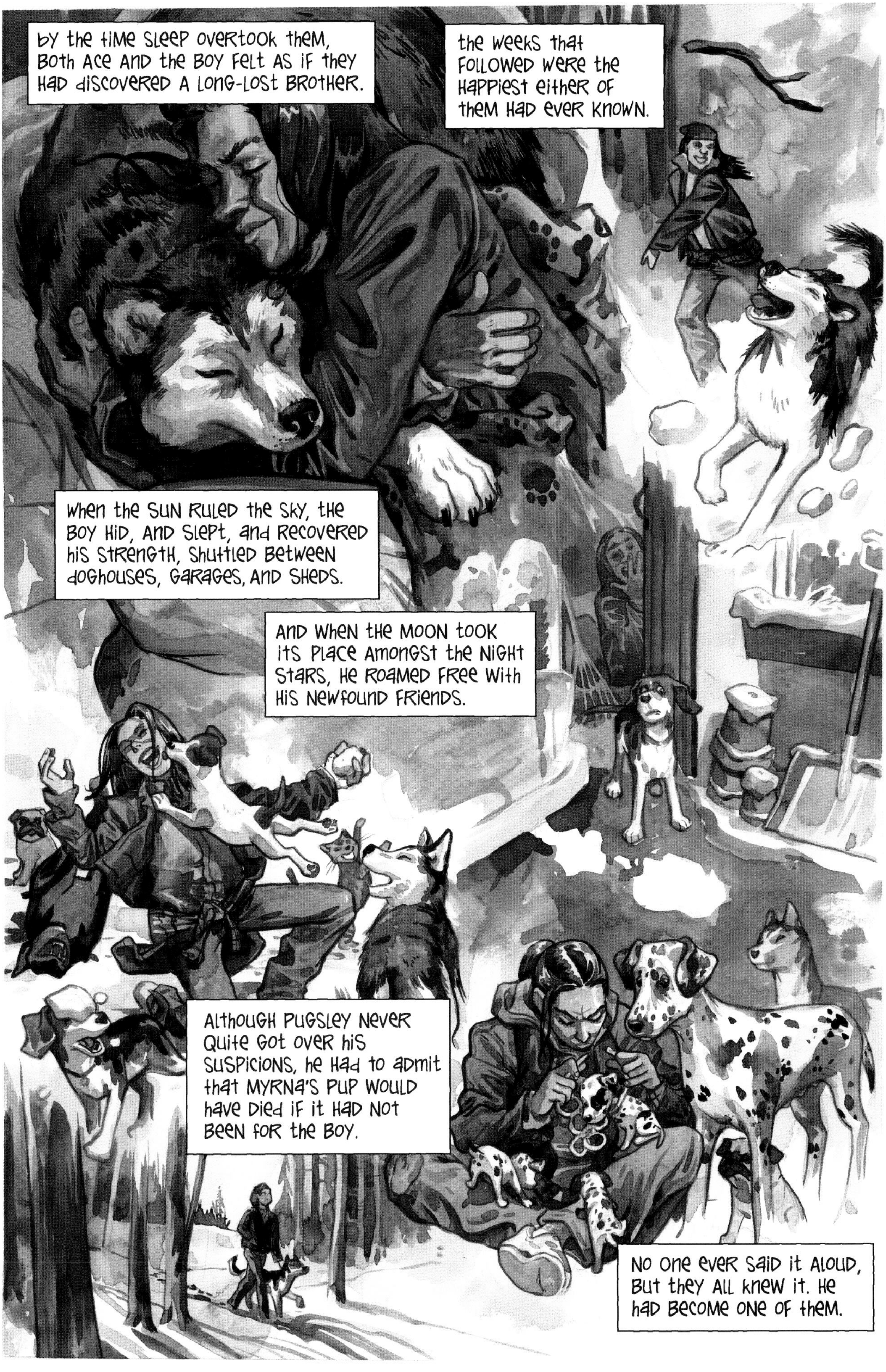
by the time sleep overtook them, Both Ace and the Boy felt as if they had discovered a long-lost brother.
the weeks that followed were the happiest either of them had ever known.
when the sun ruled the sky, the Boy hid, and slept, and recovered his strength, shuttled between doghouses, garages, and sheds.
And when the moon took its place amongst the night stars, he roamed free with his newfound friends.
Although Pugsley never quite got over his suspicions, he had to admit that Myrna's pup would have died if it had not been for the Boy.
No one ever said it aloud, But they all knew it. He had become one of them.

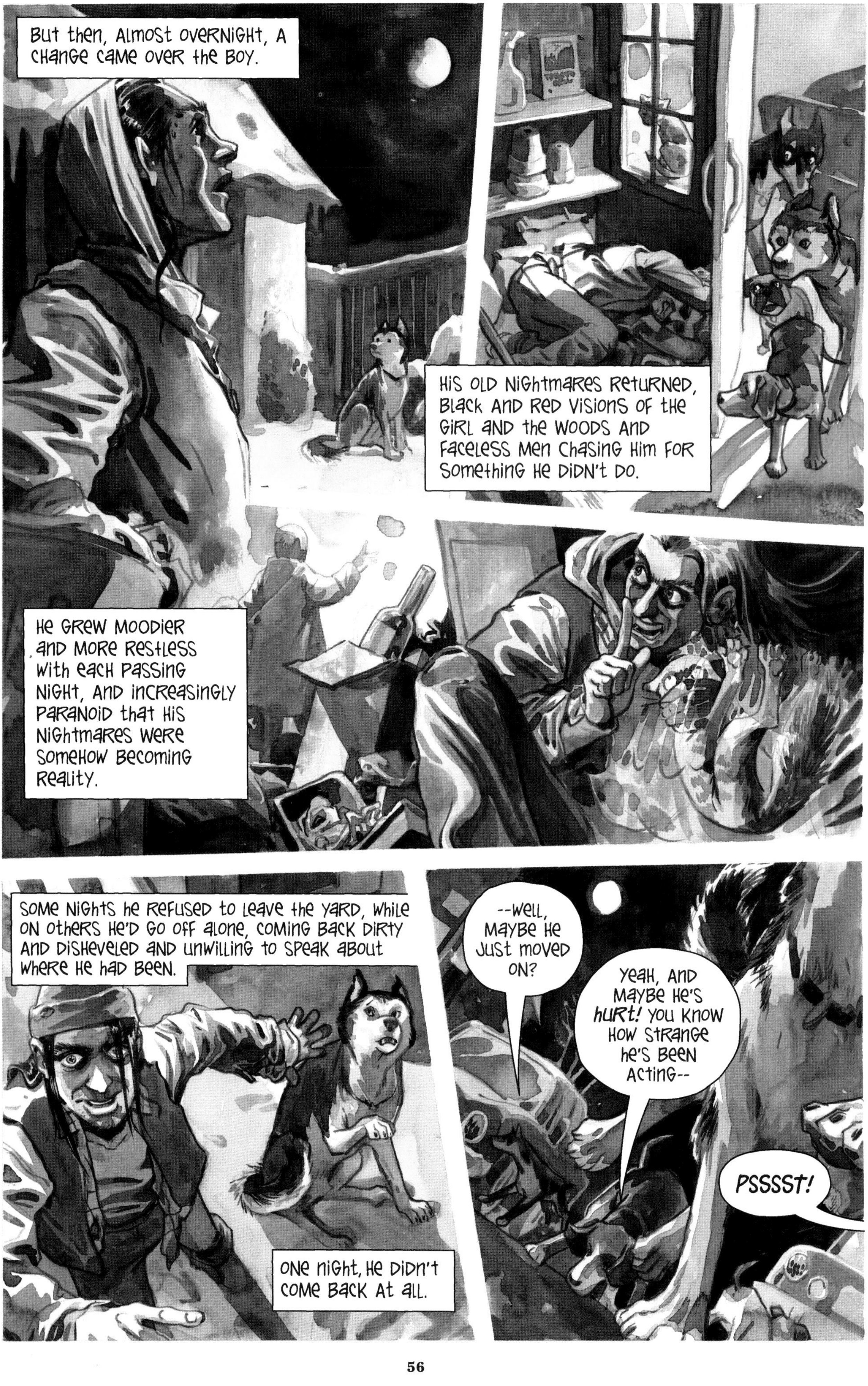

But then, almost overnight, a change came over the boy.
His old nightmares returned, black and red visions of the girl and the woods and faceless men chasing him for something he didn't do.
He grew moodier and more restless with each passing night, and increasingly paranoid that his nightmares were somehow becoming reality.
Some nights he refused to leave the yard, while on others he'd go off alone, coming back dirty and disheveled and unwilling to speak about where he had been.
One night, he didn't come back at all.
--Well, maybe he just moved on?
Yeah, and maybe he's *hurt!* You know how strange he's been acting--
PSSSST!

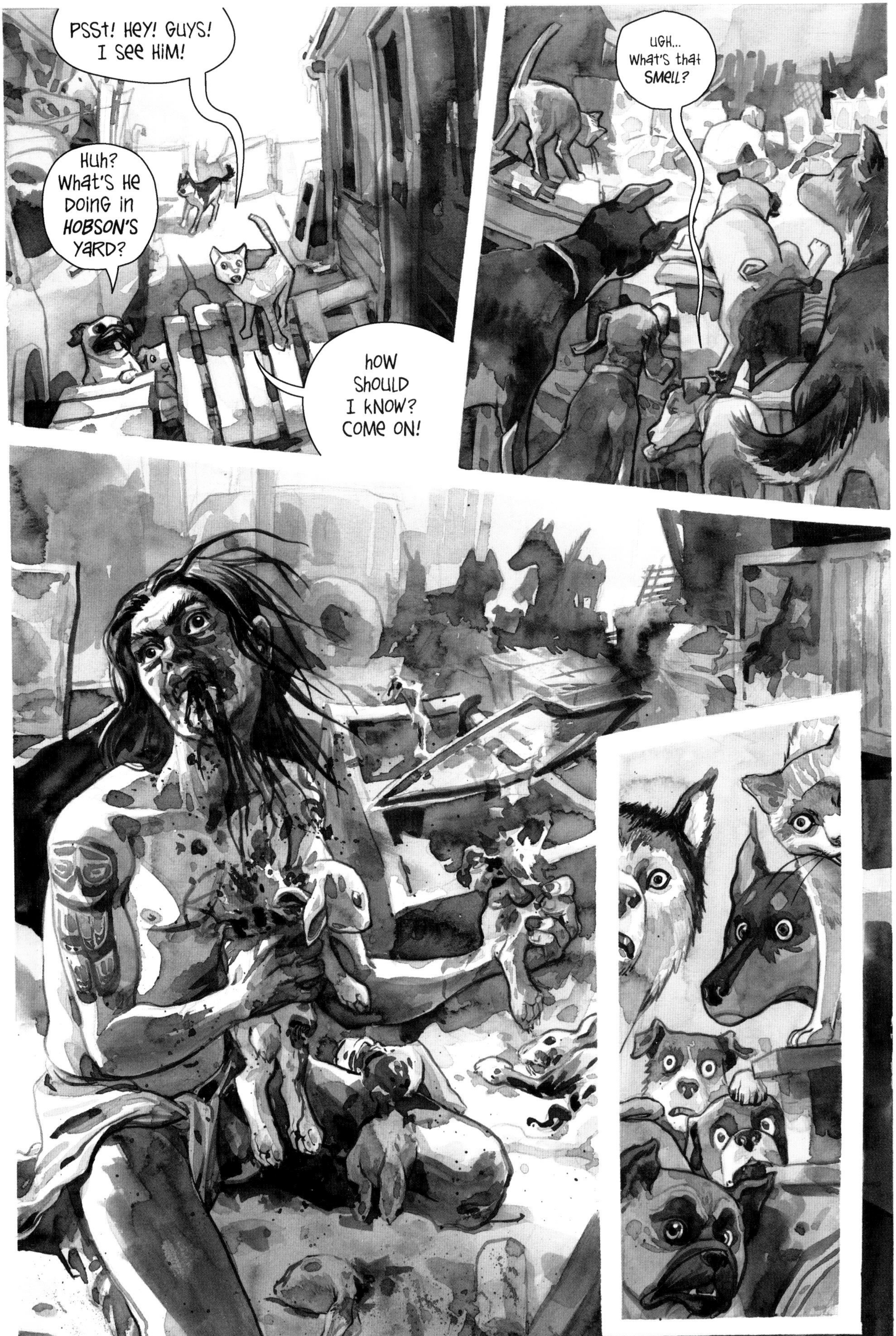
PSSt! Hey! GUYS! I See HIM!
Huh? What's He Doing in HOBSON'S YARD?
how SHOULD I kNOW? COMe ON!
UGH... What's that SMELL?

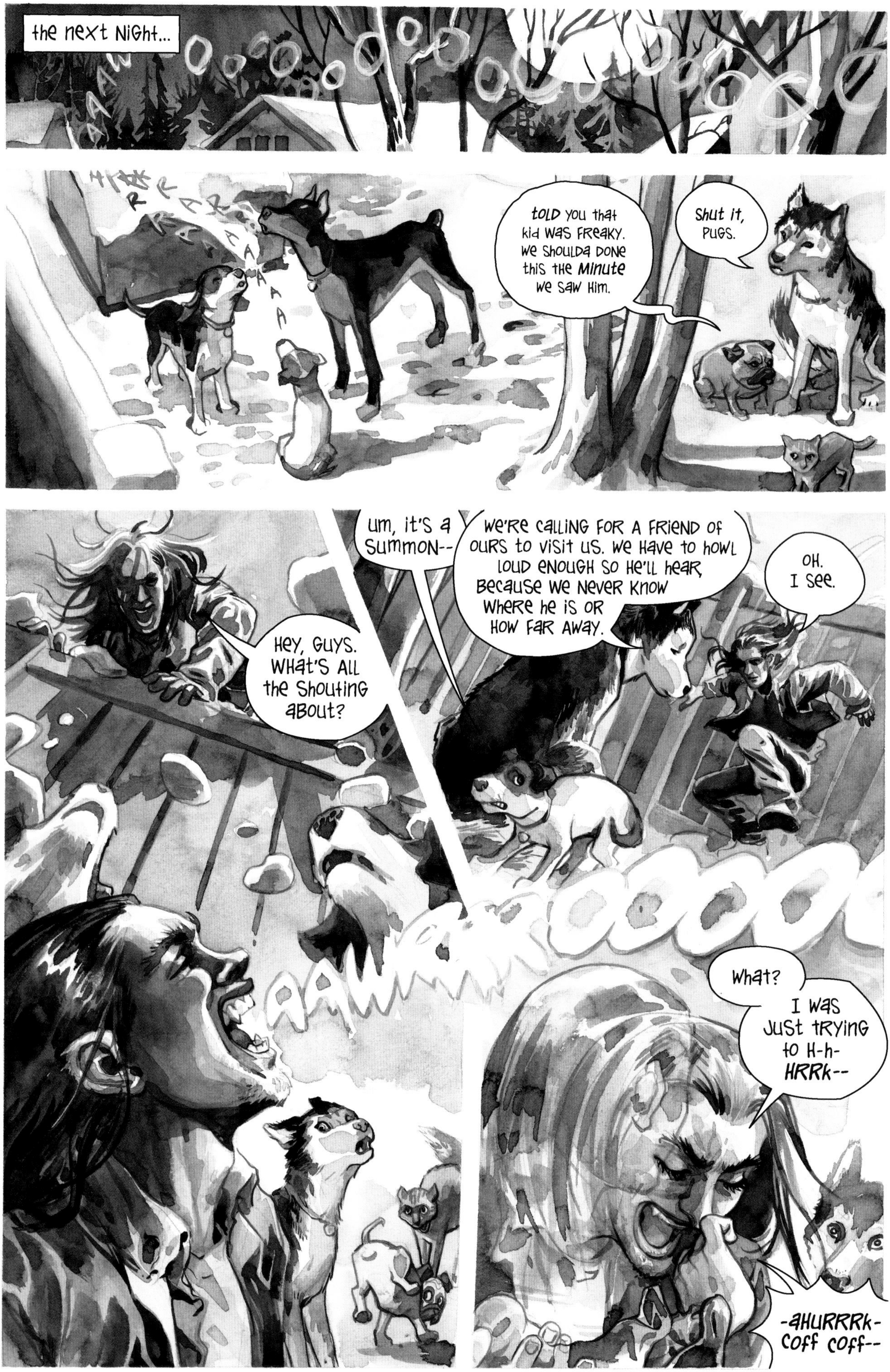

the next Night...
AAWOOOOOOOOOOOOOOOOOOOOOOOO
told you that kid was freaky. we shoulda done this the minute we saw him.
Shut it, Pugs.
Hey, guys. What's all the shouting about?
um, it's a summon--
we're calling for a friend of ours to visit us. we have to howl loud enough so he'll hear, because we never know where he is or how far away.
oh. I see.
What?
I was just trying to H-h-HRRk--
-ahurrrk-coff coff--

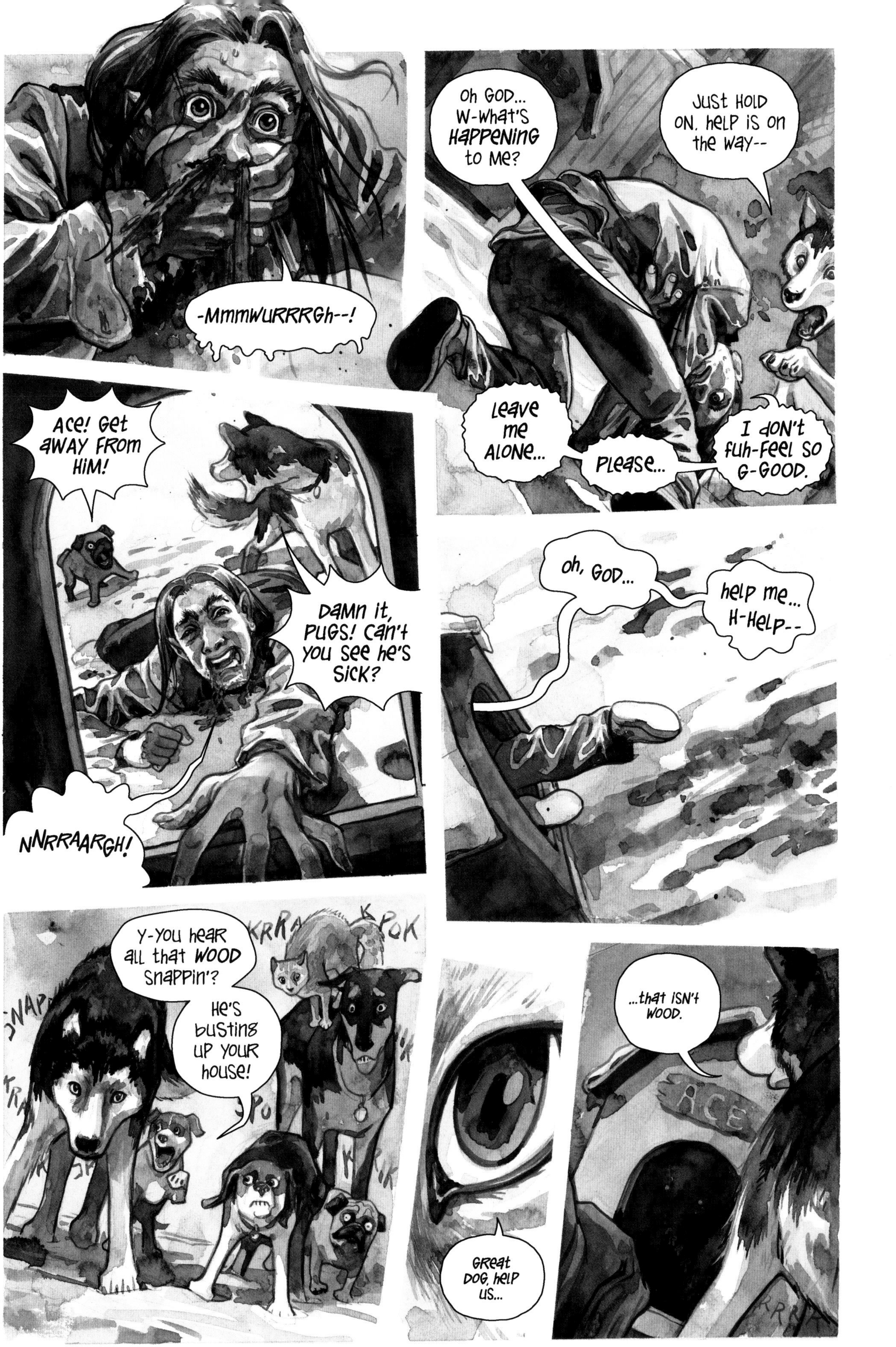
-MmmWURRRGh--!
Oh GOD... W-what's HAPPENING to me?
Just HOLD ON. help is on the way--
Leave me ALONE...
Please...
I don't fuh-feel so G-GOOD.
Ace! Get away FROM HIM!
Damn it, PUGS! Can't you see he's sick?
NNRRAARGH!
oh, GOD...
help me... H-Help--
Y-You hear all that WOOD snappin'?
He's busting up YOUR house!
KRRA
KPOK
...that isn't WOOD.
Great Dog, help us...
ACE

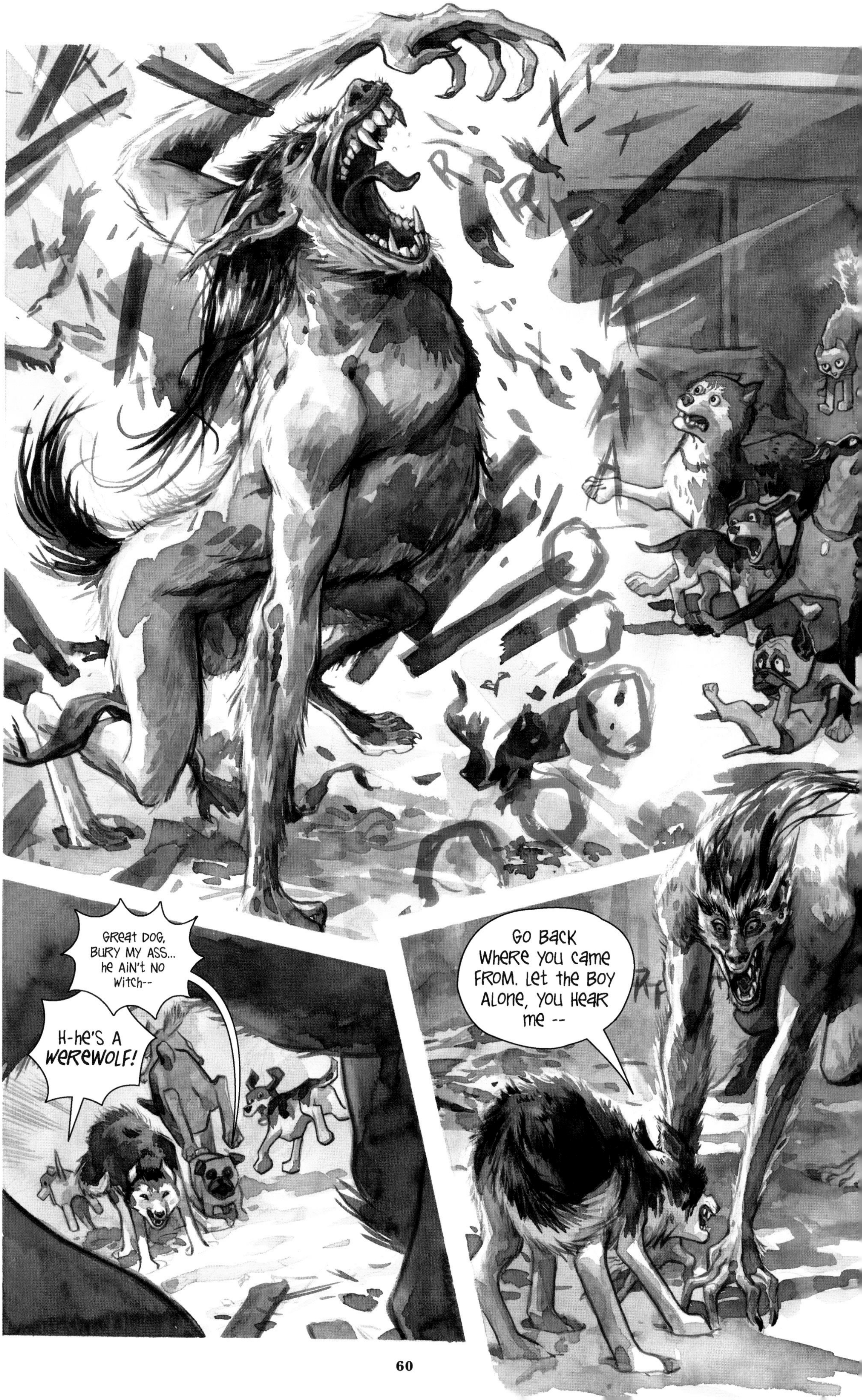
Great dog, bury my ass... he ain't no witch--
H-he's a *werewolf!*
Go back where you came from. Let the boy alone, you hear me --

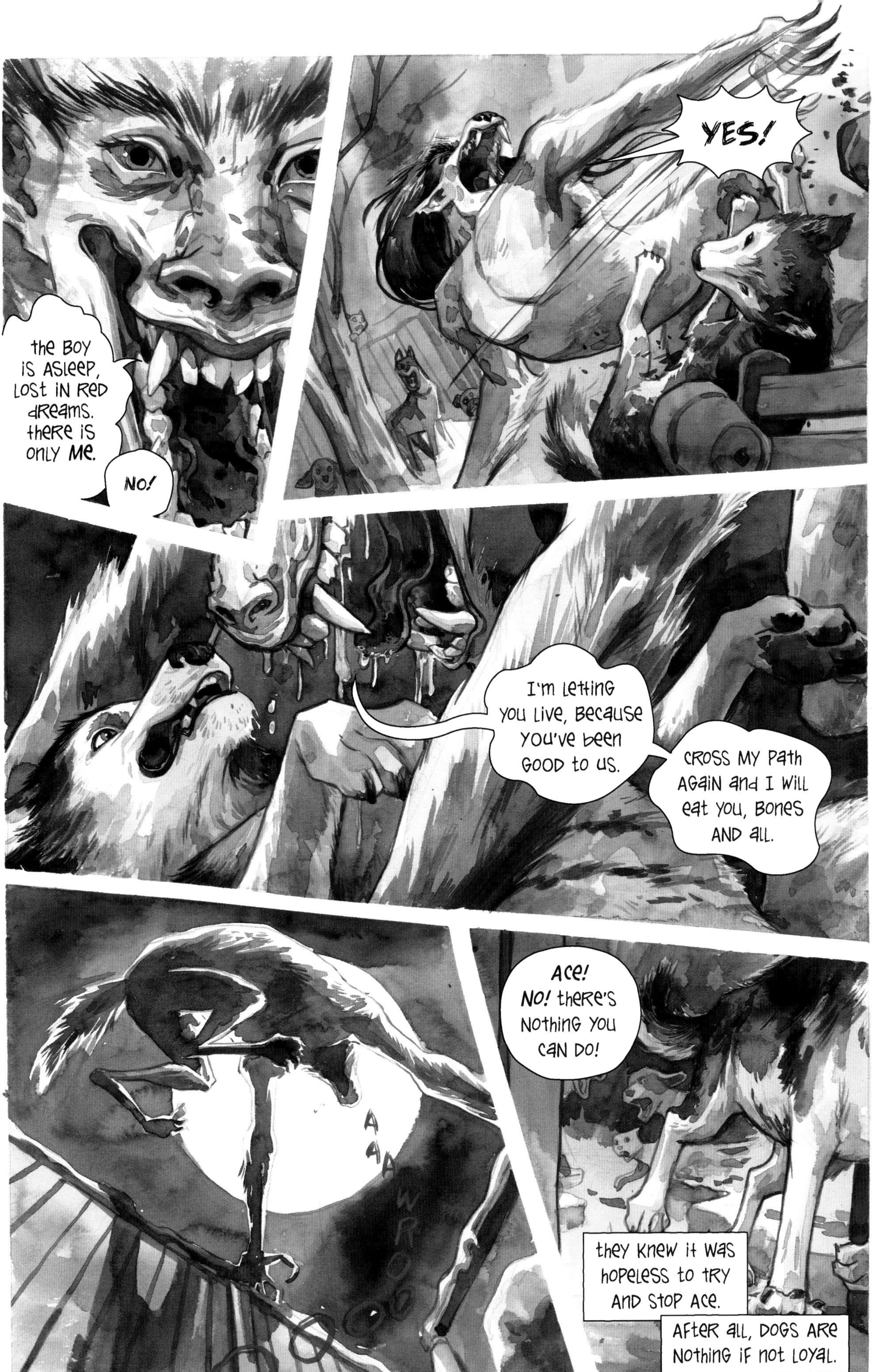
the Boy is asleep, lost in red dreams. there is only **me**.
No!
YES!
I'm letting you live, because you've been good to us.
cross my path again and I will eat you, Bones and all.
Ace! *No!* there's nothing you can do!
they knew it was hopeless to try and stop Ace.
After all, dogs are nothing if not loyal.

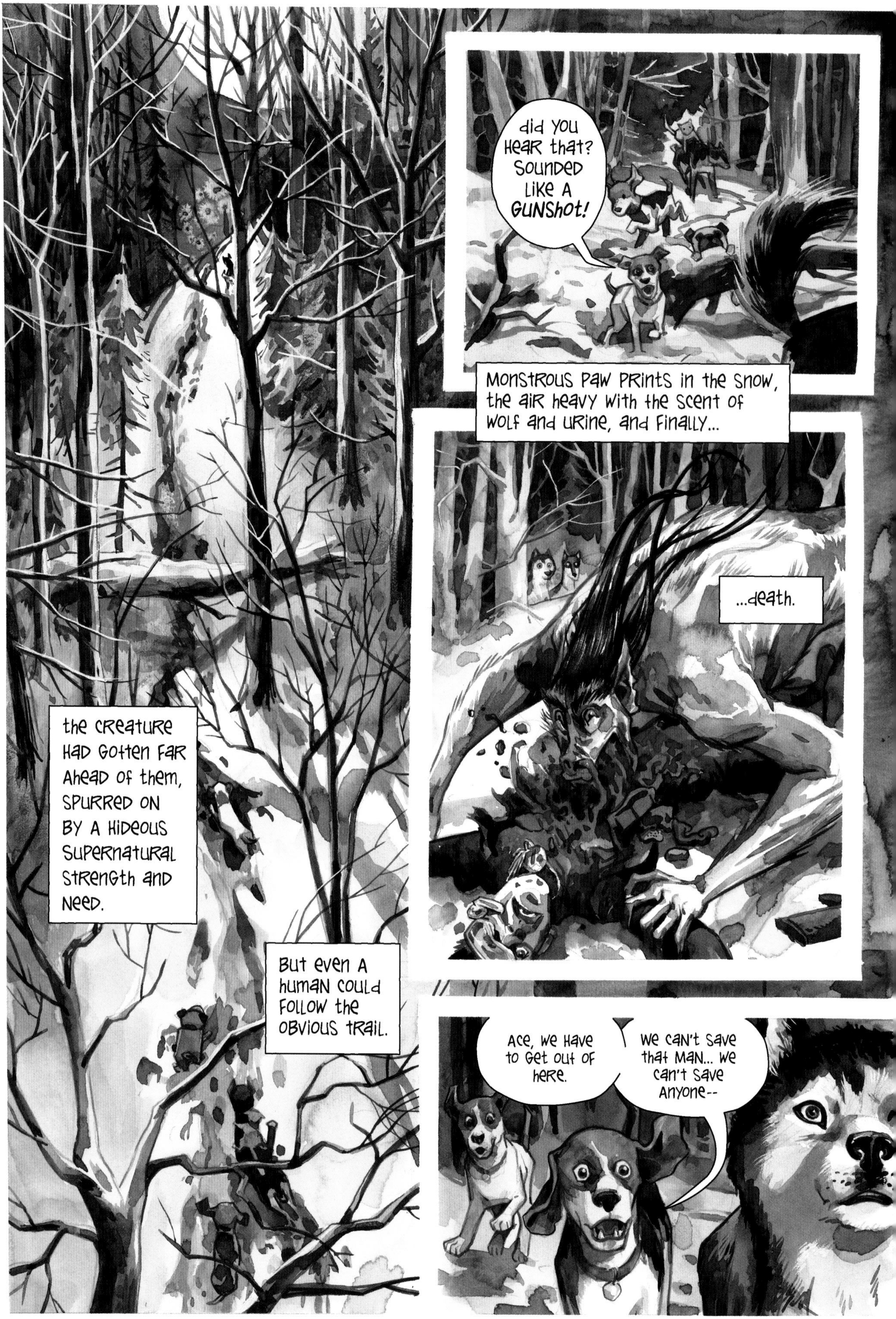
the creature had gotten far ahead of them, spurred on by a hideous supernatural strength and need.
But even a human could follow the obvious trail.
did you hear that? sounded like a gunshot!
Monstrous paw prints in the snow, the air heavy with the scent of wolf and urine, and finally...
...death.
Ace, we have to get out of here.
We can't save that man... we can't save anyone--

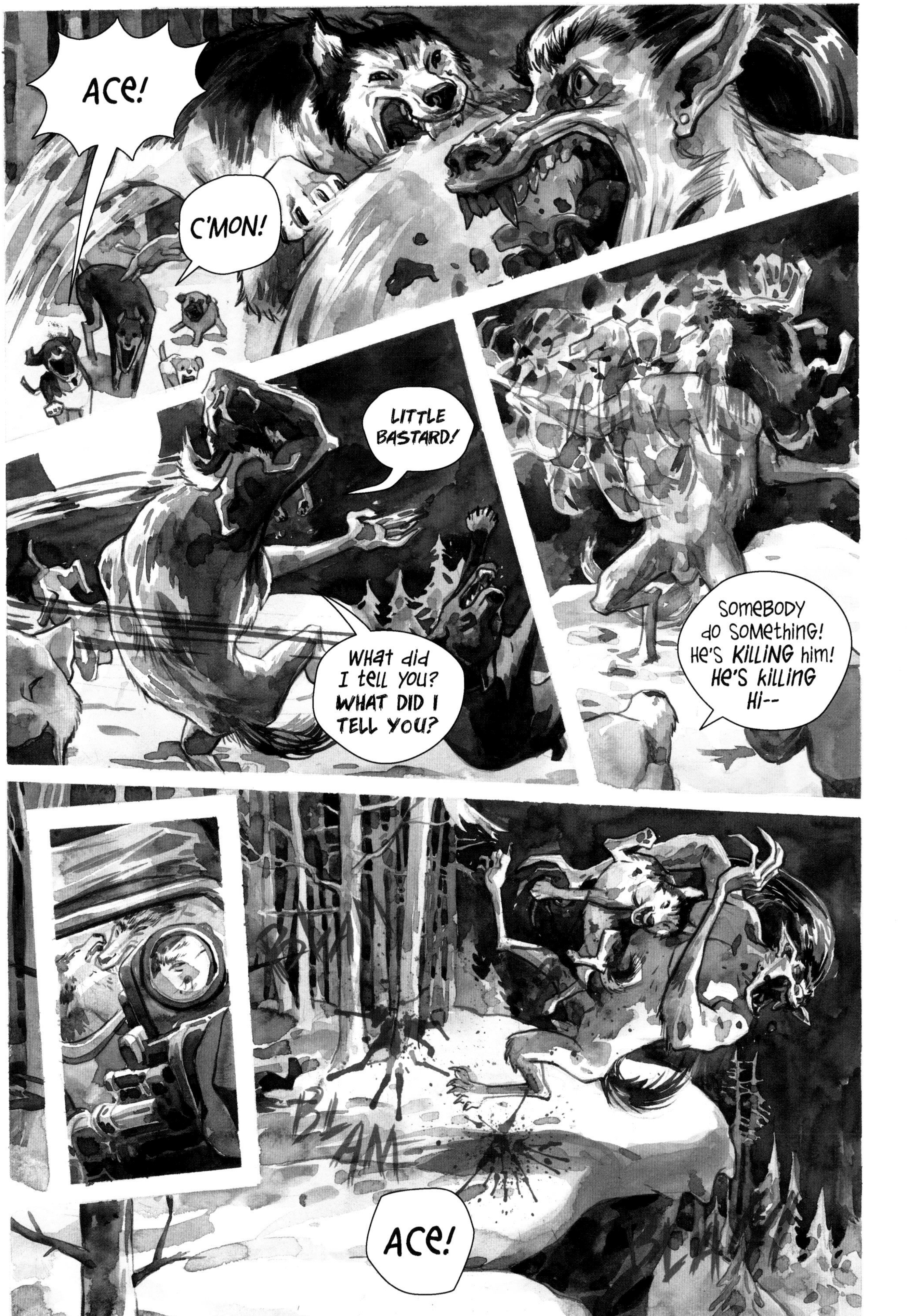
ACE!
C'MON!
LITTLE BASTARD!
WHAT DID I TELL YOU? WHAT DID I TELL YOU?
SOMEBODY DO SOMETHING! HE'S KILLING HIM! HE'S KILLING HI--
BLAM
ACE!

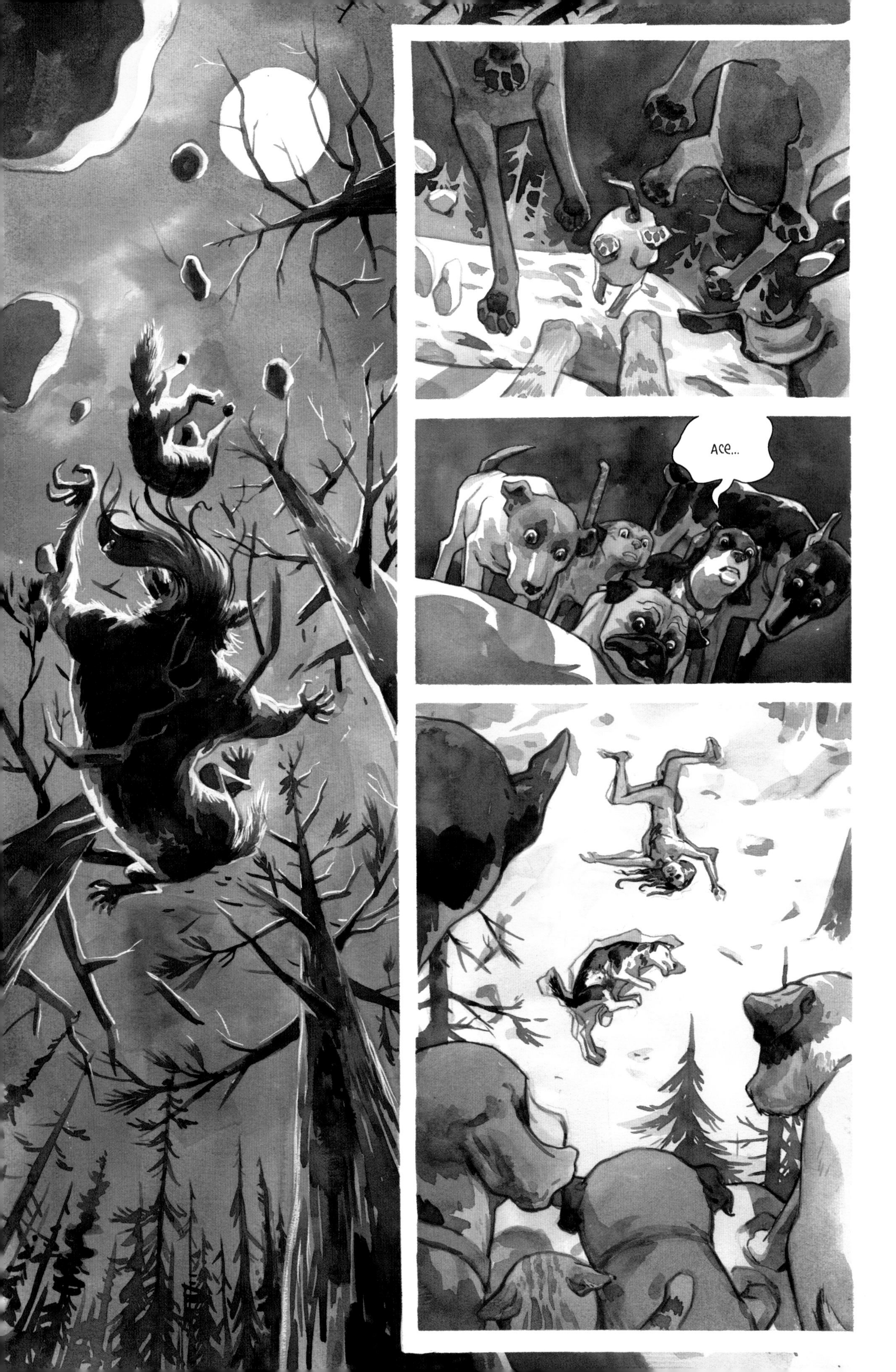

Ace...

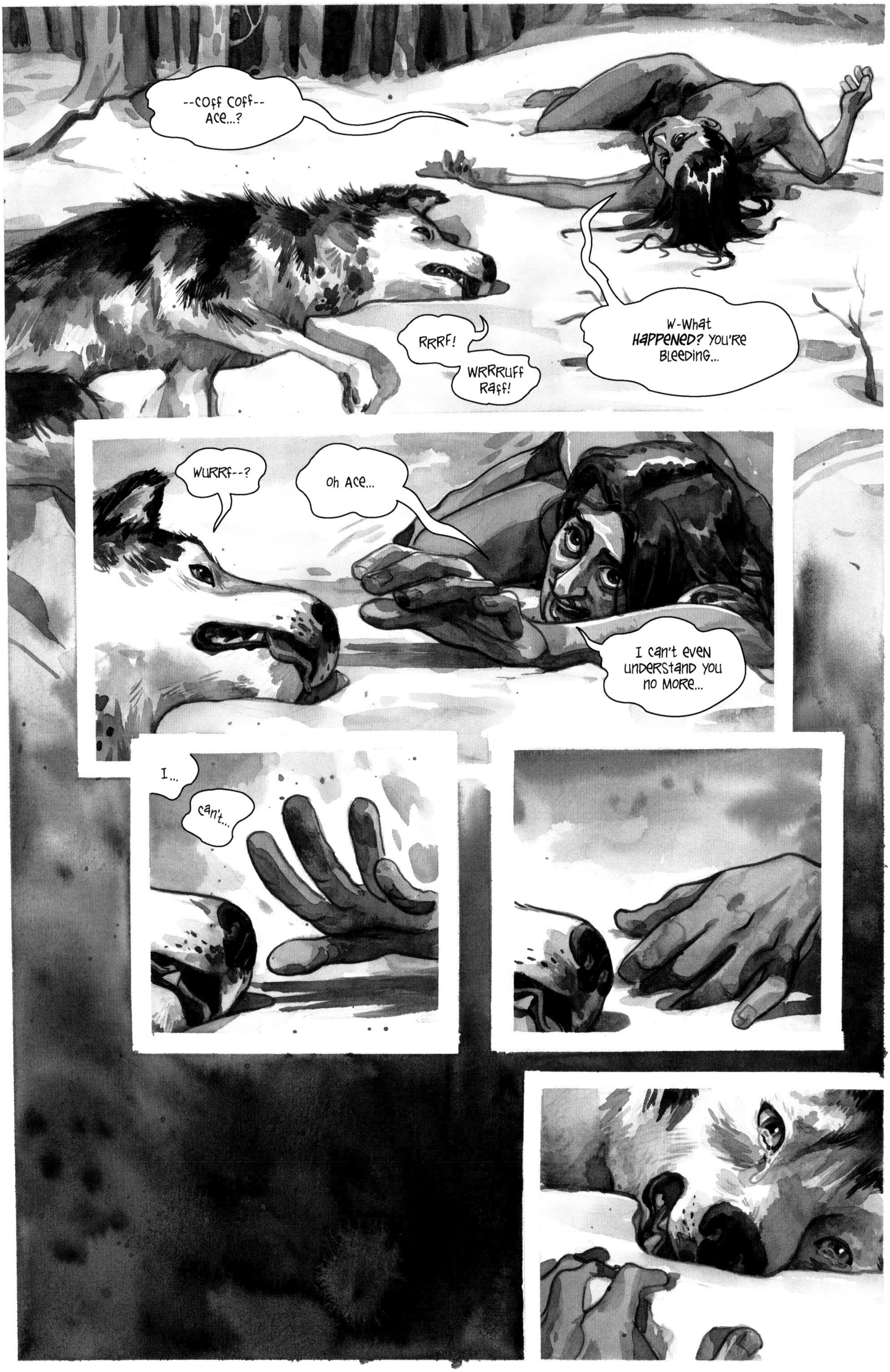
--COFF COFF--
ACE...?
W-WHAT HAPPENED? YOU'RE BLEEDING...
RRRF!
WRRRUFF RAFF!
WURRF--?
OH ACE...
I CAN'T EVEN UNDERSTAND YOU NO MORE...
I...
CAN'T...

YO! OVER HERE!

YEAH, IT'S HIM ALL RIGHT.

POOR BASTARD.

DON'T FEEL TOO SORRY FOR HIM. YOU SAW WHAT HE DID TO DANNY.

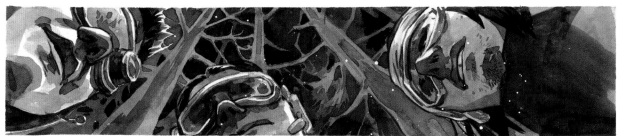

WHAT ABOUT THE HUSKY? HE LOOKS PRETTY BAD.

YOU WANNA WASTE A SILVER BULLET ON SOME MUTT, YOU GO RIGHT AHEAD.

YEAH. YOU GOT A POINT THERE.

SORRY, BOY.

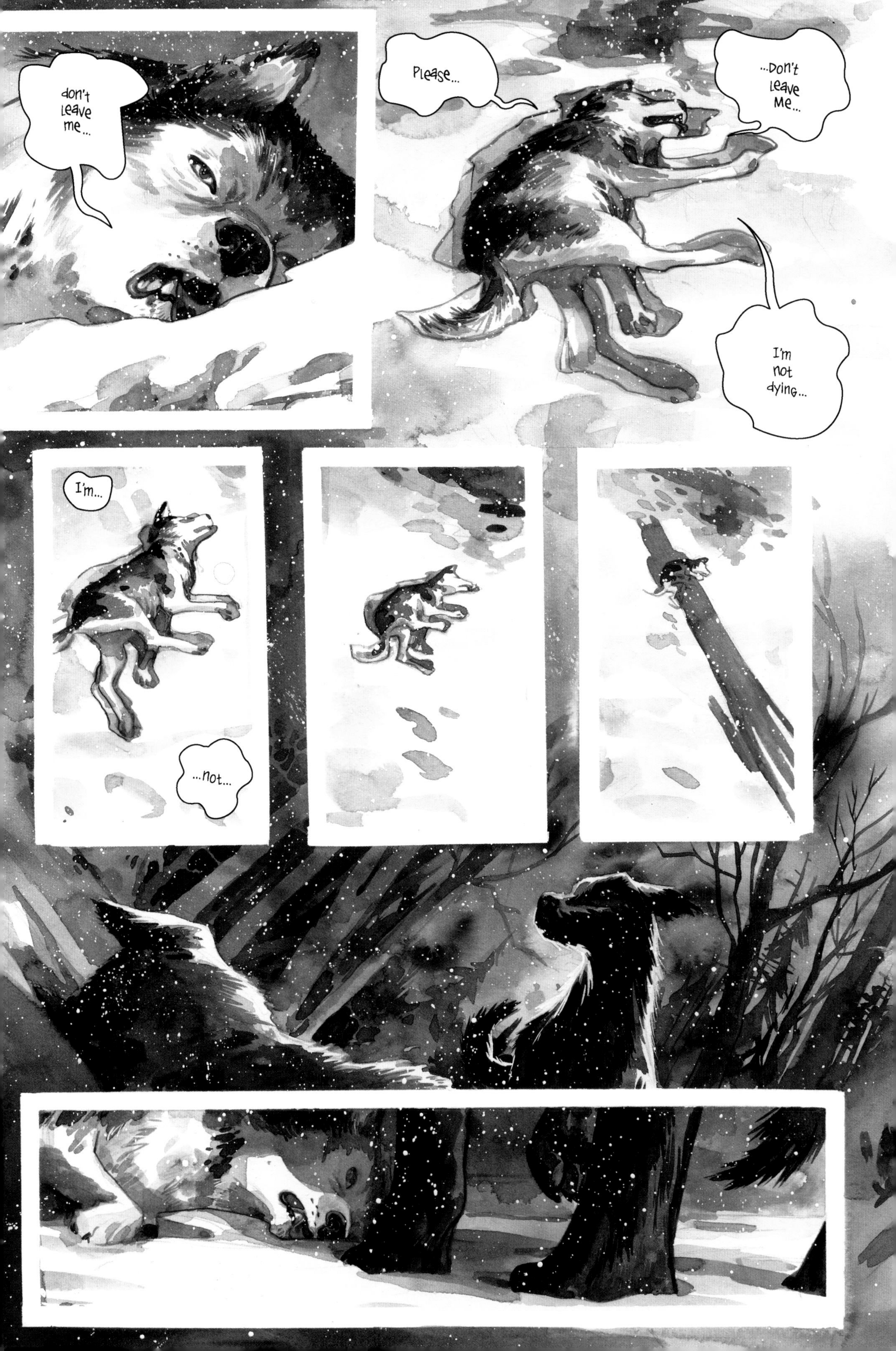
don't leave me...
Please...
...Don't leave me...
I'm not dying...
I'm...
...not...

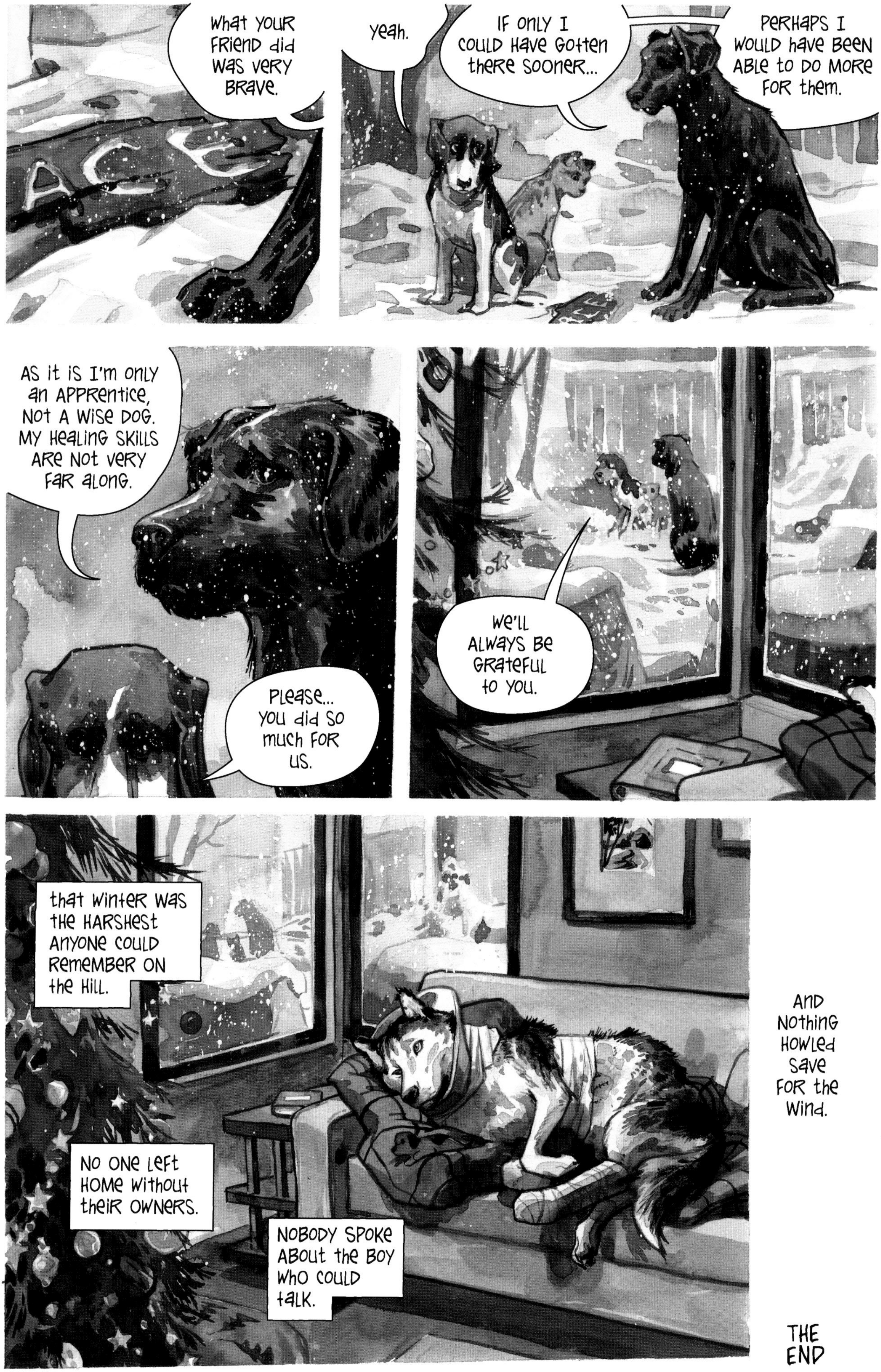
What your friend did was very brave.
Yeah.
If only I could have gotten there sooner...
Perhaps I would have been able to do more for them.
As it is I'm only an apprentice, not a wise dog. My healing skills are not very far along.
Please... you did so much for us.
We'll always be grateful to you.
That winter was the harshest anyone could remember on the Hill.
No one left home without their owners.
Nobody spoke about the boy who could talk.
And nothing howled save for the wind.
THE END

THE GATHERING STORM

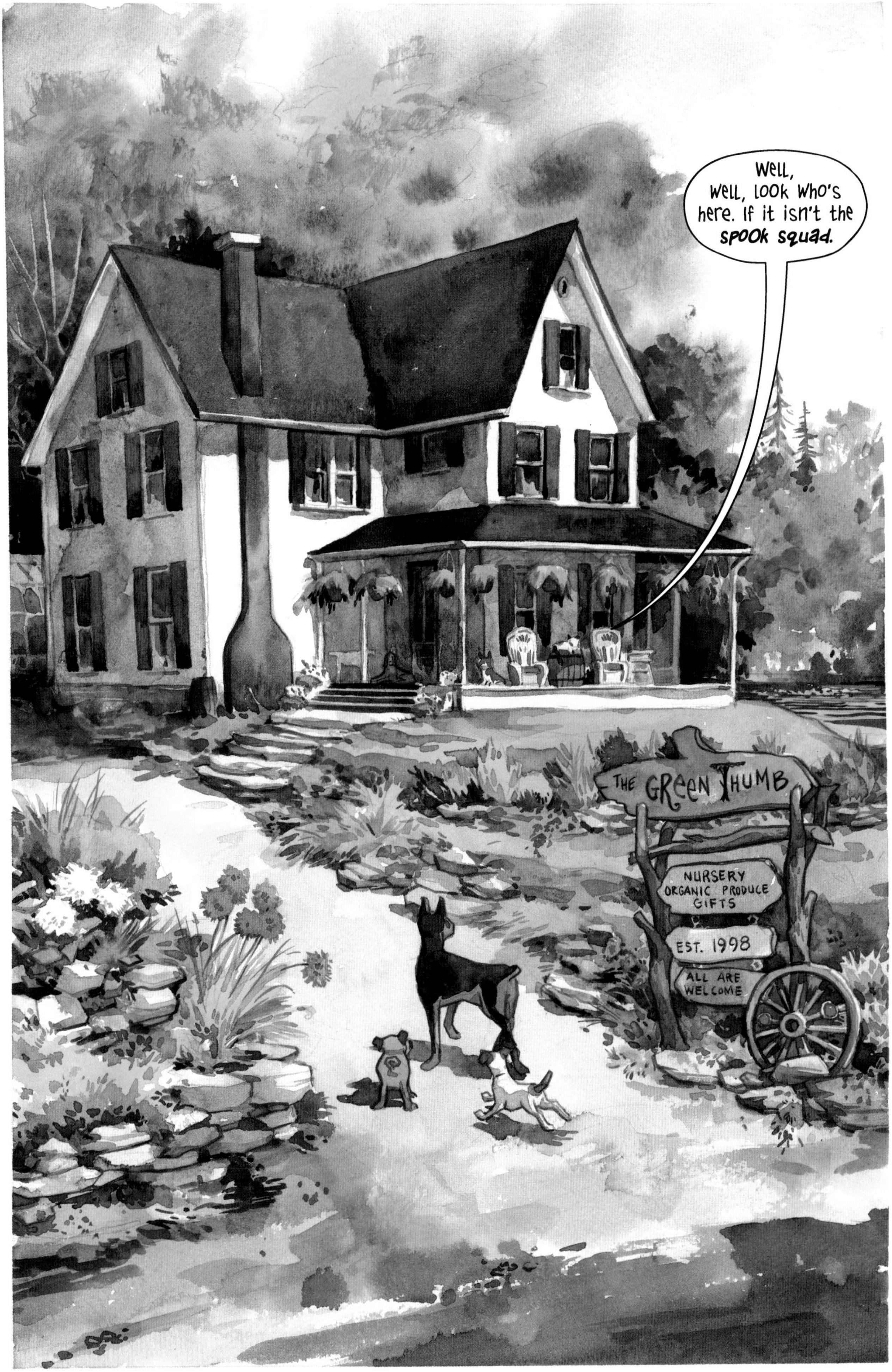
Well,
Well, look who's here. If it isn't the spook squad.
THE GREEN THUMB
NURSERY
ORGANIC PRODUCE
GIFTS
EST. 1998
ALL ARE WELCOME

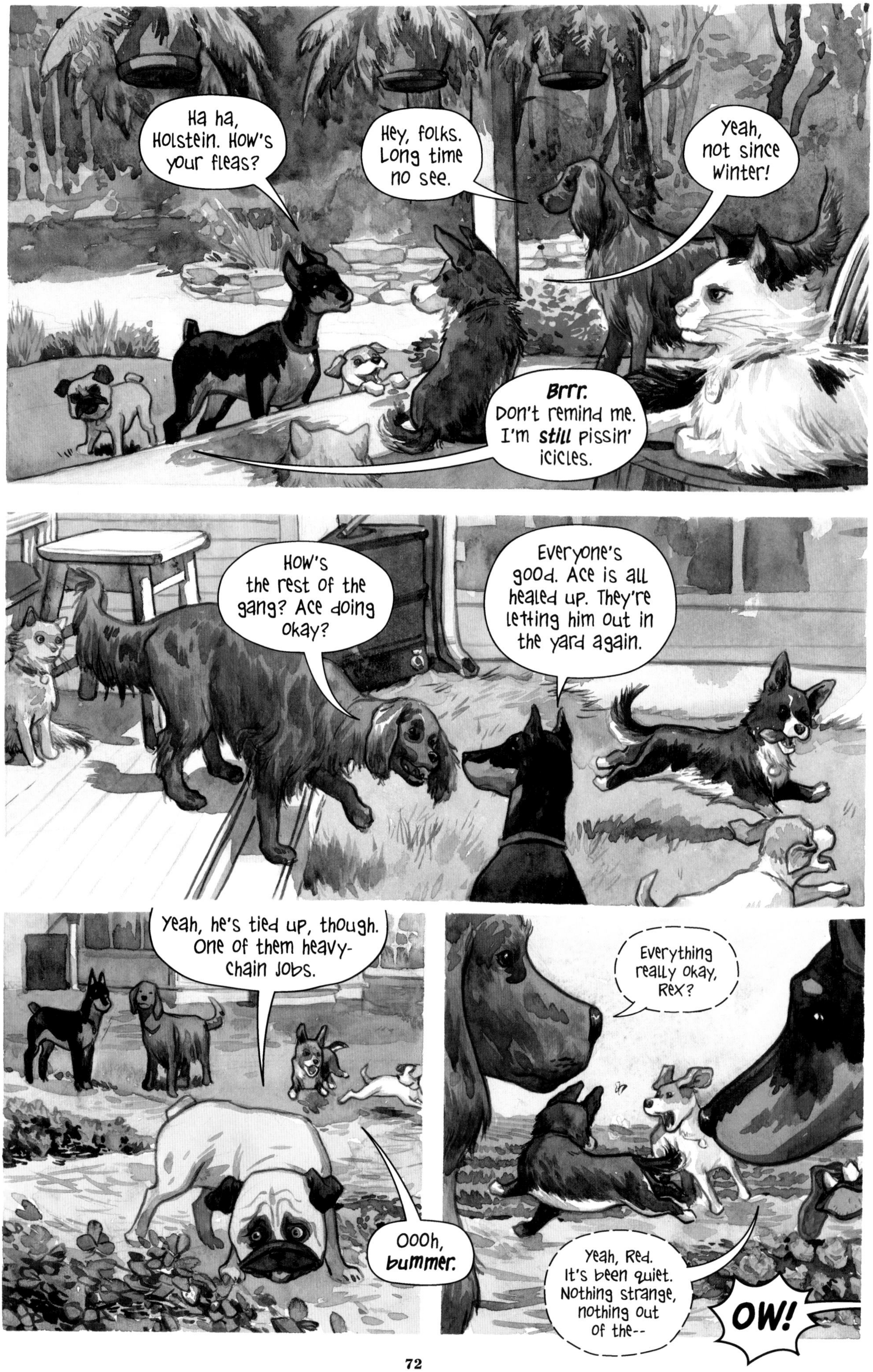
Ha ha, Holstein. How's your fleas?
Hey, folks. Long time no see.
Yeah, not since winter!
Brrr. Don't remind me. I'm still pissin' icicles.
How's the rest of the gang? Ace doing okay?
Everyone's good. Ace is all healed up. They're letting him out in the yard again.
Yeah, he's tied up, though. One of them heavy-chain jobs.
Oooh, bummer.
Everything really okay, Rex?
Yeah, Red. It's been quiet. Nothing strange, nothing out of the--
OW!

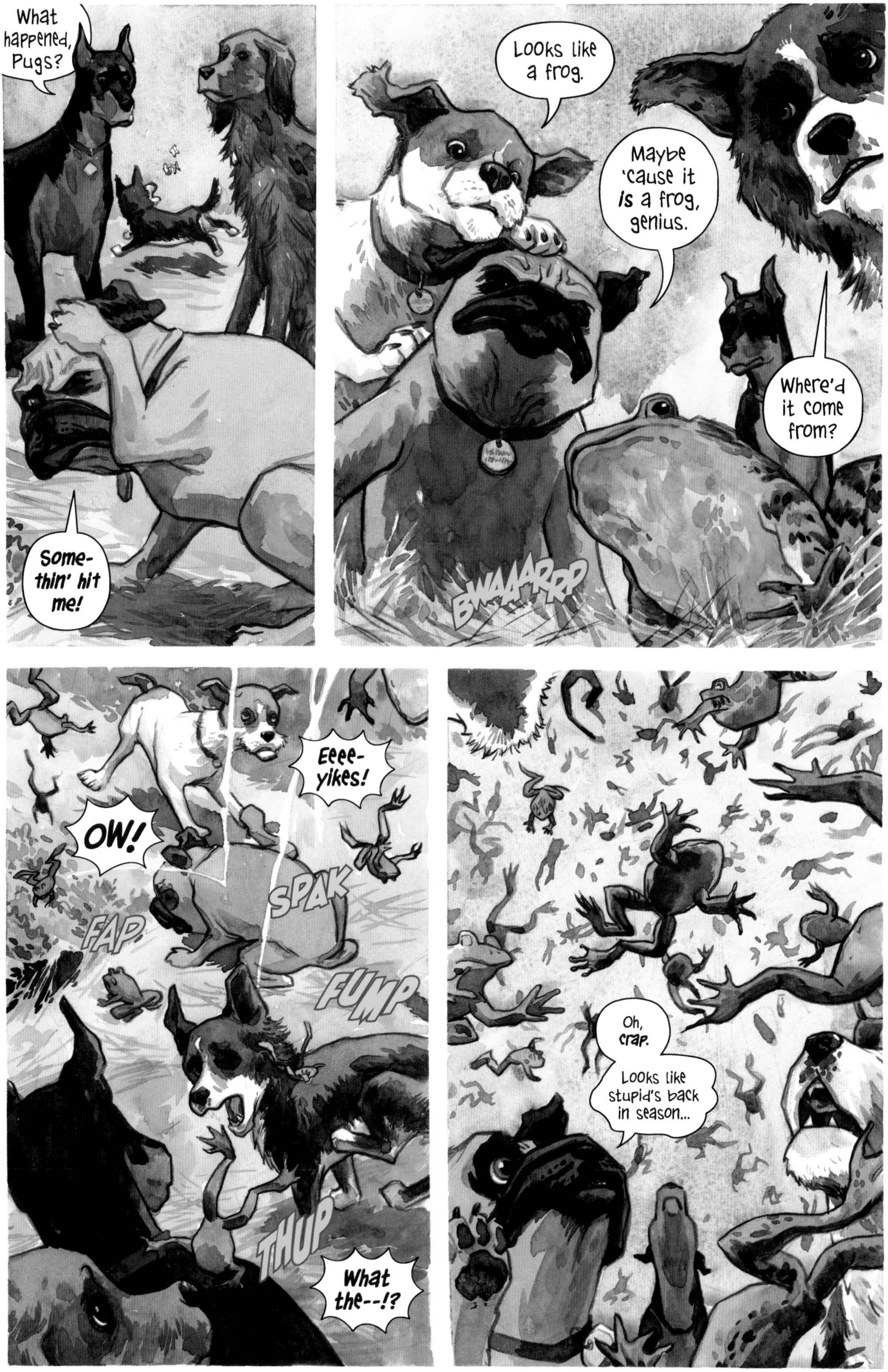
What happened, Pugs?
Some-thin' hit me!
Looks like a frog.
Maybe 'cause it is a frog, genius.
Where'd it come from?
BWAAARRP
Eeee-yikes!
OW!
SPAK
FAP
FUMP
THUP
What the--!?
Oh, crap.
Looks like stupid's back in season...

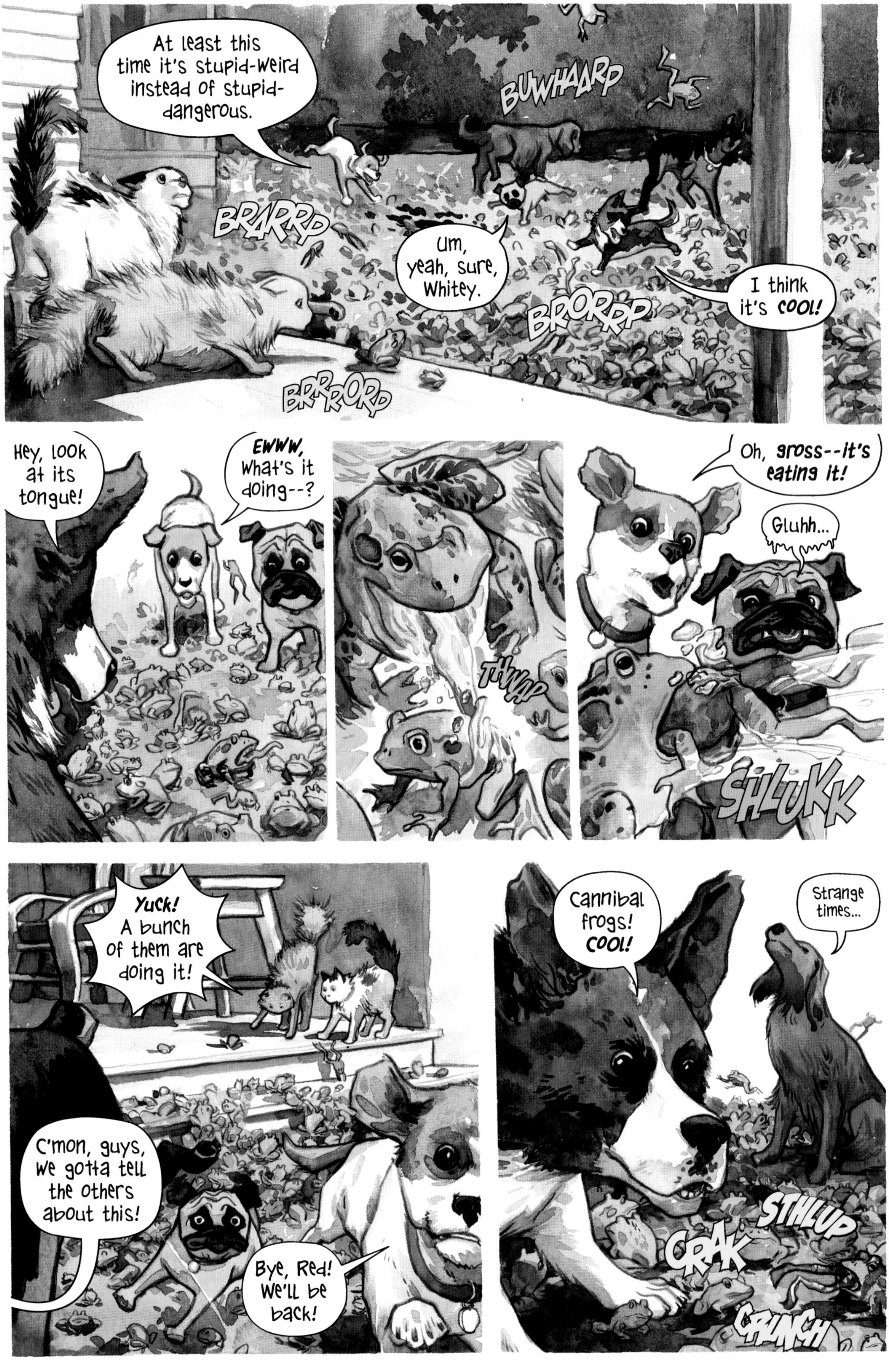
At least this time it's stupid-weird instead of stupid-dangerous.
BUWHAARP
BRARRP
Um, yeah, sure, Whitey.
I think it's COOL!
BRORRP
BRRRORP
Hey, look at its tongue!
EWWW, What's it doing--?
THWAP
Oh, gross--it's eating it!
Gluhh...
SHLUKK
Yuck! A bunch of them are doing it!
C'mon, guys, we gotta tell the others about this!
Bye, Red! We'll be back!
Cannibal frogs! COOL!
Strange times...
STHLUP
CRAK
CRUNCH

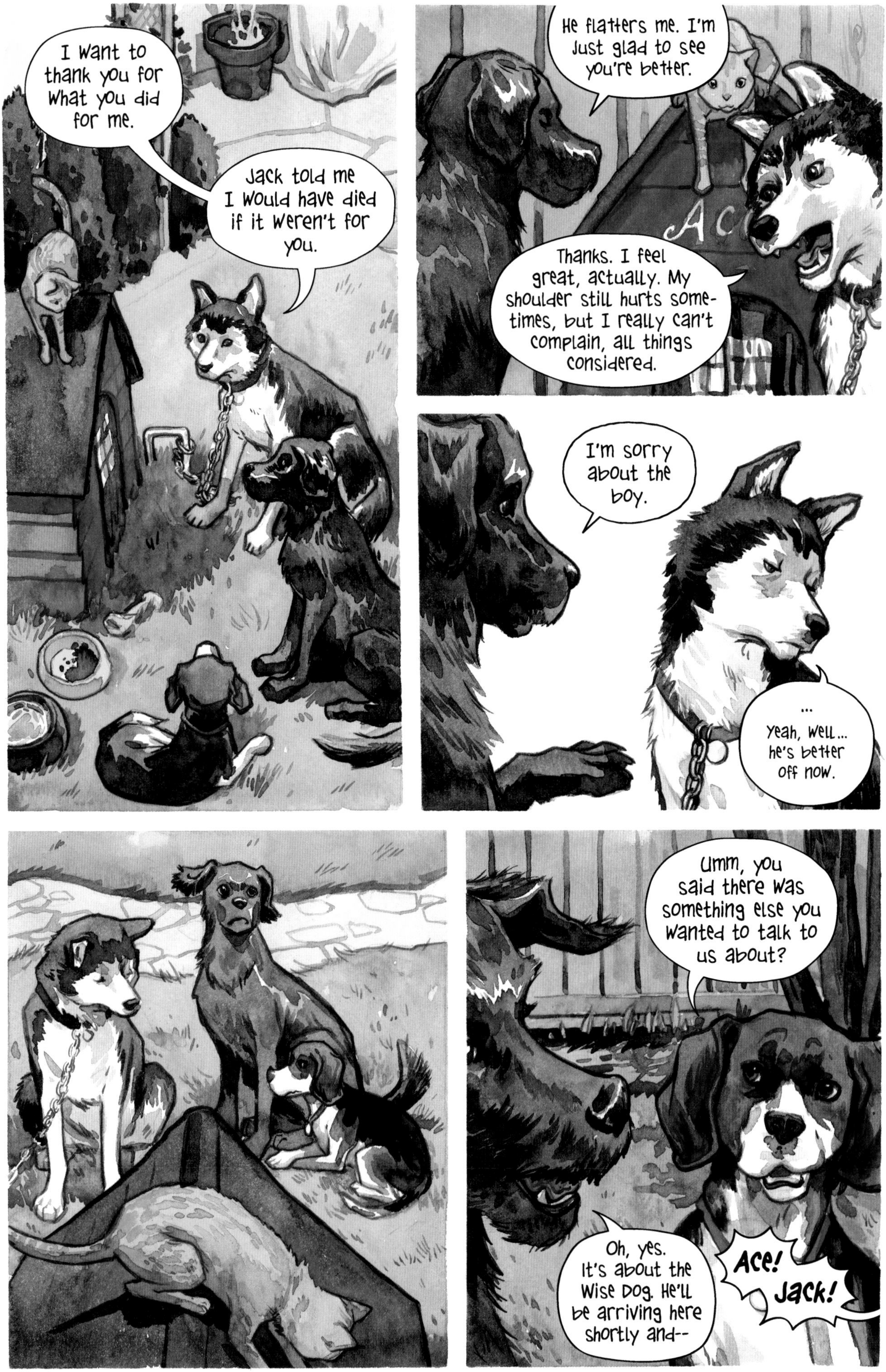
I want to thank you for what you did for me.
Jack told me I would have died if it weren't for you.
He flatters me. I'm just glad to see you're better.
Thanks. I feel great, actually. My shoulder still hurts sometimes, but I really can't complain, all things considered.
I'm sorry about the boy.
... Yeah, well... he's better off now.
Umm, you said there was something else you wanted to talk to us about?
Oh, yes. It's about the Wise Dog. He'll be arriving here shortly and--
Ace! Jack!

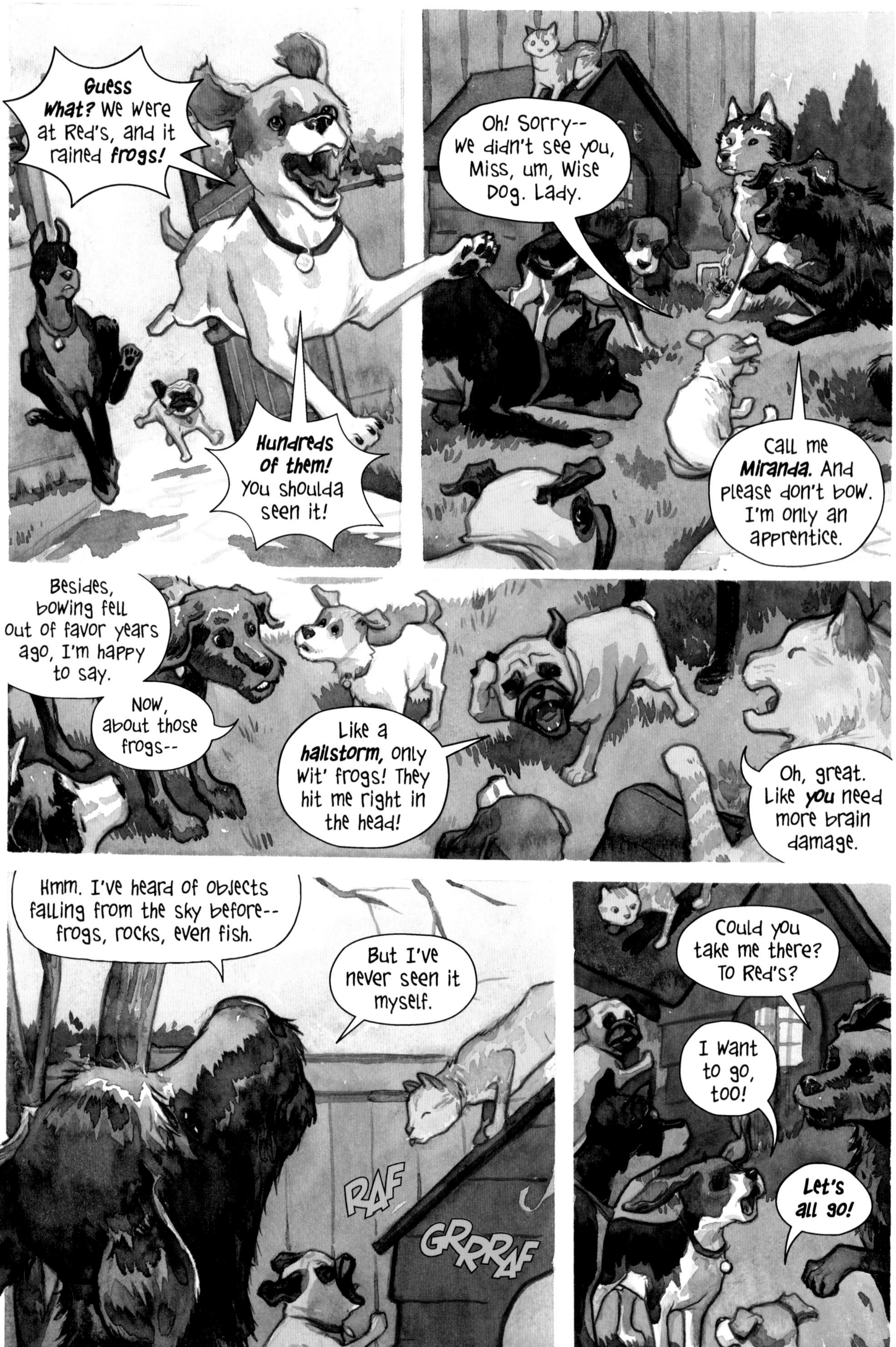
Guess What? We were at Red's, and it rained frogs!
Hundreds of them! You shoulda seen it!
Oh! Sorry-- We didn't see you, Miss, um, Wise Dog. Lady.
Call me Miranda. And please don't bow. I'm only an apprentice.
Besides, bowing fell out of favor years ago, I'm happy to say.
Now, about those frogs--
Like a hailstorm, only wit' frogs! They hit me right in the head!
Oh, great. Like you need more brain damage.
Hmm. I've heard of objects falling from the sky before-- frogs, rocks, even fish.
But I've never seen it myself.
RAF
GRRRAF
Could you take me there? To Red's?
I want to go, too!
Let's all go!

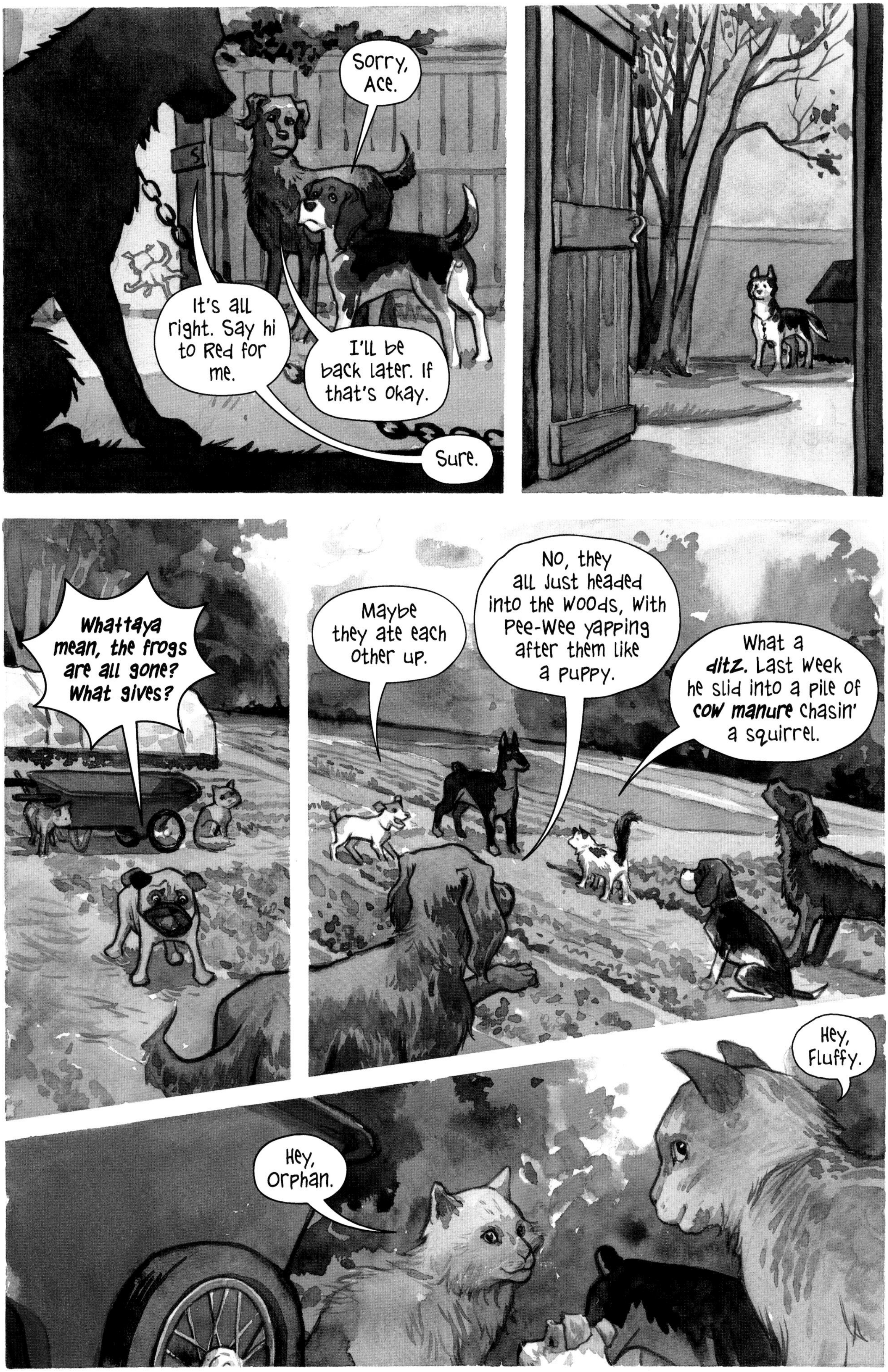
Sorry, Ace.
It's all right. Say hi to Red for me.
I'll be back later. If that's okay.
Sure.
Whattaya mean, the frogs are all gone? What gives?
Maybe they ate each other up.
No, they all just headed into the woods, with Pee-Wee yapping after them like a puppy.
What a ditz. Last week he slid into a pile of cow manure chasin' a squirrel.
Hey, Fluffy.
Hey, Orphan.

WELL, I'd better go find them, if I'm to make a full report.

Hey, WE can be a *hunting party!*

Have fun. If you see Pee-Wee, make sure he's not stuck in a gopher hole or anything.

Huh. No sign of 'em anywhere. HOW fast can frogs hop, anyway?

I'd say pretty fast, from the looks of it.

Bleagh. It smells so... froggy.

Yeah, it's everywhere. Hard to sniff out anything else.

There *IS* something else...

Sulfur.

Is that normal?

Don't ask *me*. What do I look like, a bloodhound?

Hey, guys...I found something.

Oh, hell.

Somebody better go get Red.

PEE-WEE
RED-GREEN
I LIVE AT THE GREEN NURSER

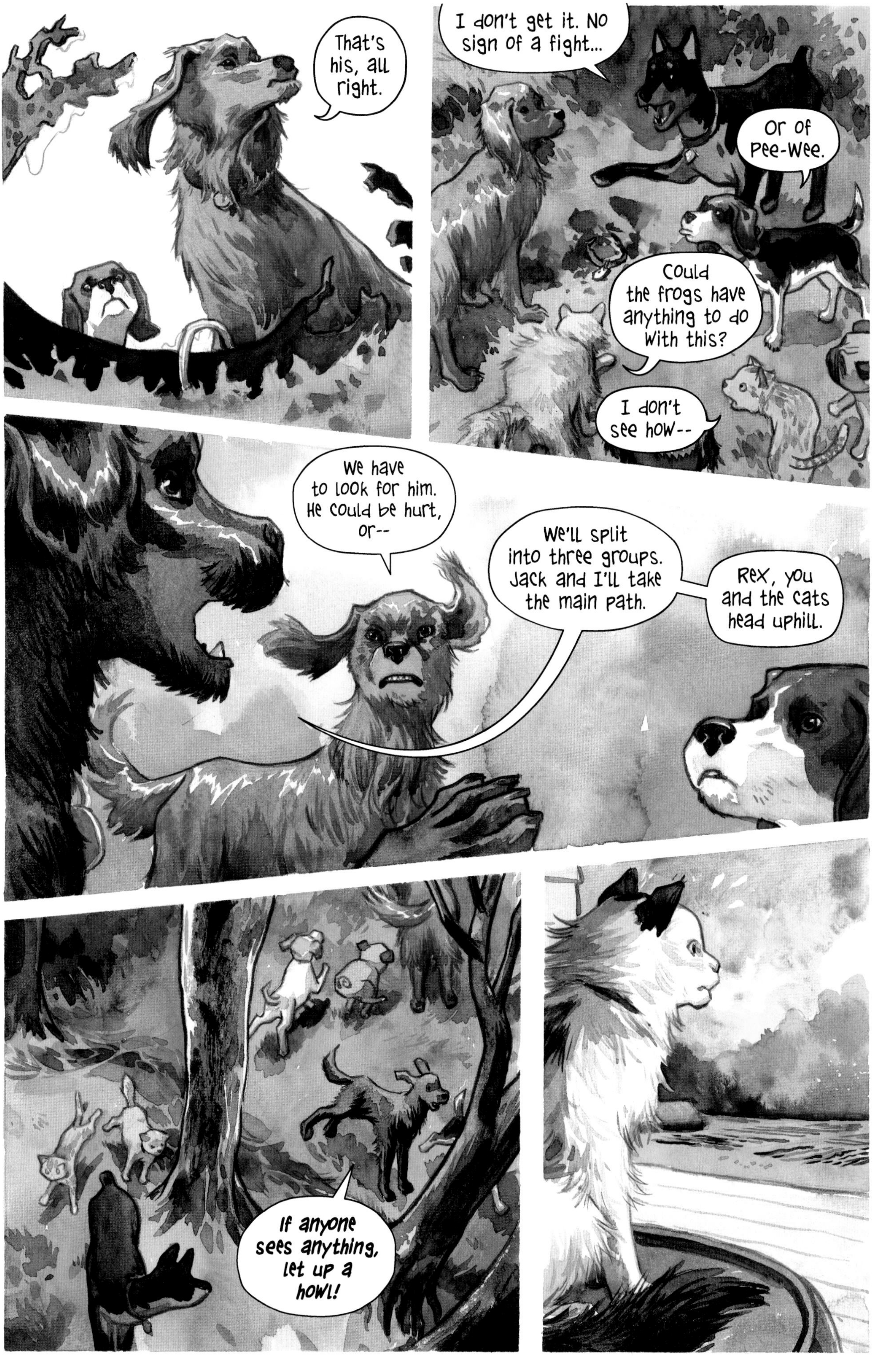

That's his, all right.
I don't get it. No sign of a fight...
Or of Pee-Wee.
Could the frogs have anything to do with this?
I don't see how--
We have to look for him. He could be hurt, or--
We'll split into three groups. Jack and I'll take the main path.
Rex, you and the cats head uphill.
If anyone sees anything, let up a howl!

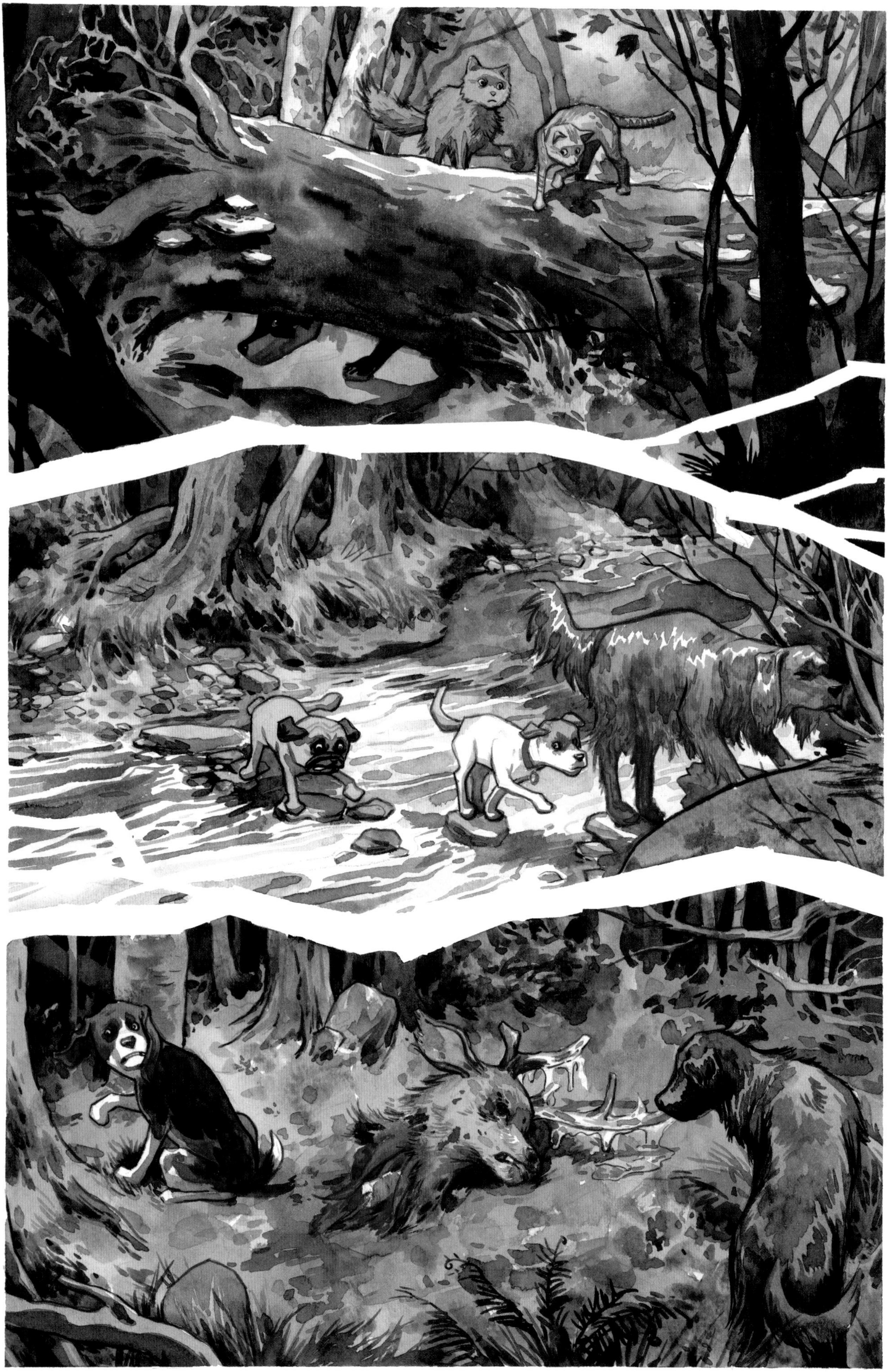

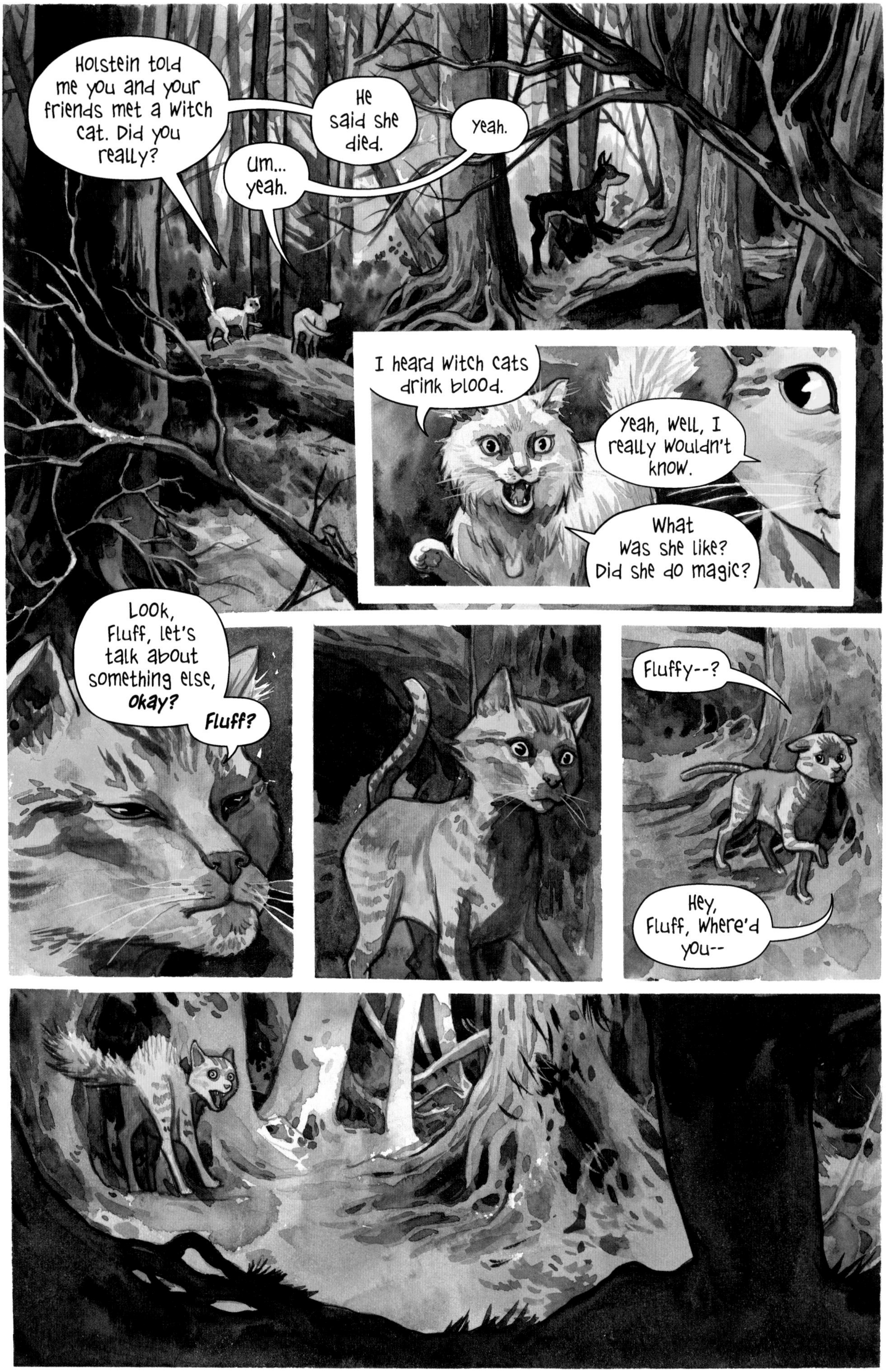

Holstein told me you and your friends met a witch cat. Did you really?
Um... yeah.
He said she died.
Yeah.
I heard witch cats drink blood.
Yeah, well, I really wouldn't know.
What was she like? Did she do magic?
Look, Fluff, let's talk about something else, **okay?**
Fluff?
Fluffy--?
Hey, Fluff, where'd you--

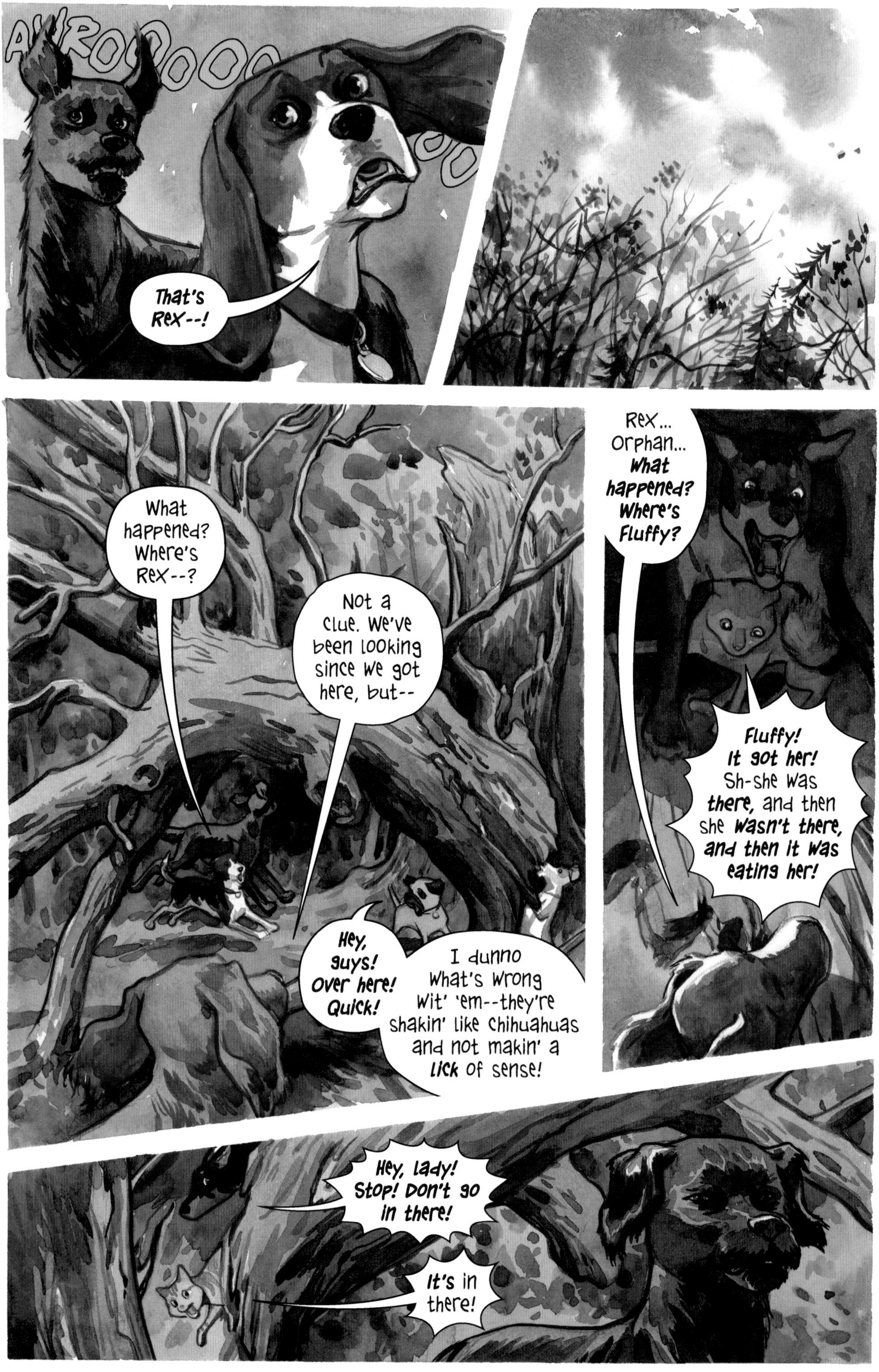
AWROOOOOOOOO
That's Rex--!
What happened? Where's Rex--?
Not a clue. We've been looking since we got here, but--
Hey, guys! Over here! Quick!
I dunno what's wrong wit' 'em--they're shakin' like Chihuahuas and not makin' a lick of sense!
Rex... Orphan... What happened? Where's Fluffy?
Fluffy! It got her! Sh-she was there, and then she wasn't there, and then it was eating her!
Hey, lady! Stop! Don't go in there!
It's in there!

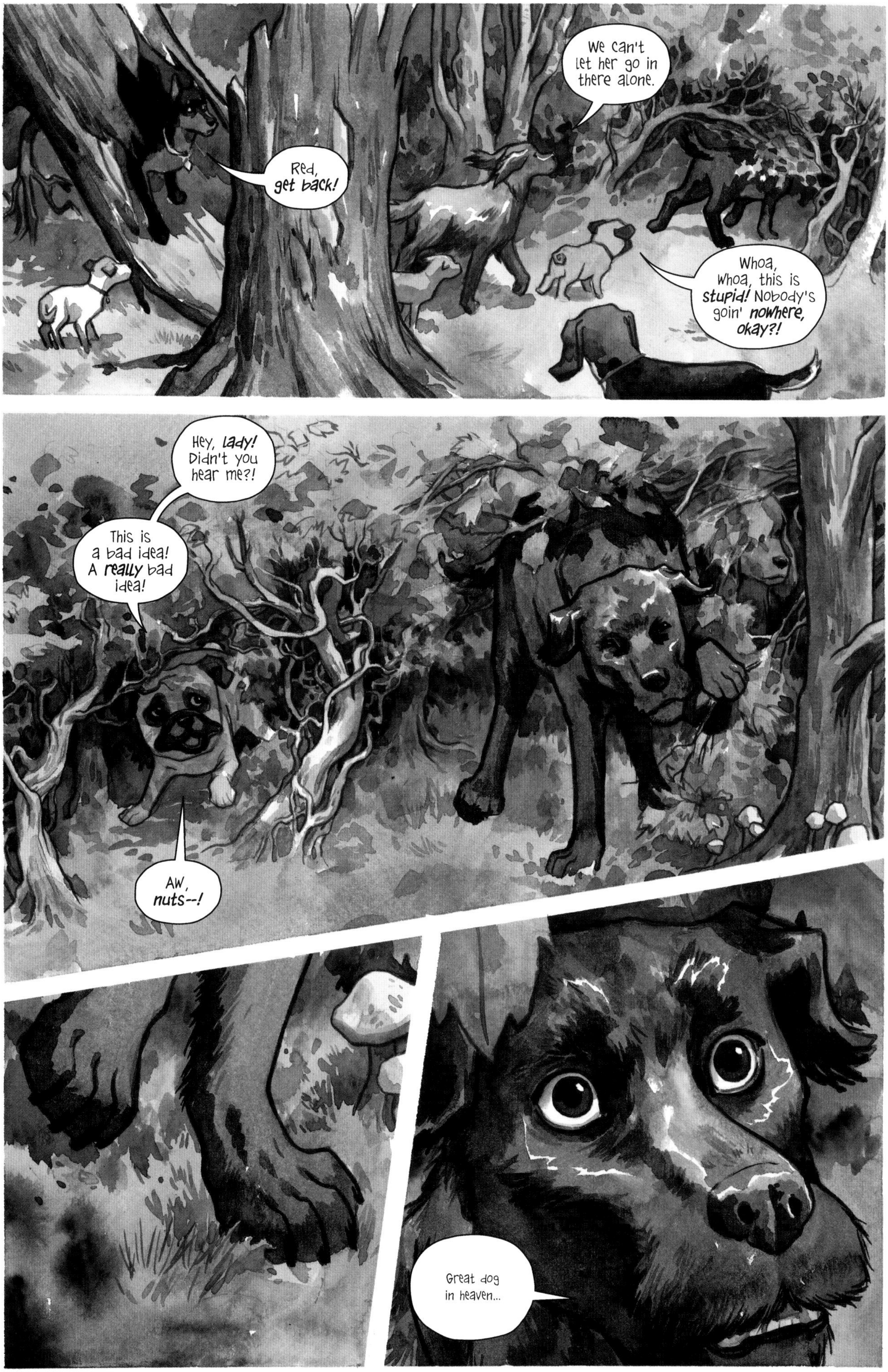

We can't let her go in there alone.
Red, **get back!**
Whoa, whoa, this is ***stupid!*** Nobody's goin' ***nowhere, okay?!***
Hey, ***lady!*** Didn't you hear me?!
This is a bad idea! A ***really*** bad idea!
Aw, ***nuts--!***
Great dog in heaven...

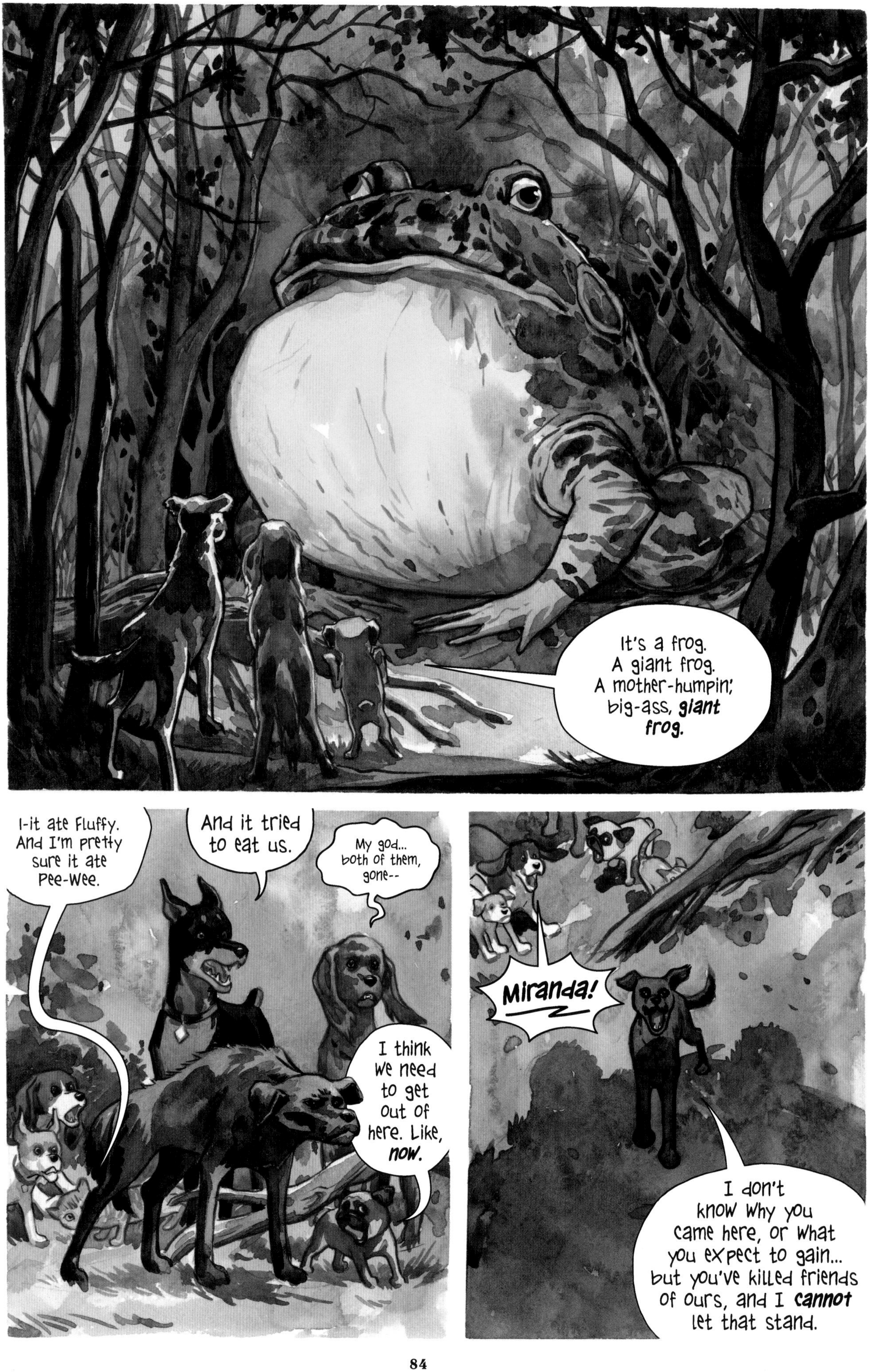
It's a frog. A giant frog. A mother-humpin', big-ass, **giant frog.**
I-it ate Fluffy. And I'm pretty sure it ate Pee-Wee.
And it tried to eat us.
My god... both of them, gone--
I think we need to get out of here. Like, **now.**
Miranda!
I don't know why you came here, or what you expect to gain... but you've killed friends of ours, and I **cannot** let that stand.

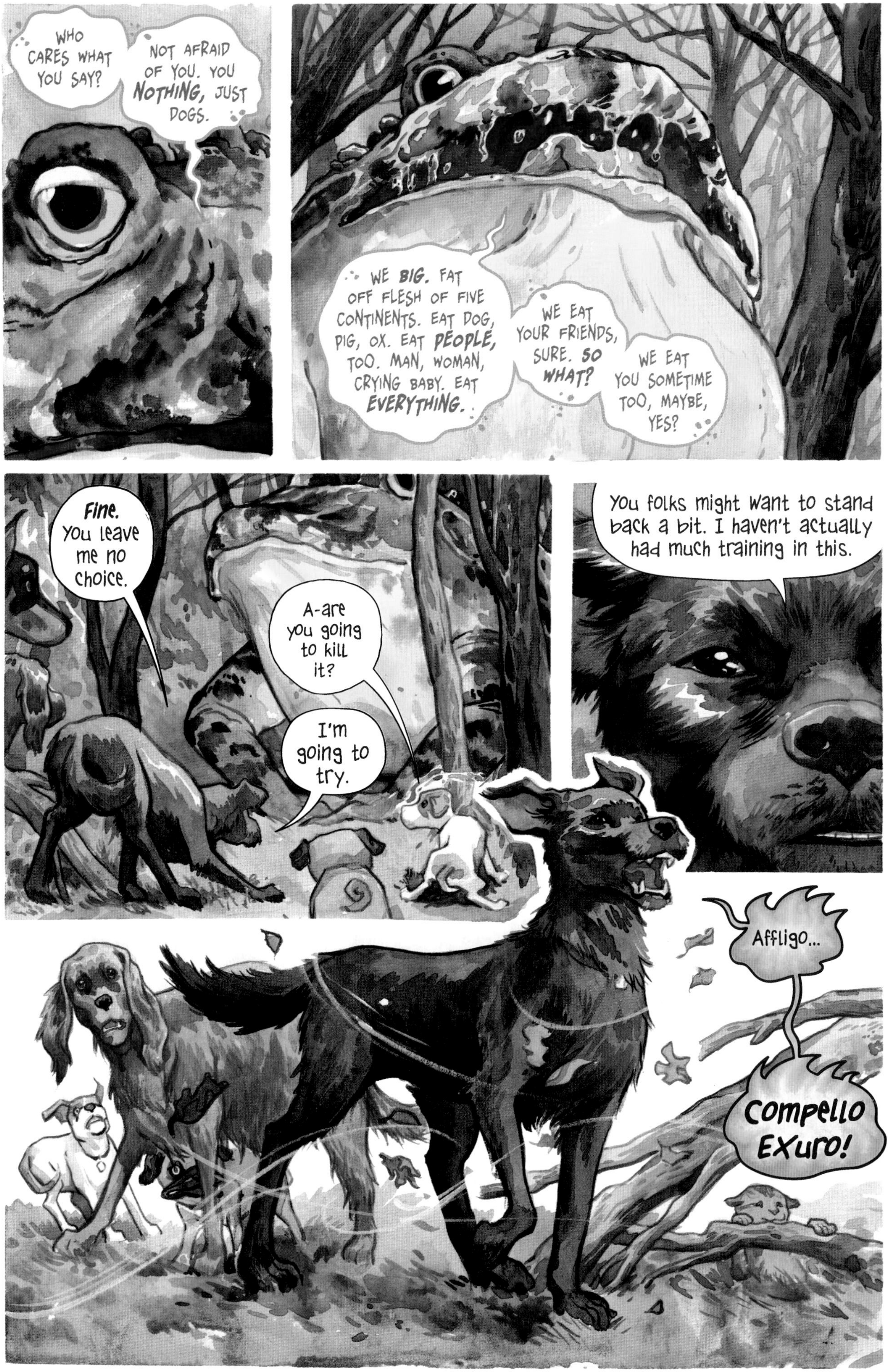
WHO CARES WHAT YOU SAY?
NOT AFRAID OF YOU. YOU NOTHING, JUST DOGS.
WE BIG. EAT OFF FLESH OF FIVE CONTINENTS. EAT DOG, PIG, OX. EAT PEOPLE, TOO. MAN, WOMAN, CRYING BABY. EAT EVERYTHING.
WE EAT YOUR FRIENDS, SURE. SO WHAT?
WE EAT YOU SOMETIME TOO, MAYBE, YES?
Fine. You leave me no choice.
A-are you going to kill it?
I'm going to try.
You folks might want to stand back a bit. I haven't actually had much training in this.
Affligo...
Compello Exuro!

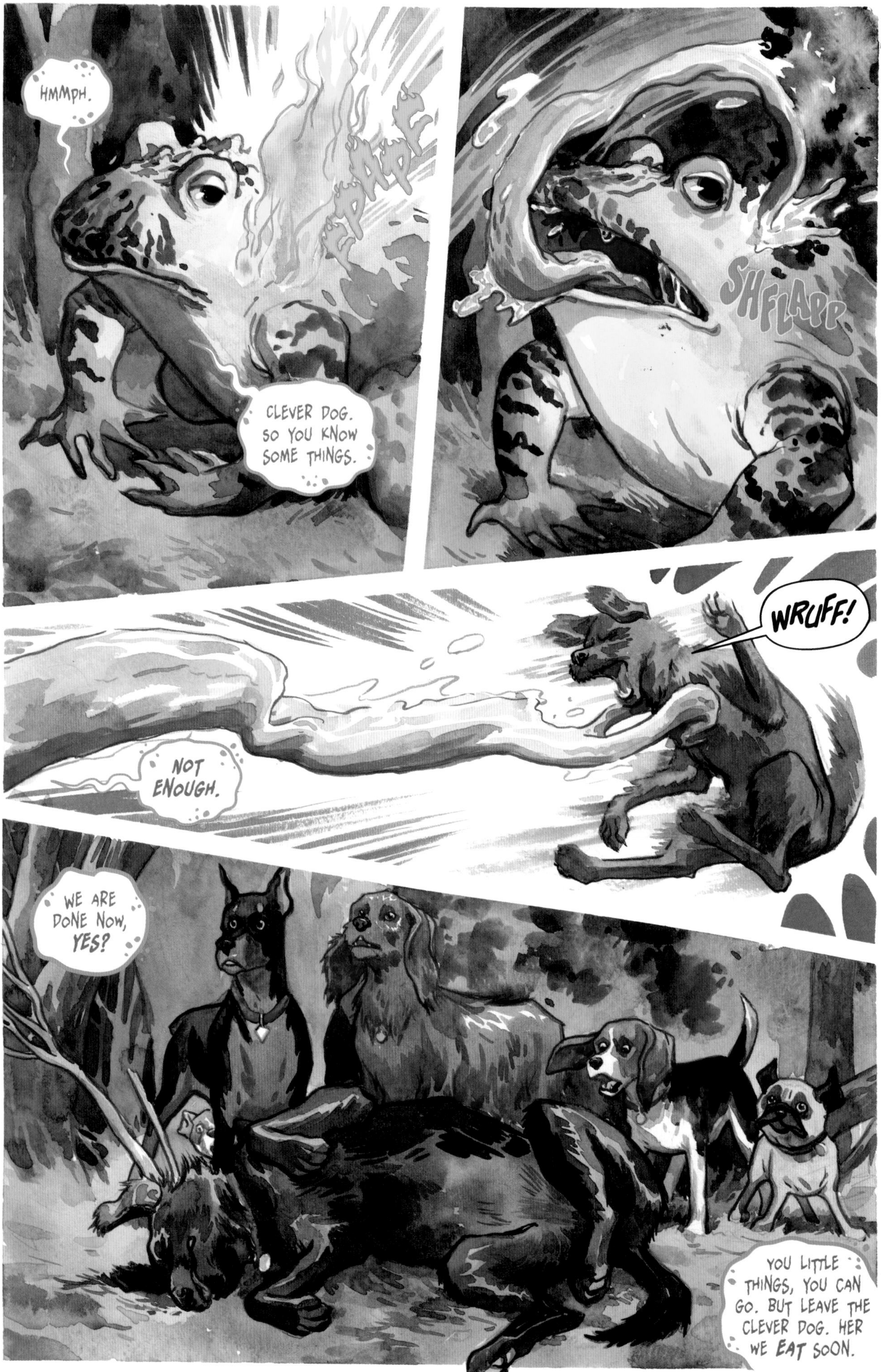
HMMPH.
FPAPF
CLEVER DOG. SO YOU KNOW SOME THINGS.
SHFLAPP
WRUFF!
NOT ENOUGH.
WE ARE DONE NOW, YES?
YOU LITTLE THINGS, YOU CAN GO. BUT LEAVE THE CLEVER DOG. HER WE EAT SOON.

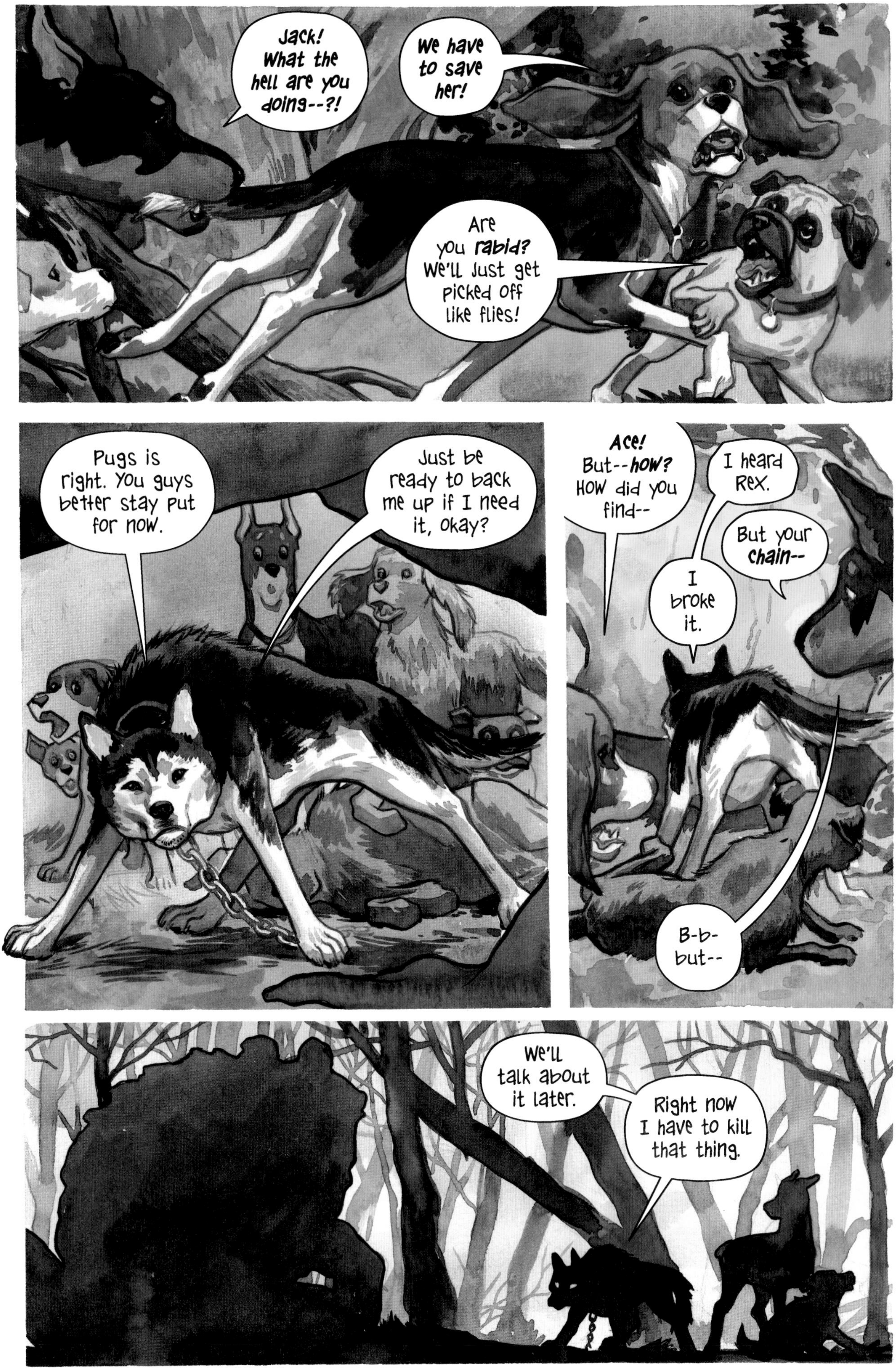
Jack! What the hell are you doing--?!
We have to save her!
Are you rabid? We'll just get picked off like flies!
Pugs is right. You guys better stay put for now.
Just be ready to back me up if I need it, okay?
Ace! But--how? HOW did you find--
I heard Rex.
But your chain--
I broke it.
B-b-but--
We'll talk about it later.
Right now I have to kill that thing.

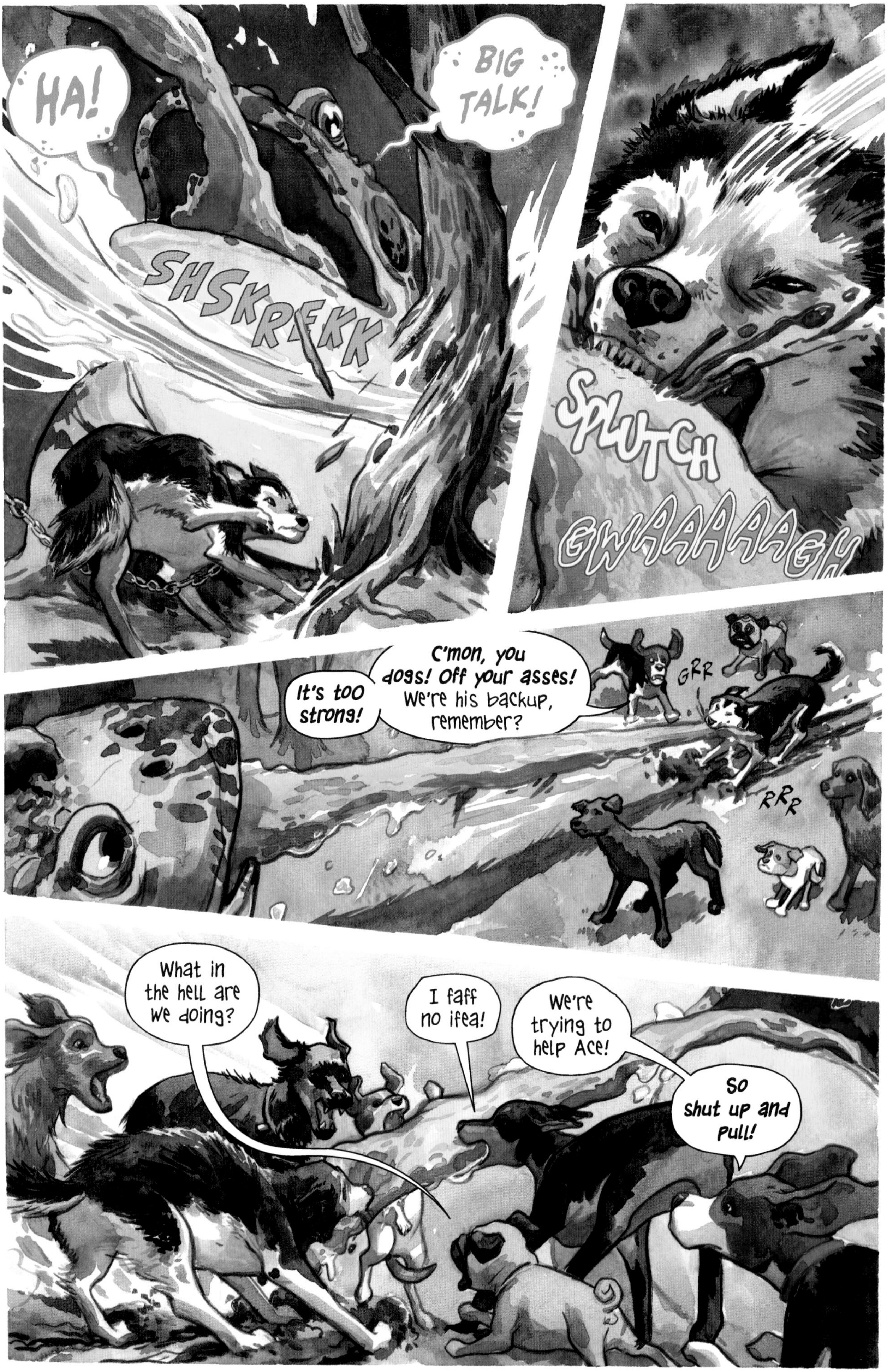
HA!
BIG TALK!
SHSKREKK
SPLUTCH
GWAAAAAAGH
It's too strong!
C'mon, you dogs! Off your asses! We're his backup, remember?
GRR
RRR
What in the hell are we doing?
I faff no ifea!
We're trying to help Ace!
So shut up and pull!

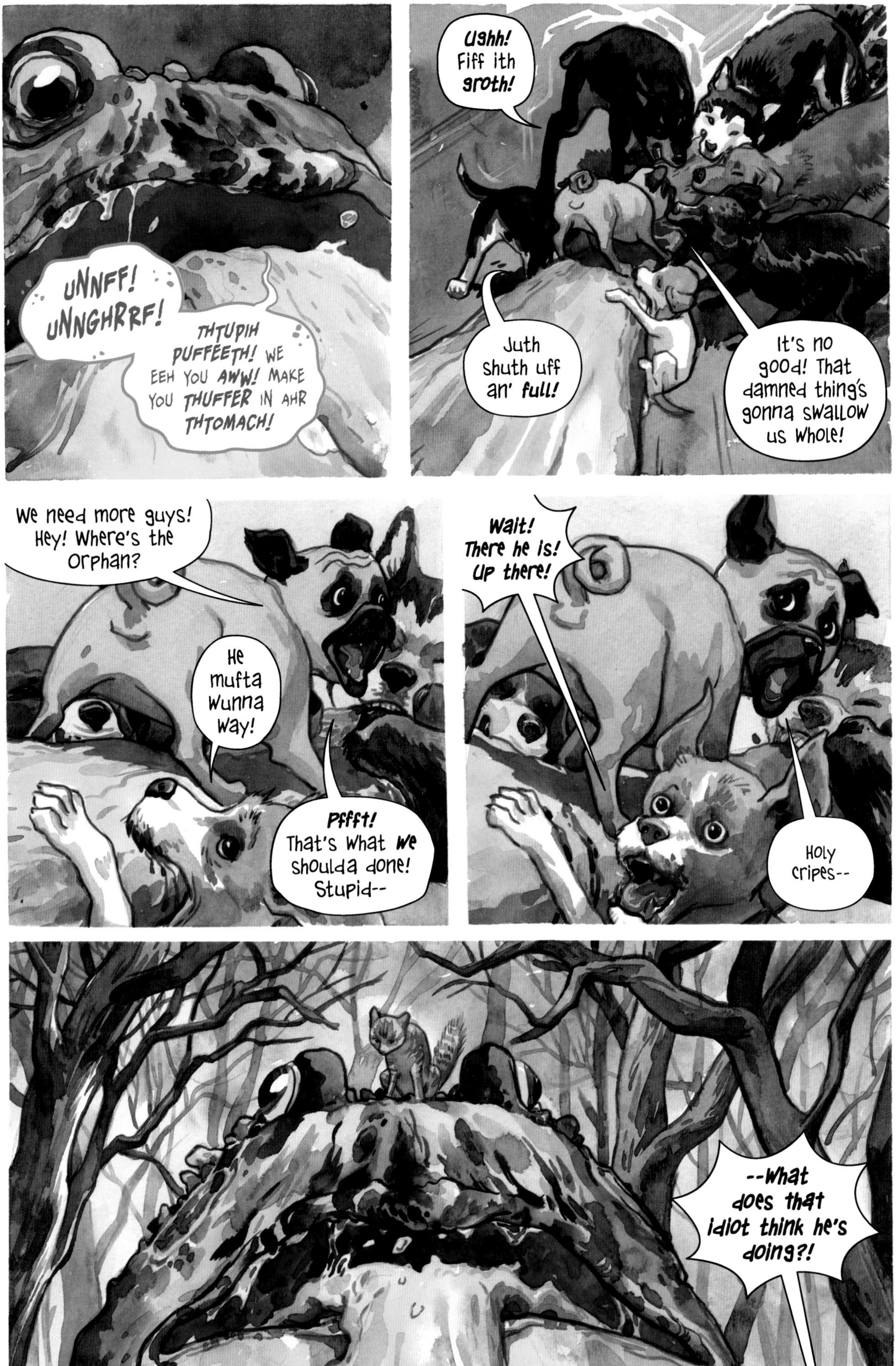
UNNFF! UNNGHRRF!
THTUPIH PUFFEETH! WE EEH YOU AWW! MAKE YOU THUFFER IN AHR THTOMACH!
Ughh! Fiff ith groth!
Juth shuth uff an' full!
It's no good! That damned thing's gonna swallow us whole!
We need more guys! Hey! Where's the Orphan?
He mufta wunna way!
Pffft! That's what we shoulda done! Stupid--
Wait! There he is! Up there!
Holy cripes--
--What does that idiot think he's doing?!

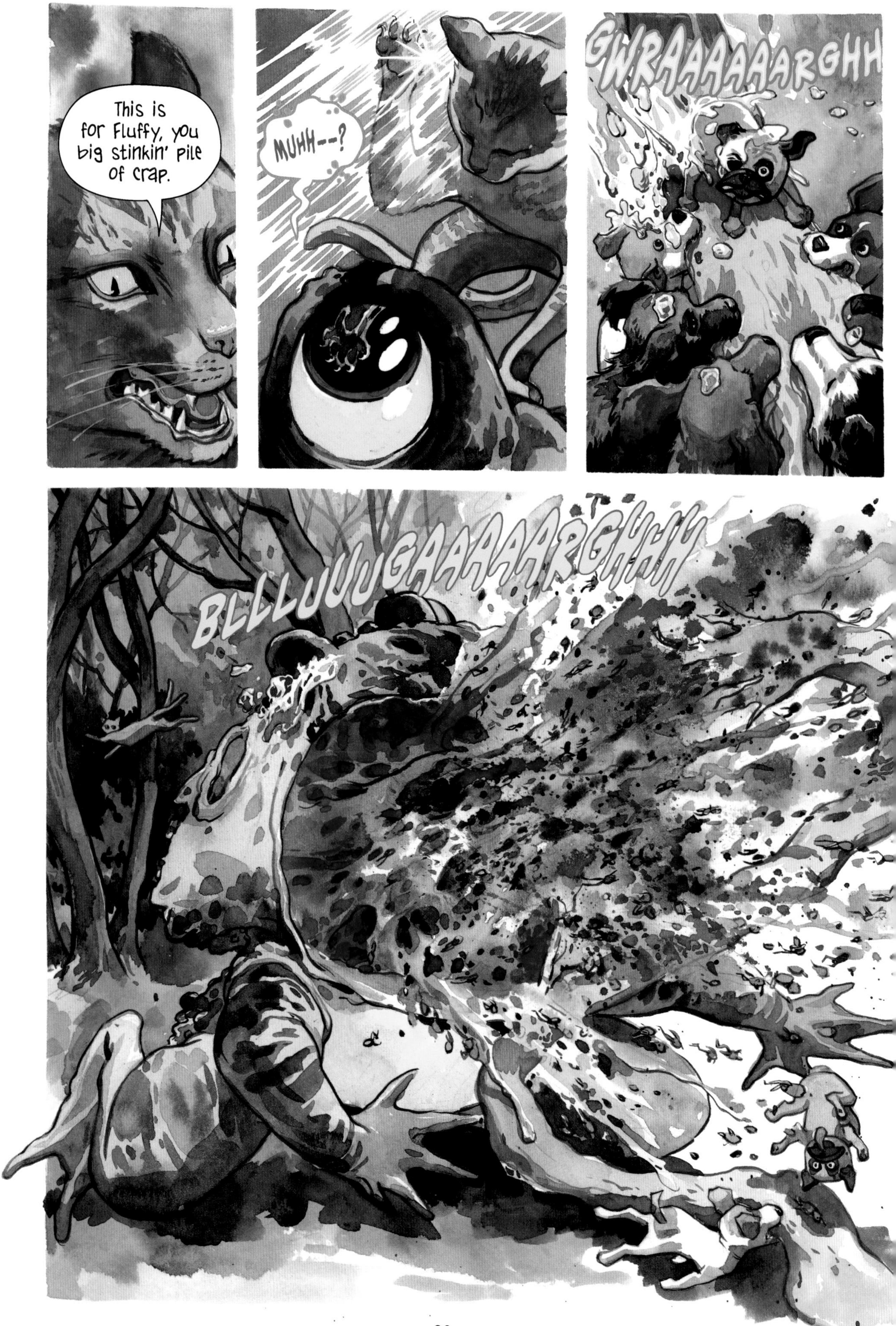
This is for Fluffy, you big stinkin' pile of crap.
MUHH--?
GWRAAAAAAARGHH
BLLUUUGAAAAARGHHH

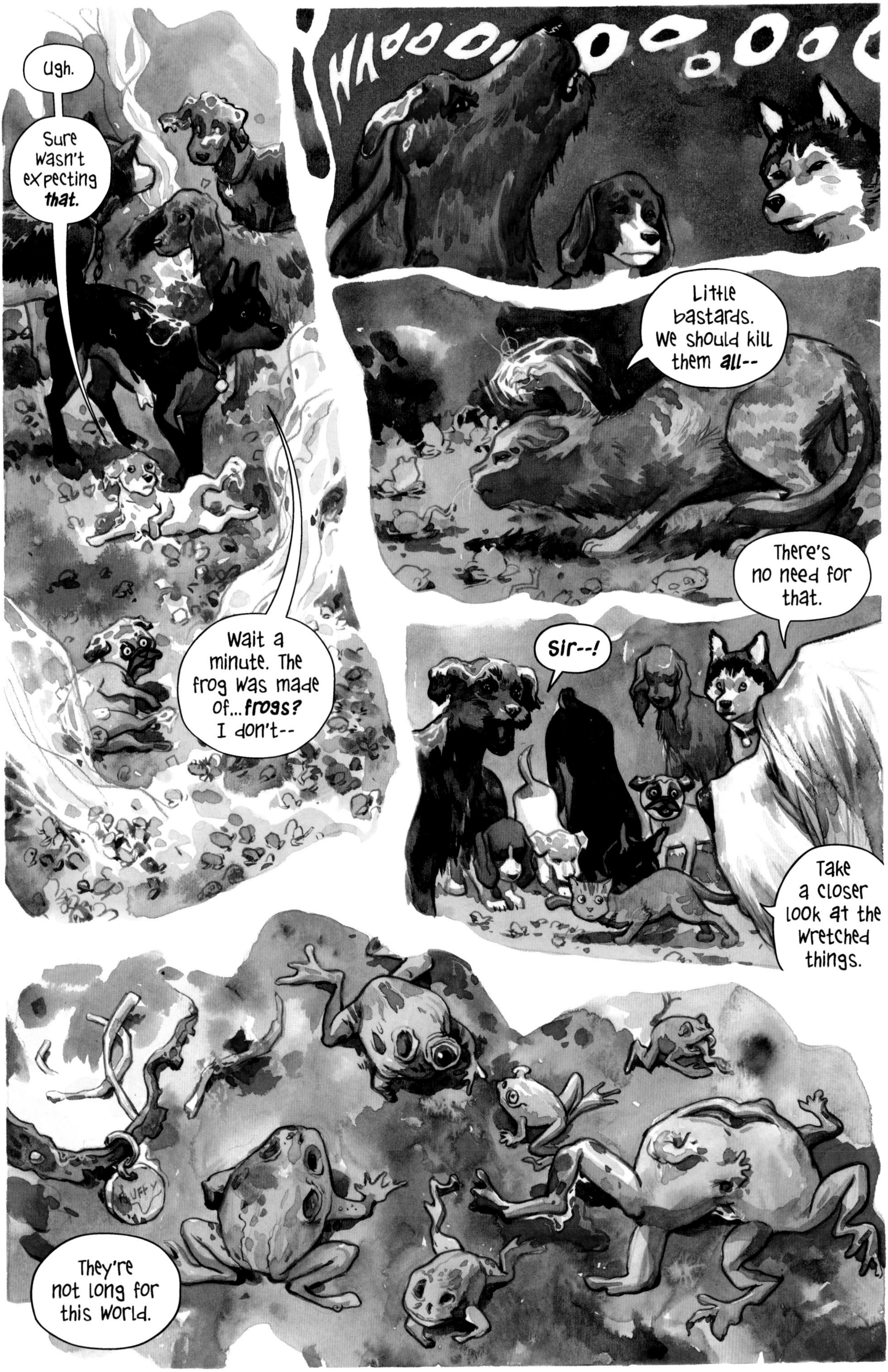

Ugh.
Sure wasn't expecting ***that.***
Wait a minute. The frog was made of... ***frogs?*** I don't--
Little bastards. We should kill them ***all--***
There's no need for that.
Sir--!
Take a closer look at the wretched things.
They're not long for this world.

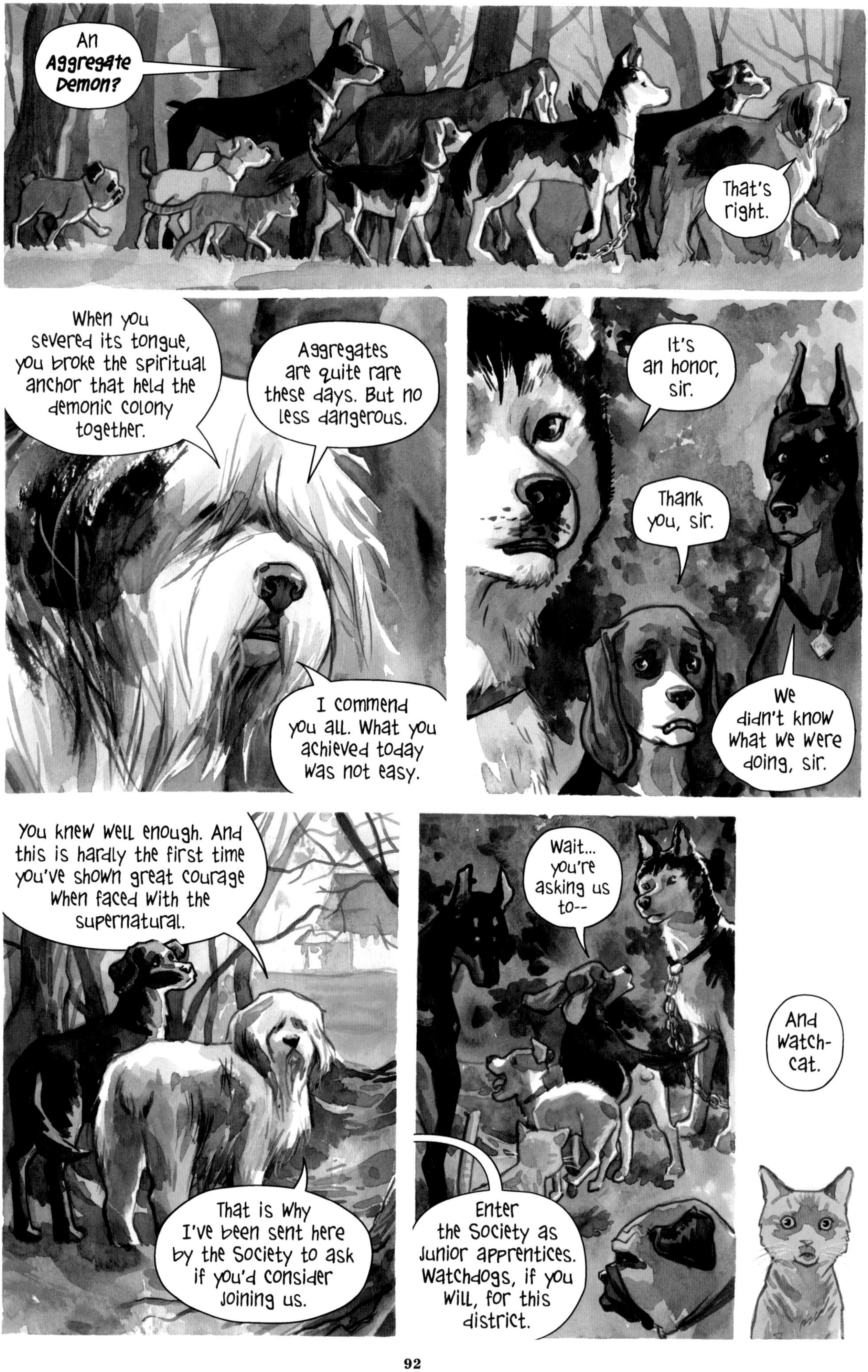
An Aggregate Demon?
That's right.
When you severed its tongue, you broke the spiritual anchor that held the demonic colony together.
Aggregates are quite rare these days. But no less dangerous.
I commend you all. What you achieved today was not easy.
It's an honor, sir.
Thank you, sir.
We didn't know what we were doing, sir.
You knew well enough. And this is hardly the first time you've shown great courage when faced with the supernatural.
That is why I've been sent here by the Society to ask if you'd consider joining us.
Wait... you're asking us to--
Enter the Society as junior apprentices. Watchdogs, if you will, for this district.
And Watch-cat.

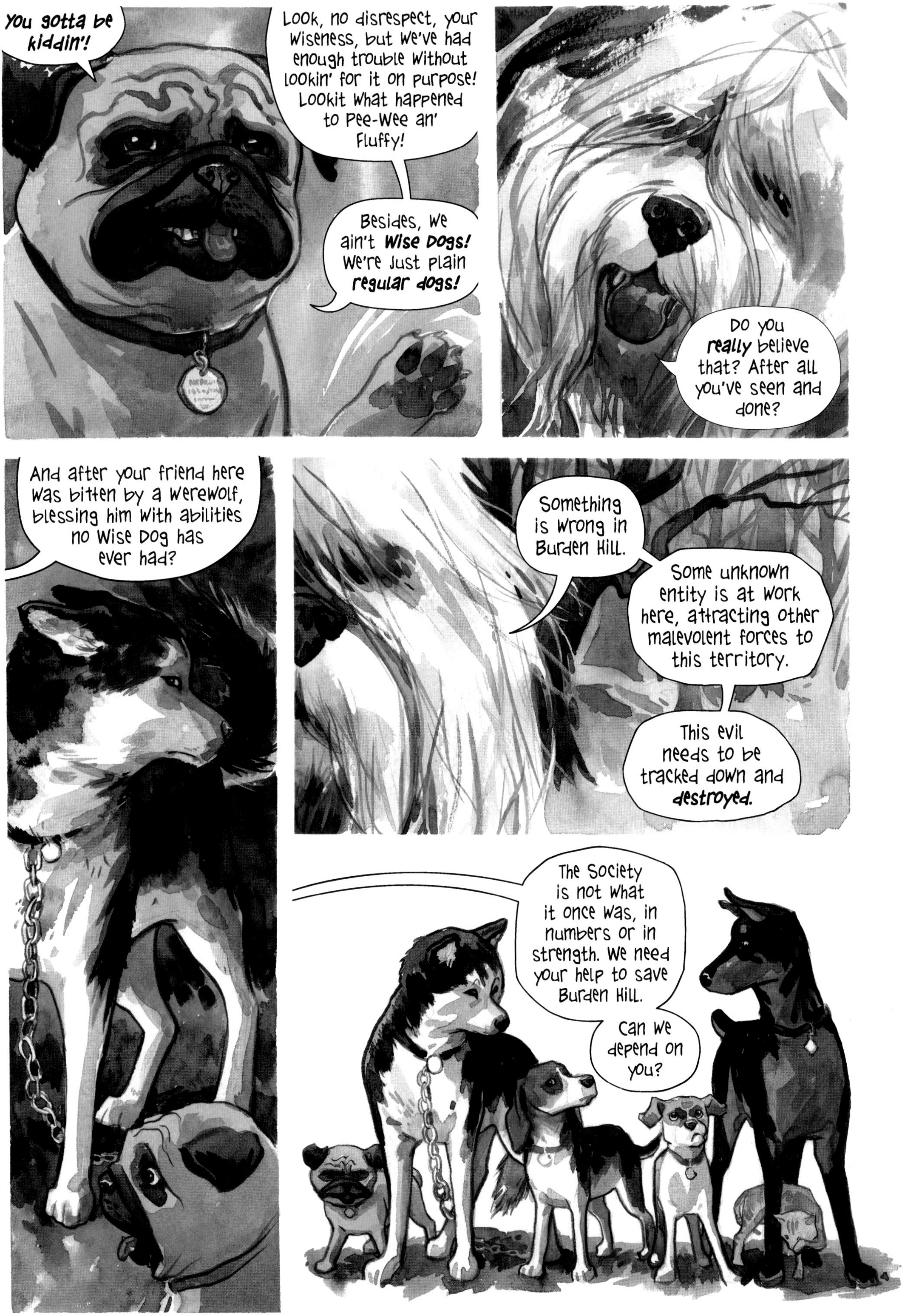
You gotta be kiddin'!
Look, no disrespect, your Wiseness, but we've had enough trouble without lookin' for it on purpose! Lookit what happened to Pee-Wee an' Fluffy!
Besides, we ain't Wise Dogs! We're just plain regular dogs!
Do you really believe that? After all you've seen and done?
And after your friend here was bitten by a werewolf, blessing him with abilities no Wise Dog has ever had?
Something is wrong in Burden Hill.
Some unknown entity is at work here, attracting other malevolent forces to this territory.
This evil needs to be tracked down and destroyed.
The Society is not what it once was, in numbers or in strength. We need your help to save Burden Hill.
Can we depend on you?

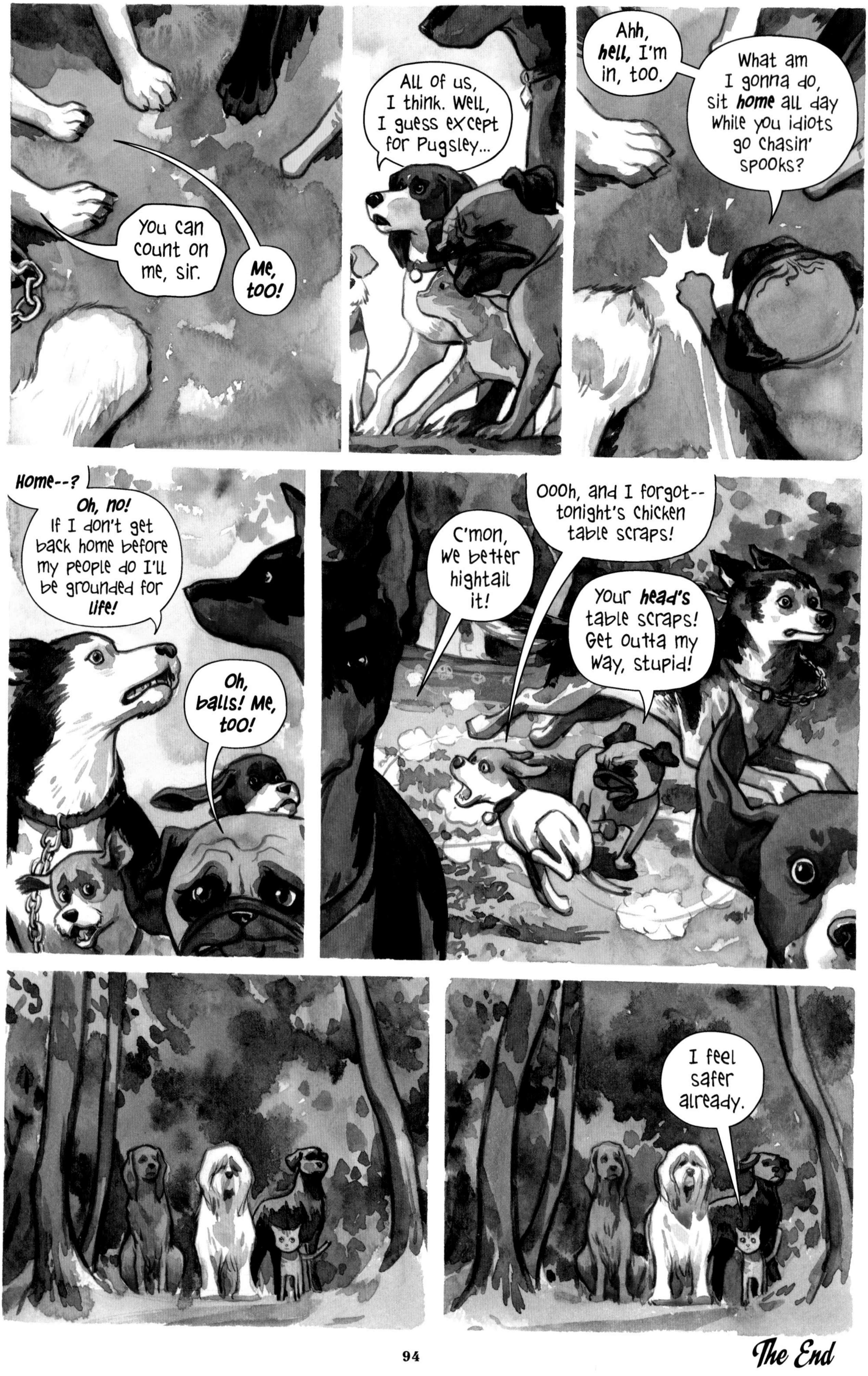
You can count on me, sir.
Me, too!
All of us, I think. Well, I guess except for Pugsley...
Ahh, hell, I'm in, too.
What am I gonna do, sit home all day while you idiots go chasin' spooks?
Home--?
Oh, no! If I don't get back home before my people do I'll be grounded for life!
Oh, balls! Me, too!
C'mon, we better hightail it!
Oooh, and I forgot-- tonight's chicken table scraps!
Your head's table scraps! Get outta my way, stupid!
I feel safer already.
The End

LOST

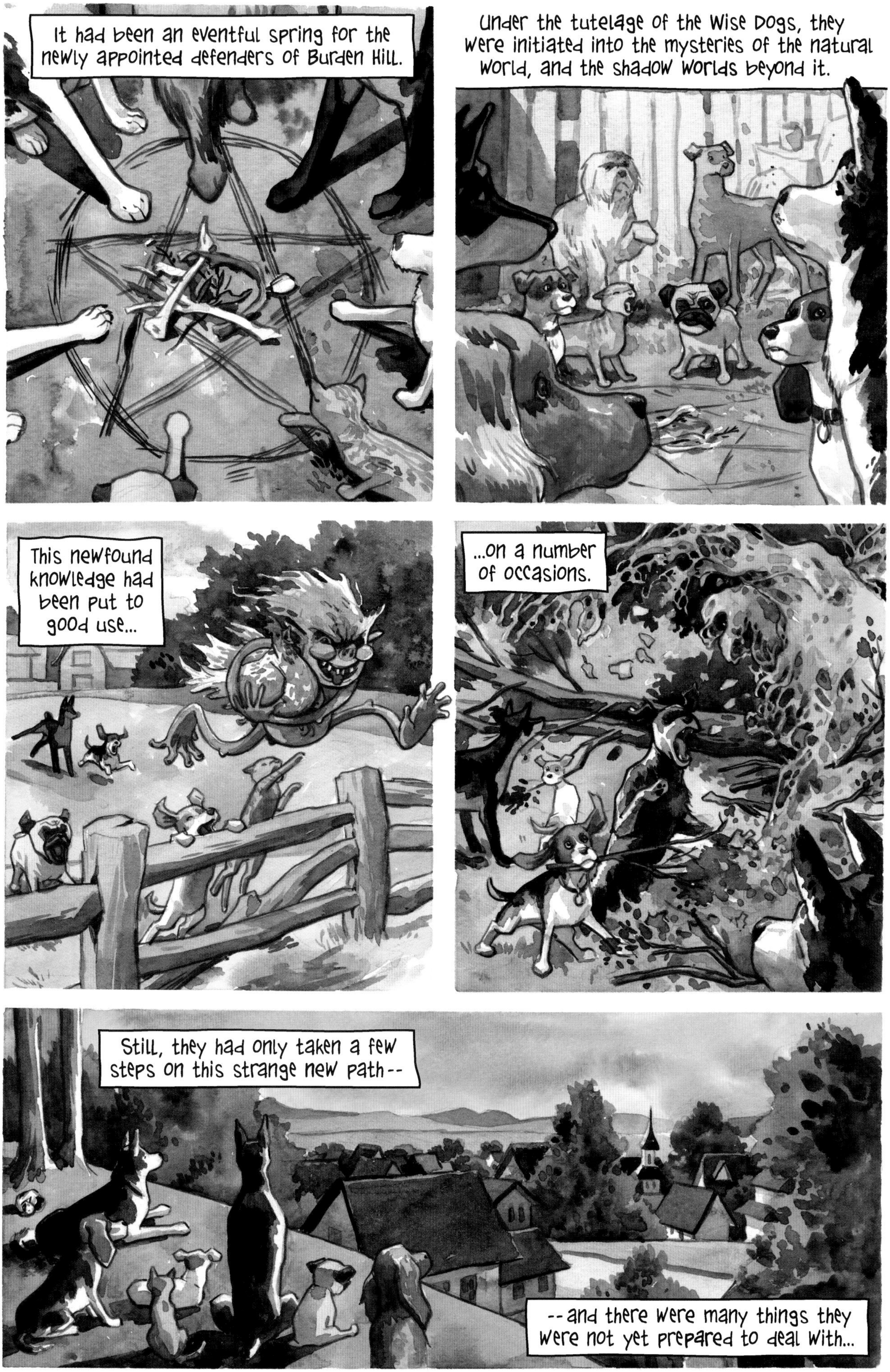
It had been an eventful spring for the newly appointed defenders of Burden Hill.
Under the tutelage of the Wise Dogs, they were initiated into the mysteries of the natural world, and the shadow worlds beyond it.
This newfound knowledge had been put to good use...
...on a number of occasions.
Still, they had only taken a few steps on this strange new path--
--and there were many things they were not yet prepared to deal with...

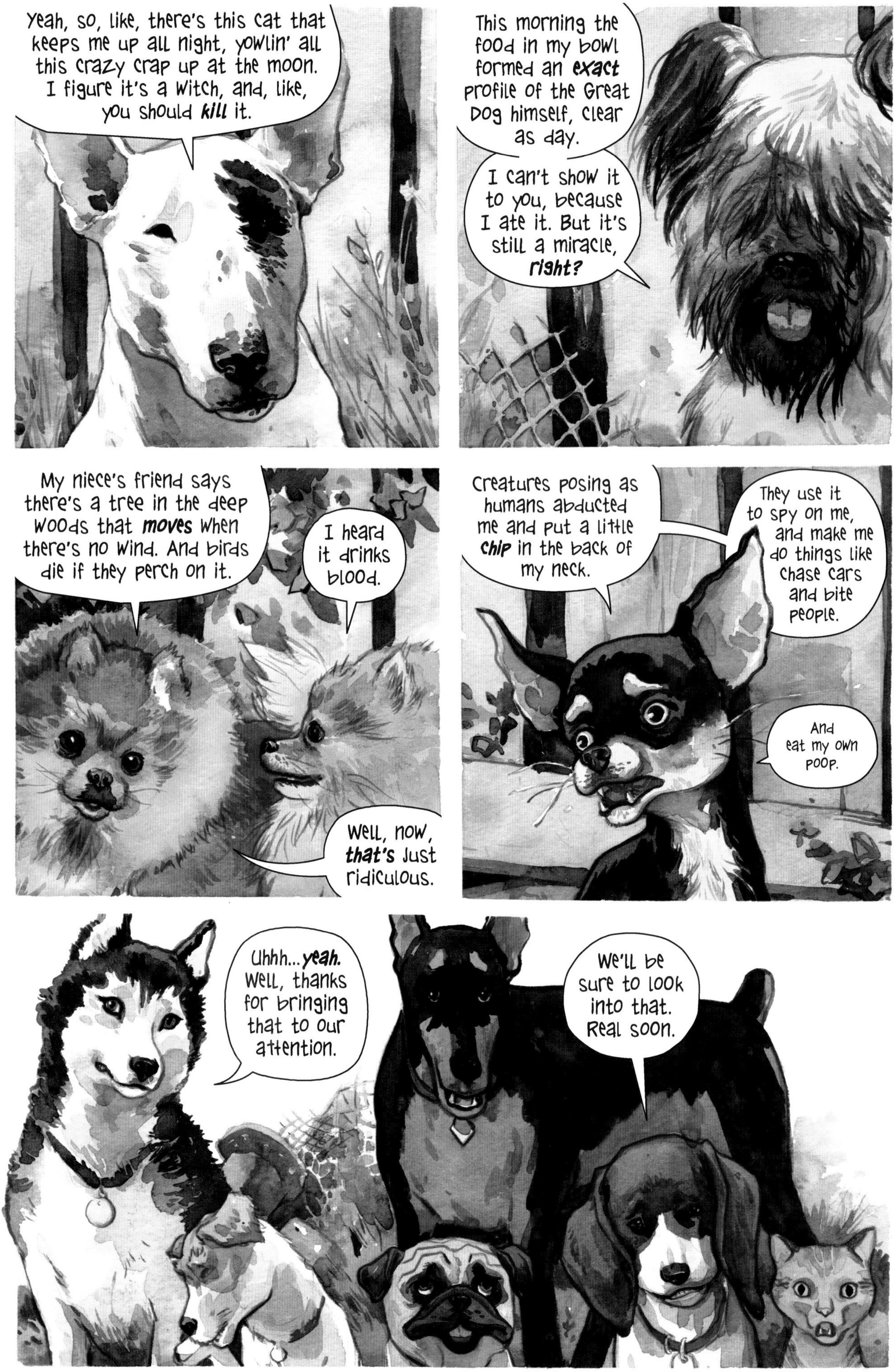
Yeah, so, like, there's this cat that keeps me up all night, yowlin' all this crazy crap up at the moon. I figure it's a witch, and, like, you should *kill* it.
This morning the food in my bowl formed an **exact** profile of the Great Dog himself, clear as day.
I can't show it to you, because I ate it. But it's still a miracle, ***right?***
My niece's friend says there's a tree in the deep woods that **moves** when there's no wind. And birds die if they perch on it.
I heard it drinks blood.
Well, now, ***that's*** just ridiculous.
Creatures posing as humans abducted me and put a little ***chip*** in the back of my neck.
They use it to spy on me, and make me do things like chase cars and bite people.
And eat my own poop.
Uhhh... ***yeah.*** Well, thanks for bringing that to our attention.
We'll be sure to look into that. Real soon.

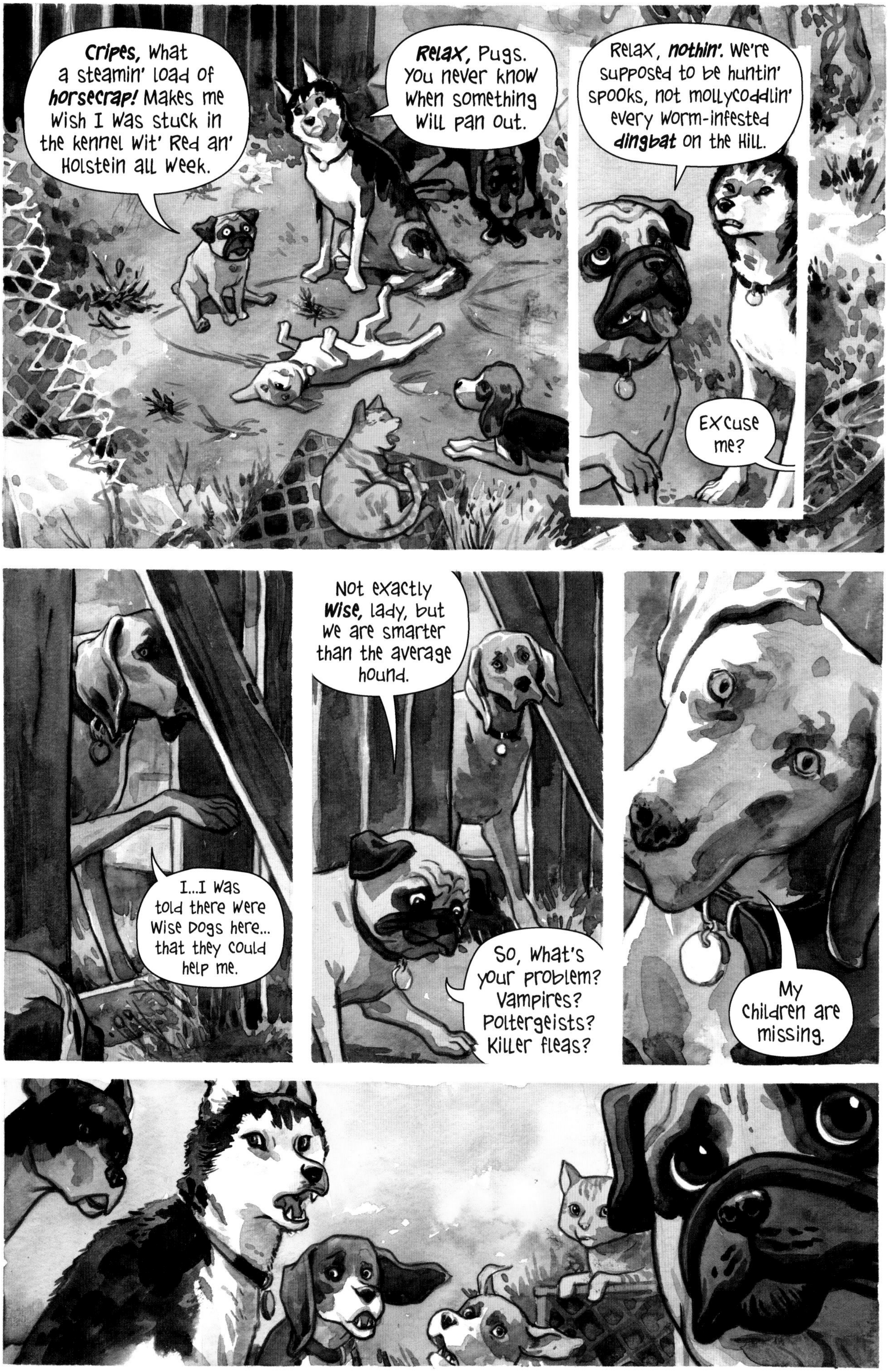
Cripes, what a steamin' load of horsecrap! Makes me wish I was stuck in the kennel wit' Red an' Holstein all week.
Relax, Pugs. You never know when something will pan out.
Relax, nothin'. We're supposed to be huntin' spooks, not mollycoddlin' every worm-infested dingbat on the Hill.
Excuse me?
I...I was told there were wise dogs here... that they could help me.
Not exactly wise, lady, but we are smarter than the average hound.
So, what's your problem? Vampires? Poltergeists? Killer fleas?
My children are missing.

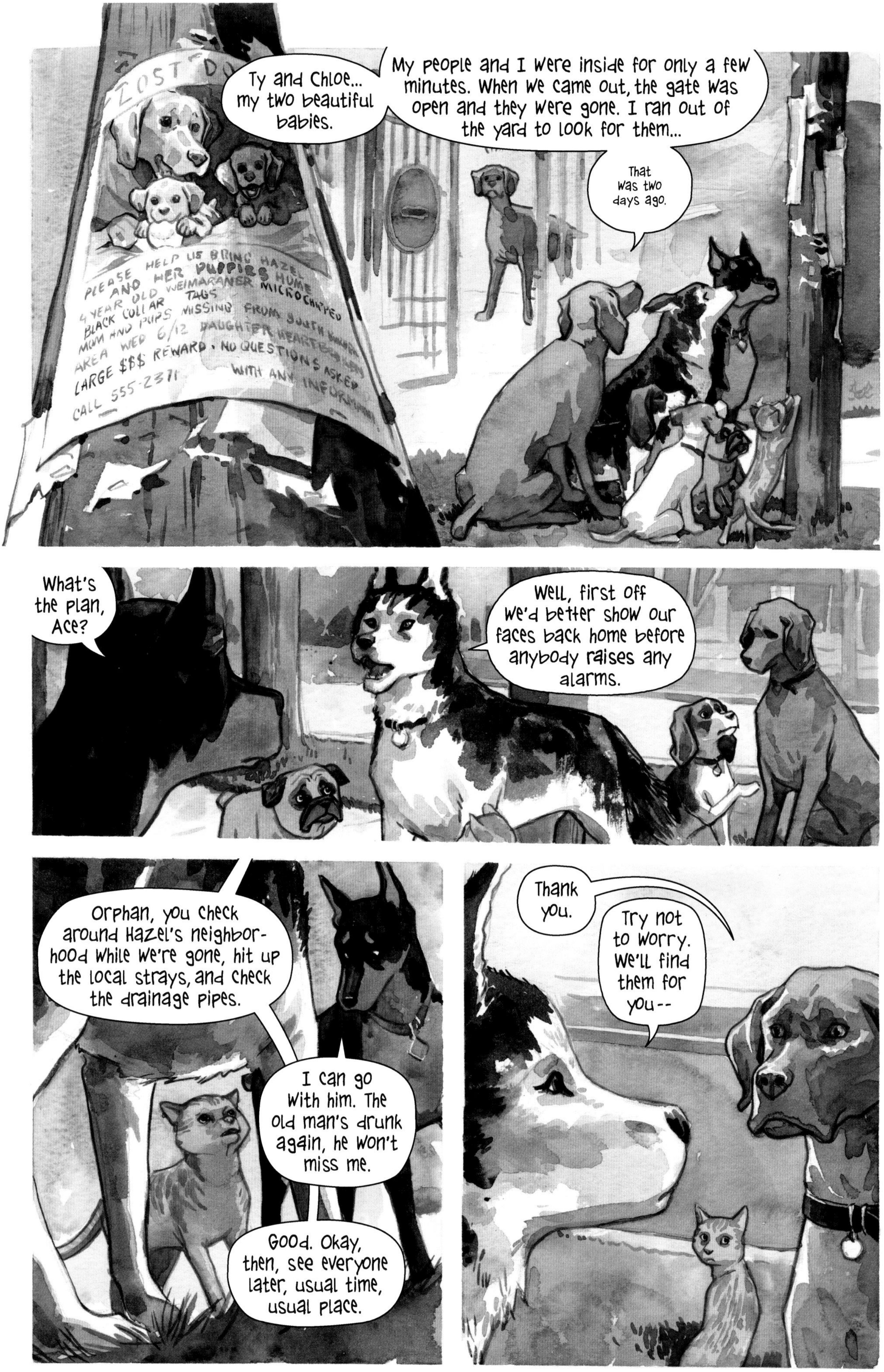
PLEASE HELP US BRING HAZEL
AND HER PUPPIES HOME
4 YEAR OLD WEIMARANER MICROCHIPPED
BLACK COLLAR TAGS
MOM AND PUPS MISSING FROM
AREA WED 6/12
LARGE $$$ REWARD. NO QUESTIONS ASKED
CALL 555-2371 WITH ANY
Ty and Chloe... my two beautiful babies.
My people and I were inside for only a few minutes. When we came out, the gate was open and they were gone. I ran out of the yard to look for them...
That was two days ago.
What's the plan, Ace?
Well, first off we'd better show our faces back home before anybody raises any alarms.
Orphan, you check around Hazel's neighbor-hood while we're gone, hit up the local strays, and check the drainage pipes.
I can go with him. The old man's drunk again, he won't miss me.
Good. Okay, then, see everyone later, usual time, usual place.
Thank you.
Try not to worry. We'll find them for you--

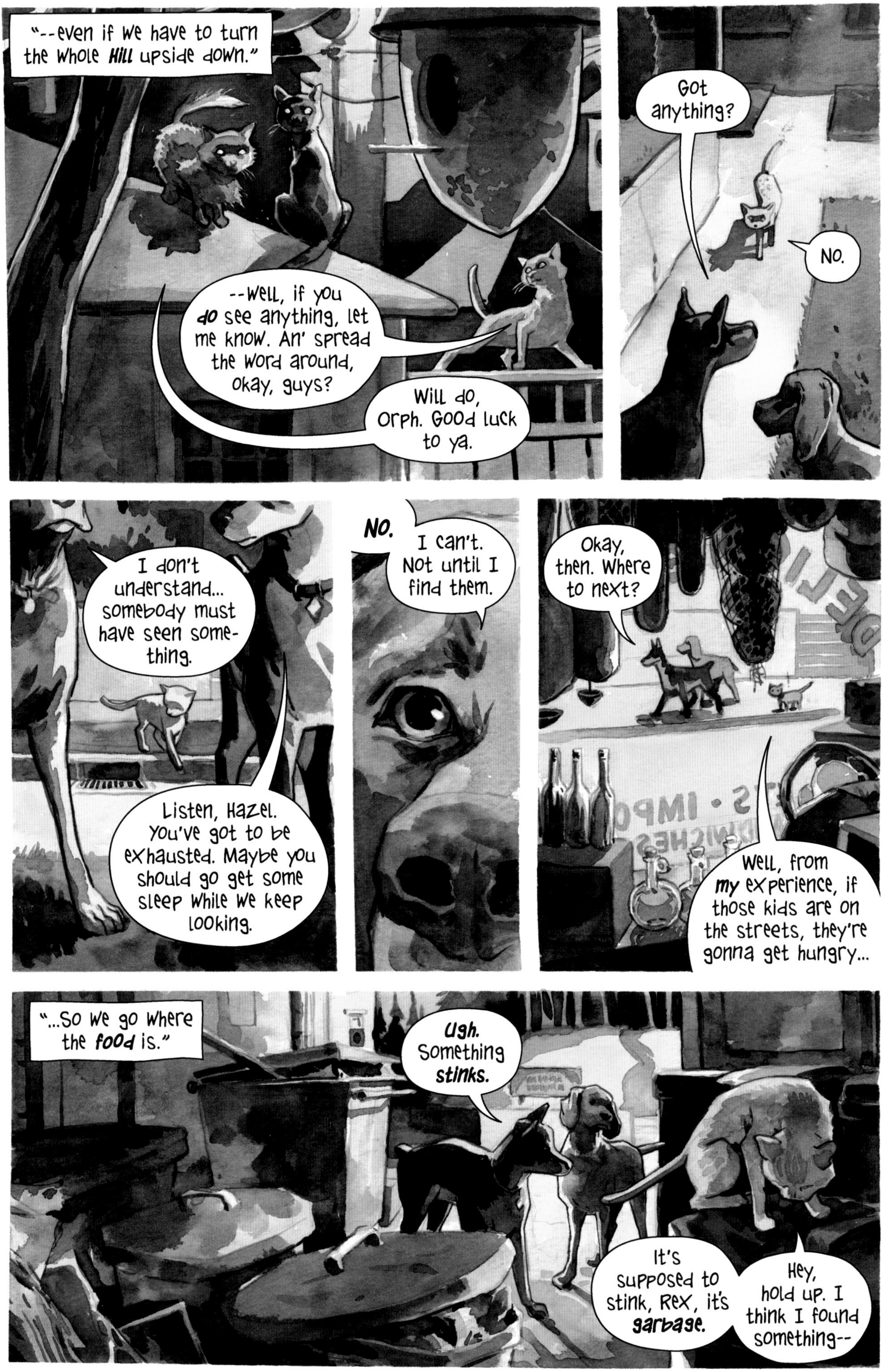
"--even if we have to turn the whole **Hill** upside down."
--Well, if you ***do*** see anything, let me know. An' spread the word around, okay, guys?
Will do, Orph. Good luck to ya.
Got anything?
No.
I don't understand... somebody must have seen some-thing.
Listen, Hazel. You've got to be exhausted. Maybe you should go get some sleep while we keep looking.
NO.
I can't. Not until I find them.
Okay, then. Where to next?
DELI
Well, from ***my*** experience, if those kids are on the streets, they're gonna get hungry...
"...So we go where the ***food*** is."
Ugh. Something ***stinks.***
It's supposed to stink, Rex, it's ***garbage.***
Hey, hold up. I think I found something--

HRRRSSSTH!?

MREEEOWWR!

My eats! **Mine!** **Scram** or I take **both** your faces off!

Think I'm kidding? **C'mon!** Who's first, huh? **Who's first for no face?**

Hey, hey, **calm down,** tough guy! We're not looking for food **or** a fight--

Please, we don't want any trouble. We're looking for my children.

Maybe you've seen them--?

Yeah, **right.** Think I'm **stupid?** I'll take **your** face off, too, lady!

HOKE!

Come along.

But, **Ma--**

But, **nothing.** You come along now, 'less you want your ears notched for you.

I'm sorry about your young'uns, miss.

There's a place in the east woods, out past the Old Cracked Oak, called **the Devil's Well.**

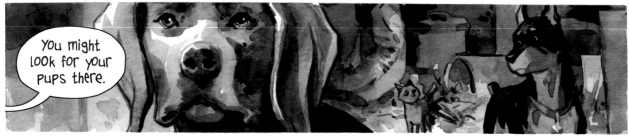

You might look for your pups there.

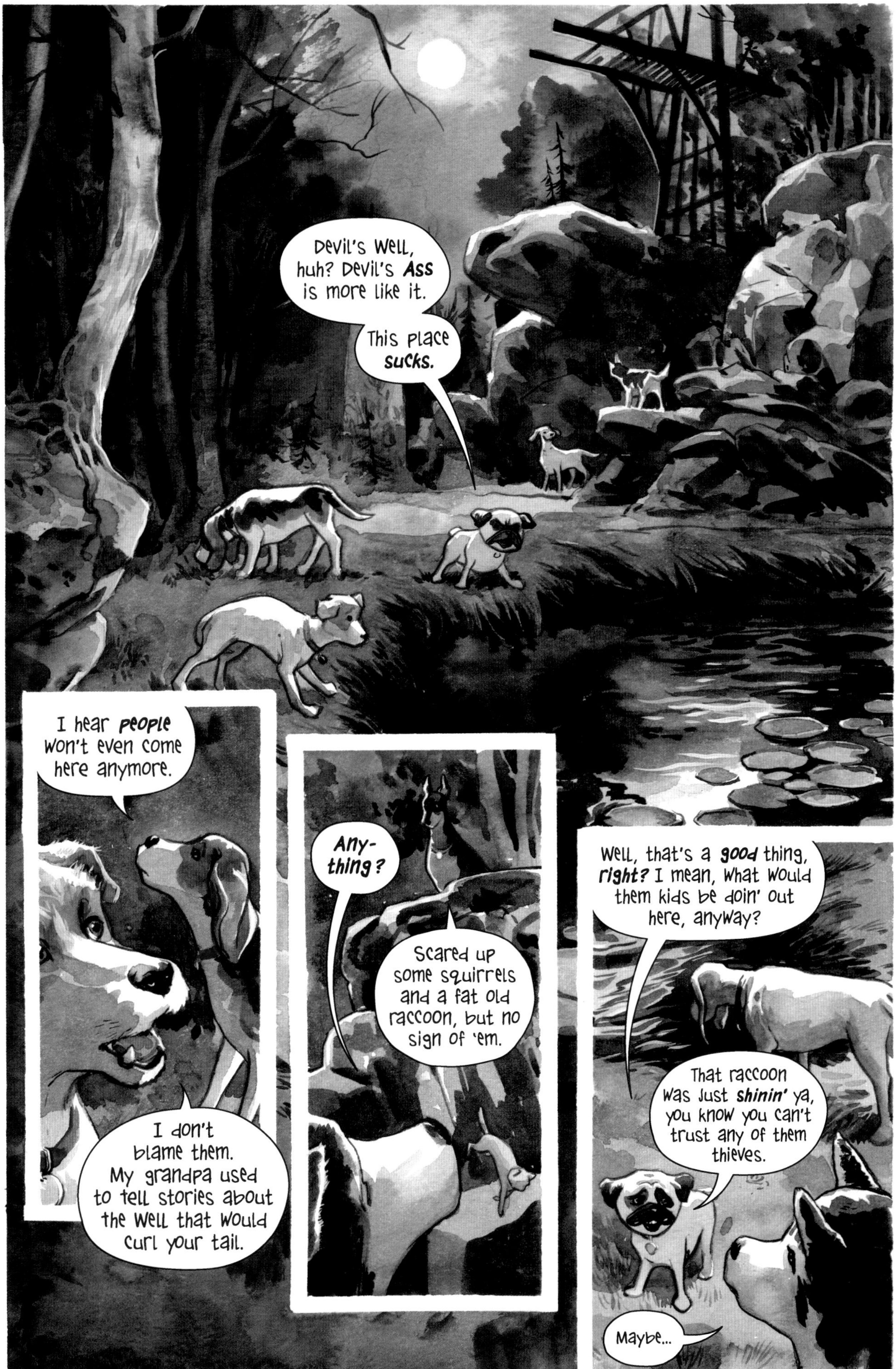
Devil's Well, huh? Devil's **Ass** is more like it.
This place **sucks.**
I hear ***people*** won't even come here anymore.
I don't blame them. My grandpa used to tell stories about the well that would curl your tail.
Any-thing?
Scared up some squirrels and a fat old raccoon, but no sign of 'em.
Well, that's a ***good*** thing, ***right?*** I mean, what would them kids be doin' out here, anyway?
That raccoon was just ***shinin'*** ya, you know you can't trust any of them thieves.
Maybe...

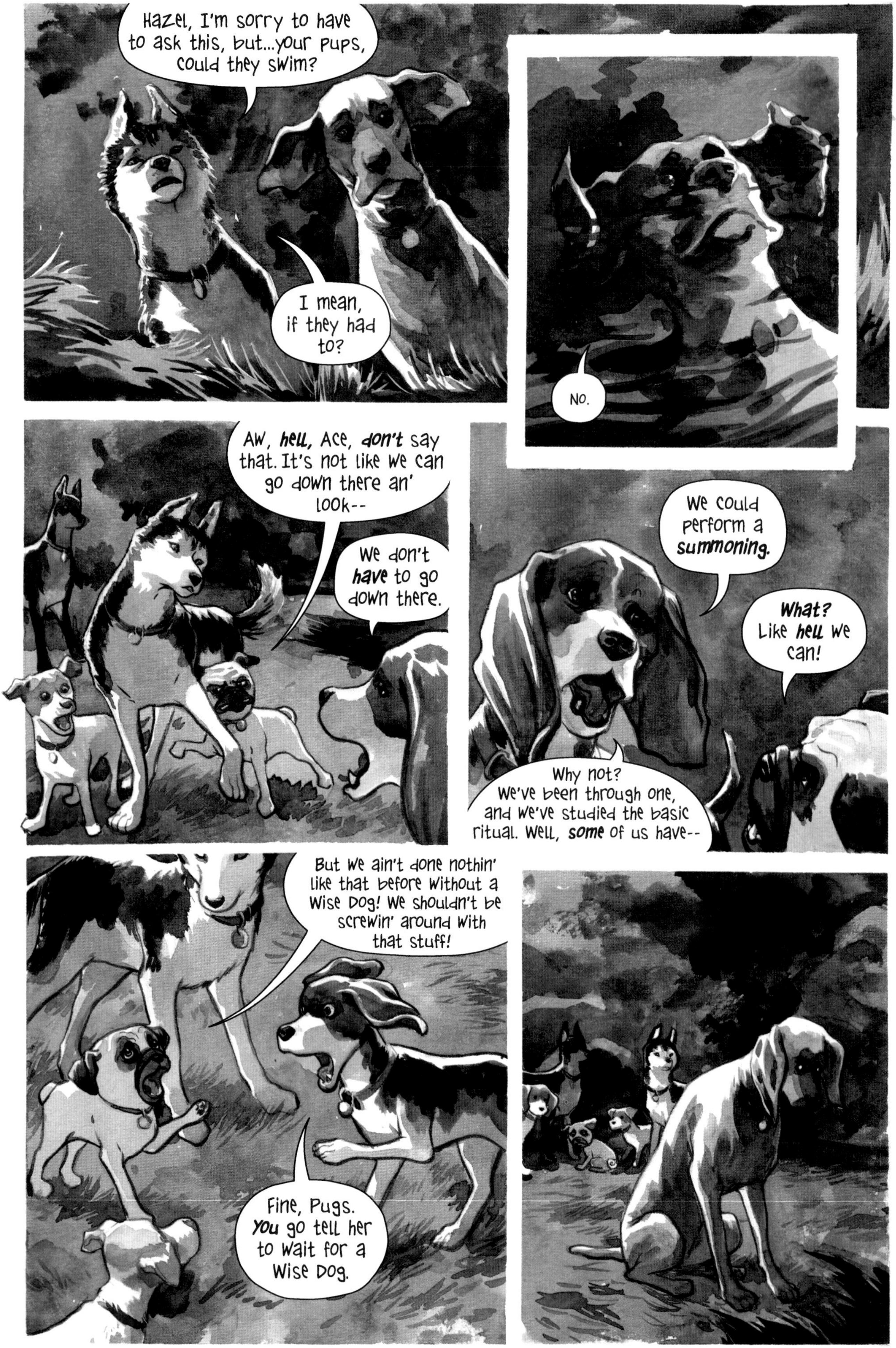
Hazel, I'm sorry to have to ask this, but...your pups, could they swim?
I mean, if they had to?
No.
Aw, **hell,** Ace, **don't** say that. It's not like we can go down there an' look--
We don't **have** to go down there.
We could perform a **summoning.**
What? Like **hell** we can!
Why not? We've been through one, and we've studied the basic ritual. Well, **some** of us have--
But we ain't done nothin' like that before without a Wise Dog! We shouldn't be screwin' around with that stuff!
Fine, Pugs. **You** go tell her to wait for a Wise Dog.

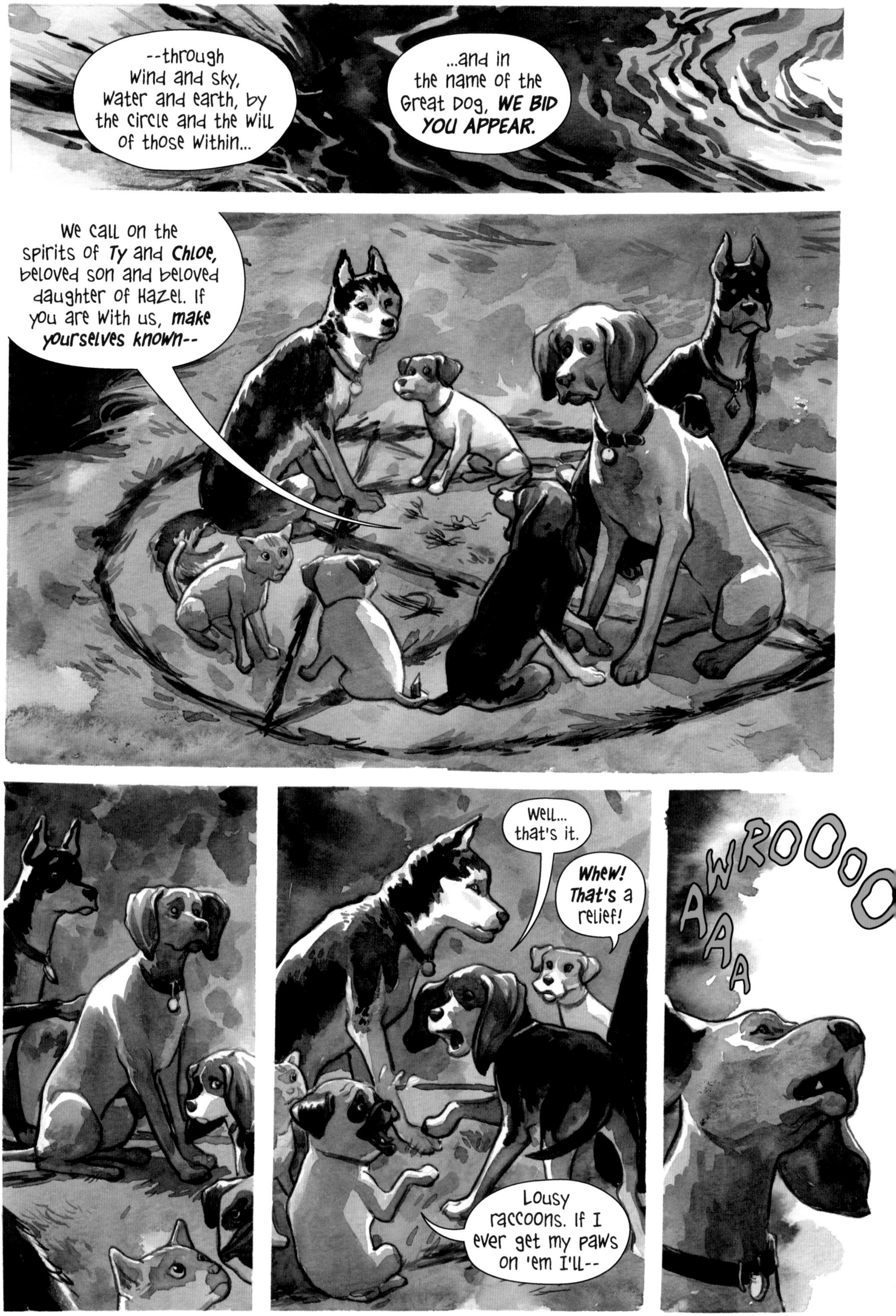
--through wind and sky, water and earth, by the circle and the will of those within...
...and in the name of the Great Dog, WE BID YOU APPEAR.
We call on the spirits of Ty and Chloe, beloved son and beloved daughter of Hazel. If you are with us, make yourselves known--
Well... that's it.
Whew! That's a relief!
Lousy raccoons. If I ever get my paws on 'em I'll--
AWROOOOOAAA

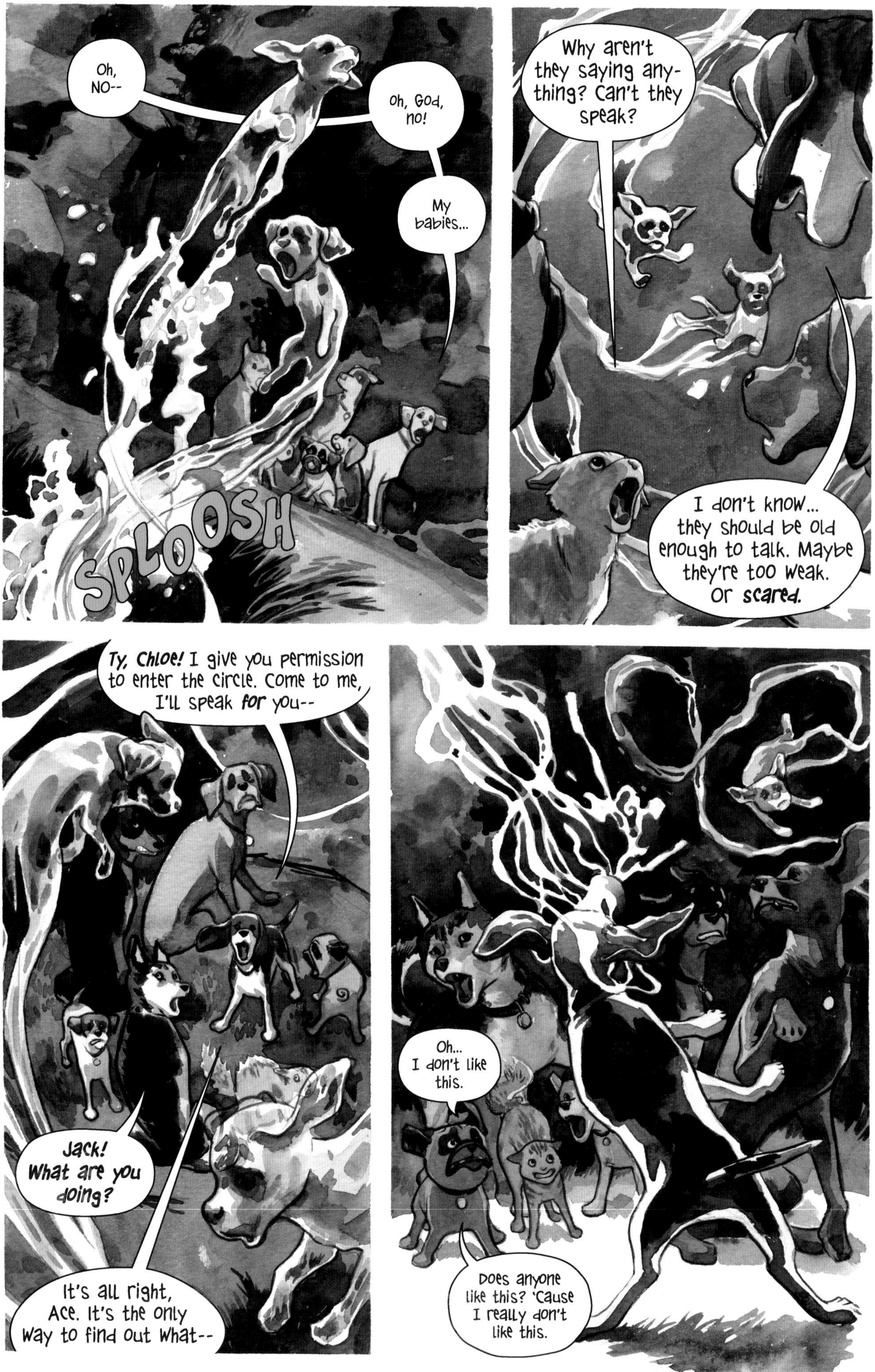
Oh, NO--
Oh, God, no!
My babies...
SPLOOSH
Why aren't they saying anything? Can't they speak?
I don't know... they should be old enough to talk. Maybe they're too weak. Or *scared.*
Ty, Chloe! I give you permission to enter the circle. Come to me, I'll speak *for* you--
Jack! What are you doing?
It's all right, Ace. It's the only way to find out what--
Oh... I don't like this.
Does anyone like this? 'Cause I really don't like this.

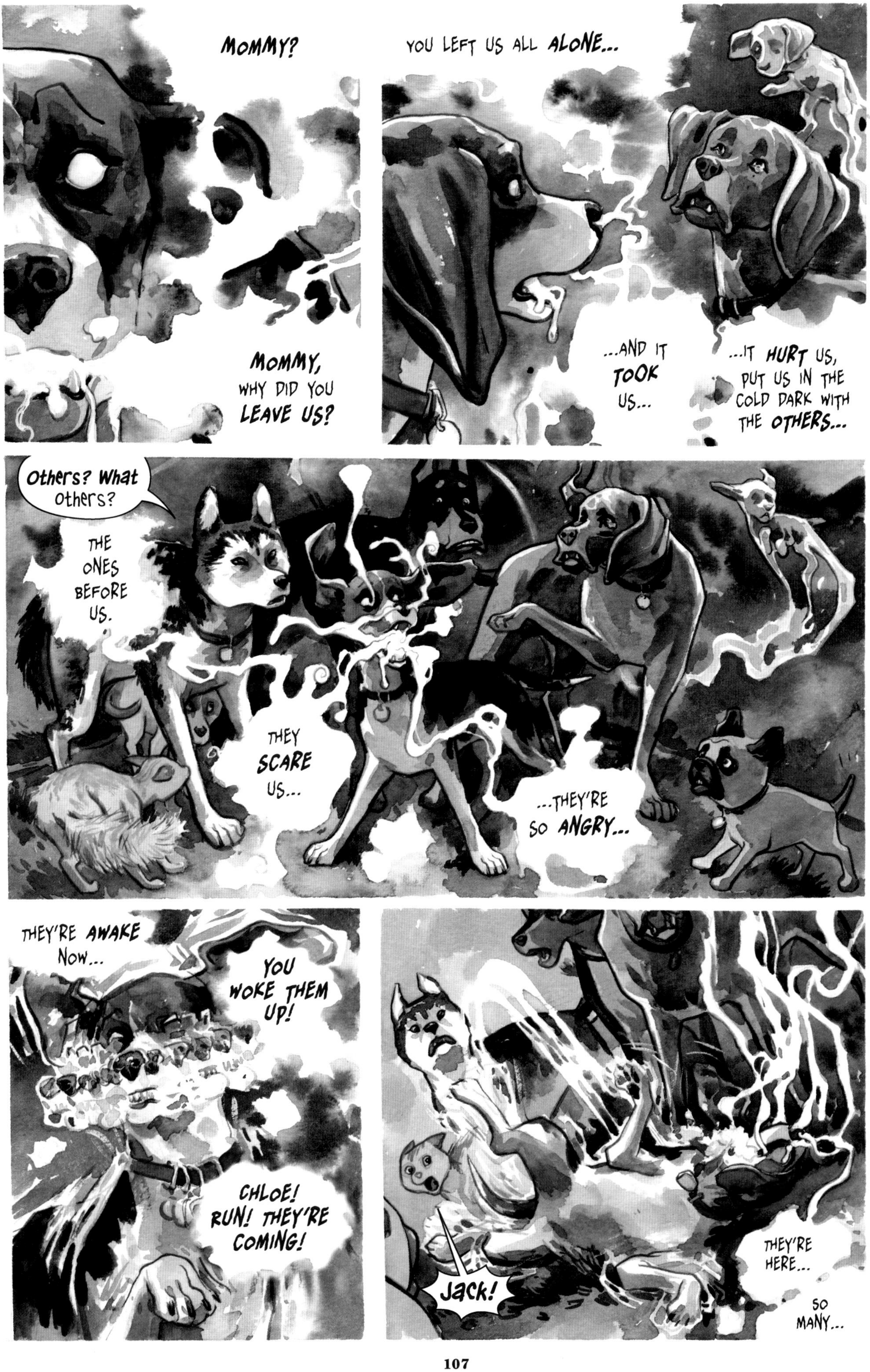
MOMMY?
MOMMY, WHY DID YOU LEAVE US?
YOU LEFT US ALL ALONE...
...AND IT TOOK US...
...IT HURT US, PUT US IN THE COLD DARK WITH THE OTHERS...
Others? What others?
THE ONES BEFORE US.
THEY SCARE US...
...THEY'RE SO ANGRY...
THEY'RE AWAKE NOW...
YOU WOKE THEM UP!
CHLOE! RUN! THEY'RE COMING!
Jack!
THEY'RE HERE...
SO MANY...

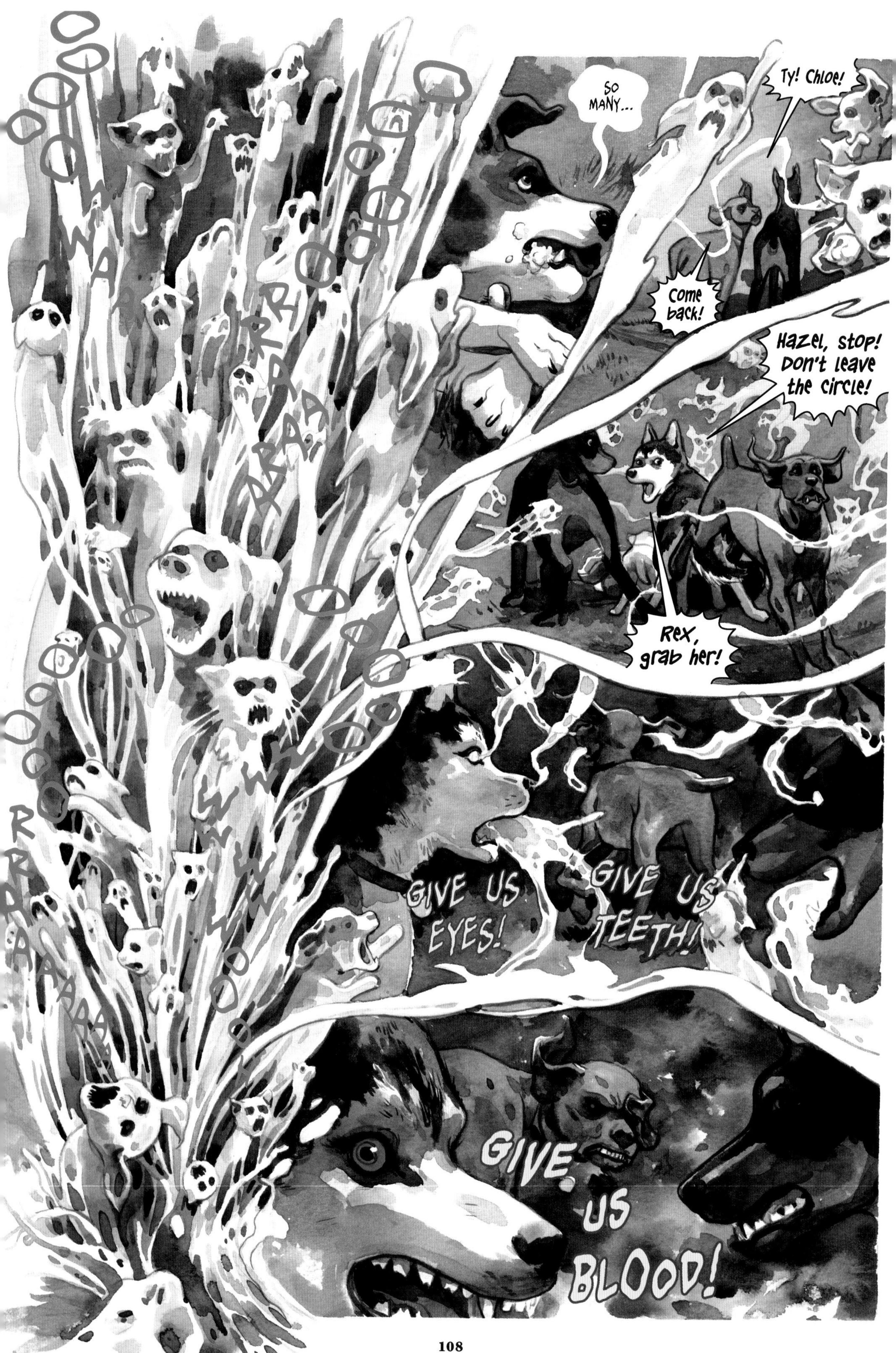

SO MANY...
Ty! Chloe!
Come back!
Hazel, stop! Don't leave the circle!
Rex, grab her!
GIVE US EYES!
GIVE US TEETH!
GIVE US BLOOD!

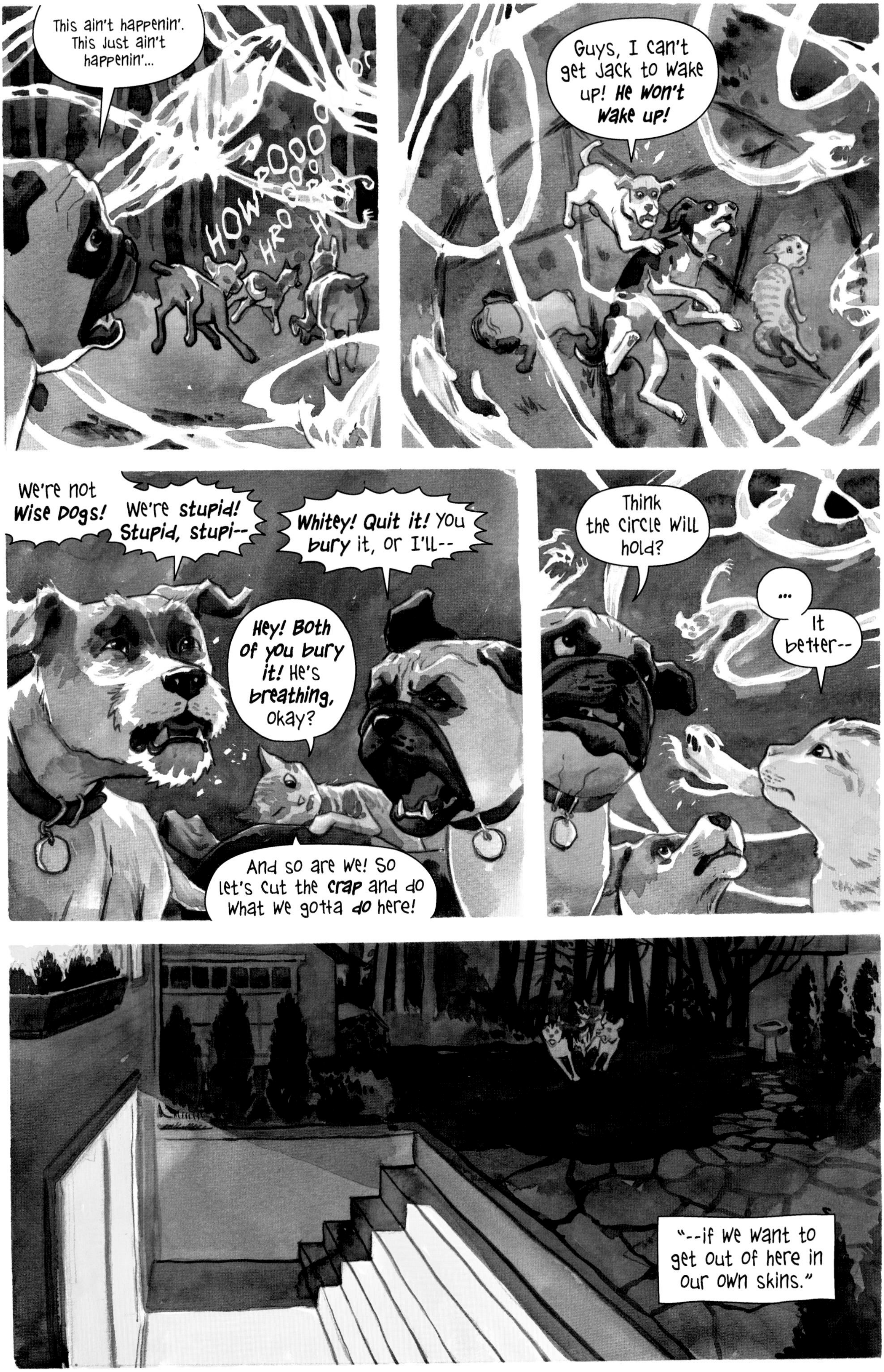
This ain't happenin'. This just ain't happenin'...
Guys, I can't get Jack to wake up! He won't wake up!
We're not Wise Dogs!
We're stupid! Stupid, stupi--
Whitey! Quit it! You bury it, or I'll--
Hey! Both of you bury it! He's breathing, okay?
And so are we! So let's cut the crap and do what we gotta do here!
Think the circle will hold?
...
It better--
"--if we want to get out of here in our own skins."

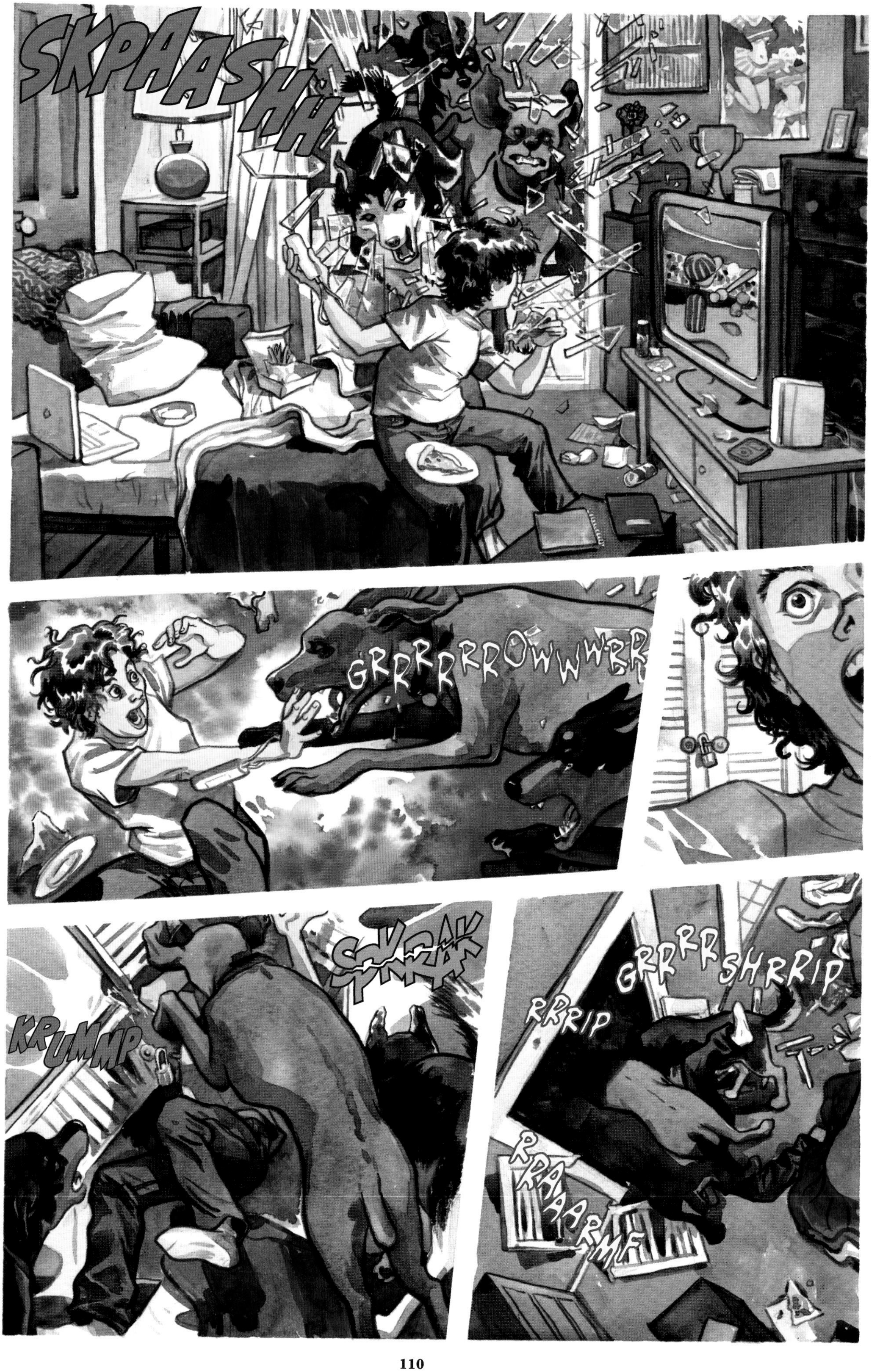
SKPAASHH
GRRRRRROWWWRR
KRUMMP
SKRAK
RRRIP
GRRRR SHRRIP
RRAAARMF

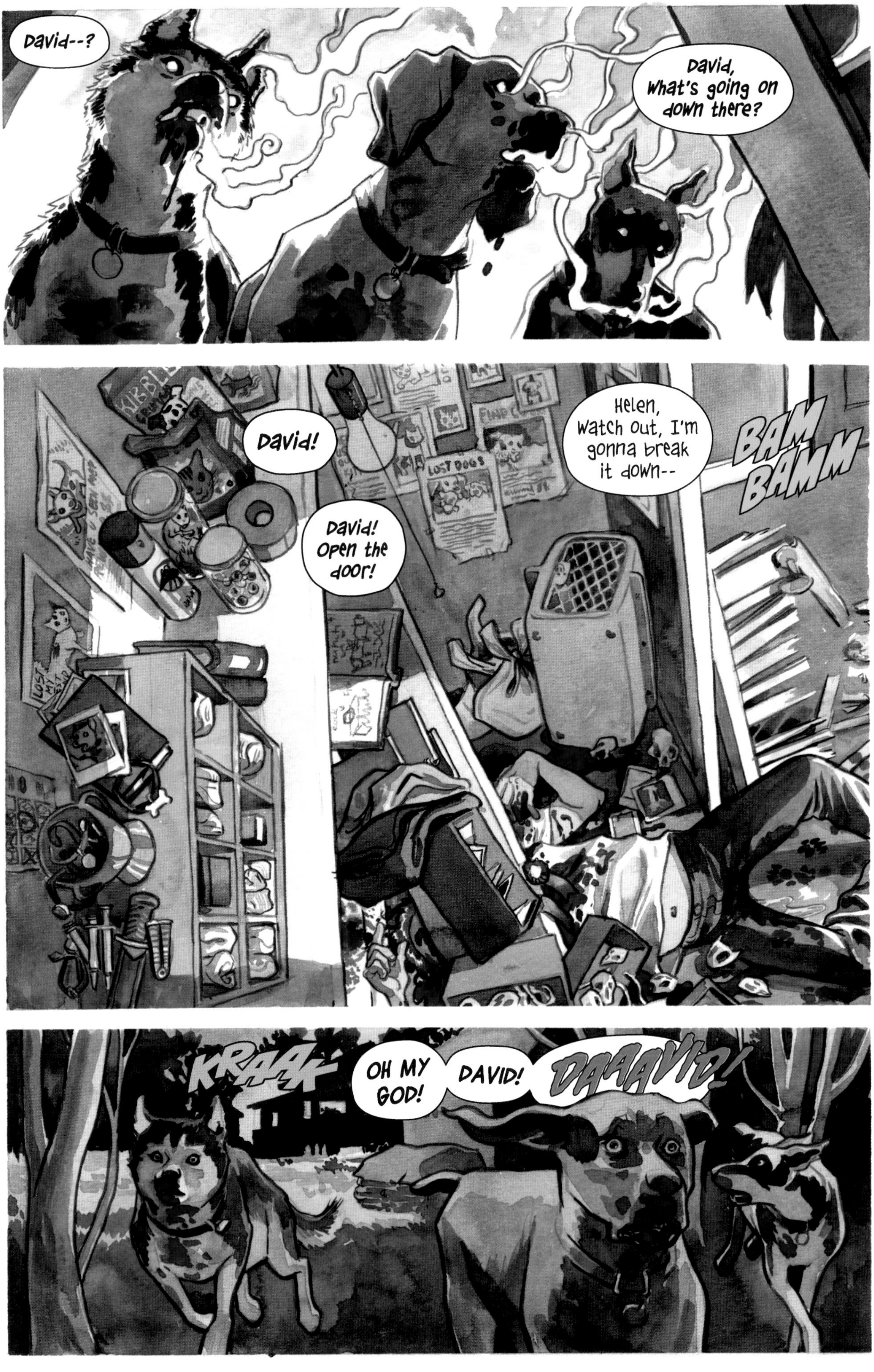

David--?
David, what's going on down there?
David!
David! Open the door!
Helen, watch out, I'm gonna break it down--
BAM BAMM
KRAAK
OH MY GOD!
DAVID!
DAAAVID!

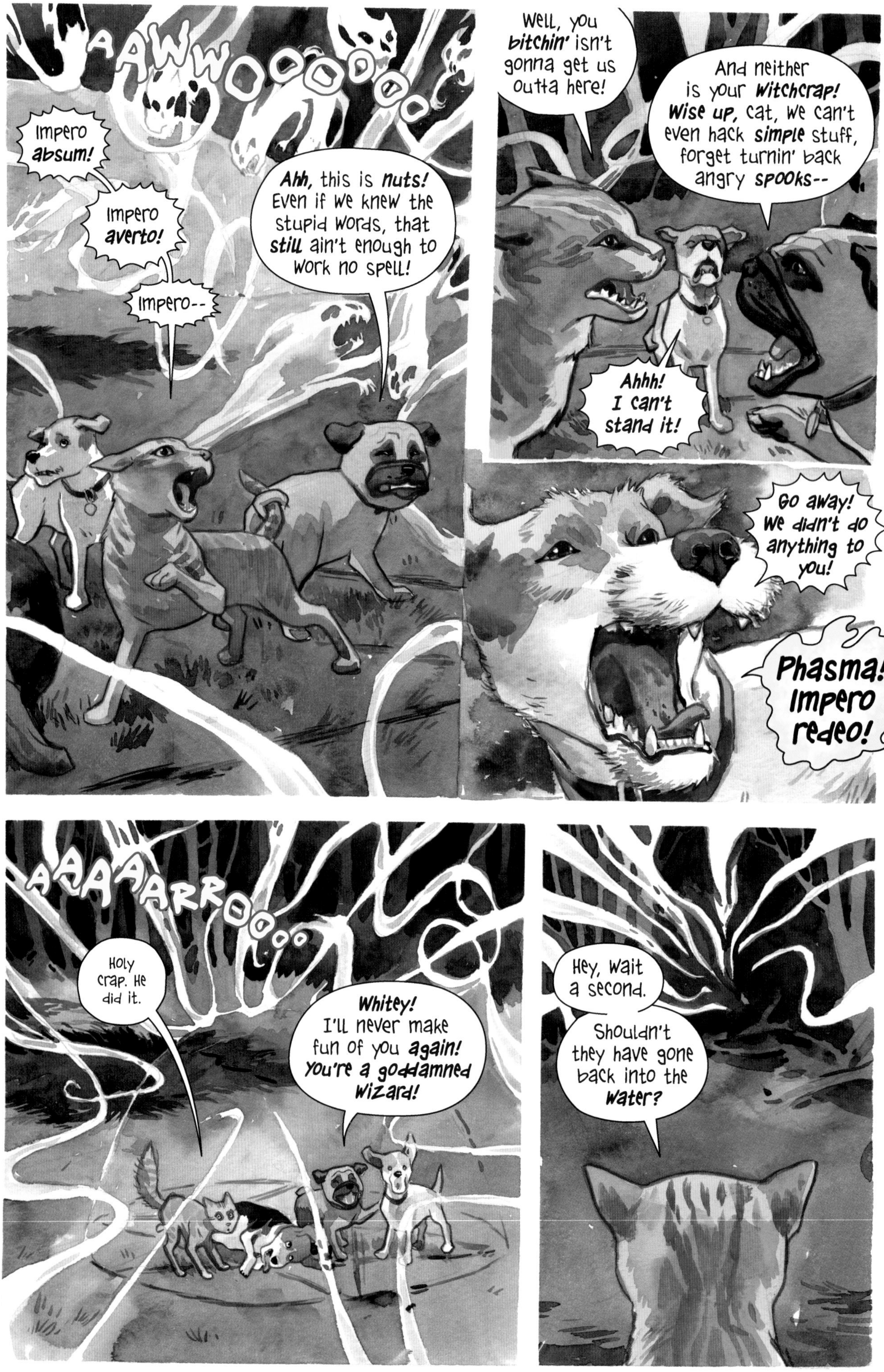
AAWWOOOOOO
Impero absum!
Impero averto!
Impero--
Ahh, this is nuts! Even if we knew the stupid words, that still ain't enough to work no spell!
Well, you bitchin' isn't gonna get us outta here!
And neither is your witchcrap! Wise up, cat, we can't even hack simple stuff, forget turnin' back angry spooks--
Ahhh! I can't stand it!
Go away! We didn't do anything to you!
Phasma! Impero redeo!
AAAAARROOOOO
Holy crap. He did it.
Whitey! I'll never make fun of you again! You're a goddamned wizard!
Hey, wait a second.
Shouldn't they have gone back into the water?

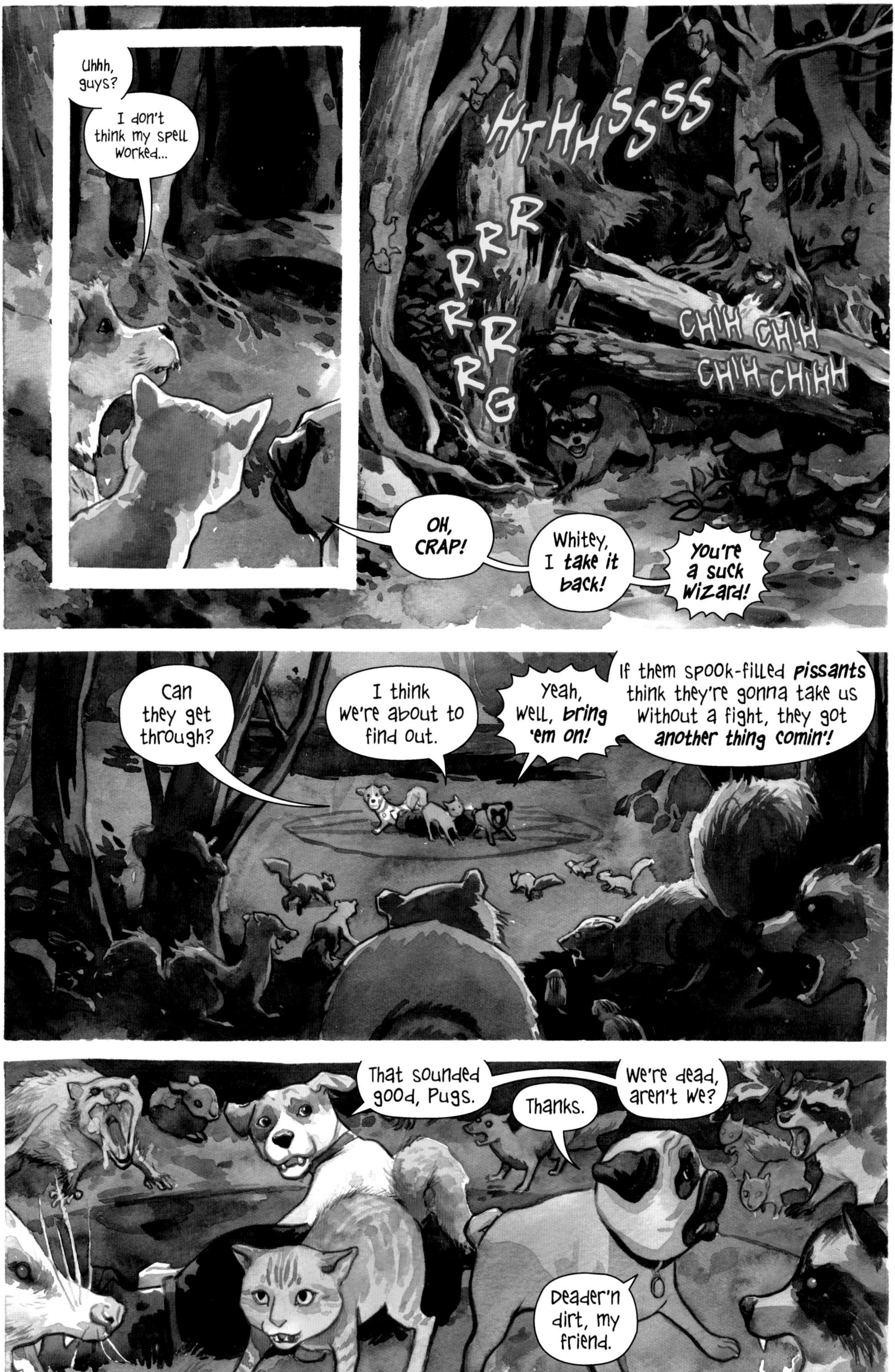
Uhhh, guys?
I don't think my spell worked...
HTHHSSSS
RRRRRRRG
CHIH CHIH CHIH CHIHH
OH, CRAP!
Whitey, I take it back!
You're a suck wizard!
Can they get through?
I think we're about to find out.
Yeah, well, bring 'em on!
If them spook-filled pissants think they're gonna take us without a fight, they got another thing comin'!
That sounded good, Pugs.
Thanks.
We're dead, aren't we?
Deader'n dirt, my friend.

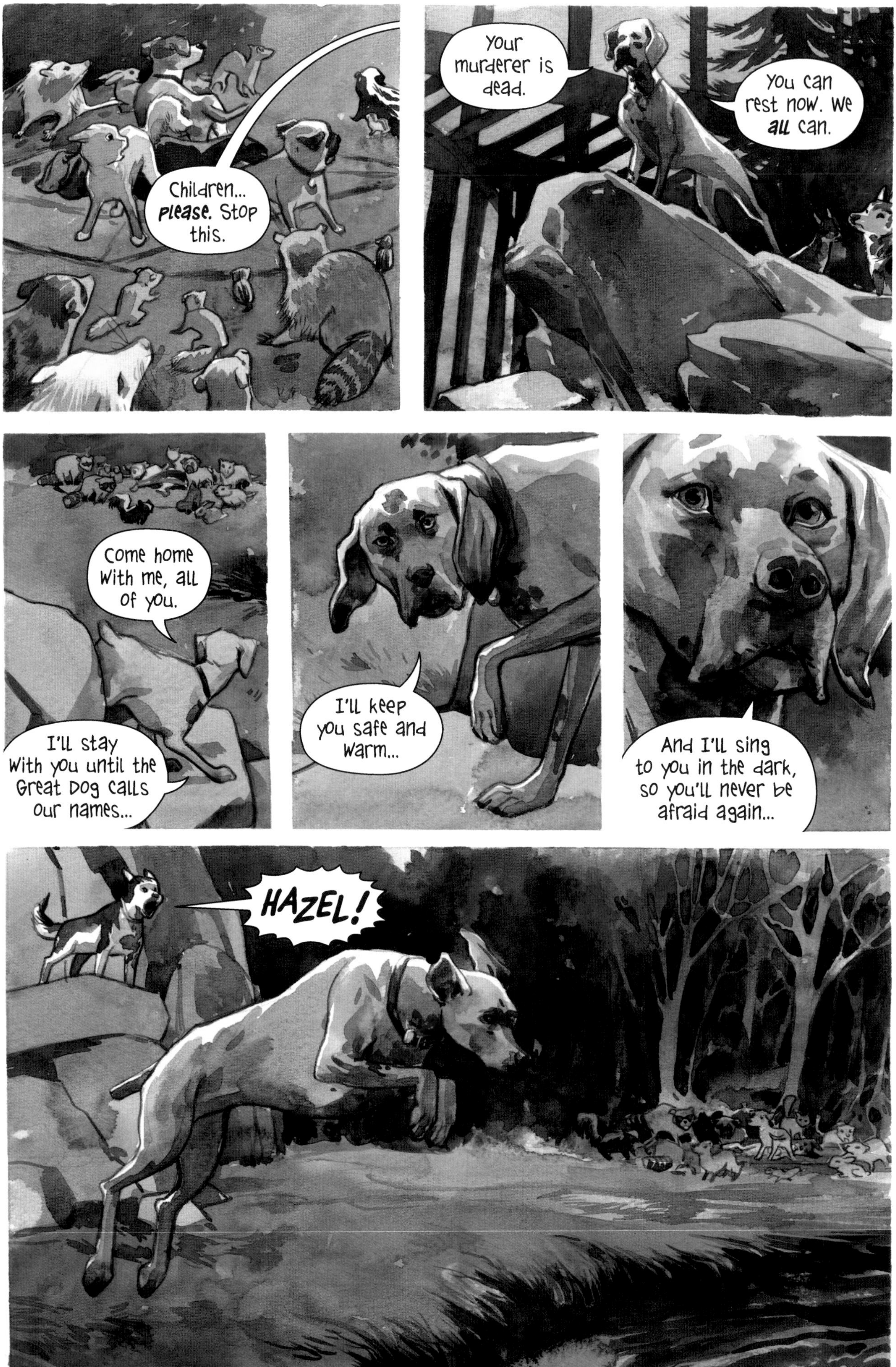
Children... please. Stop this.
Your murderer is dead.
You can rest now. We all can.
Come home with me, all of you.
I'll stay with you until the Great Dog calls our names...
I'll keep you safe and warm...
And I'll sing to you in the dark, so you'll never be afraid again...
HAZEL!

NO! Ace, don't--!

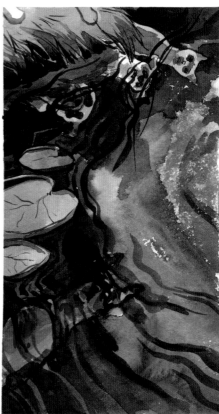

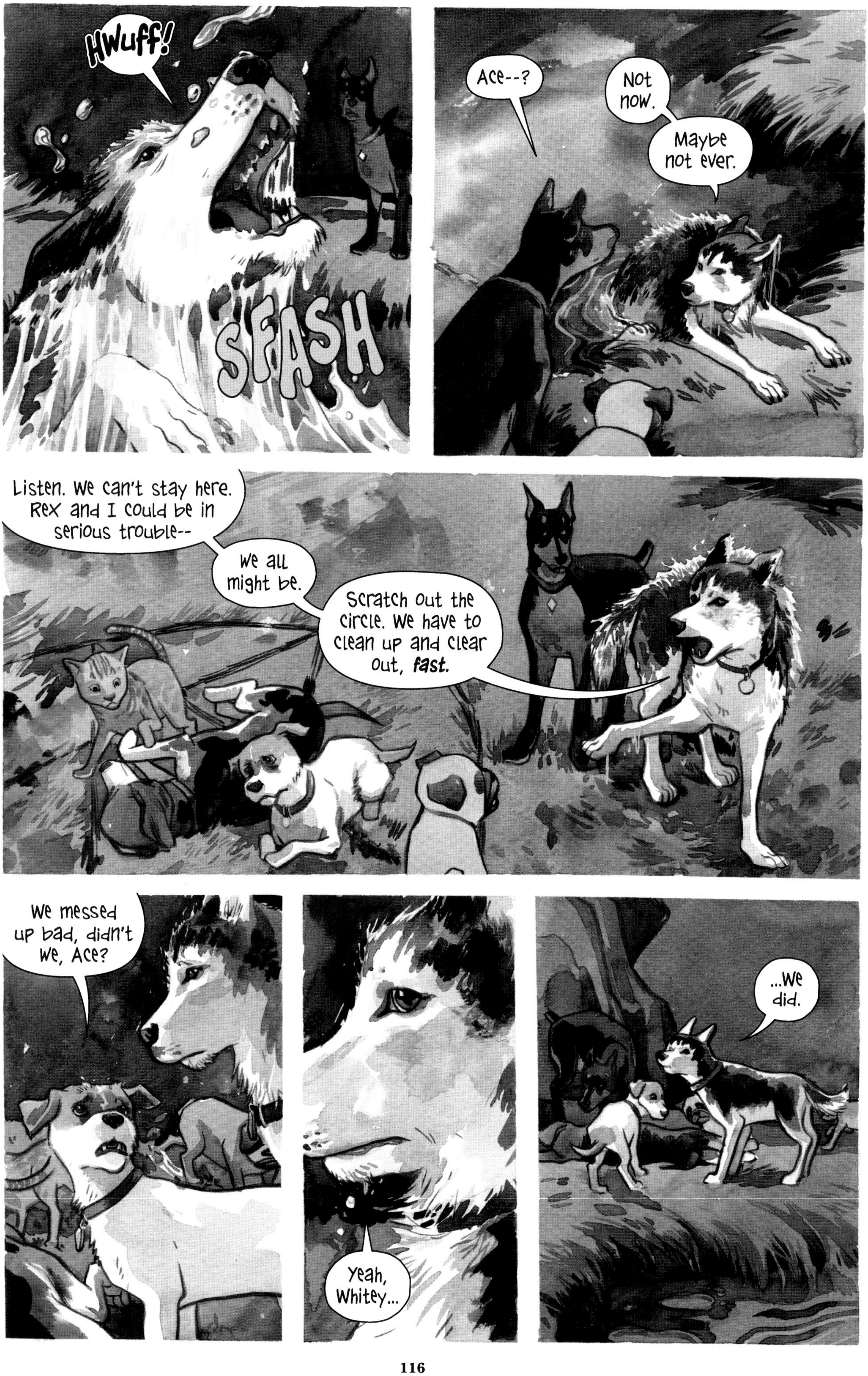
HWuff!
SFASH
Ace--?
Not now.
Maybe not ever.
Listen. We can't stay here. Rex and I could be in serious trouble--
We all might be.
Scratch out the circle. We have to clean up and clear out, *fast.*
We messed up bad, didn't we, Ace?
Yeah, Whitey...
...We did.

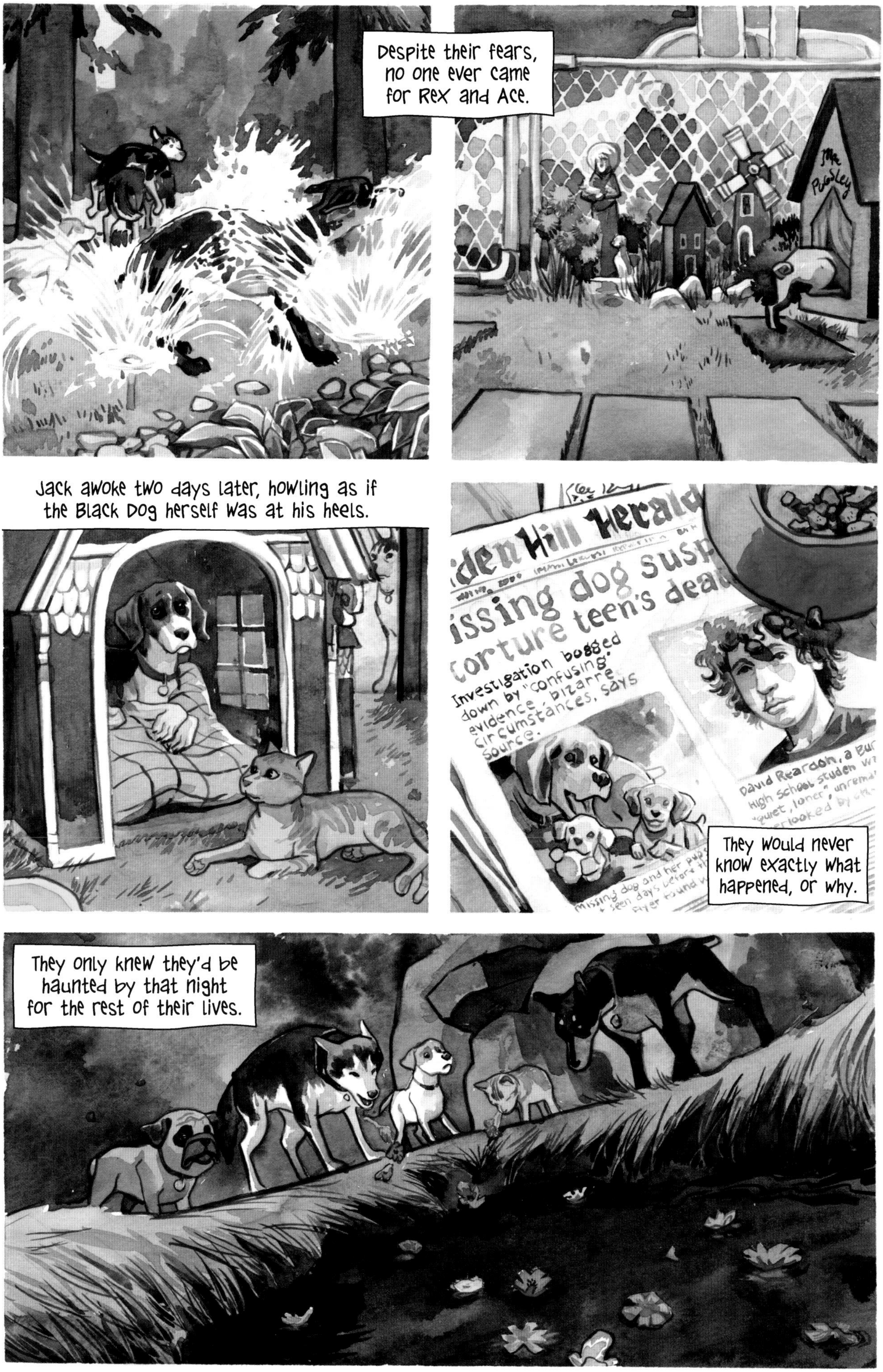
Despite their fears, no one ever came for Rex and Ace.
Jack awoke two days later, howling as if the Black Dog herself was at his heels.
Investigation bogged down by "confusing, bizarre evidence, circumstances," says source.
They would never know exactly what happened, or why.
They only knew they'd be haunted by that night for the rest of their lives.

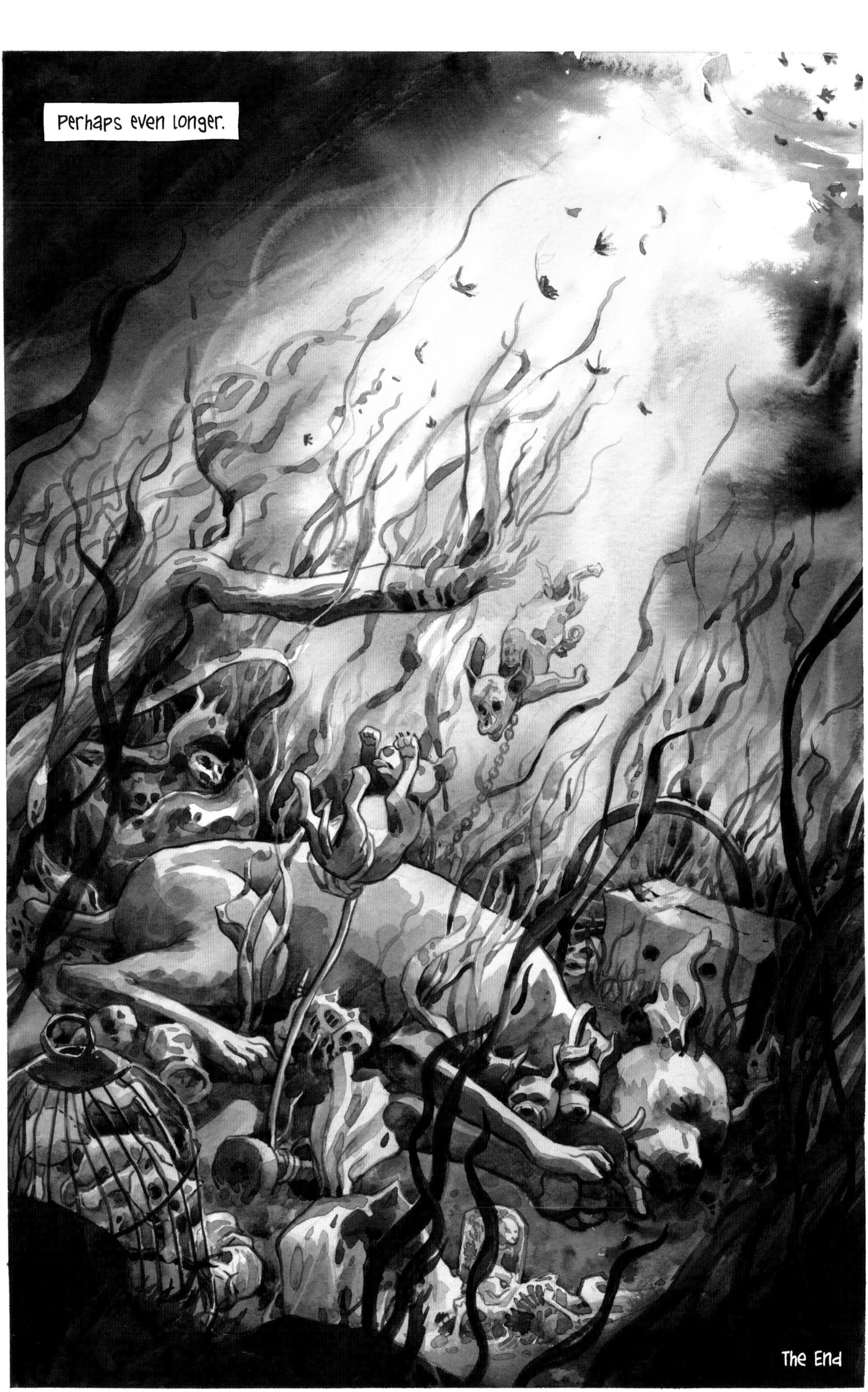
Perhaps even longer.
The End

SOMETHING WHISKERED
THIS WAY **COMES**

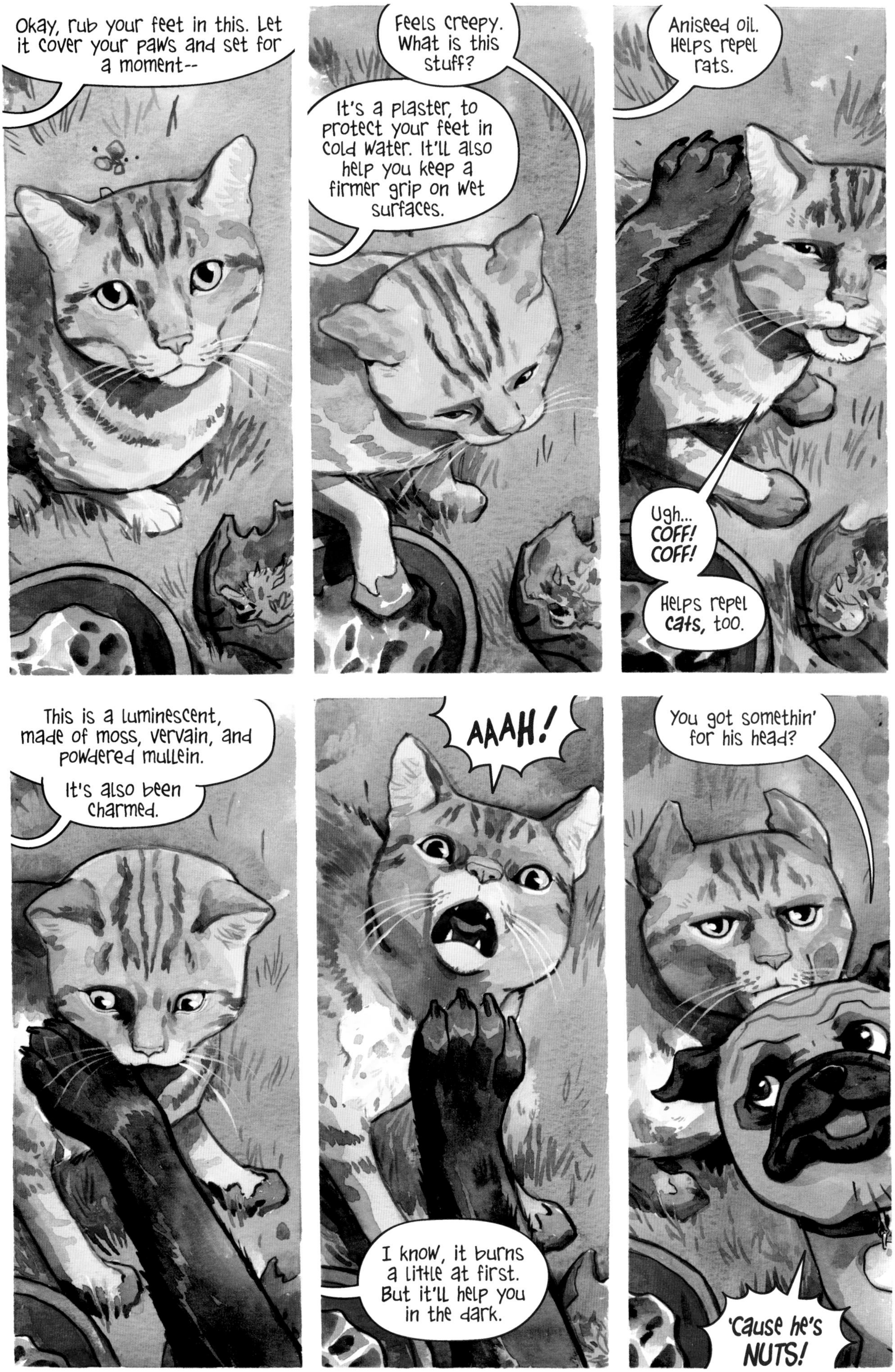
Okay, rub your feet in this. Let it cover your paws and set for a moment--
Feels creepy. What is this stuff?
It's a plaster, to protect your feet in cold water. It'll also help you keep a firmer grip on wet surfaces.
Aniseed oil. Helps repel rats.
Ugh... COFF! COFF!
Helps repel cats, too.
This is a luminescent, made of moss, vervain, and powdered mullein.
It's also been charmed.
AAAH!
I know, it burns a little at first. But it'll help you in the dark.
You got somethin' for his head?
'Cause he's NUTS!

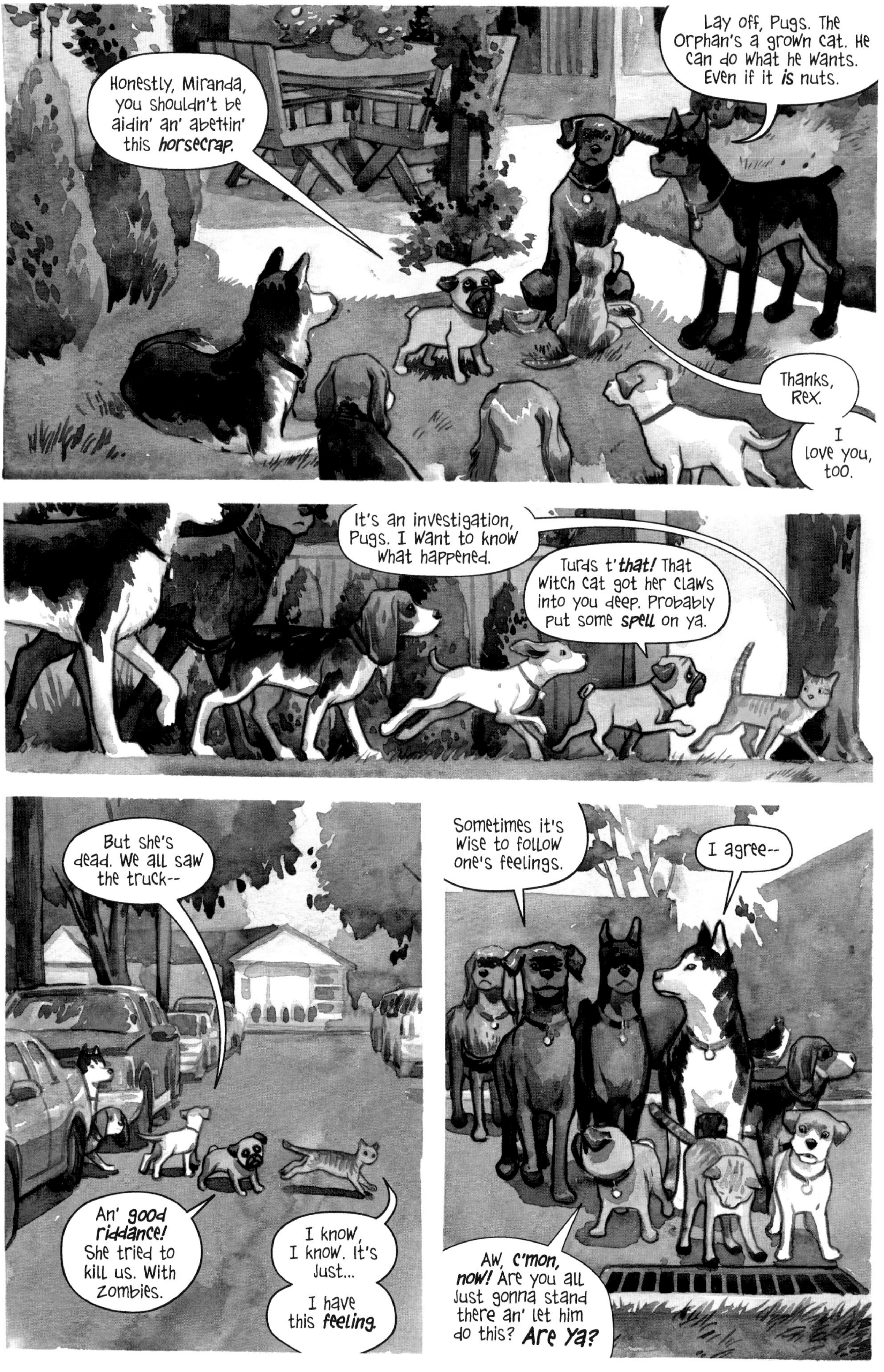
Honestly, Miranda, you shouldn't be aidin' an' abettin' this horsecrap.
Lay off, Pugs. The Orphan's a grown cat. He can do what he wants. Even if it is nuts.
Thanks, Rex.
I love you, too.
It's an investigation, Pugs. I want to know what happened.
Turds t'that! That witch cat got her claws into you deep. Probably put some spell on ya.
But she's dead. We all saw the truck--
An' good riddance! She tried to kill us. With zombies.
I know, I know. It's just...
I have this feeling.
Sometimes it's wise to follow one's feelings.
I agree--
Aw, c'mon, now! Are you all just gonna stand there an' let him do this? Are ya?

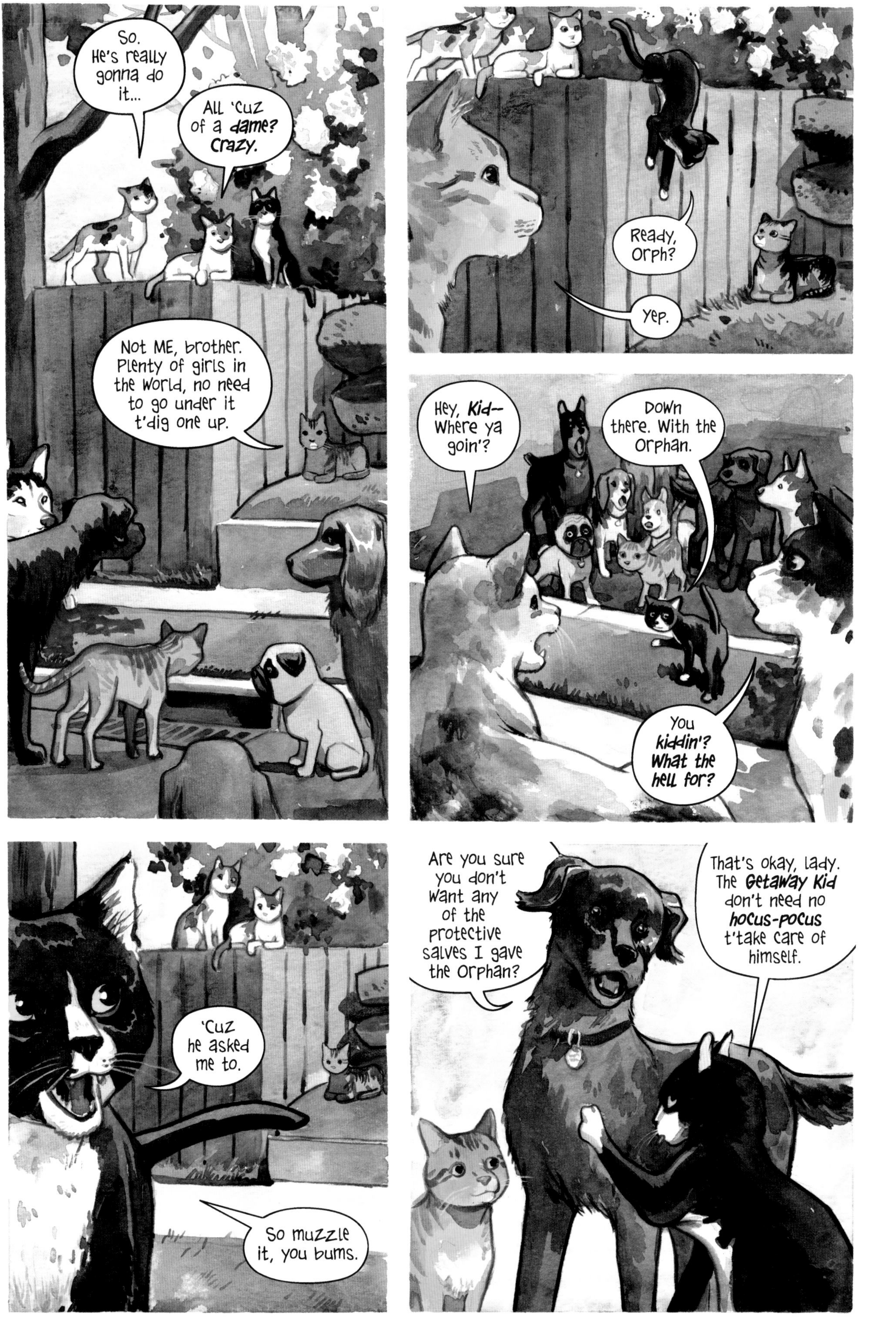
So. He's really gonna do it...
All 'cuz of a dame? Crazy.
Not ME, brother. Plenty of girls in the world, no need to go under it t'dig one up.
Ready, Orph?
Yep.
Hey, Kid-- Where ya goin'?
Down there. With the Orphan.
You kiddin'? What the hell for?
'Cuz he asked me to.
So muzzle it, you bums.
Are you sure you don't want any of the protective salves I gave the Orphan?
That's okay, lady. The Getaway Kid don't need no hocus-pocus t'take care of himself.

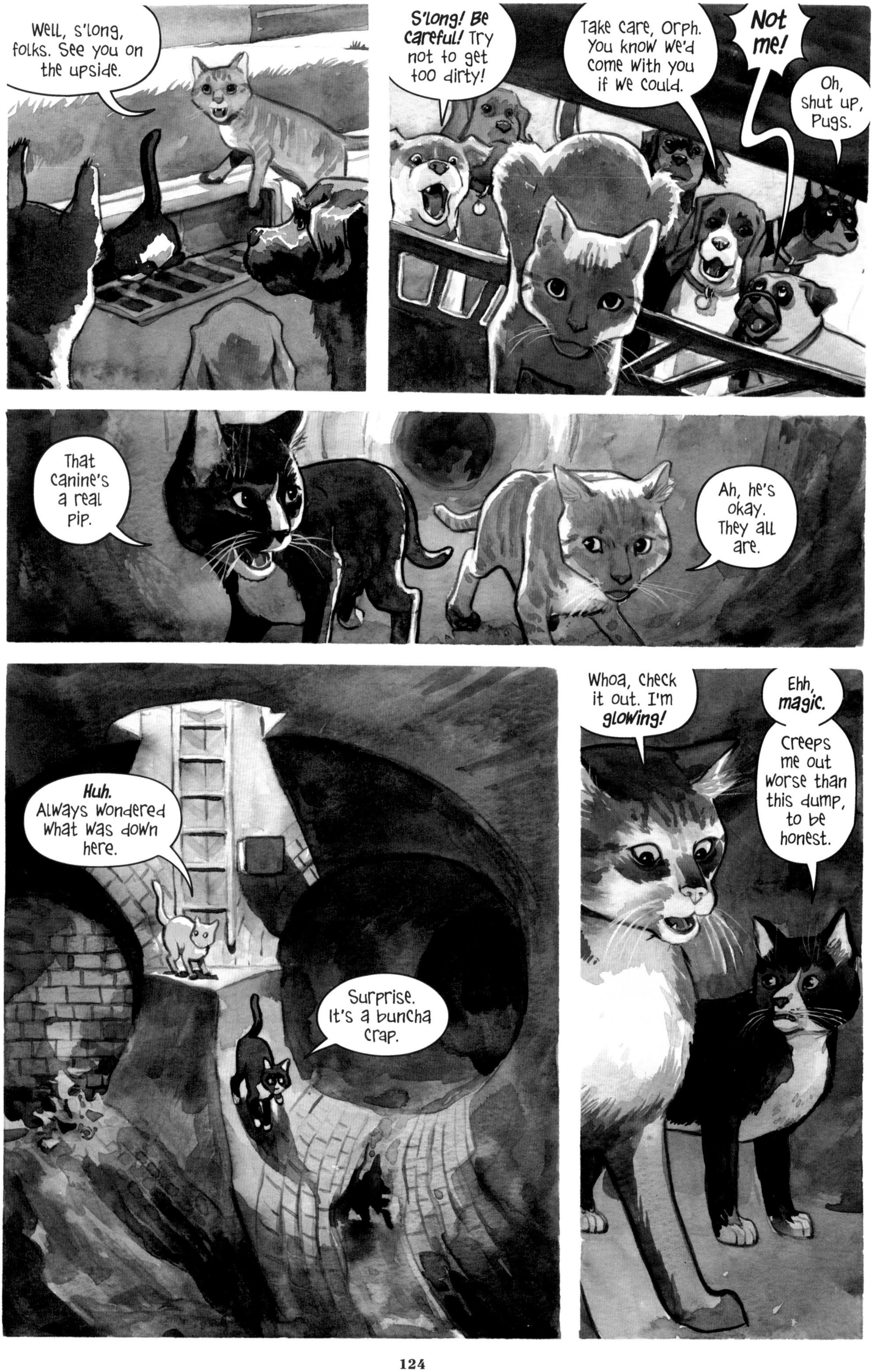
Well, s'long, folks. See you on the upside.
S'long! Be careful! Try not to get too dirty!
Take care, Orph. You know we'd come with you if we could.
Not me!
Oh, shut up, Pugs.
That canine's a real pip.
Ah, he's okay. They all are.
Huh. Always wondered what was down here.
Surprise. It's a buncha crap.
Whoa, check it out. I'm ***glowing!***
Ehh, ***magic.***
Creeps me out worse than this dump, to be honest.

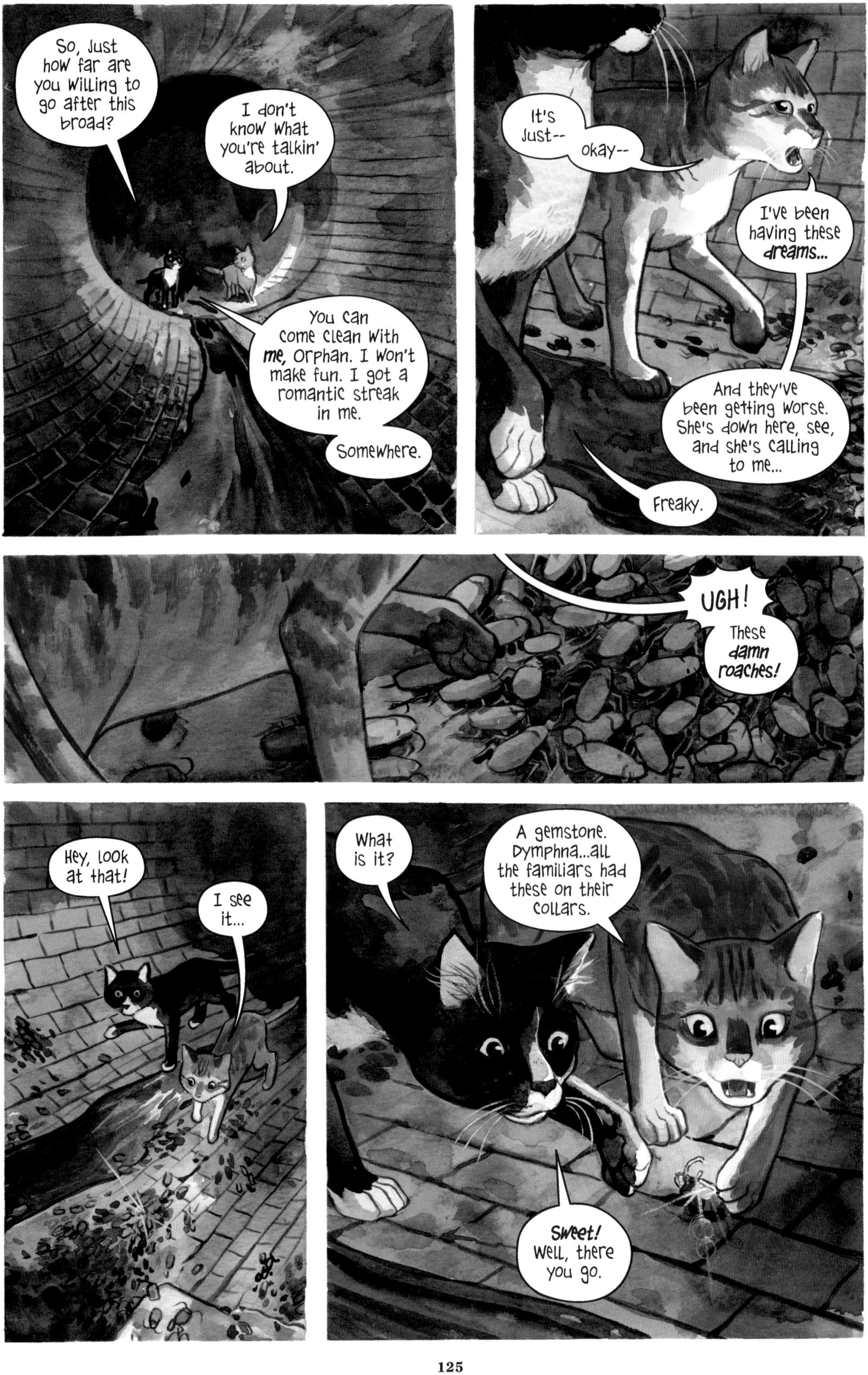
So, Just how far are you willing to go after this broad?
I don't know what you're talkin' about.
You can come clean with *me,* Orphan. I won't make fun. I got a romantic streak in me.
Somewhere.
It's Just--
okay--
I've been having these ***dreams...***
And they've been getting worse. She's down here, see, and she's calling to me...
Freaky.
UGH!
These ***damn roaches!***
Hey, look at that!
I see it...
What is it?
A gemstone. Dymphna...all the familiars had these on their collars.
Sweet! Well, there you go.

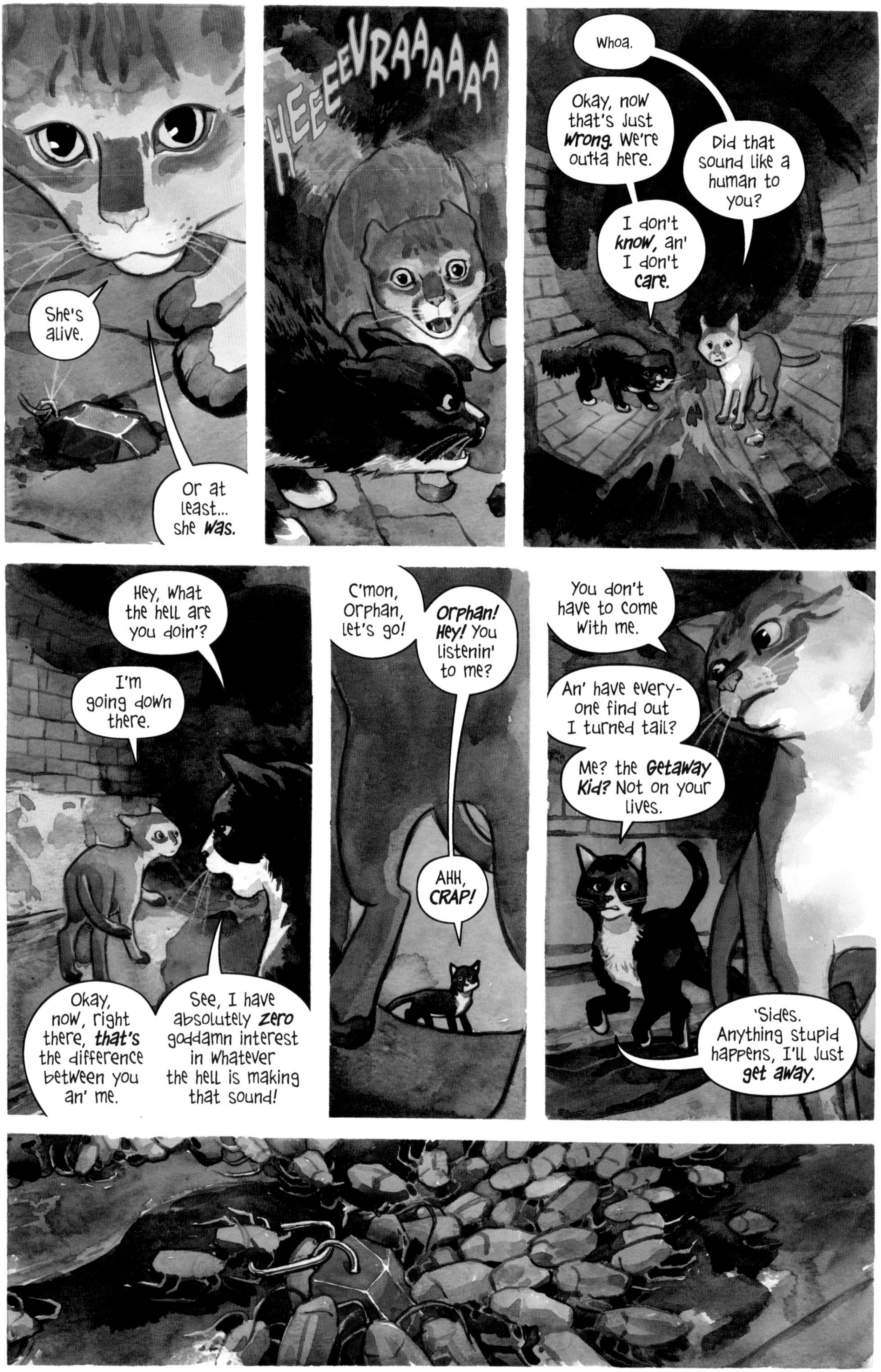
She's alive.
Or at least... she was.
HEEEEVRAAAAAAA
Whoa.
Okay, now that's just wrong. We're outta here.
Did that sound like a human to you?
I don't know, an' I don't care.
Hey, what the hell are you doin'?
I'm going down there.
Okay, now, right there, that's the difference between you an' me.
See, I have absolutely zero goddamn interest in whatever the hell is making that sound!
C'mon, Orphan, let's go!
Orphan! Hey! You listenin' to me?
AHH, CRAP!
You don't have to come with me.
An' have every-one find out I turned tail?
Me? the Getaway Kid? Not on your lives.
'Sides. Anything stupid happens, I'll just get away.

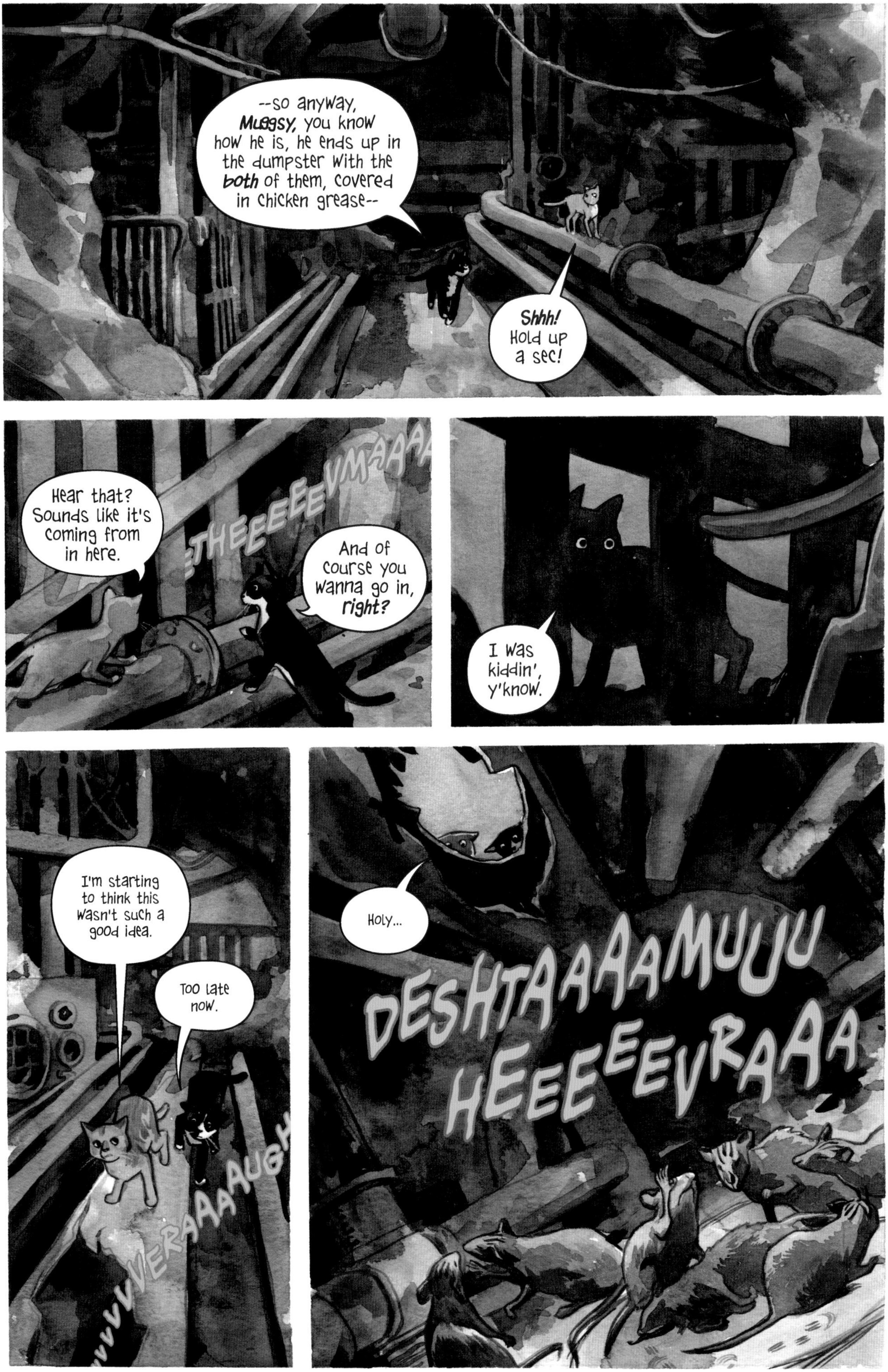
--so anyway, Muggsy, you know how he is, he ends up in the dumpster with the both of them, covered in chicken grease--
Shhh! Hold up a sec!
Hear that? Sounds like it's coming from in here.
THEEEEEVMAAA
And of course you wanna go in, right?
I was kiddin', y'know.
I'm starting to think this wasn't such a good idea.
Too late now.
VVVVVERAAAAUGH
Holy...
DESHTAAAAMUUU
HEEEEEVRAAA

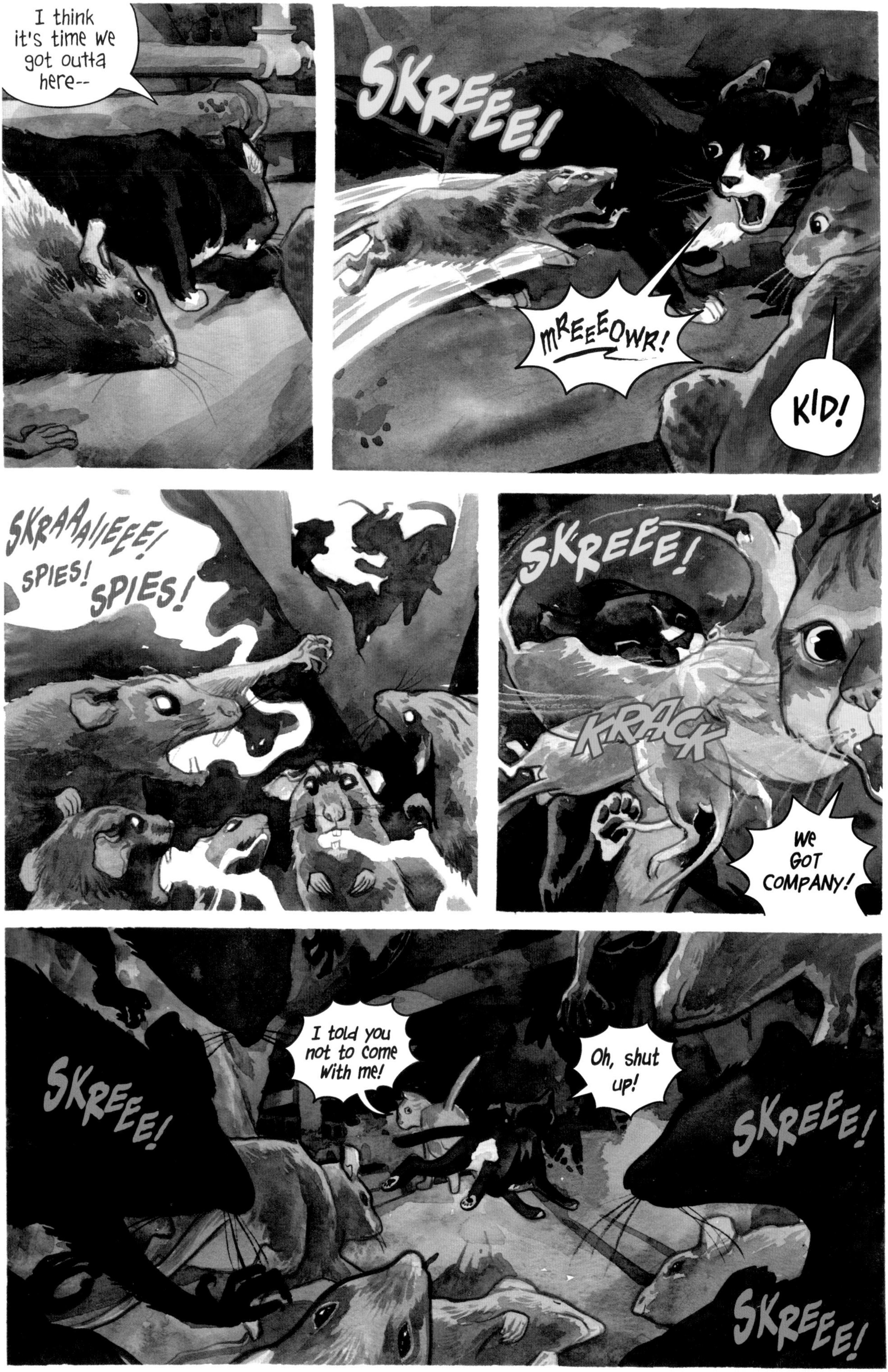
I think it's time we got outta here--
SKREEE!
MREEEOWR!
KID!
SKRAAAIIEEE!
SPIES!
SPIES!
SKREEEE!
KRACK
WE GOT COMPANY!
SKREEE!
I told you not to come with me!
Oh, shut up!
SKREEE!
SKREEE!

KID!

Sorry, Orphan! Looks like every cat for himself!

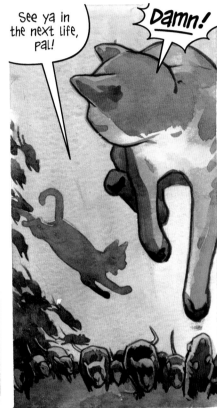

See ya in the next life, pal!

Damn!

Damn damn dammit damn--

Huh.

No one's following. Don't know if that's good or--

CRIK

CRAK

SKRAKK

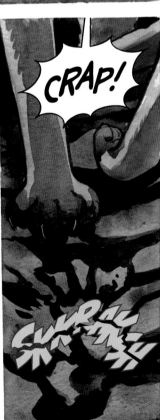

CRAP!

CUNRAL NNTN XU

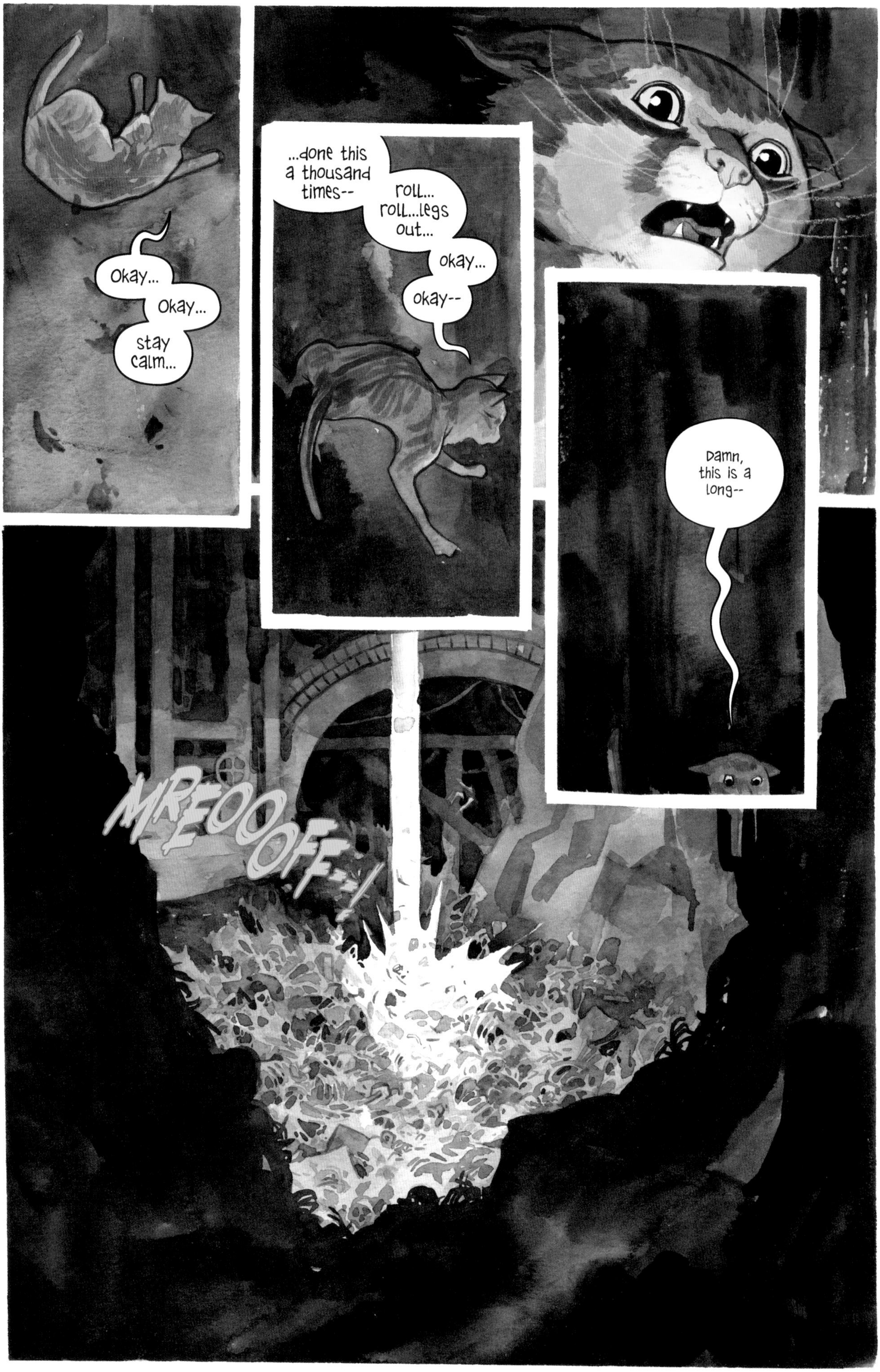

Okay...
Okay...
stay calm...
...done this a thousand times--
roll... roll...legs out...
okay...
okay--
Damn, this is a long--
MREOOOFF--!

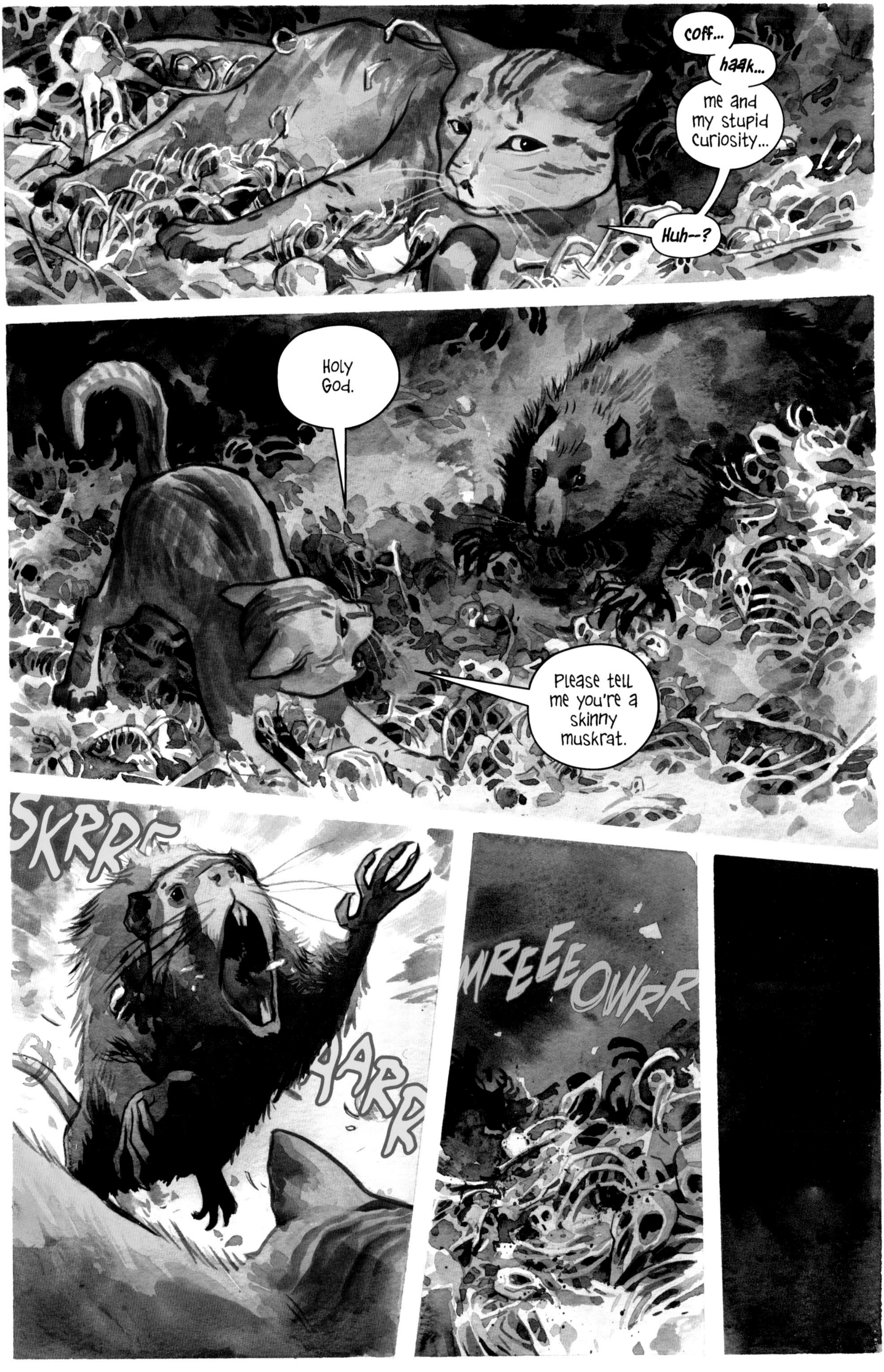
coff...
haak...
me and my stupid curiosity...
Huh--?
Holy God.
Please tell me you're a skinny muskrat.
SKRRE
AARR
MREEEOWRR

Orphan?

Orphan...?

Dymphna...?

What in Sekhmet's name are you doing here?

Um... it's a long story.

I'm... investigating stuff.

Rats.

You came looking for me, didn't you?

I don't know what you're talking about. I'm investigating. I'm a Junior apprentice in the Wise Dog Society now.

Don't be ridiculous. They'd never let a cat in.

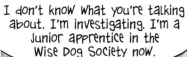

They let *me* in.

Things must be quite desperate for them if that's true.

Gee, **thanks.** Glad to see you, too.

Well, that does explain the luminescent you have on you. Did you prepare it yourself?

Me? Nah, I'm lousy at that stuff.

Why are you looking at me like that?

Hmm? Oh, nothing.

132

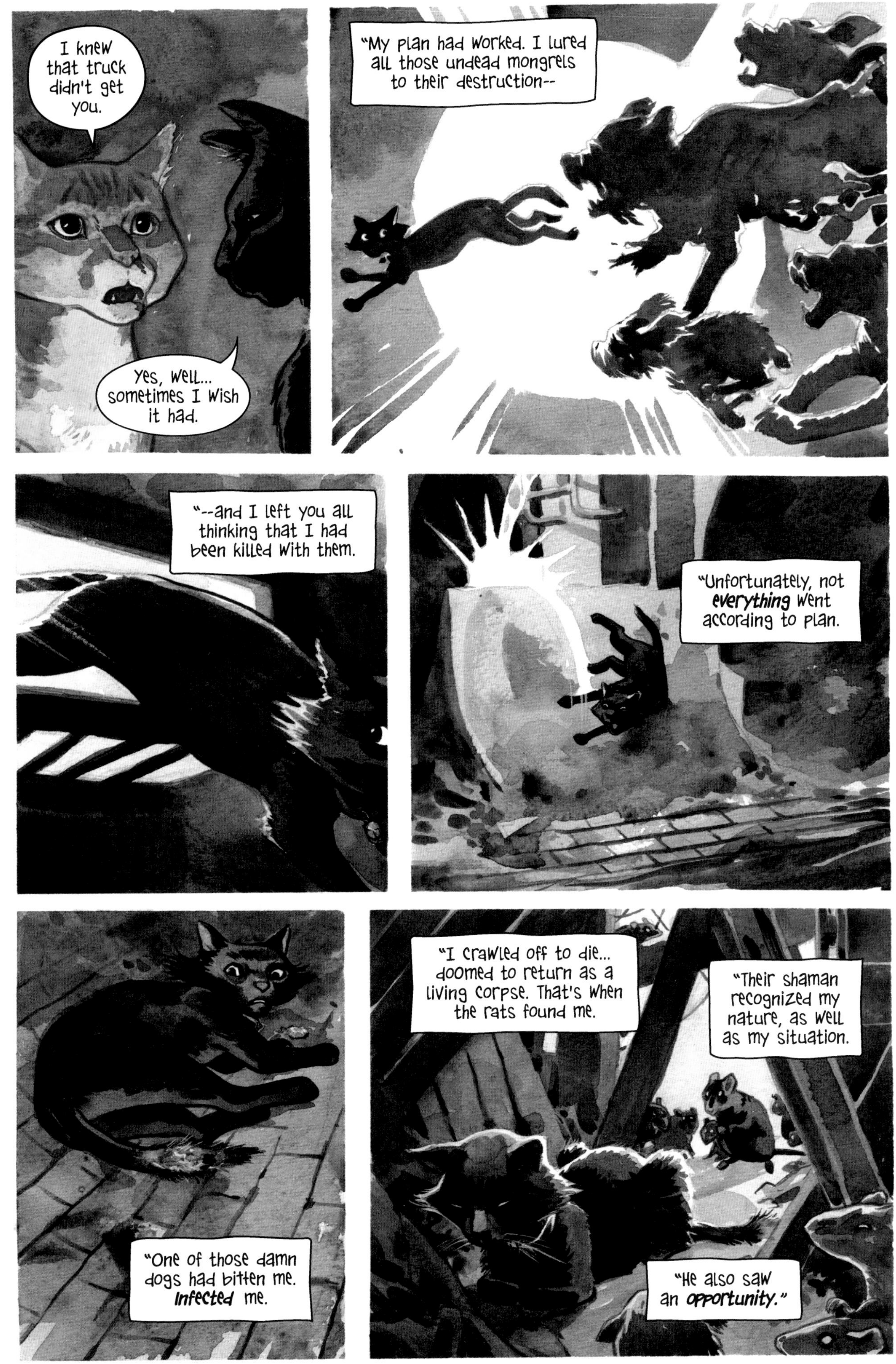
I knew that truck didn't get you.
Yes, well... sometimes I wish it had.
"My plan had worked. I lured all those undead mongrels to their destruction--
"--and I left you all thinking that I had been killed with them.
"Unfortunately, not *everything* went according to plan.
"One of those damn dogs had bitten me. *Infected* me.
"I crawled off to die... doomed to return as a living corpse. That's when the rats found me.
"Their shaman recognized my nature, as well as my situation.
"He also saw an *opportunity.*"

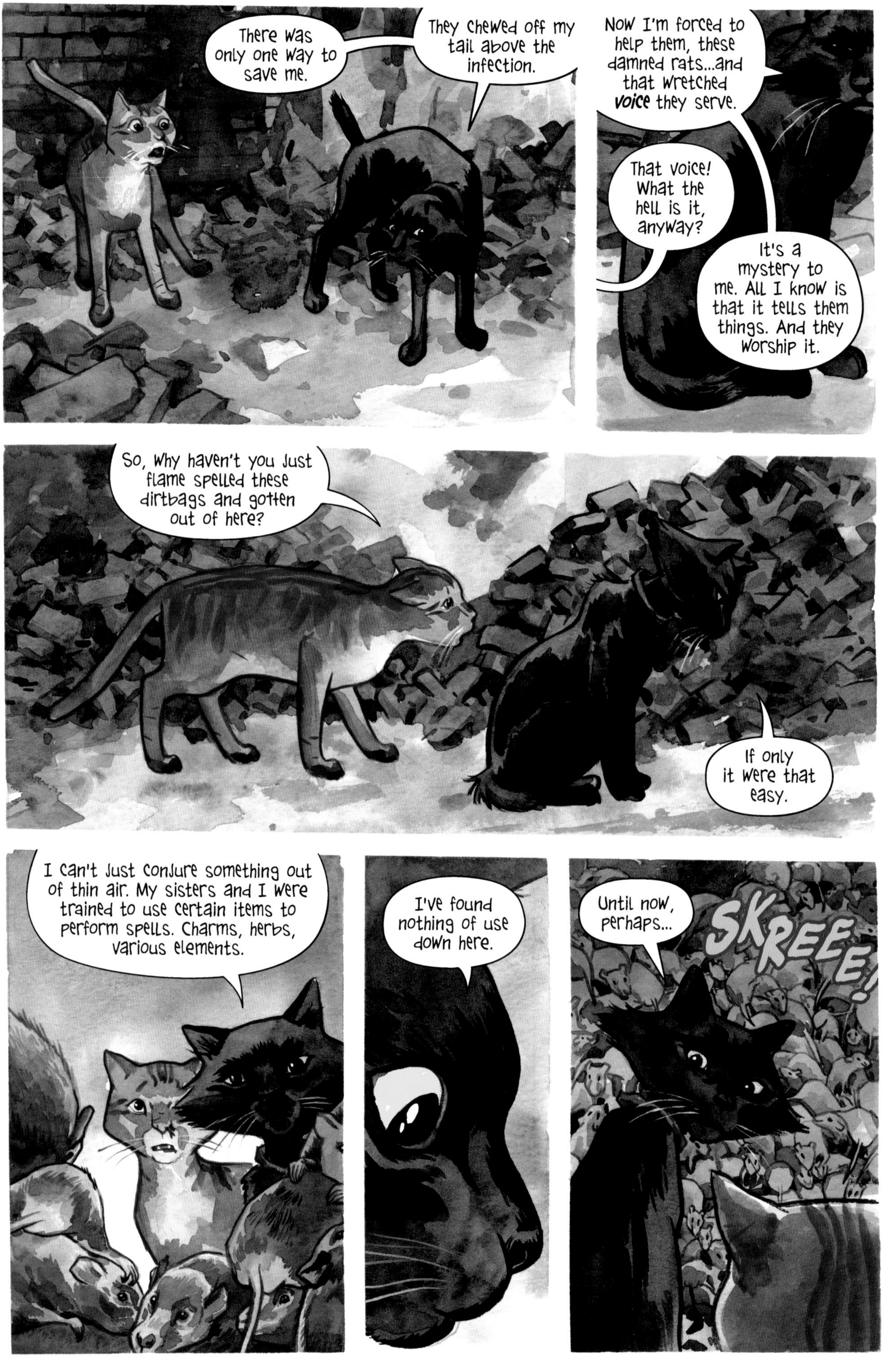
There was only one way to save me.
They chewed off my tail above the infection.
Now I'm forced to help them, these damned rats...and that wretched **voice** they serve.
That voice! What the hell is it, anyway?
It's a mystery to me. All I know is that it tells them things. And they worship it.
So, why haven't you just flame spelled these dirtbags and gotten out of here?
If only it were that easy.
I can't just conjure something out of thin air. My sisters and I were trained to use certain items to perform spells. Charms, herbs, various elements.
I've found nothing of use down here.
Until now, perhaps...
SKREEEE!

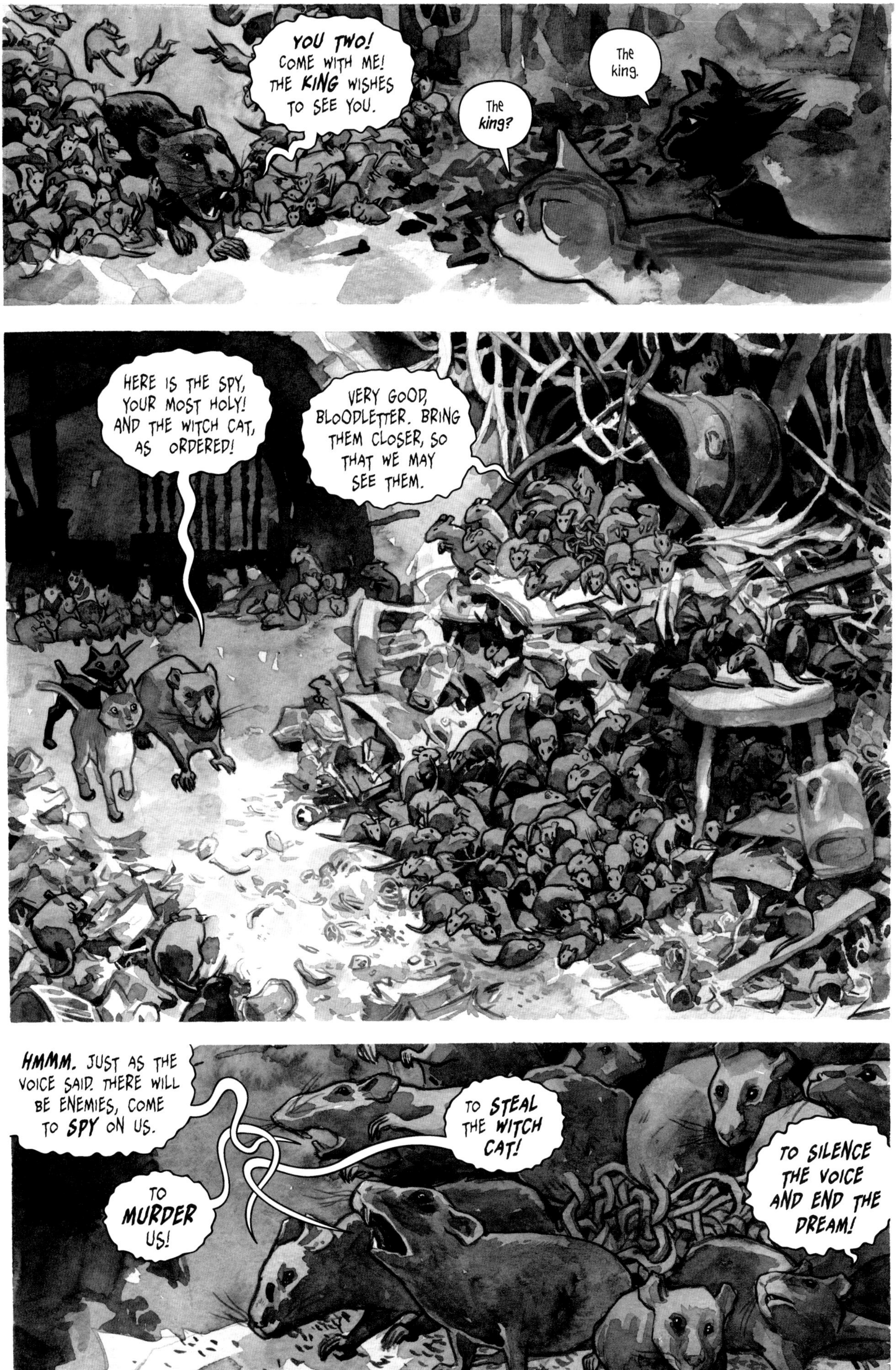
YOU TWO! COME WITH ME! THE KING WISHES TO SEE YOU.
The king?
The king.
HERE IS THE SPY, YOUR MOST HOLY! AND THE WITCH CAT, AS ORDERED!
VERY GOOD, BLOODLETTER. BRING THEM CLOSER, SO THAT WE MAY SEE THEM.
HMMM. JUST AS THE VOICE SAID. THERE WILL BE ENEMIES, COME TO SPY ON US.
TO MURDER US!
TO STEAL THE WITCH CAT!
TO SILENCE THE VOICE AND END THE DREAM!

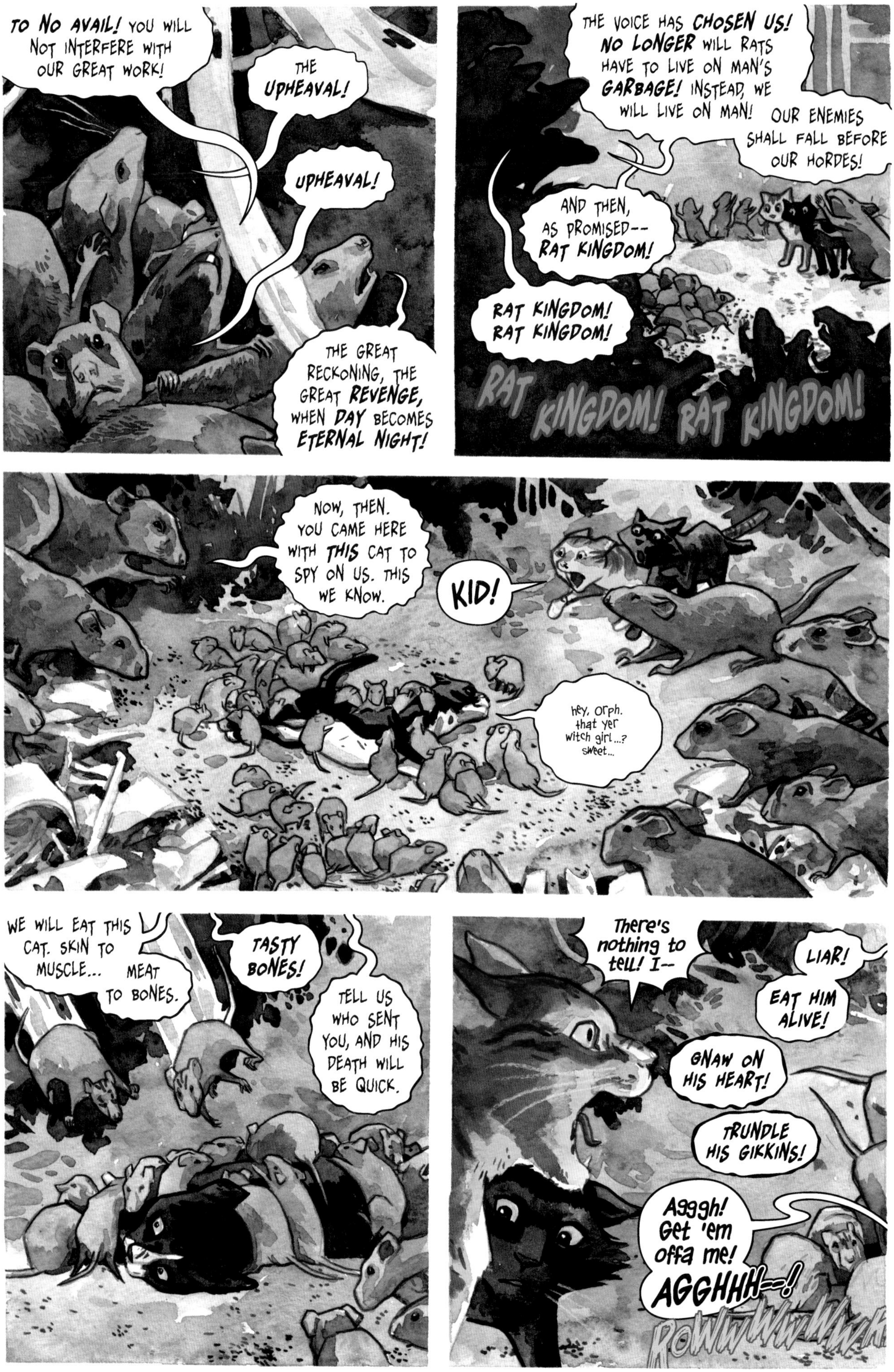

TO NO AVAIL! YOU WILL NOT INTERFERE WITH OUR GREAT WORK!
THE UPHEAVAL!
UPHEAVAL!
THE GREAT RECKONING, THE GREAT REVENGE, WHEN DAY BECOMES ETERNAL NIGHT!
THE VOICE HAS CHOSEN US! NO LONGER WILL RATS HAVE TO LIVE ON MAN'S GARBAGE! INSTEAD, WE WILL LIVE ON MAN!
OUR ENEMIES SHALL FALL BEFORE OUR HORDES!
AND THEN, AS PROMISED-- RAT KINGDOM!
RAT KINGDOM! RAT KINGDOM!
RAT KINGDOM! RAT KINGDOM!
NOW, THEN. YOU CAME HERE WITH THIS CAT TO SPY ON US. THIS WE KNOW.
KID!
hey, Orph. that yer witch girl...? sweet...
WE WILL EAT THIS CAT. SKIN TO MUSCLE... MEAT TO BONES.
TASTY BONES!
TELL US WHO SENT YOU, AND HIS DEATH WILL BE QUICK.
There's nothing to tell! I--
LIAR!
EAT HIM ALIVE!
GNAW ON HIS HEART!
TRUNDLE HIS GIKKINS!
Agggh! Get 'em offa me! AGGHHH--!

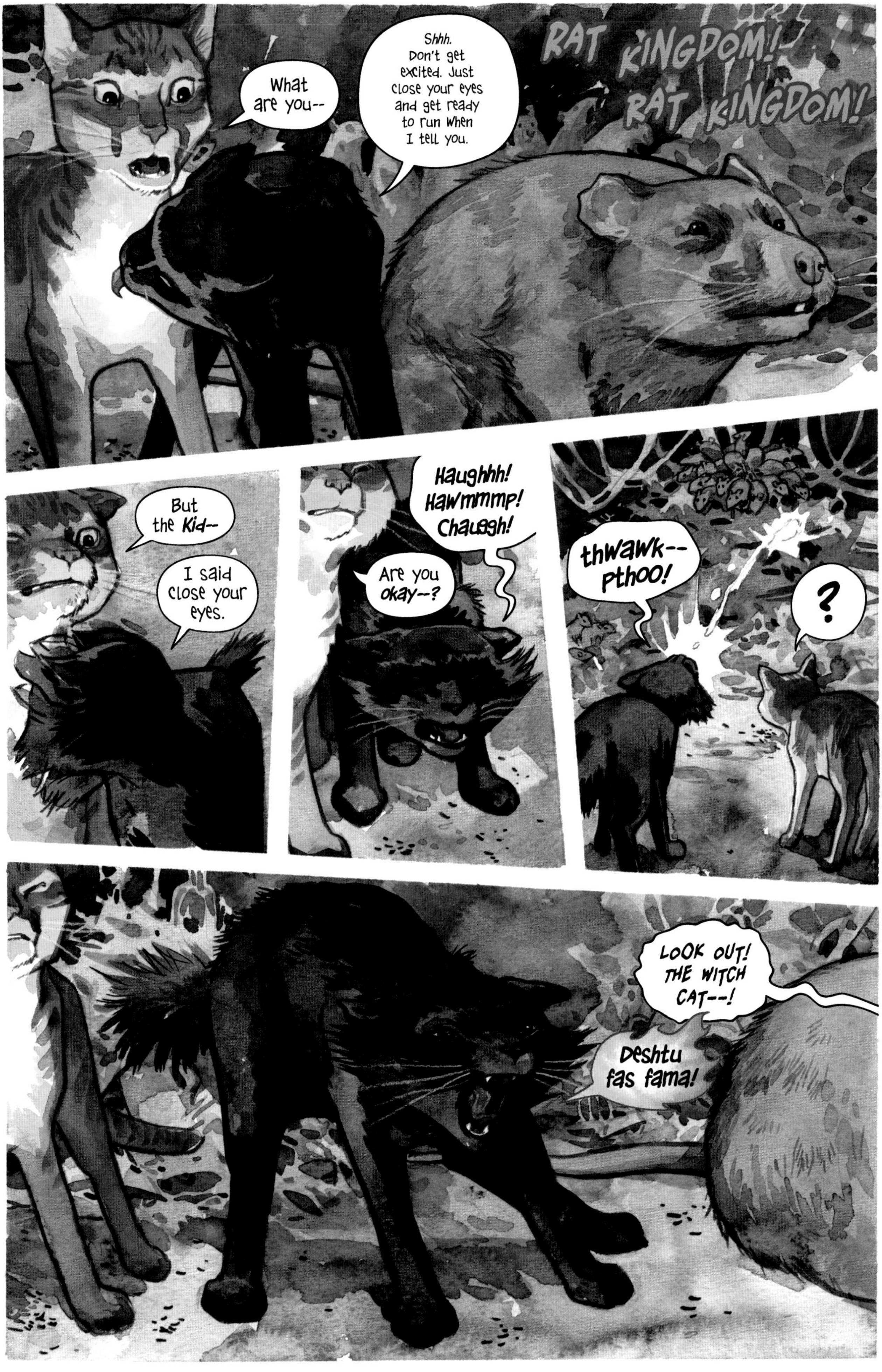
What are you--
Shhh. Don't get excited. Just close your eyes and get ready to run when I tell you.
RAT KINGDOM! RAT KINGDOM!
But the Kid--
I said close your eyes.
Haughhh! Hawmmmp! Chaughh!
Are you okay--?
thwawk--pthoo!
?
LOOK OUT! THE WITCH CAT--!
Deshtu fas fama!

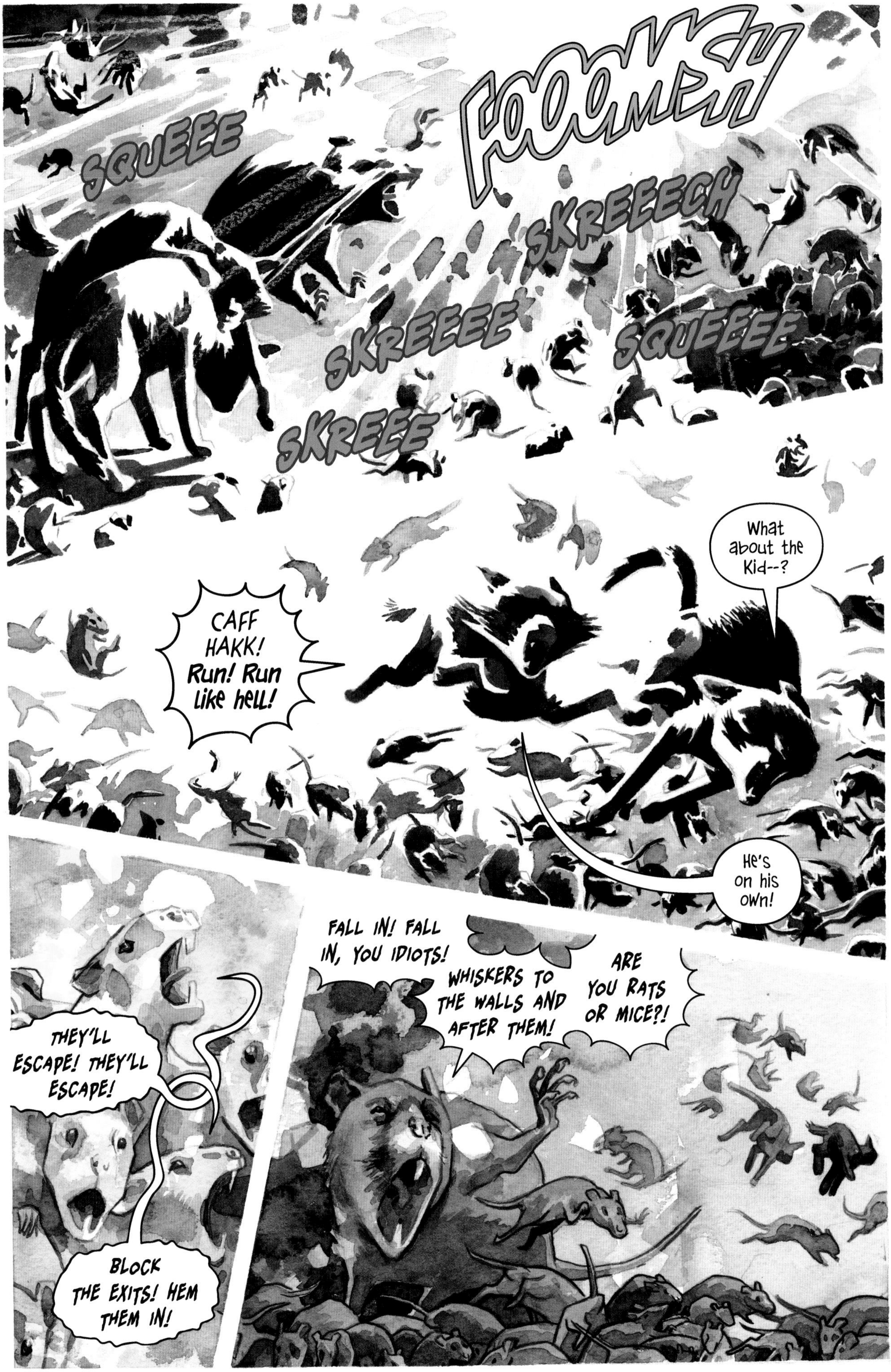
SQUEEE
FOOOMPH
SKREEECH
SKREEEE
SQUEEEE
SKREEE
CAFF HAKK! Run! Run like hell!
What about the Kid--?
He's on his own!
THEY'LL ESCAPE! THEY'LL ESCAPE!
BLOCK THE EXITS! HEM THEM IN!
FALL IN! FALL IN, YOU IDIOTS!
WHISKERS TO THE WALLS AND AFTER THEM!
ARE YOU RATS OR MICE?!

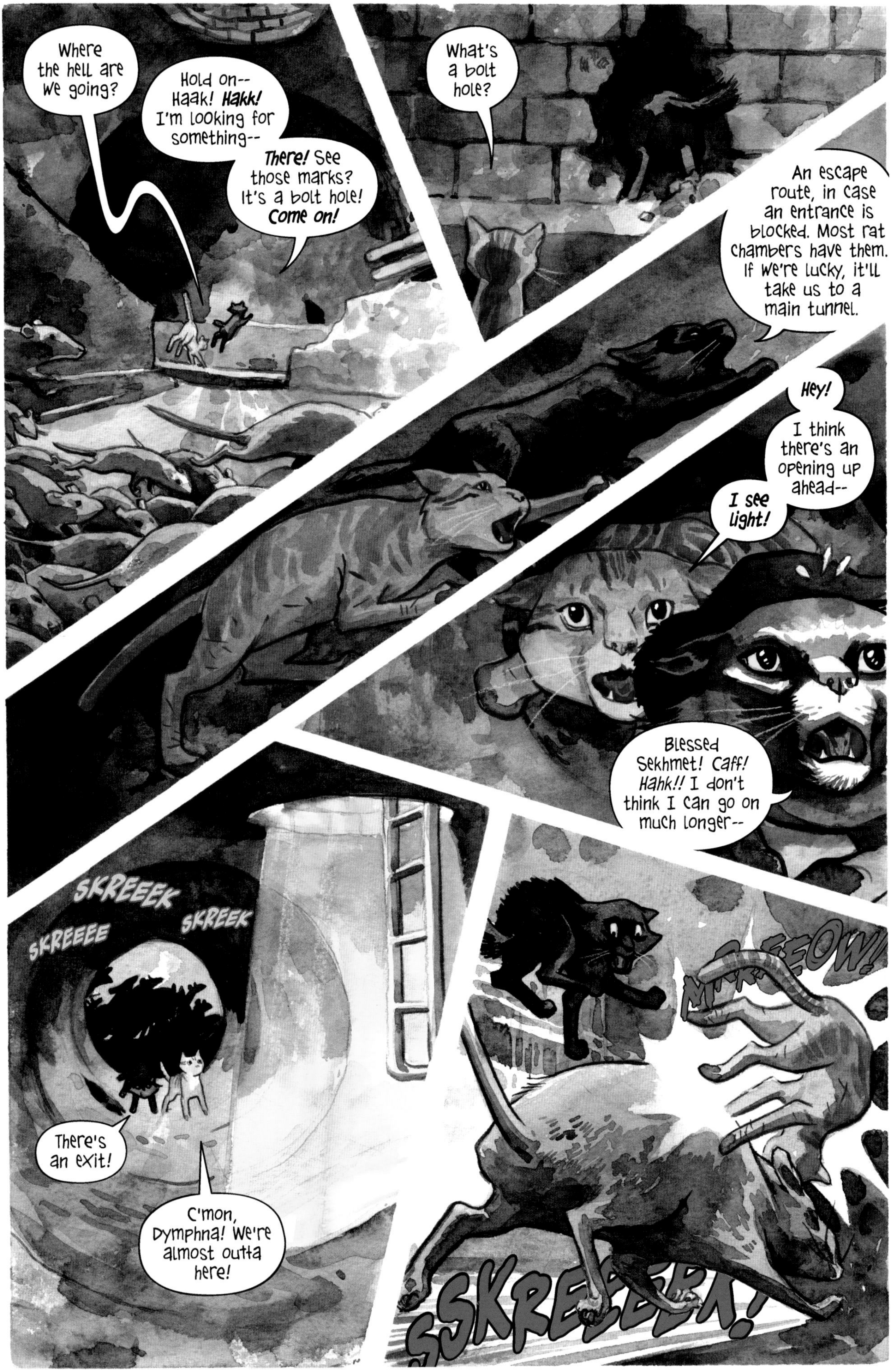

Where the hell are we going?
Hold on-- Haak! Hakk! I'm looking for something--
There! See those marks? It's a bolt hole! Come on!
What's a bolt hole?
An escape route, in case an entrance is blocked. Most rat chambers have them. If we're lucky, it'll take us to a main tunnel.
Hey!
I think there's an opening up ahead--
I see light!
Blessed Sekhmet! Caff! Hahk!! I don't think I can go on much longer--
SKREEEK
SKREEEE
SKREEK
There's an exit!
C'mon, Dymphna! We're almost outta here!

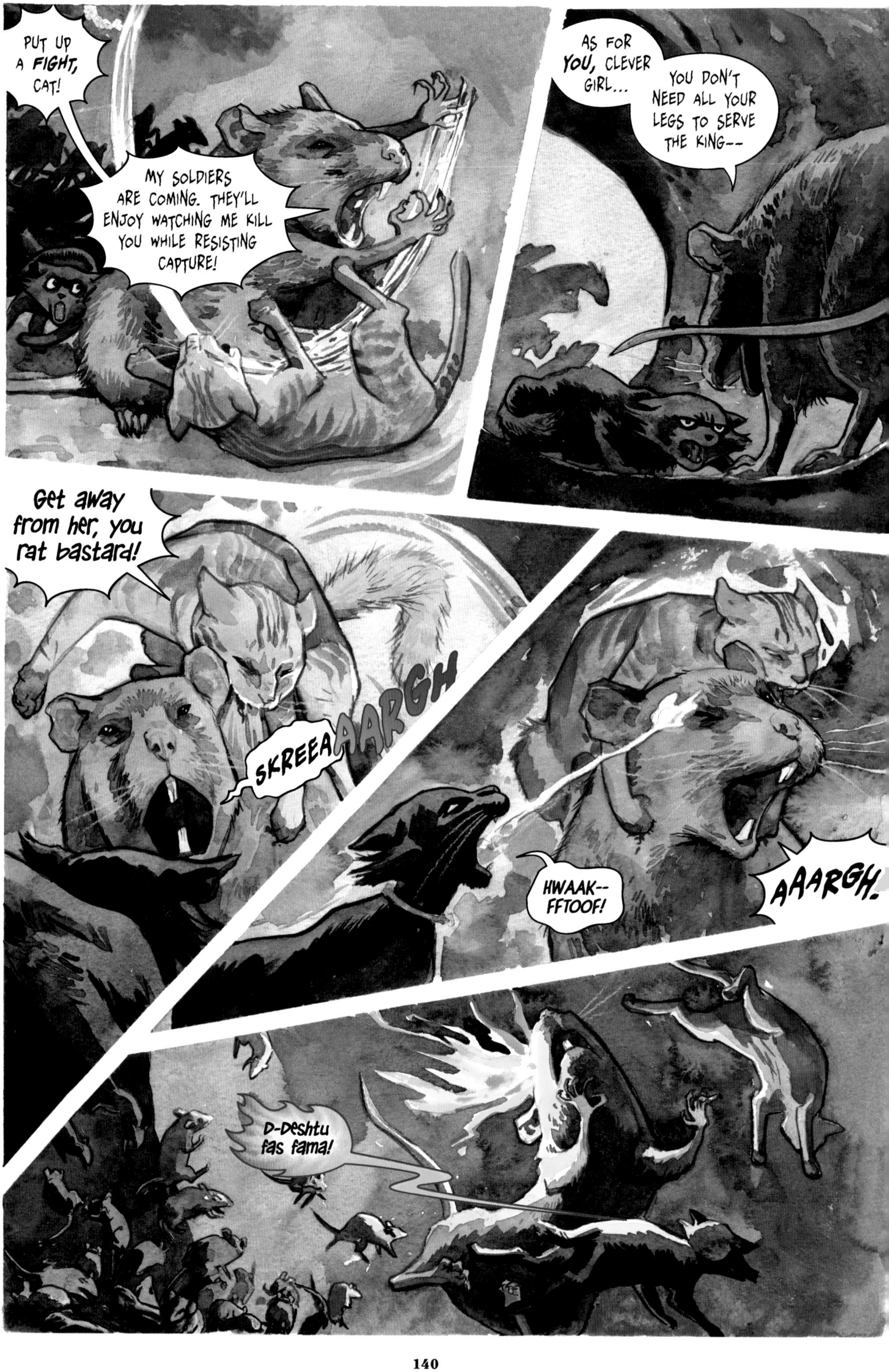
PUT UP A FIGHT, CAT!
MY SOLDIERS ARE COMING. THEY'LL ENJOY WATCHING ME KILL YOU WHILE RESISTING CAPTURE!
AS FOR YOU, CLEVER GIRL...
YOU DON'T NEED ALL YOUR LEGS TO SERVE THE KING--
Get away from her, you rat bastard!
SKREEAAARGH
HWAAK-- FFTOOF!
AAARGH!
D-Deshtu fas fama!

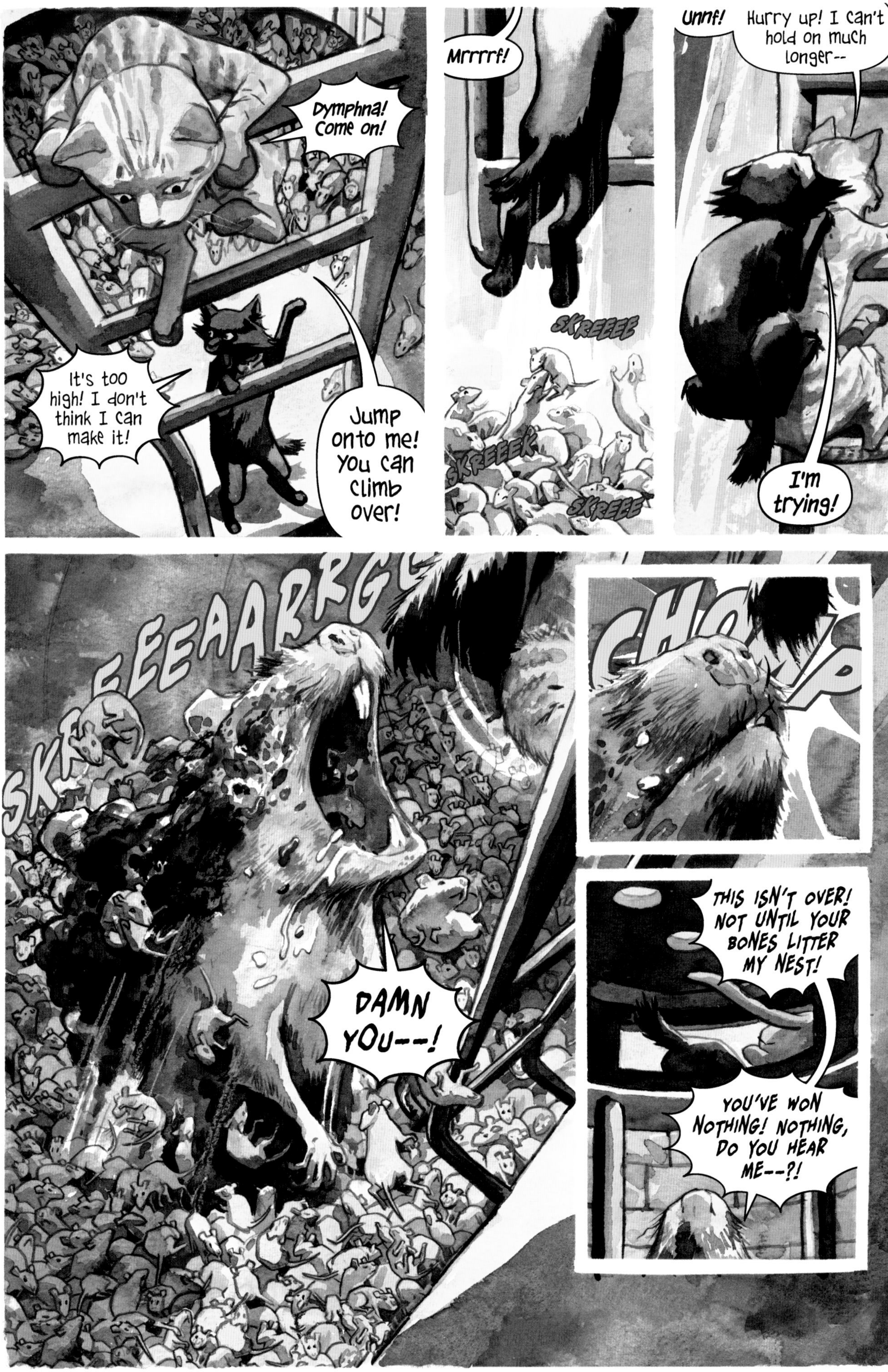

Dymphna! Come on!
It's too high! I don't think I can make it!
Jump onto me! You can climb over!
Mrrrrf!
SKREEEE
SKREEEK
SKREEE
Unnf!
Hurry up! I can't hold on much longer--
I'm trying!
SKREEEAARRGG
DAMN YOU--!
CHOMP
THIS ISN'T OVER! NOT UNTIL YOUR BONES LITTER MY NEST!
YOU'VE WON NOTHING! NOTHING, DO YOU HEAR ME--?!

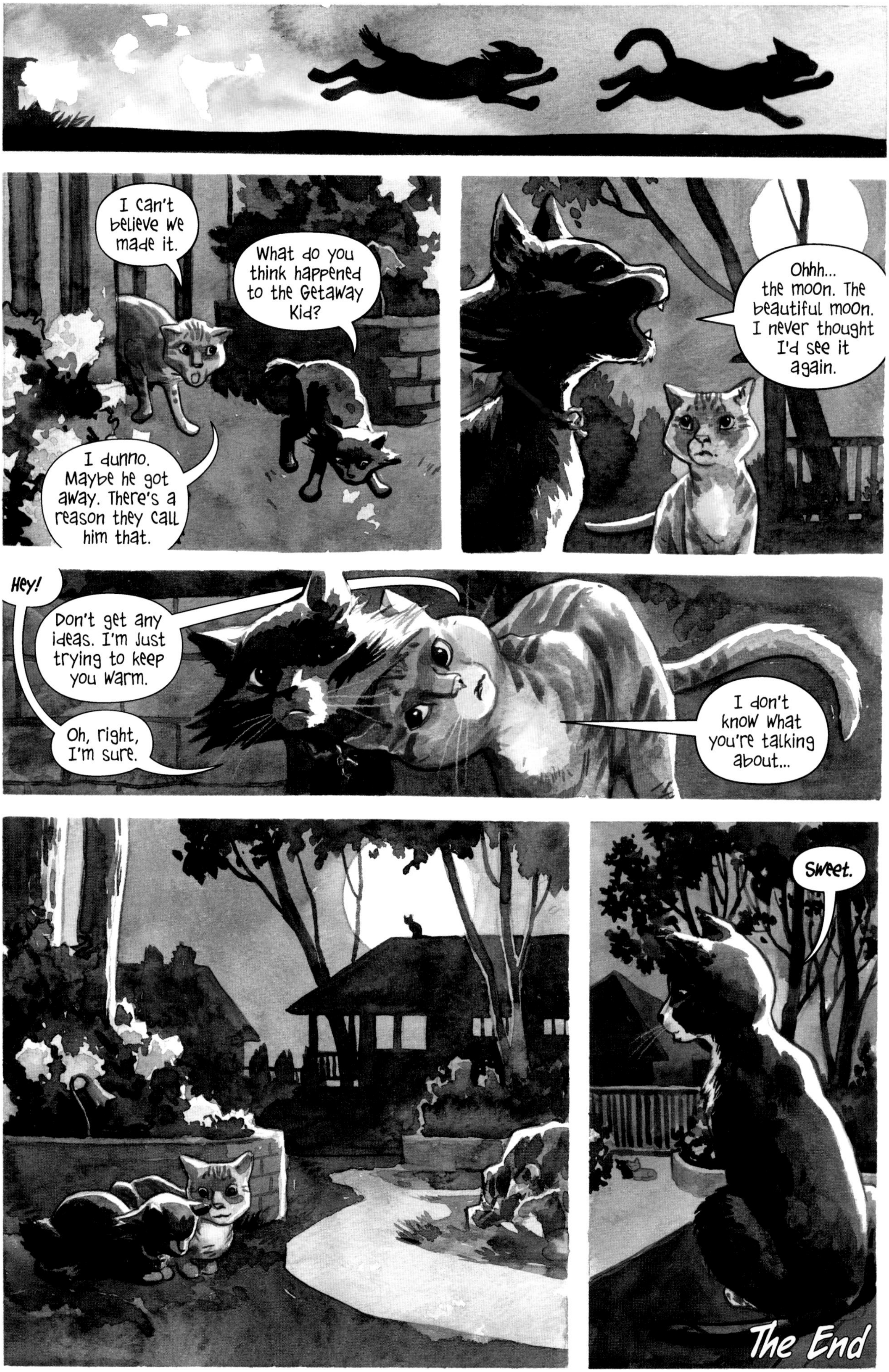
I can't believe we made it.
What do you think happened to the Getaway Kid?
I dunno. Maybe he got away. There's a reason they call him that.
Ohhh... the moon. The beautiful moon. I never thought I'd see it again.
Hey!
Don't get any ideas. I'm just trying to keep you warm.
Oh, right, I'm sure.
I don't know what you're talking about...
Sweet.
The End

GRAVE HAPPENINGS

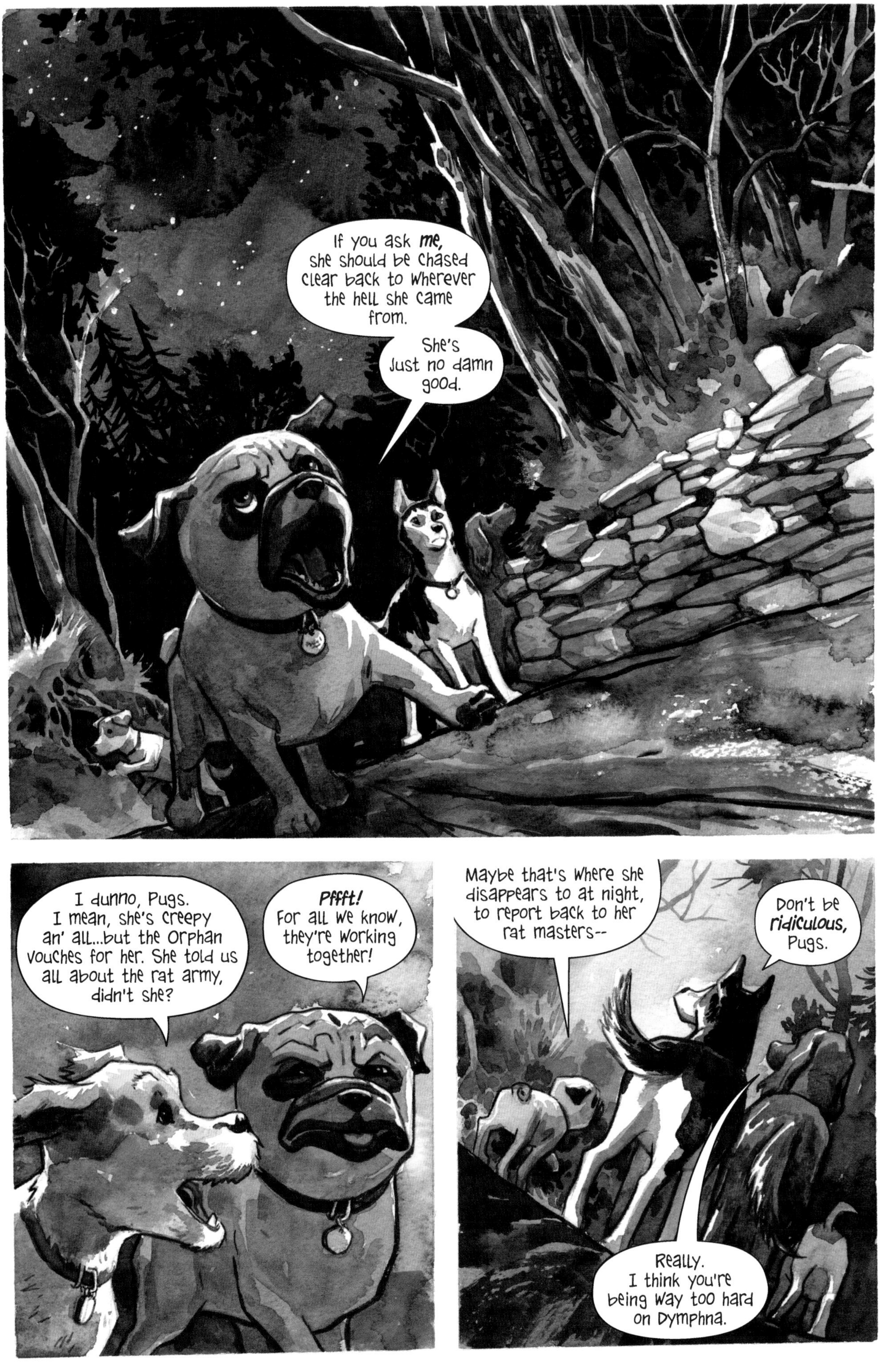
If you ask me, she should be chased clear back to wherever the hell she came from.
She's just no damn good.
I dunno, Pugs. I mean, she's creepy an' all...but the Orphan vouches for her. She told us all about the rat army, didn't she?
Pffft! For all we know, they're working together!
Maybe that's where she disappears to at night, to report back to her rat masters--
Don't be ridiculous, Pugs.
Really. I think you're being way too hard on Dymphna.

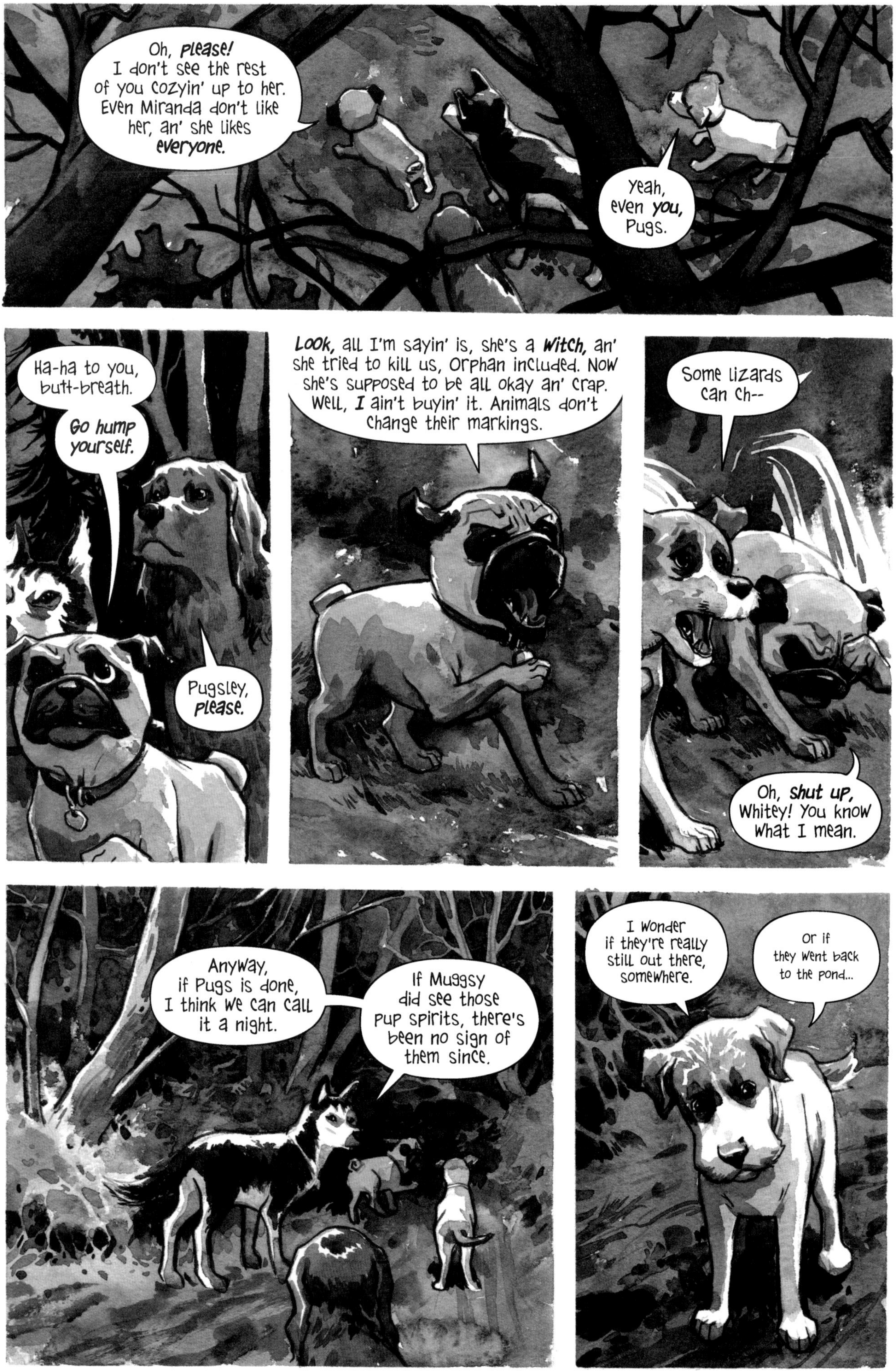

Oh, please! I don't see the rest of you cozyin' up to her. Even Miranda don't like her, an' she likes everyone.
Yeah, even you, Pugs.
Ha-ha to you, butt-breath.
Go hump yourself.
Pugsley, please.
Look, all I'm sayin' is, she's a witch, an' she tried to kill us, Orphan included. Now she's supposed to be all okay an' crap. Well, I ain't buyin' it. Animals don't change their markings.
Some lizards can ch--
Oh, shut up, Whitey! You know what I mean.
Anyway, if Pugs is done, I think we can call it a night.
If Muggsy did see those pup spirits, there's been no sign of them since.
I wonder if they're really still out there, somewhere.
Or if they went back to the pond...

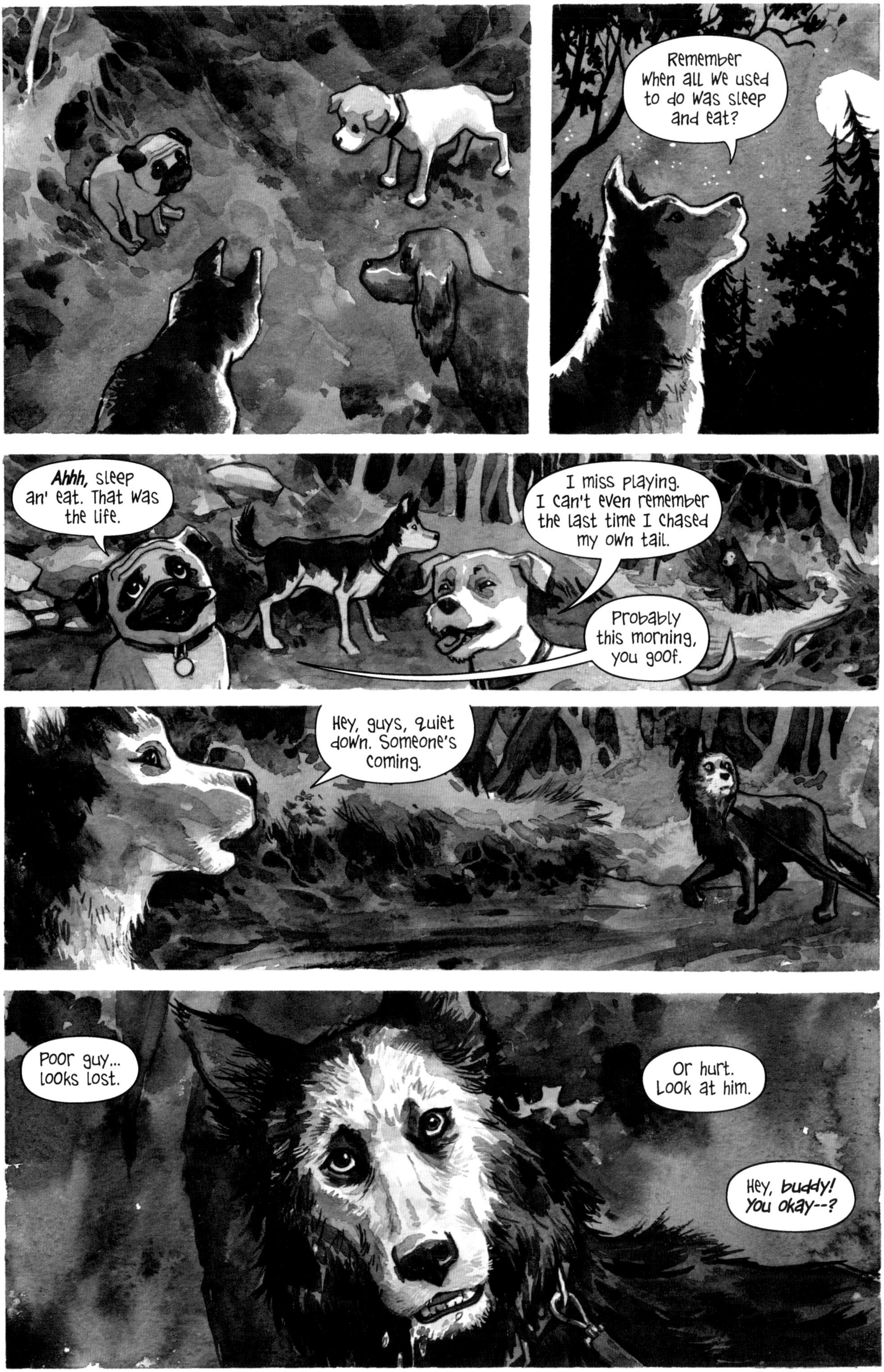

Remember when all we used to do was sleep and eat?
Ahhh, sleep an' eat. That was the life.
I miss playing. I can't even remember the last time I chased my own tail.
Probably this morning, you goof.
Hey, guys, quiet down. Someone's coming.
Poor guy... looks lost.
Or hurt. Look at him.
Hey, ***buddy!*** *You okay--?*

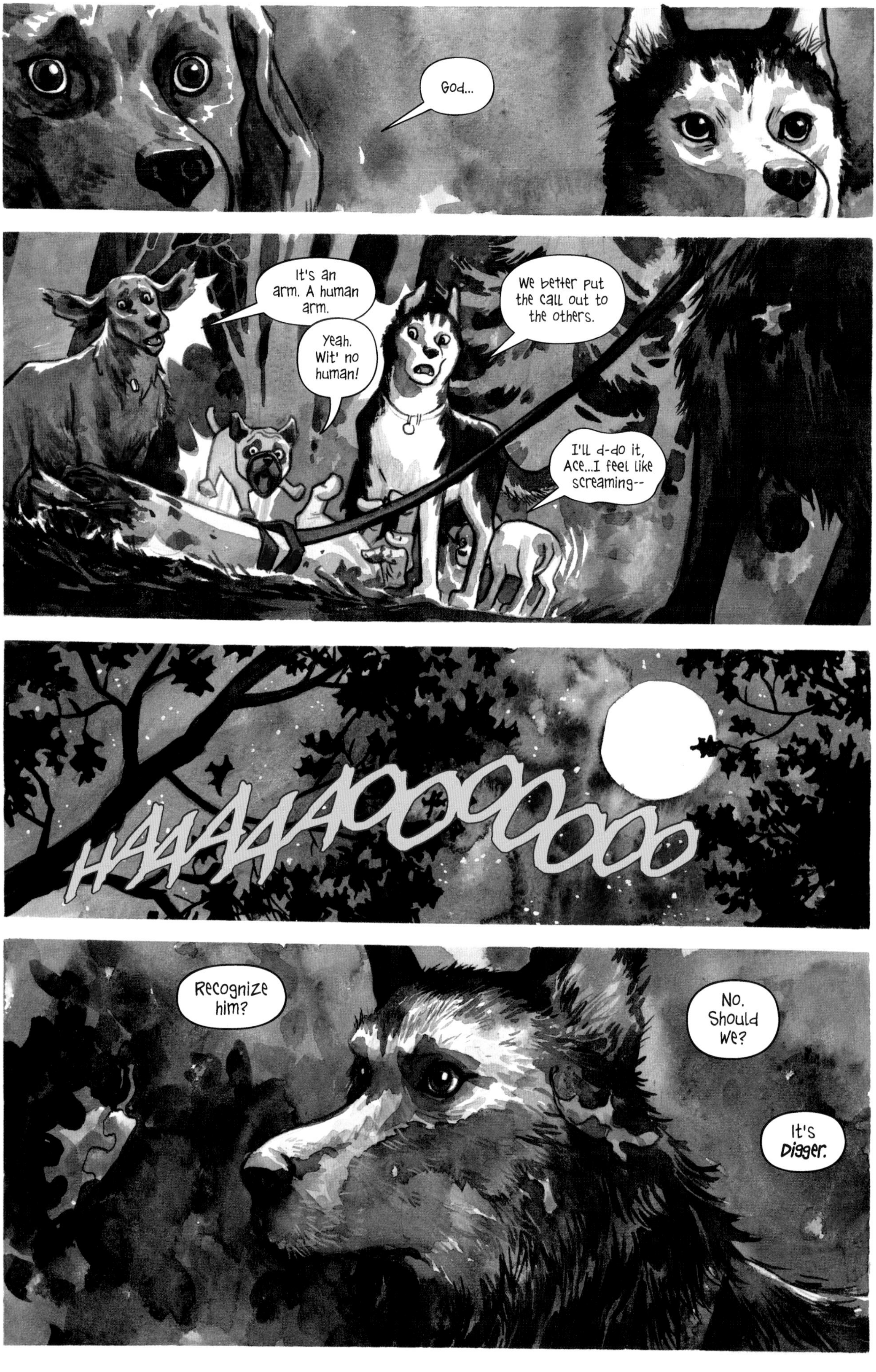
God...
It's an arm. A human arm.
Yeah. Wit' no human!
We better put the call out to the others.
I'll d-do it, Ace...I feel like screaming--
HAAAAAOOOOOOOOO
Recognize him?
No. Should we?
It's Digger.

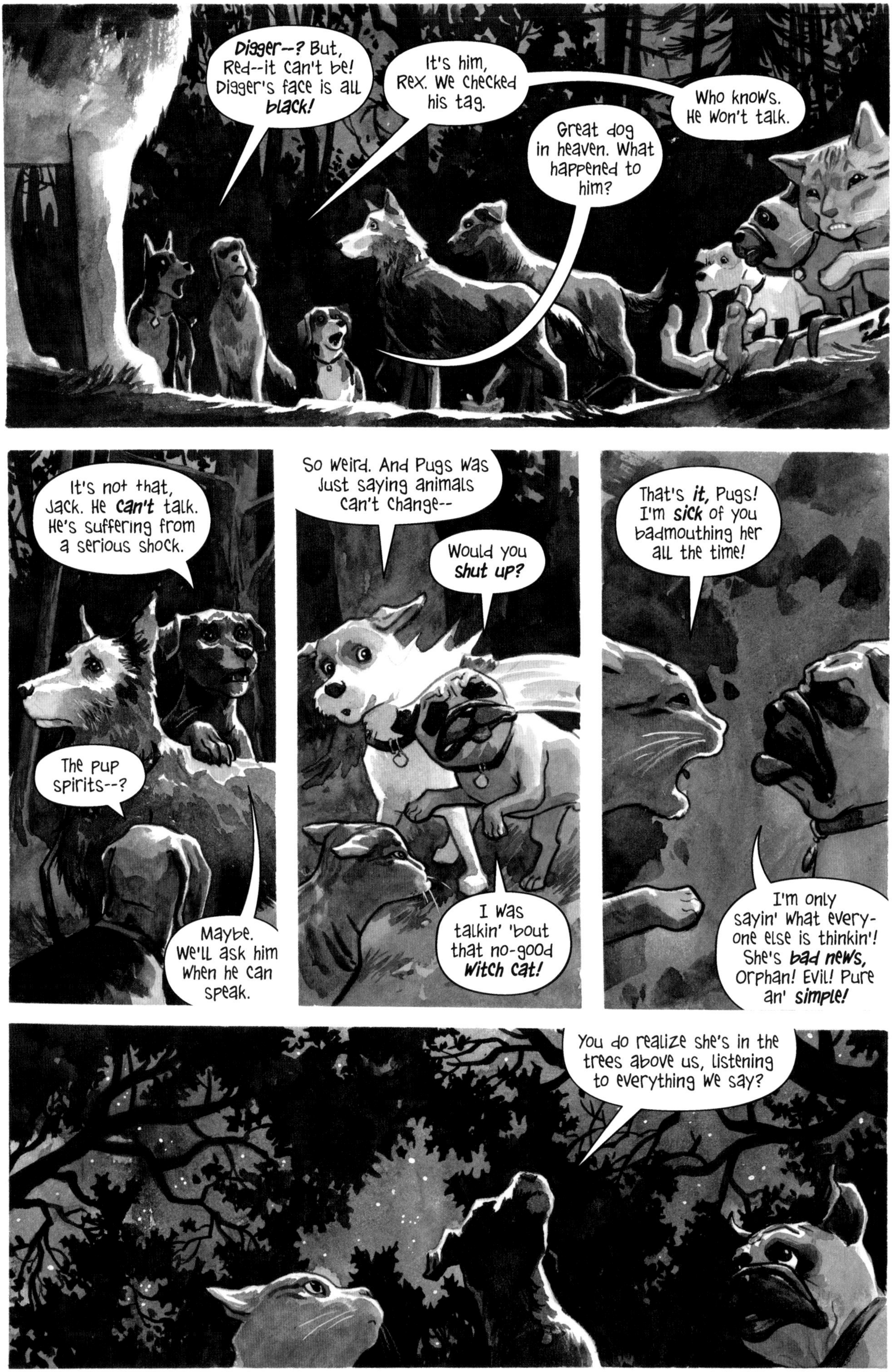
Digger--? But, Red--it can't be! Digger's face is all black!
It's him, Rex. We checked his tag.
Great dog in heaven. What happened to him?
Who knows. He won't talk.
It's not that, Jack. He can't talk. He's suffering from a serious shock.
The pup spirits--?
Maybe. We'll ask him when he can speak.
So weird. And Pugs was just saying animals can't change--
Would you shut up?
I was talkin' 'bout that no-good witch cat!
That's it, Pugs! I'm sick of you badmouthing her all the time!
I'm only sayin' what every-one else is thinkin'! She's bad news, Orphan! Evil! Pure an' simple!
You do realize she's in the trees above us, listening to everything we say?

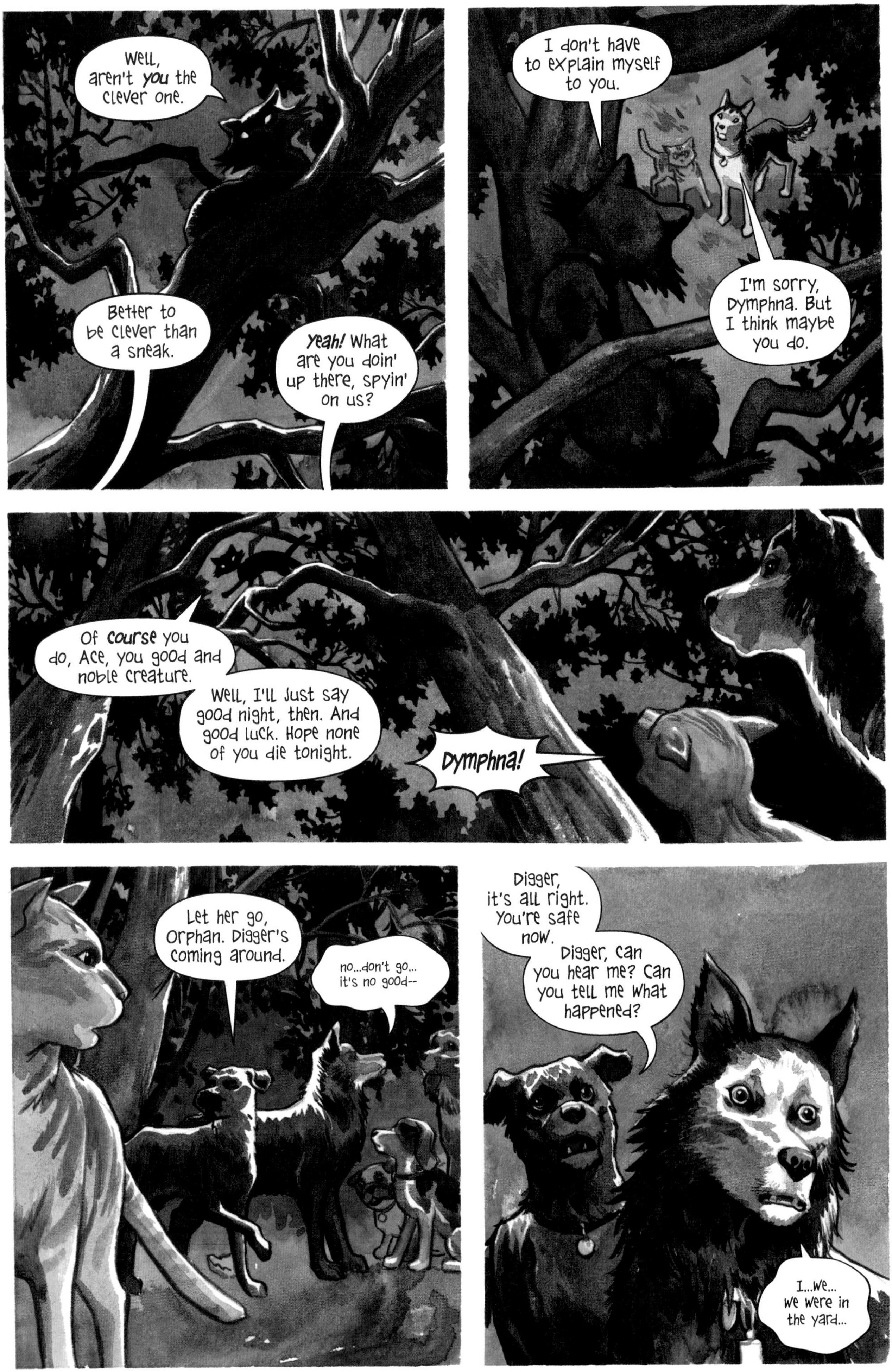
Well, aren't you the clever one.
Better to be clever than a sneak.
Yeah! What are you doin' up there, spyin' on us?
I don't have to explain myself to you.
I'm sorry, Dymphna. But I think maybe you do.
Of course you do, Ace, you good and noble creature.
Well, I'll just say good night, then. And good luck. Hope none of you die tonight.
Dymphna!
Let her go, Orphan. Digger's coming around.
no...don't go... it's no good--
Digger, it's all right. You're safe now.
Digger, can you hear me? Can you tell me what happened?
I...we... we were in the yard...

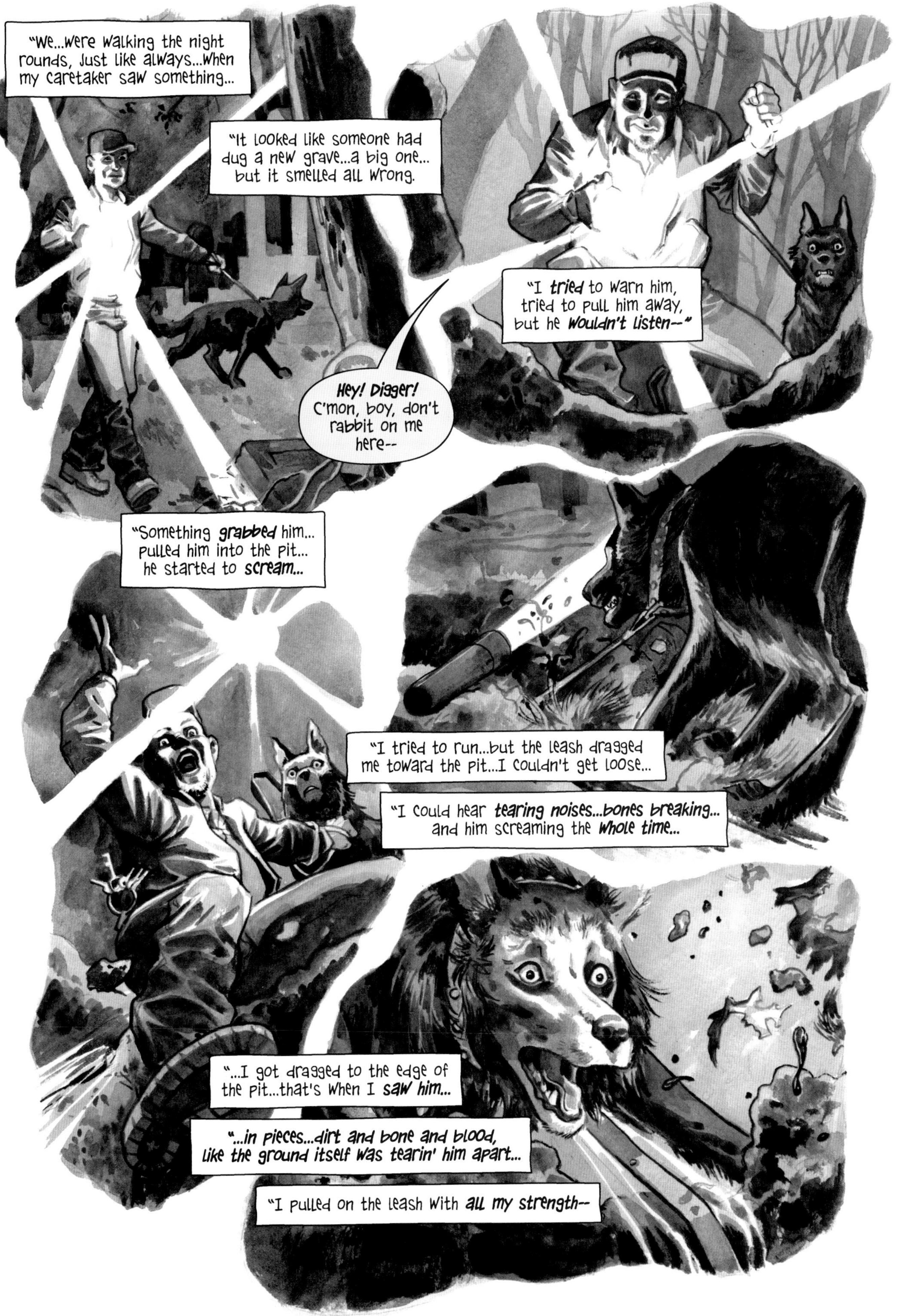
"We...were walking the night rounds, just like always...when my caretaker saw something...
"It looked like someone had dug a new grave...a big one... but it smelled all wrong.
Hey! Digger! C'mon, boy, don't rabbit on me here--
"I tried to warn him, tried to pull him away, but he wouldn't listen--"
"Something grabbed him... pulled him into the pit... he started to scream...
"I tried to run...but the leash dragged me toward the pit...I couldn't get loose...
"I could hear tearing noises...bones breaking... and him screaming the whole time...
"...I got dragged to the edge of the pit...that's when I saw him...
"...in pieces...dirt and bone and blood, like the ground itself was tearin' him apart...
"I pulled on the leash with all my strength--

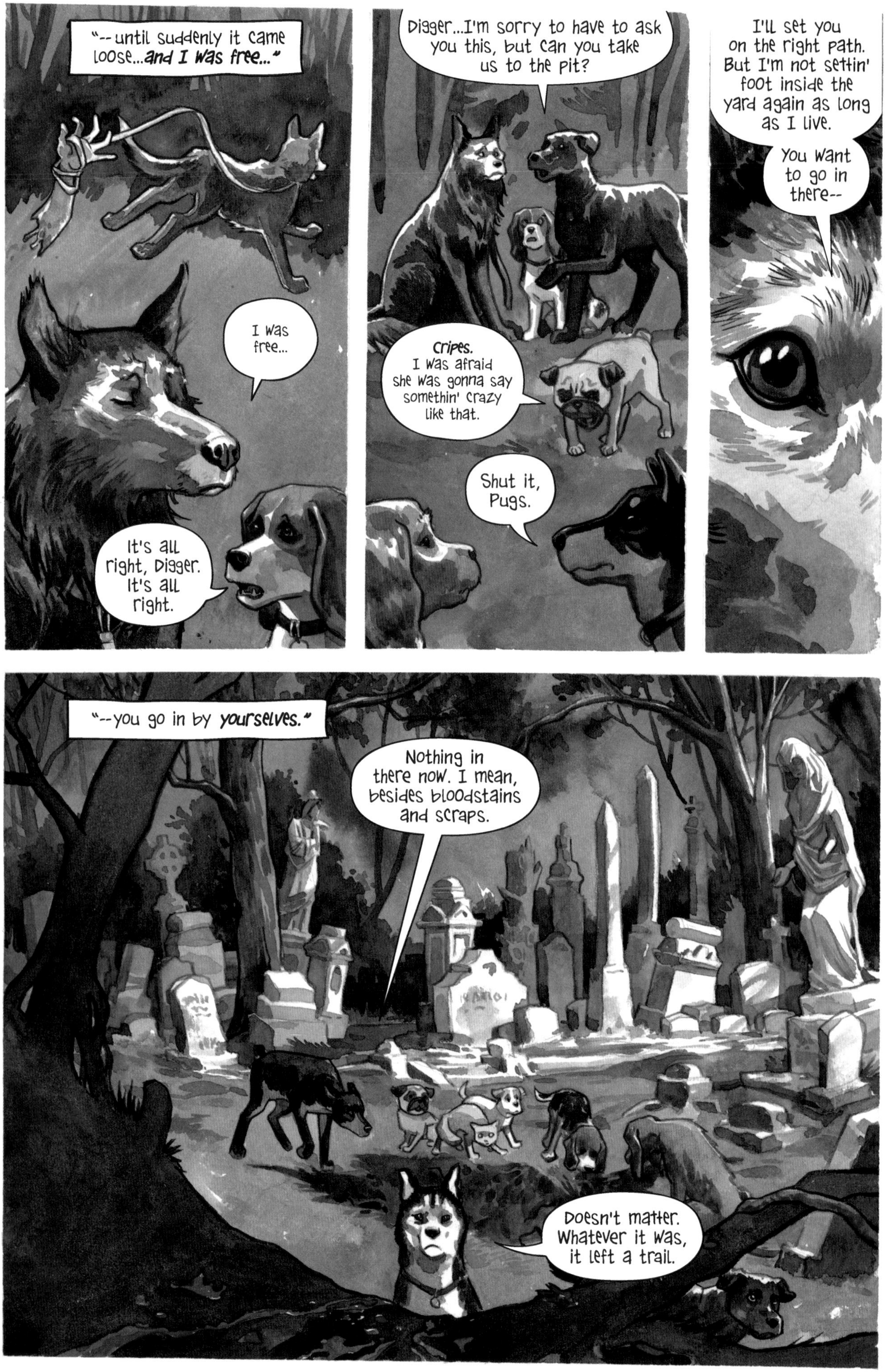
"--until suddenly it came loose...and I was free..."
I was free...
It's all right, Digger. It's all right.
Digger...I'm sorry to have to ask you this, but can you take us to the pit?
Cripes. I was afraid she was gonna say somethin' crazy like that.
Shut it, Pugs.
I'll set you on the right path. But I'm not settin' foot inside the yard again as long as I live.
You want to go in there--
"--you go in by yourselves."
Nothing in there now. I mean, besides bloodstains and scraps.
Doesn't matter. Whatever it was, it left a trail.

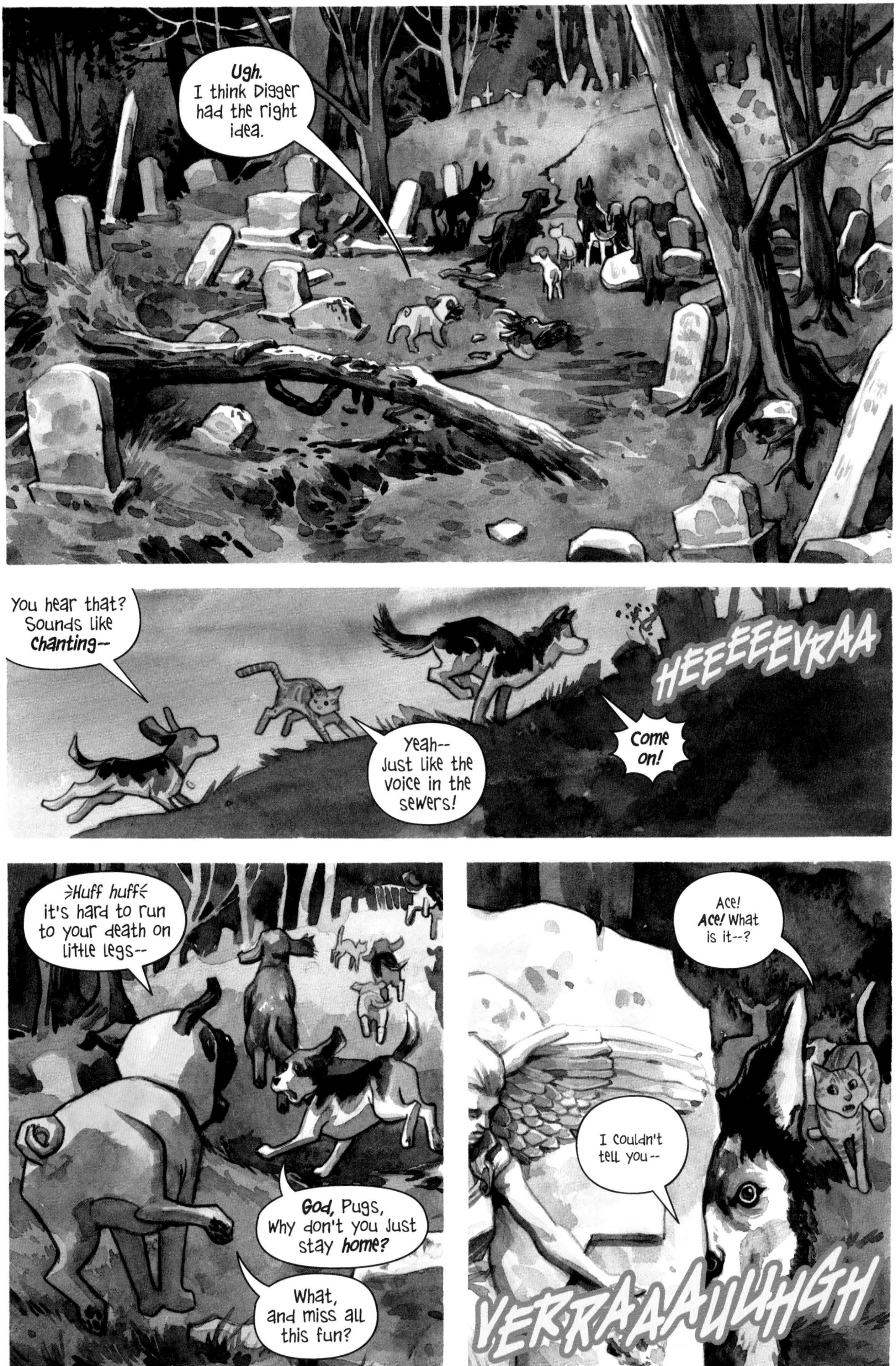
Ugh. I think Digger had the right idea.
You hear that? Sounds like Chanting--
Yeah-- Just like the voice in the sewers!
Come on!
HEEEEEVRAA
⋟Huff huff⋞ it's hard to run to your death on little legs--
God, Pugs, Why don't you just stay home?
What, and miss all this fun?
Ace! Ace! What is it--?
I couldn't tell you--
VERRAAAULHGH

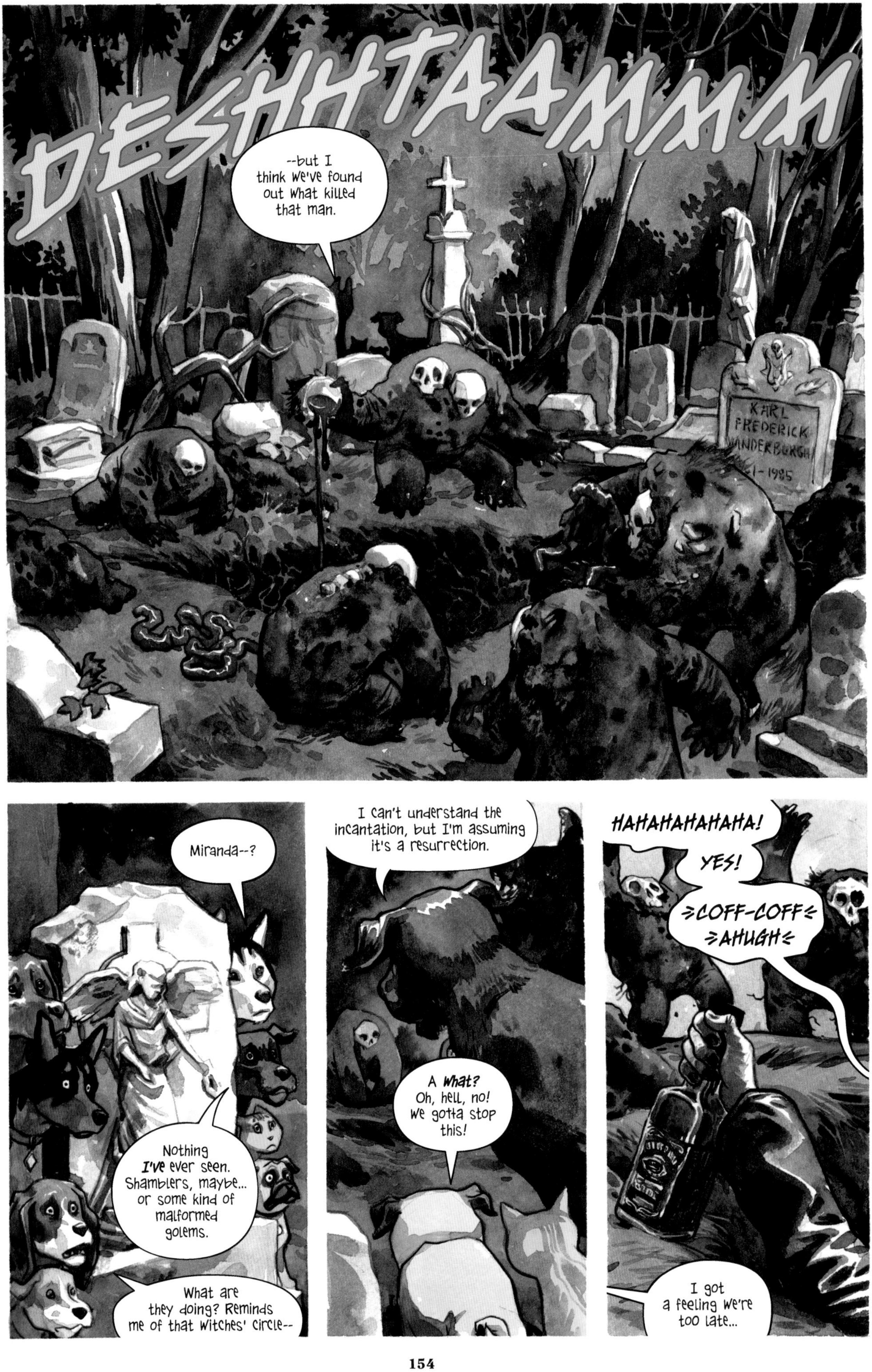
DESHHTAAMMM
--but I think we've found out what killed that man.
KARL FREDERICK VANDERBURGH
1- 1985
Miranda--?
Nothing I've ever seen. Shamblers, maybe... or some kind of malformed golems.
What are they doing? Reminds me of that witches' circle--
I can't understand the incantation, but I'm assuming it's a resurrection.
A what? Oh, hell, no! We gotta stop this!
HAHAHAHAHAHA!
YES!
COFF-COFF AHUGH
I got a feeling we're too late...

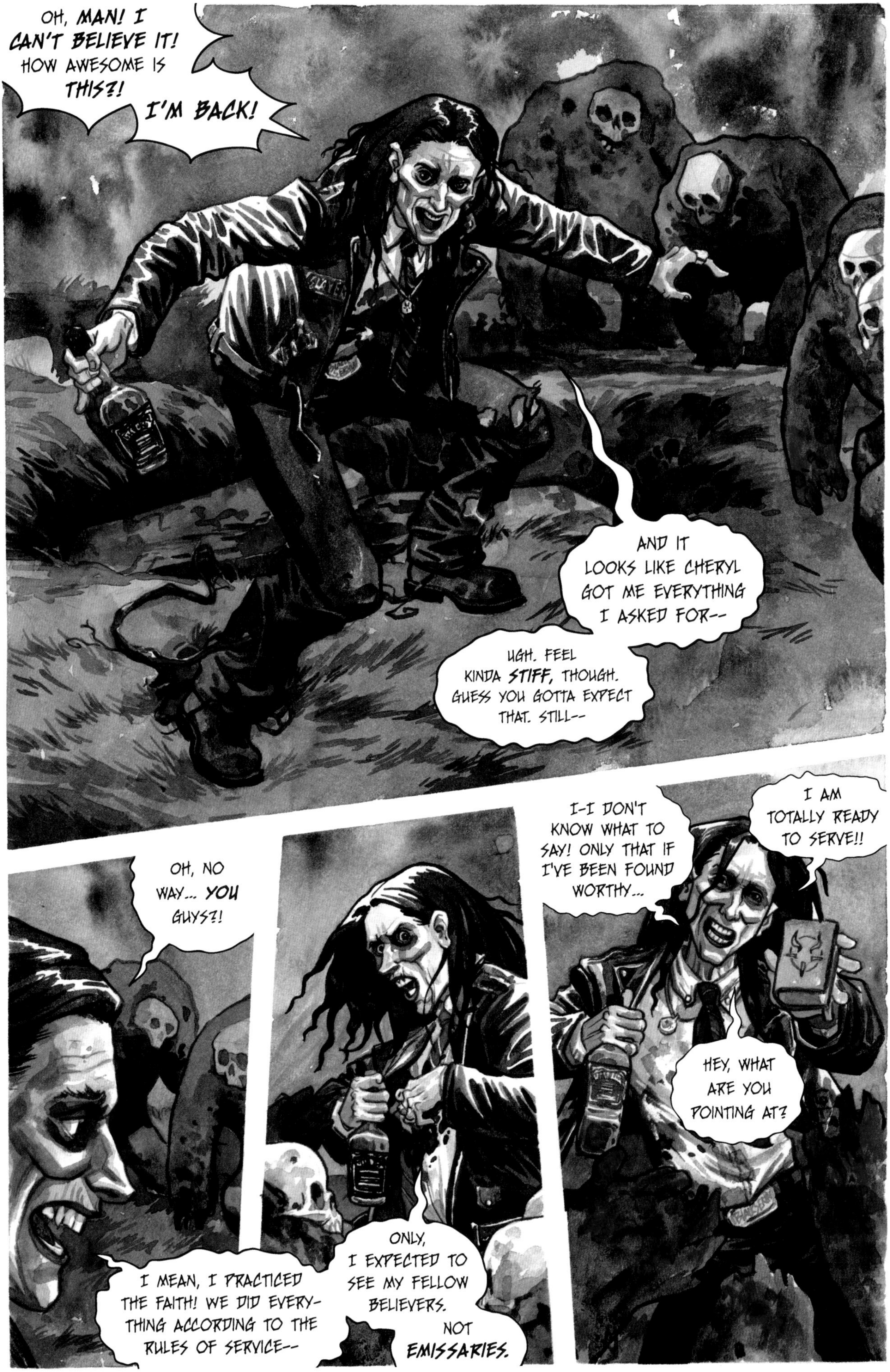
OH, MAN! I CAN'T BELIEVE IT! HOW AWESOME IS THIS?!
I'M BACK!
AND IT LOOKS LIKE CHERYL GOT ME EVERYTHING I ASKED FOR--
UGH. FEEL KINDA STIFF, THOUGH. GUESS YOU GOTTA EXPECT THAT. STILL--
OH, NO WAY... YOU GUYS?!
I MEAN, I PRACTICED THE FAITH! WE DID EVERY-THING ACCORDING TO THE RULES OF SERVICE--
ONLY, I EXPECTED TO SEE MY FELLOW BELIEVERS.
NOT EMISSARIES.
I-I DON'T KNOW WHAT TO SAY! ONLY THAT IF I'VE BEEN FOUND WORTHY...
I AM TOTALLY READY TO SERVE!!
HEY, WHAT ARE YOU POINTING AT?

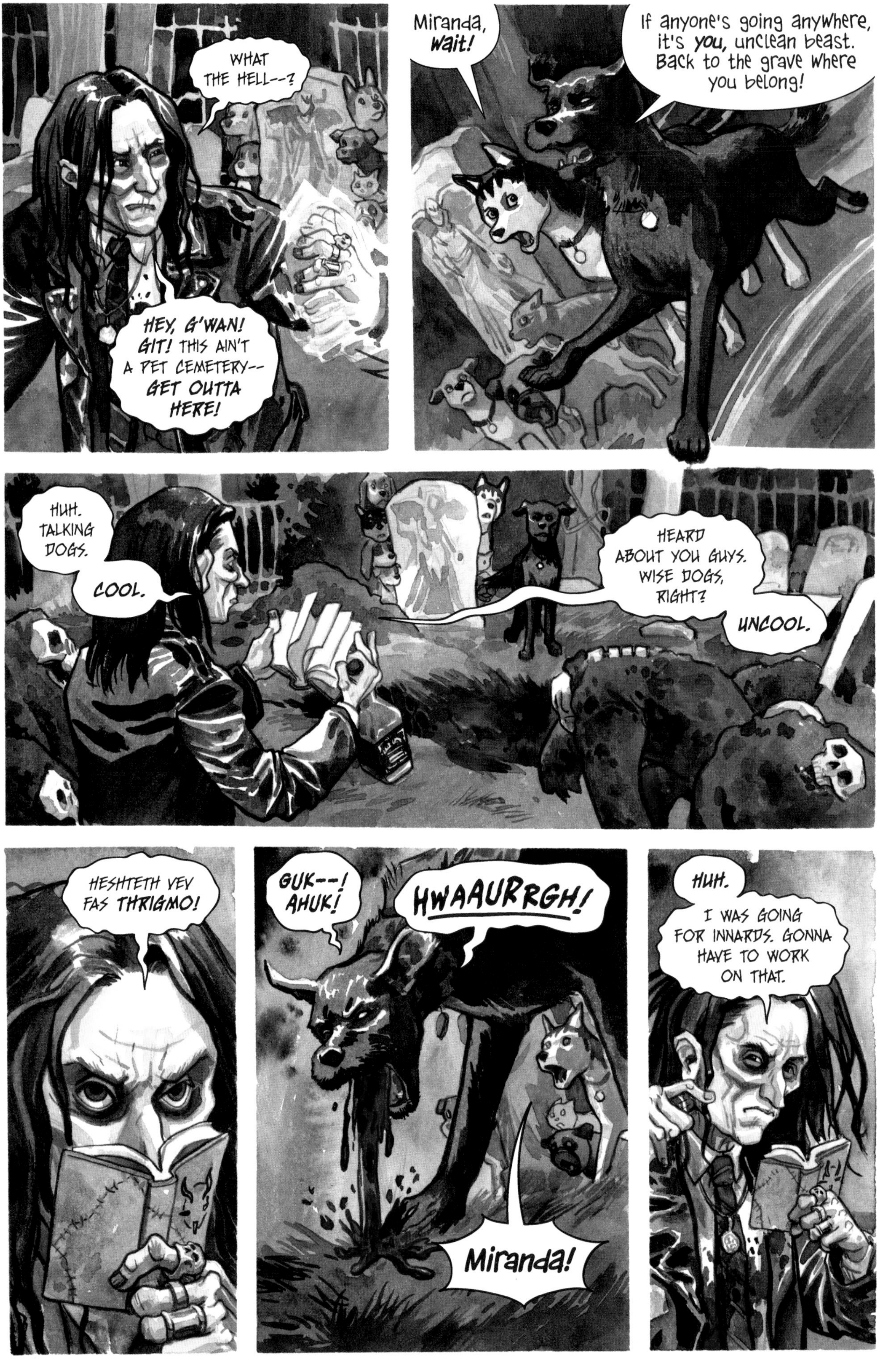
WHAT THE HELL--?
HEY, G'WAN! GIT! THIS AIN'T A PET CEMETERY-- GET OUTTA HERE!
Miranda, wait!
If anyone's going anywhere, it's you, unclean beast. Back to the grave where you belong!
HUH. TALKING DOGS.
COOL.
HEARD ABOUT YOU GUYS. WISE DOGS, RIGHT?
UNCOOL.
HESHTETH VEV FAS THRIGMO!
GUK--! AHUK!
HWAAURRGH!
Miranda!
HUH.
I WAS GOING FOR INNARDS. GONNA HAVE TO WORK ON THAT.

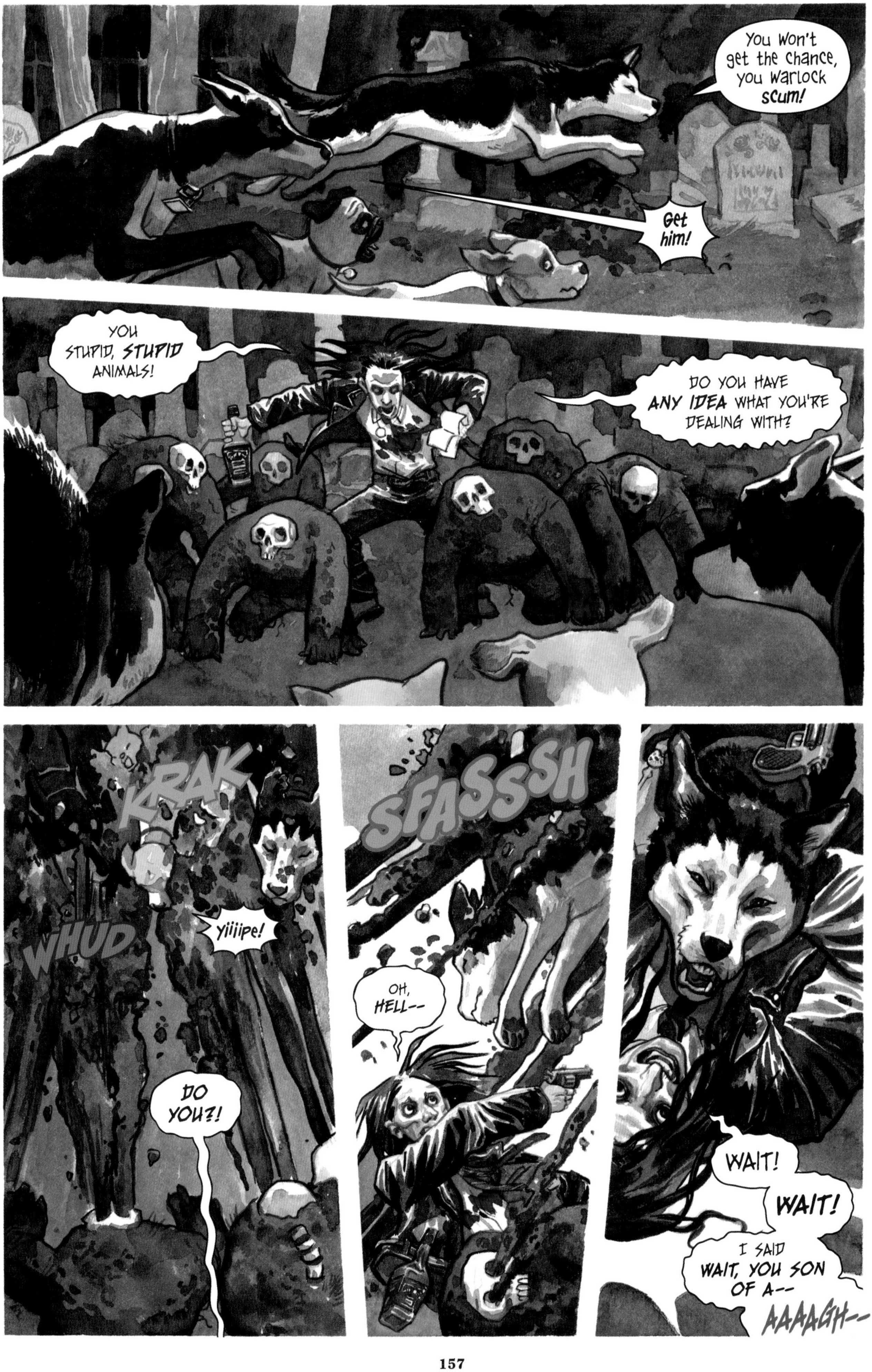
You won't get the chance, you warlock scum!
Get him!
YOU STUPID, STUPID ANIMALS!
DO YOU HAVE ANY IDEA WHAT YOU'RE DEALING WITH?
KRAK
WHUD
yiiiipe!
DO YOU?!
SFASSSH
OH, HELL--
WAIT!
WAIT!
I SAID WAIT, YOU SON OF A--
AAAAGH--

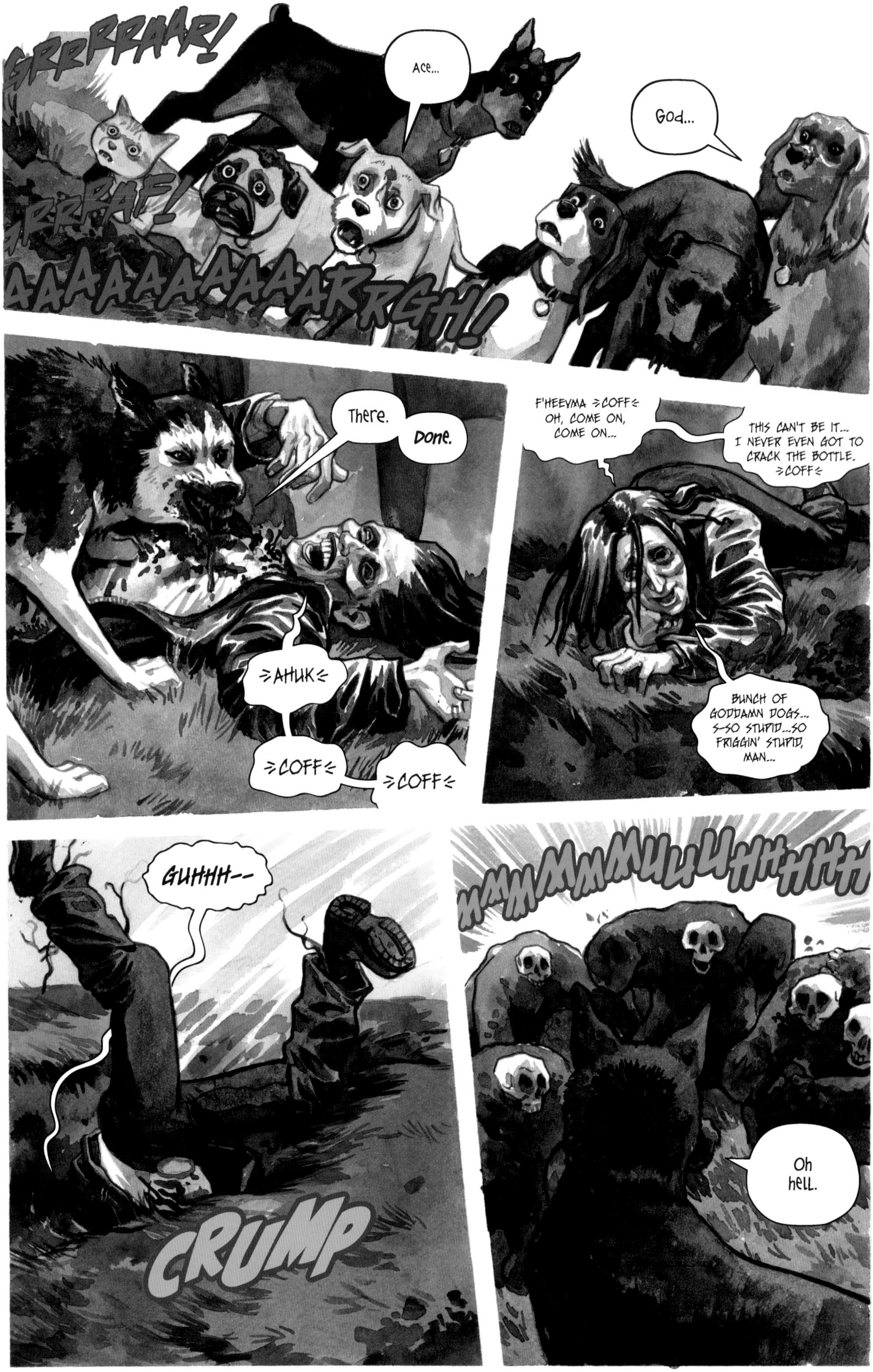
GRRRRAAR!
RRRAF!
AAAAAAAAAAARRGH!
Ace...
God...
There.
Done.
≥AHUK≤
≥COFF≤
≥COFF≤
F'HEEVMA ≥COFF≤ OH, COME ON, COME ON...
THIS CAN'T BE IT... I NEVER EVEN GOT TO CRACK THE BOTTLE. ≥COFF≤
BUNCH OF GODDAMN DOGS... S-SO STUPID...SO FRIGGIN' STUPID, MAN...
GUHHH--
CRUMP
MMMMMMMUUUHHHHHH
Oh hell.

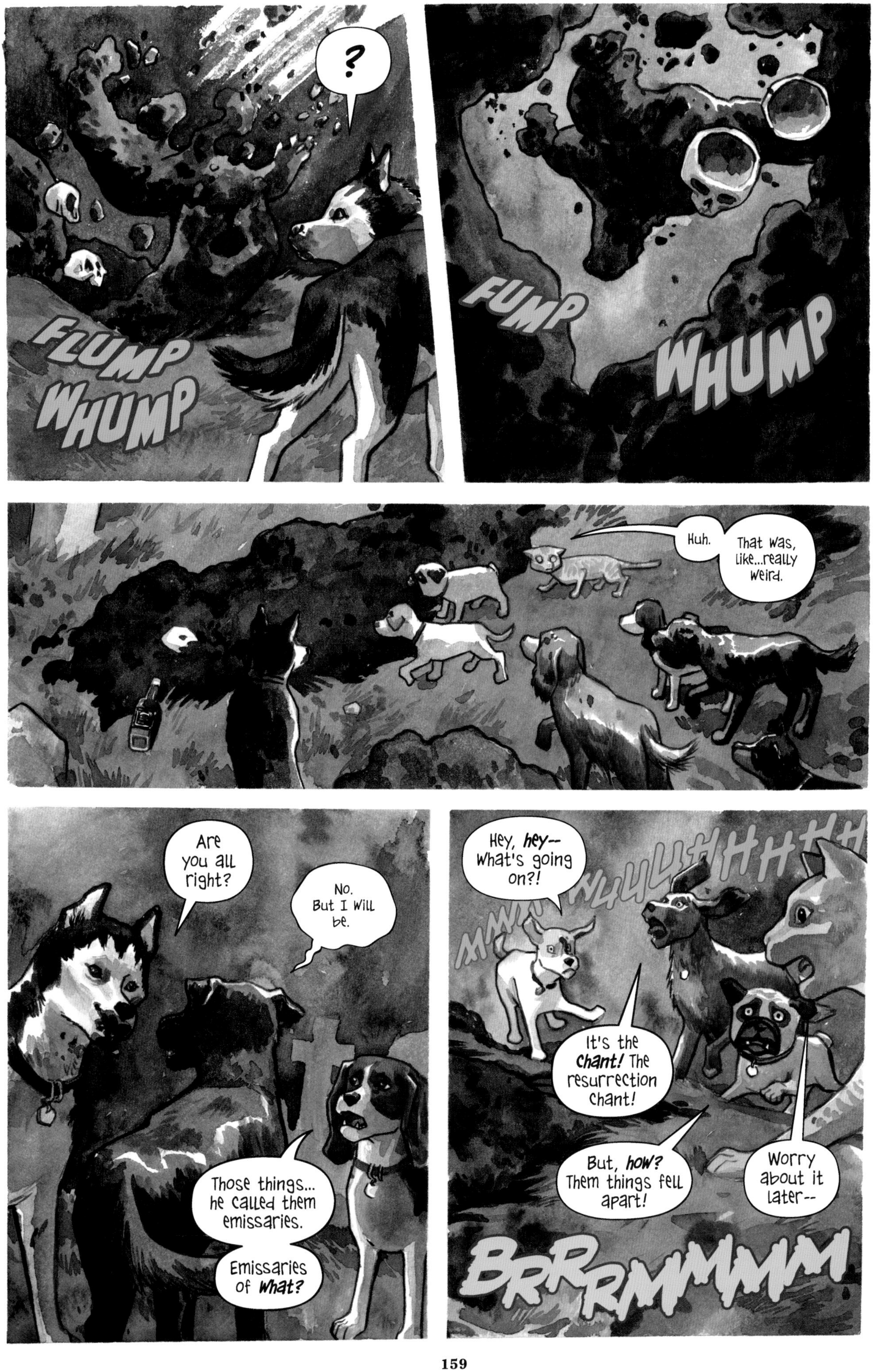
?
FLUMP
WHUMP
FUMP
WHUMP
Huh.
That was, like...really weird.
Are you all right?
No. But I will be.
Those things... he called them emissaries.
Emissaries of *what?*
Hey, *hey*-- What's going on?!
It's the *chant!* The resurrection chant!
But, *how?* Them things fell apart!
Worry about it later--
BRRRMMMMMM

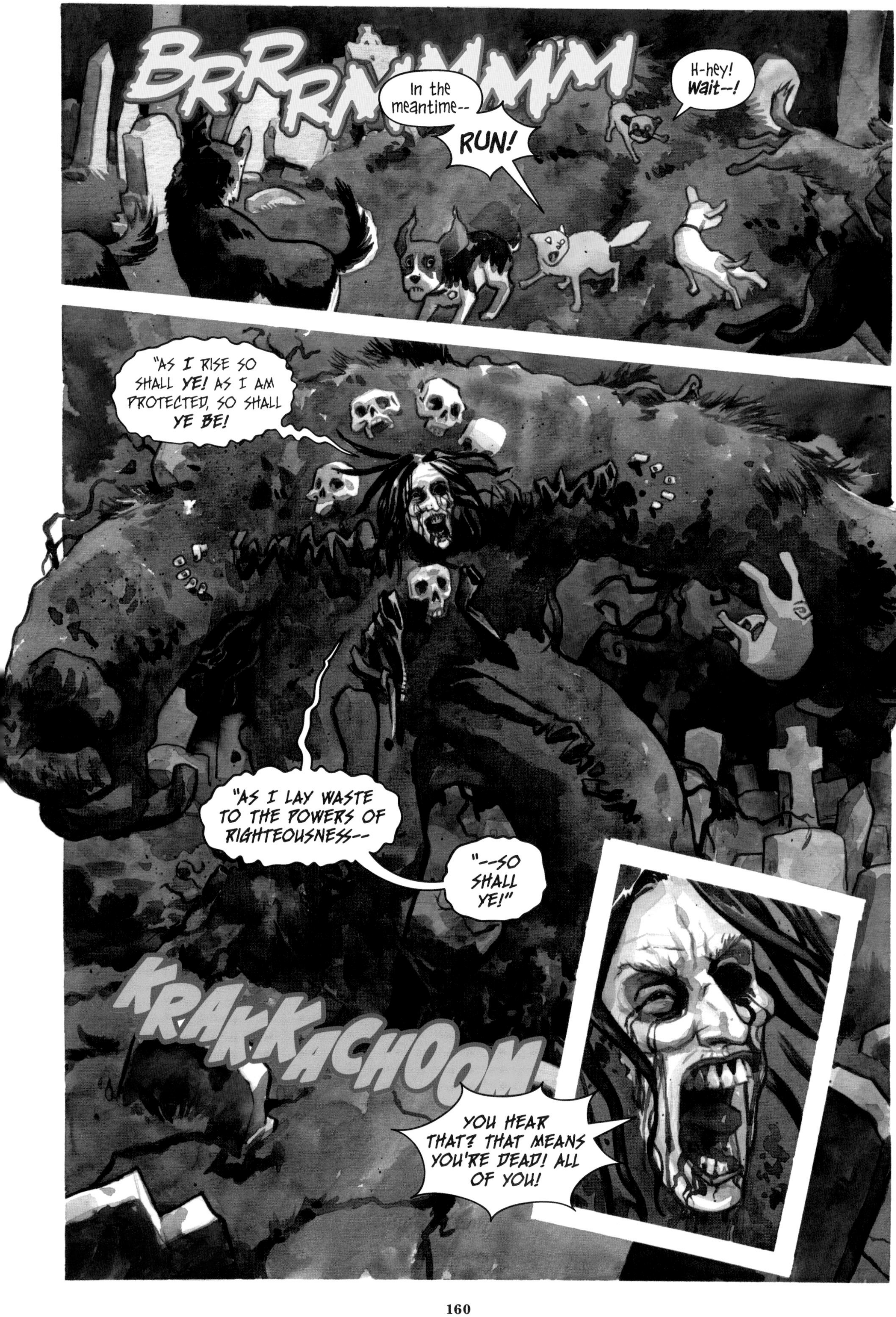
BRRRMMMM
In the meantime--
RUN!
H-hey! Wait--!
"AS I RISE SO SHALL YE! AS I AM PROTECTED, SO SHALL YE BE!
"AS I LAY WASTE TO THE POWERS OF RIGHTEOUSNESS--
"--SO SHALL YE!"
KRAKKACHOOM
YOU HEAR THAT? THAT MEANS YOU'RE DEAD! ALL OF YOU!

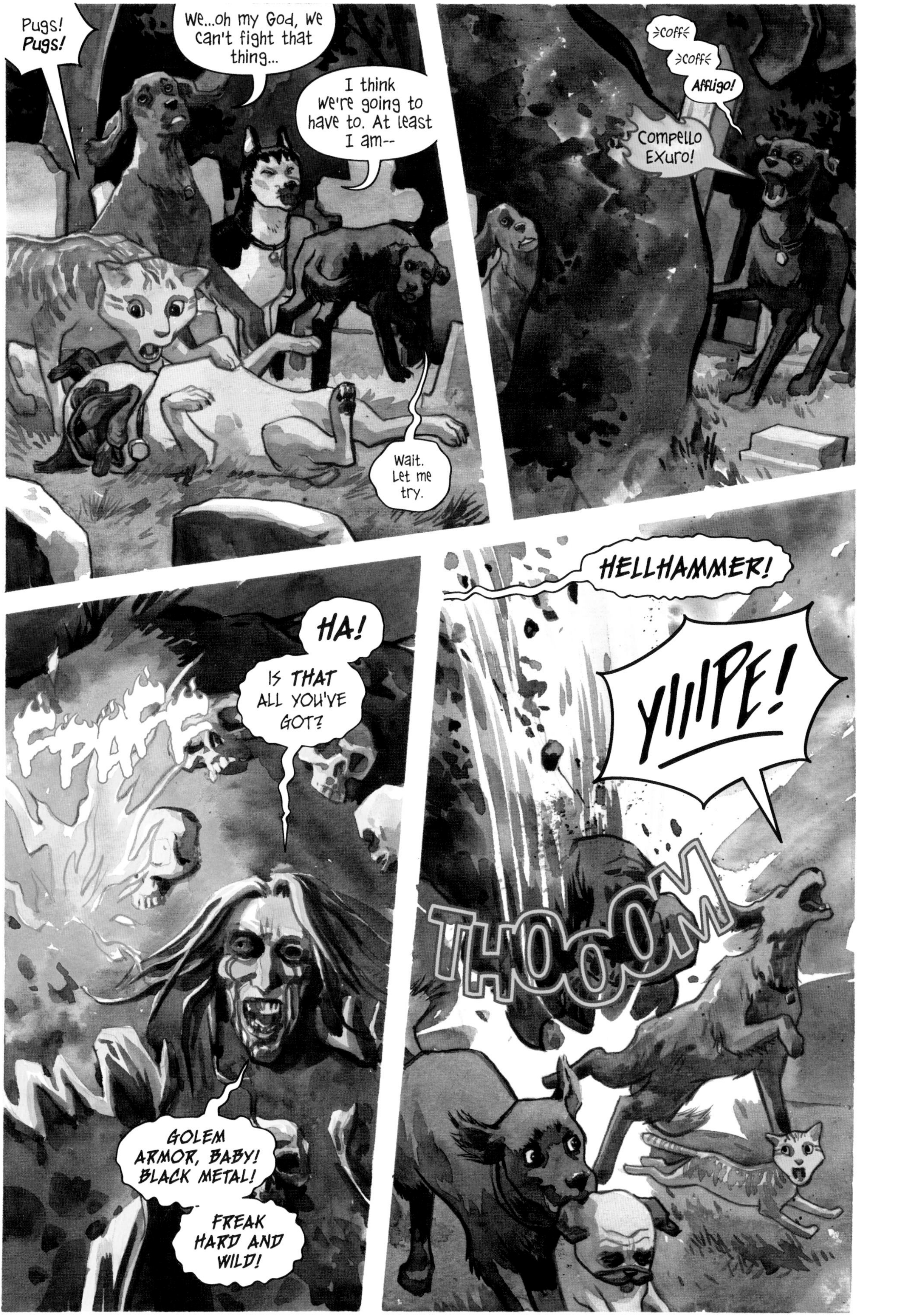
Pugs! Pugs!
We...oh my God, we can't fight that thing...
I think we're going to have to. At least I am--
Wait. Let me try.
»coff«
»coff«
Affligo!
Compello Exuro!
HA!
IS THAT ALL YOU'VE GOT?
GOLEM ARMOR, BABY! BLACK METAL!
FREAK HARD AND WILD!
HELLHAMMER!
YIIIPE!
THOOOOM

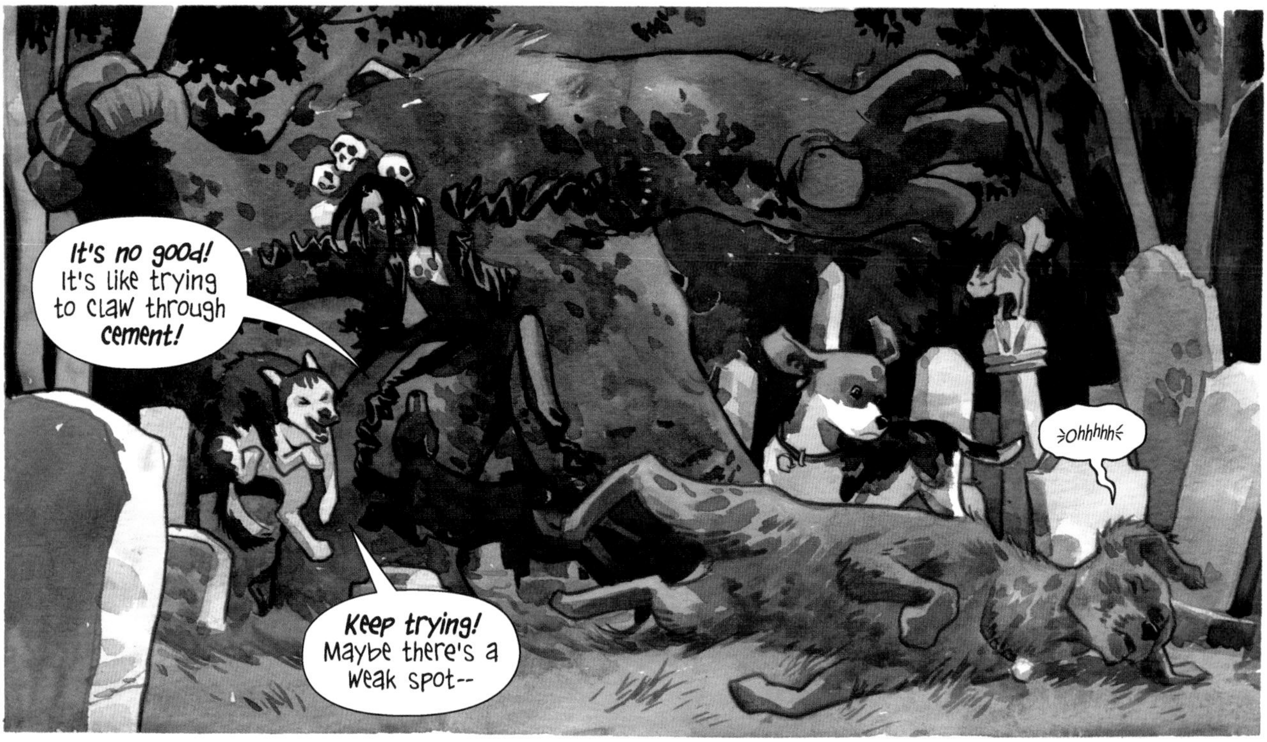
It's no good! It's like trying to claw through cement!
Keep trying! Maybe there's a weak spot--
≥Ohhhhh≤

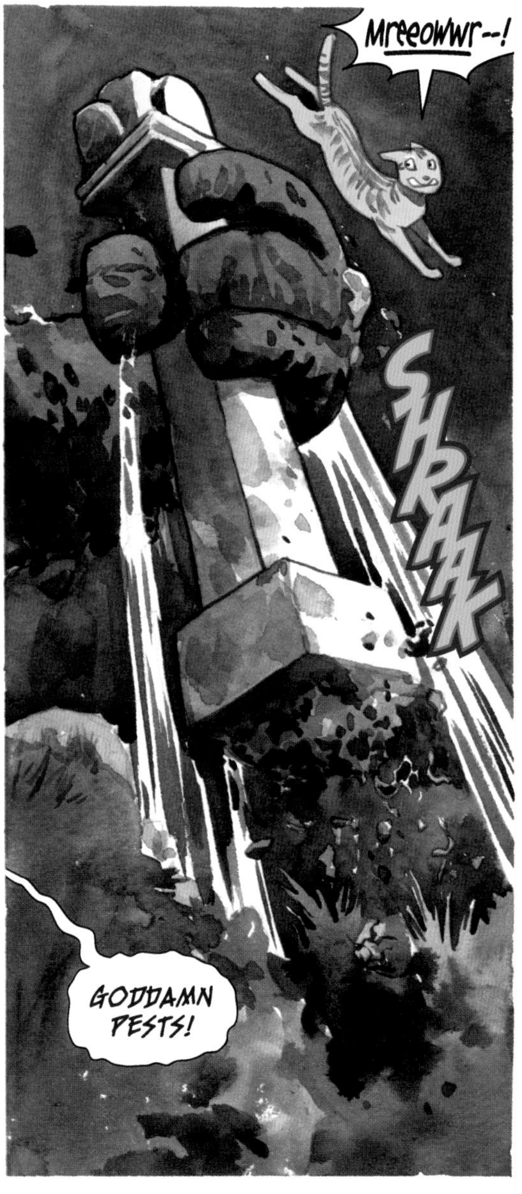
Mreeowwr--!
SHRAAK
GODDAMN PESTS!

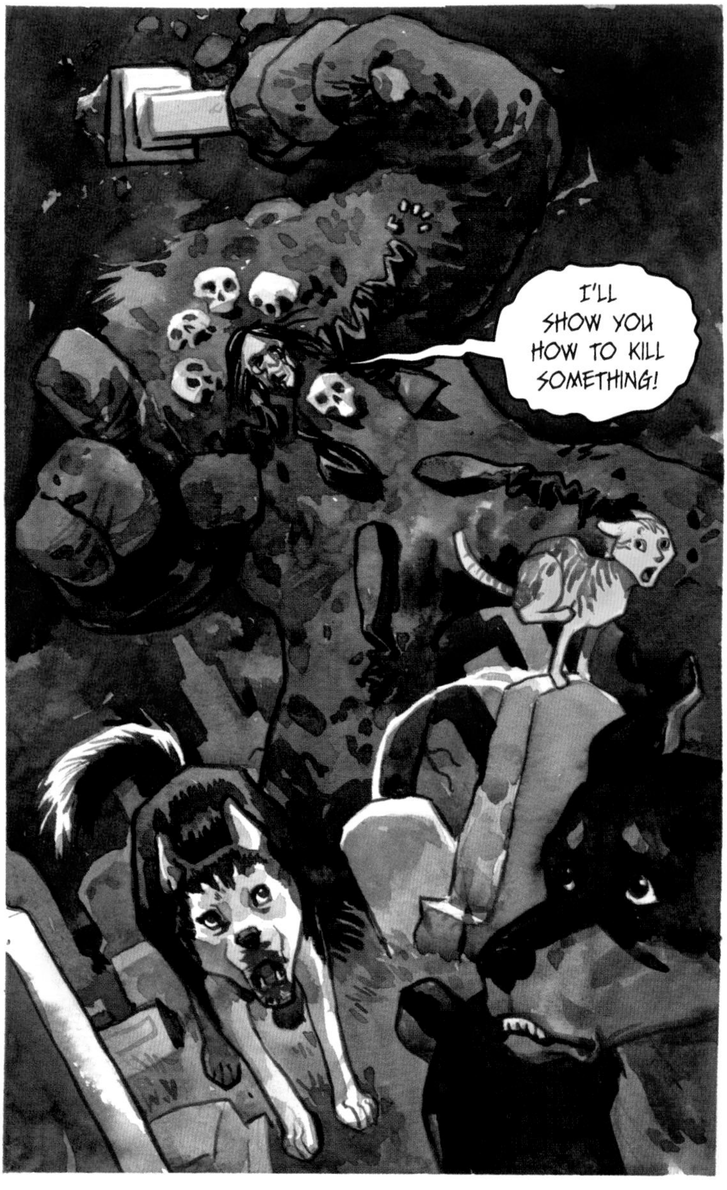
I'LL SHOW YOU HOW TO KILL SOMETHING!

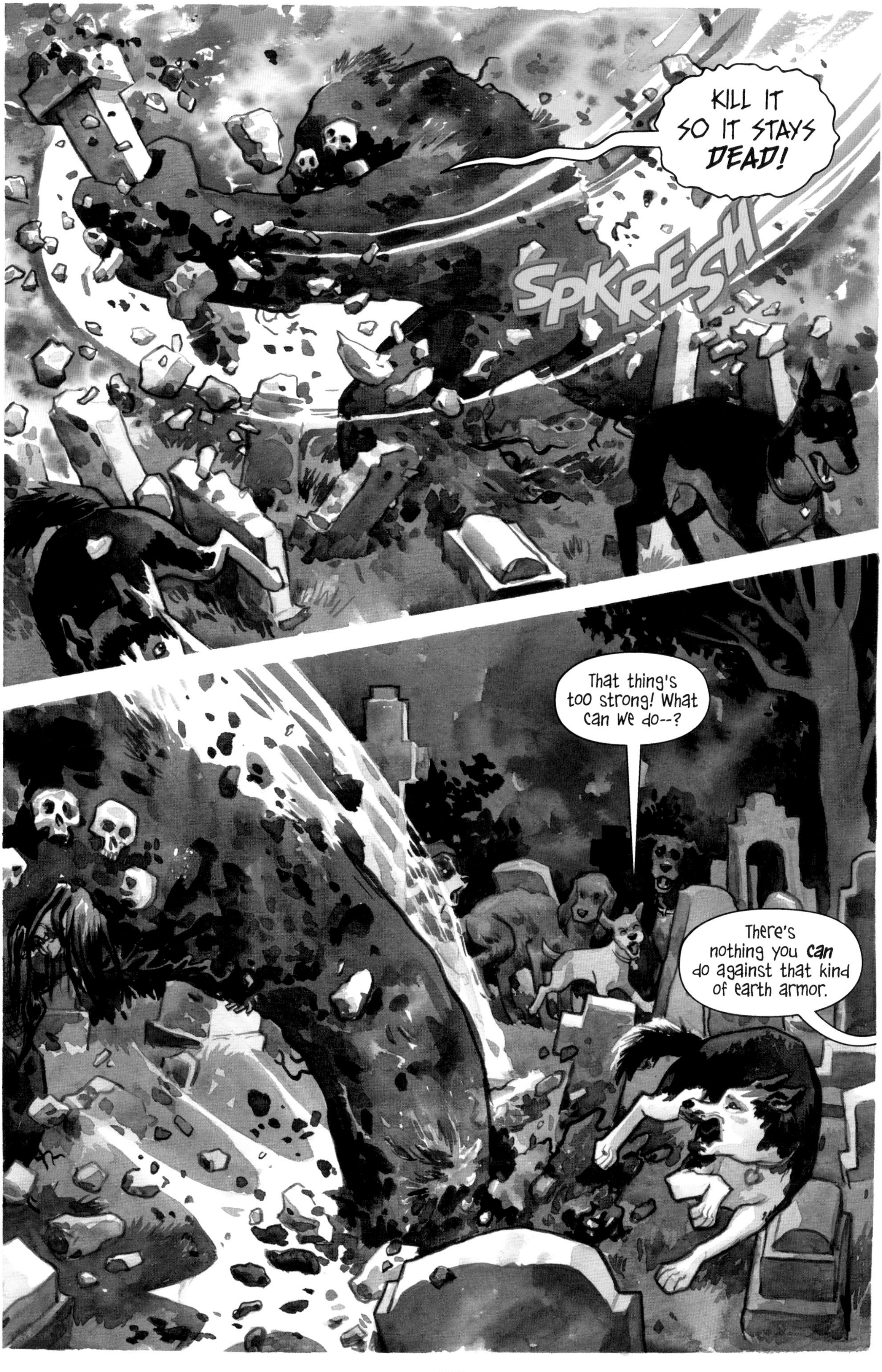
KILL IT SO IT STAYS DEAD!
SPKRESH
That thing's too strong! What can we do--?
There's nothing you can do against that kind of earth armor.

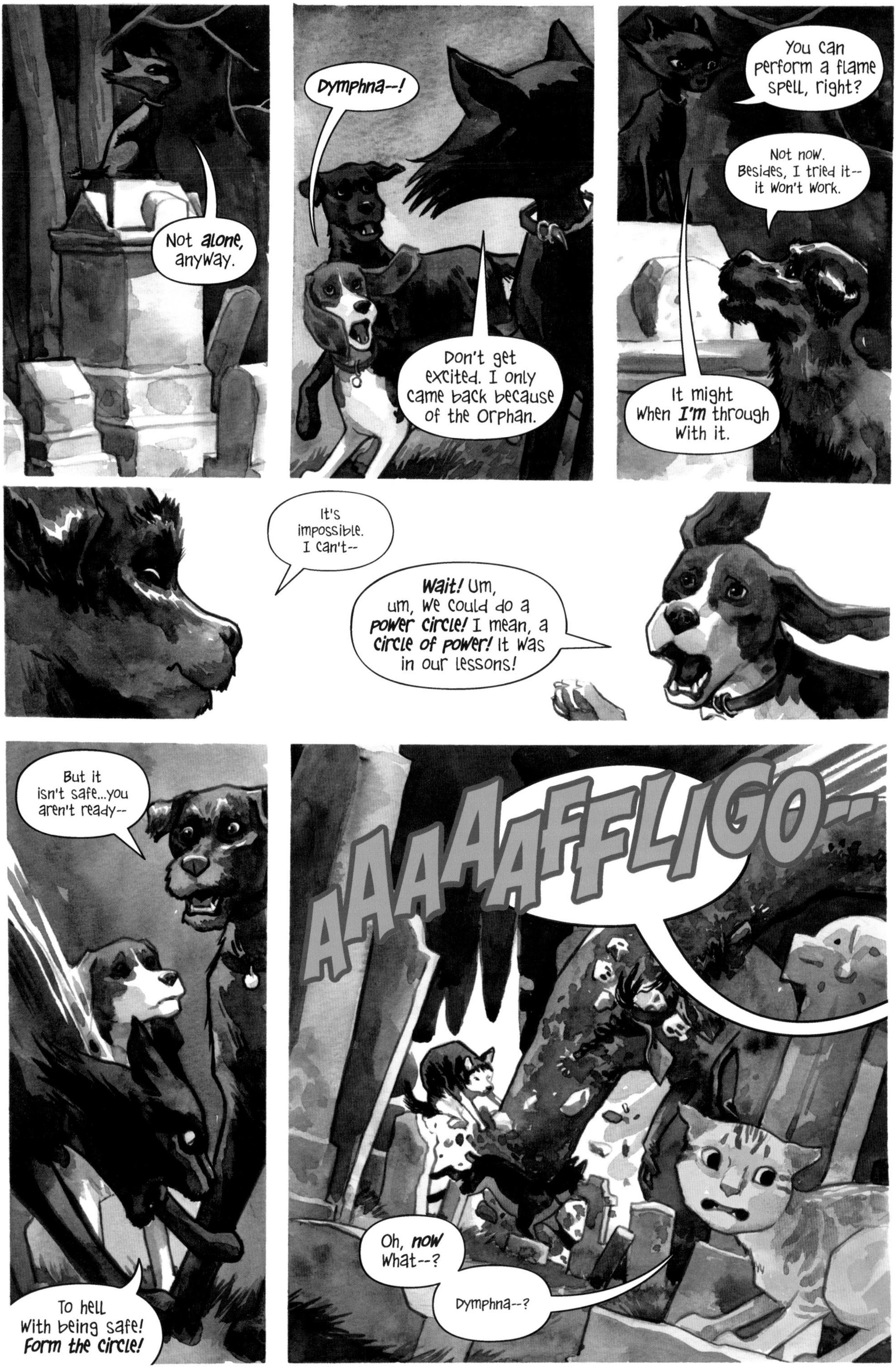

Not alone, anyway.
Dymphna--!
Don't get excited. I only came back because of the Orphan.
You can perform a flame spell, right?
Not now. Besides, I tried it--it won't work.
It might when I'm through with it.
It's impossible. I can't--
Wait! Um, um, we could do a power circle! I mean, a circle of power! It was in our lessons!
But it isn't safe...you aren't ready--
To hell with being safe! Form the circle!
AAAAAFFLIGO--
Oh, now what--?
Dymphna--?

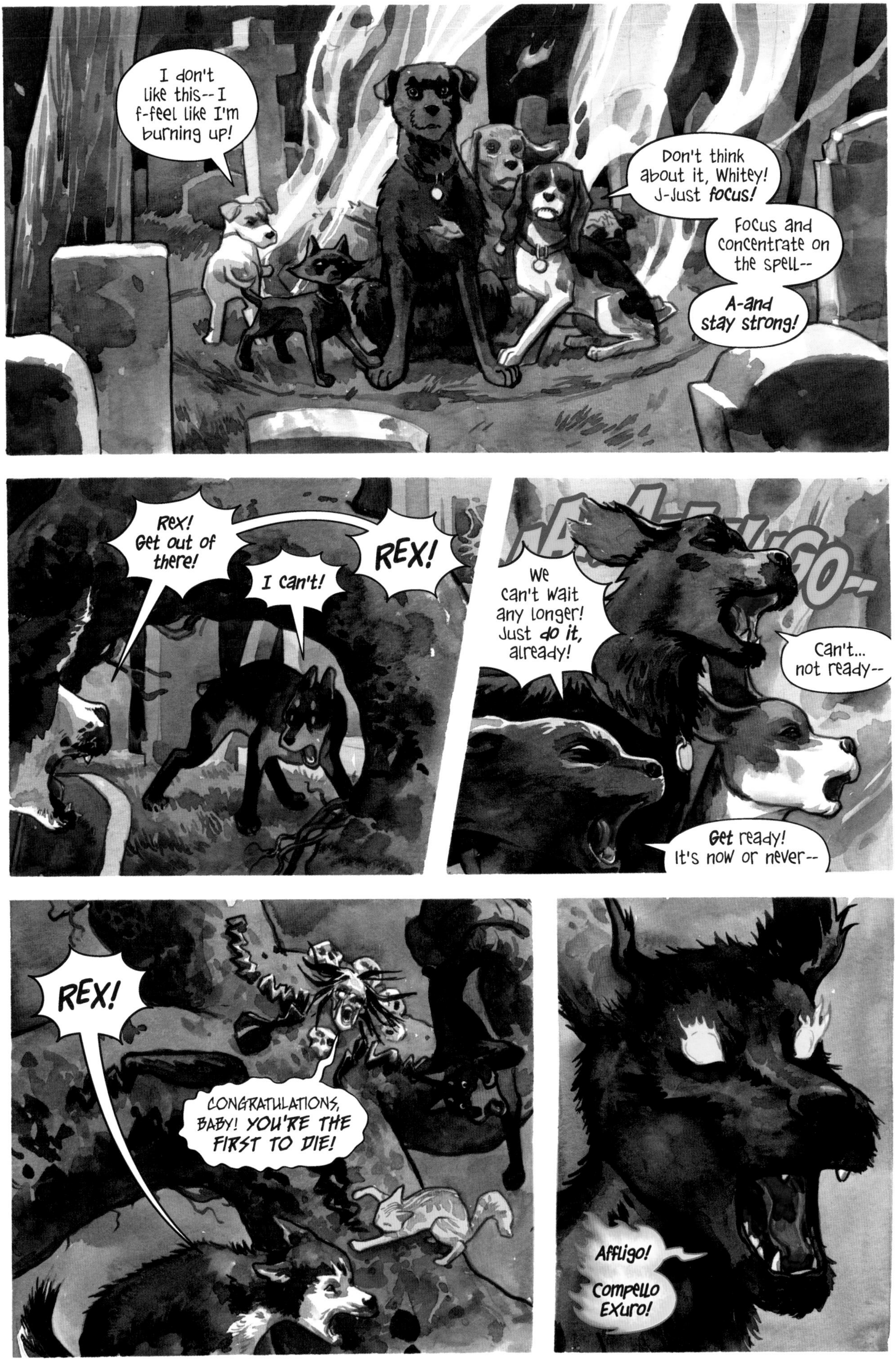
I don't like this--I f-feel like I'm burning up!
Don't think about it, Whitey! J-Just focus!
Focus and concentrate on the spell--
A-and stay strong!
Rex! Get out of there!
I can't!
REX!
We can't wait any longer! Just do it, already!
Can't... not ready--
Get ready! It's now or never--
REX!
CONGRATULATIONS, BABY! YOU'RE THE FIRST TO DIE!
Affligo!
Compello Exuro!

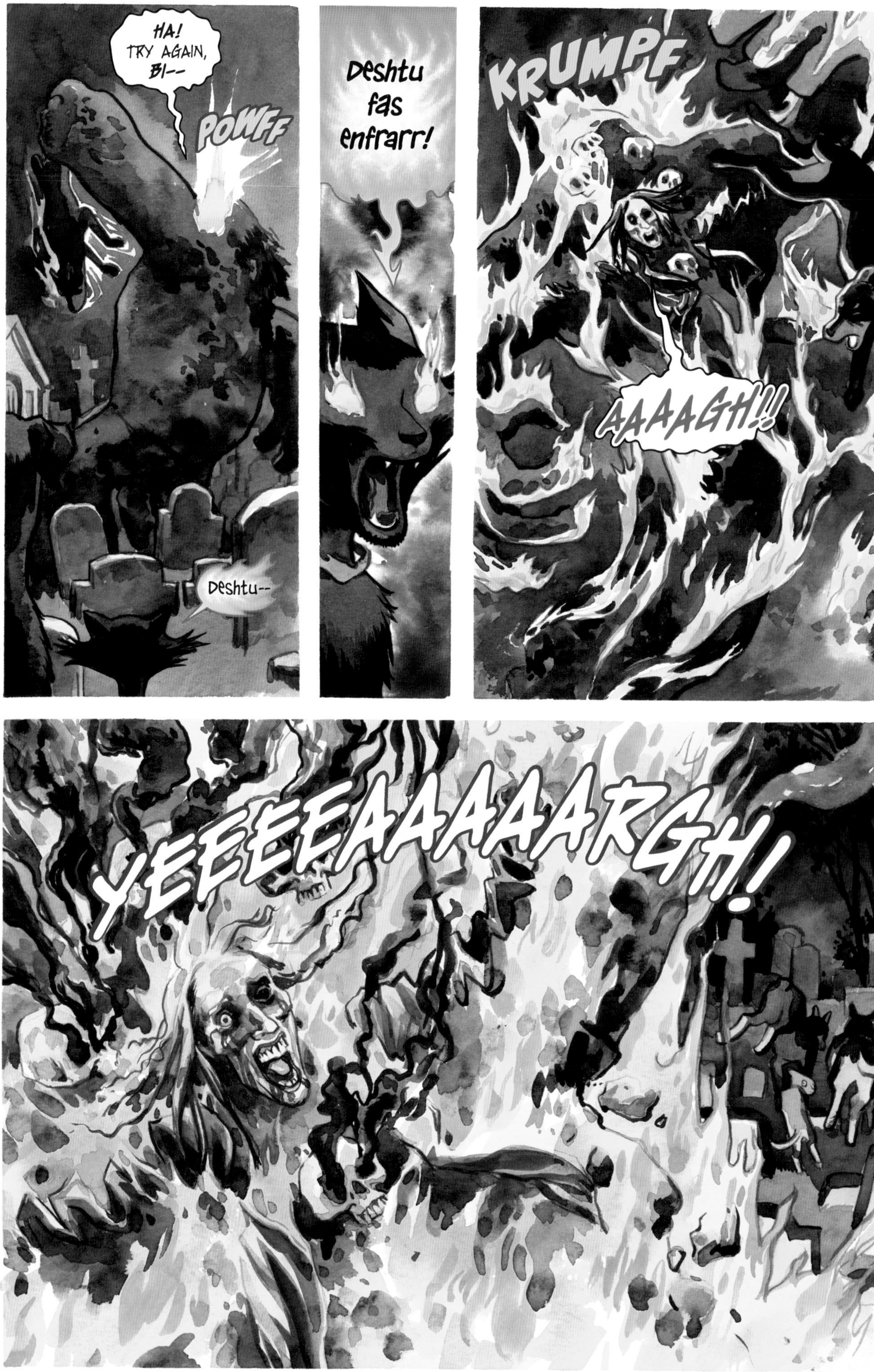
HA! TRY AGAIN, BI--
POWFF
Deshtu--
Deshtu fas enfrarr!
KRUMPF
AAAAGH!!
YEEEEAAAAAARGH!

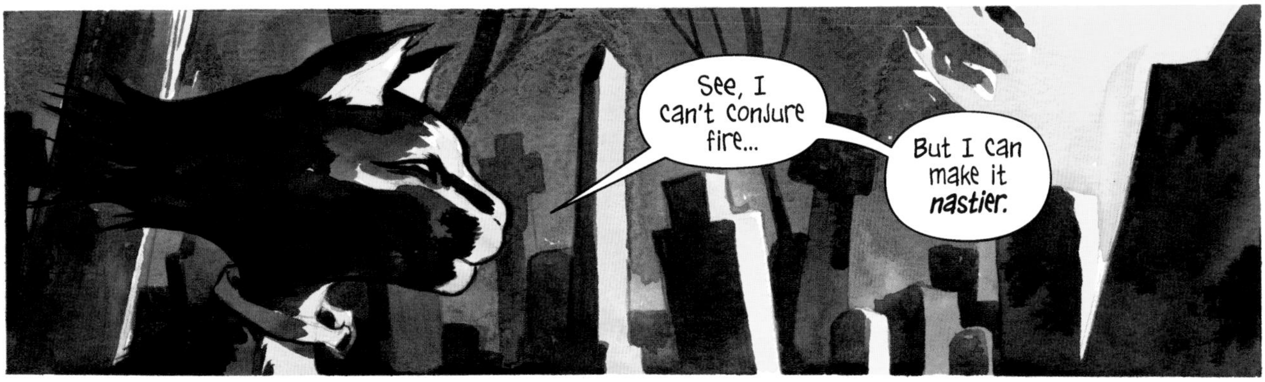
See, I can't conjure fire...
But I can make it *nastier.*

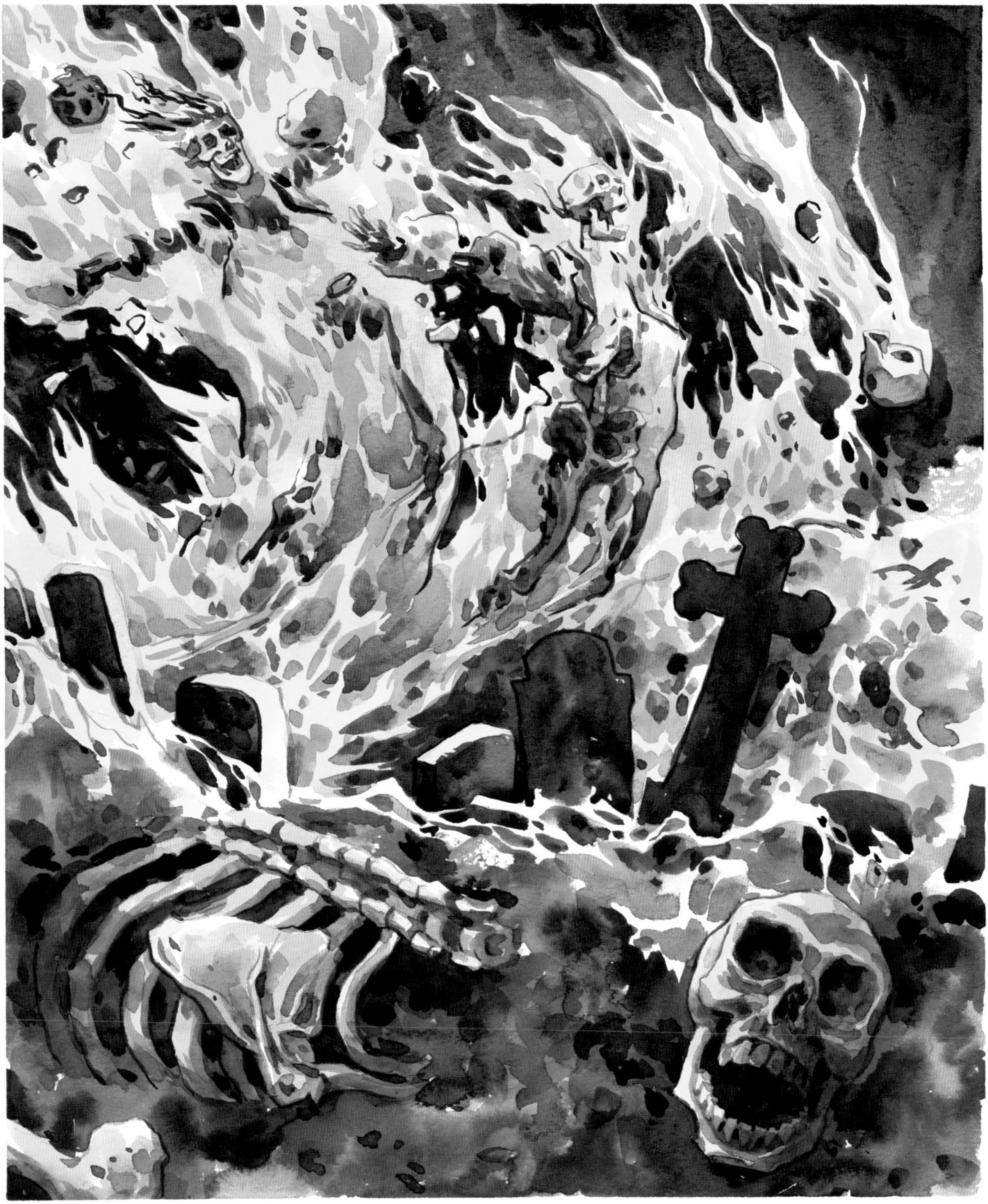

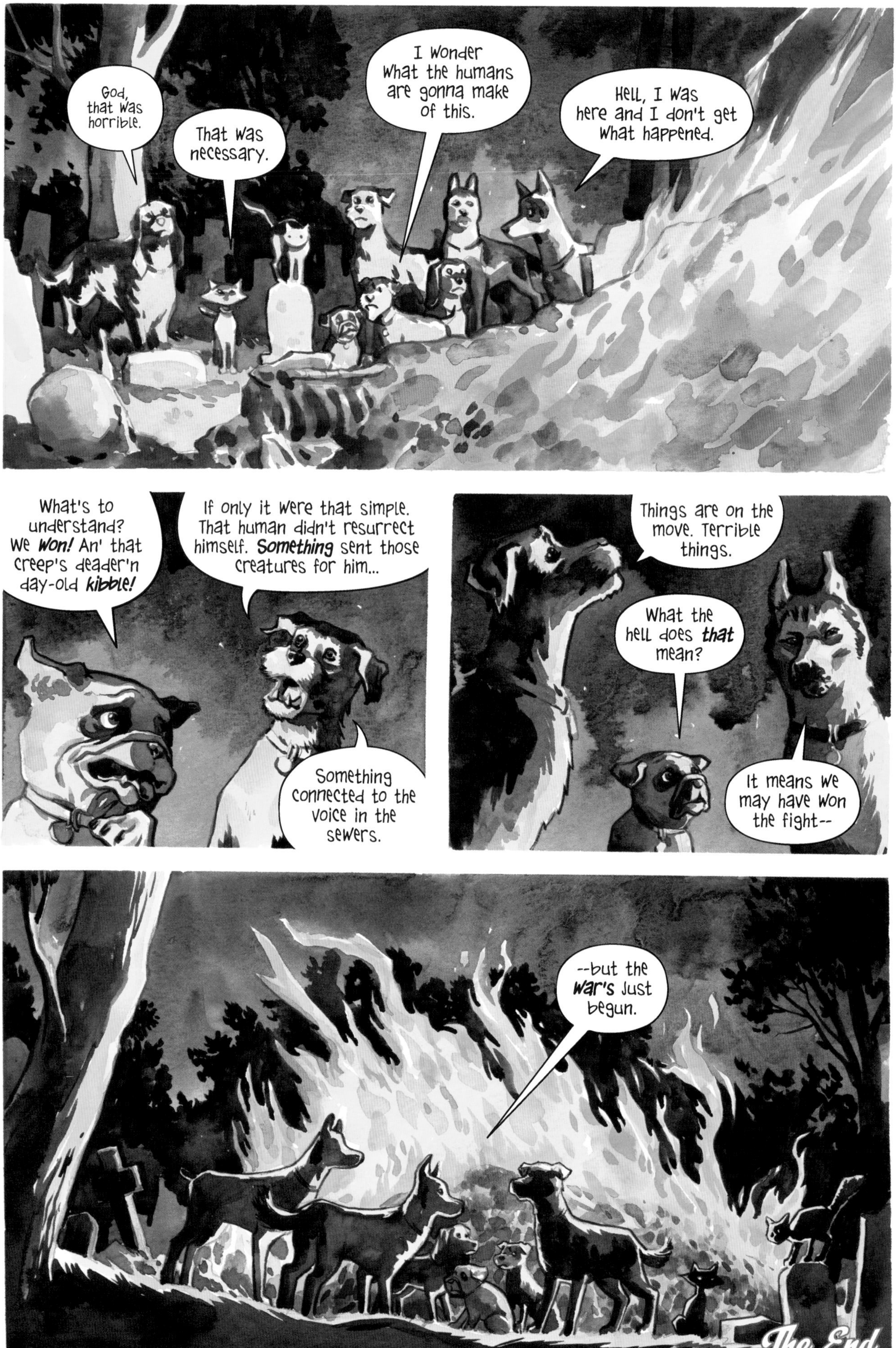
God, that was horrible.
That was necessary.
I wonder what the humans are gonna make of this.
Hell, I was here and I don't get what happened.
What's to understand? We **won!** An' that creep's deader'n day-old **kibble!**
If only it were that simple. That human didn't resurrect himself. **Something** sent those creatures for him...
Something connected to the voice in the sewers.
Things are on the move. Terrible things.
What the hell does **that** mean?
It means we may have won the fight--
--but the **war's** just begun.
The End

AFTERWORD

I~n 2003 **scott allie asked me** if I would be interested in contributing to a horror anthology he was putting together called *The Dark Horse Book of Hauntings*. I was more than interested, because it was an opportunity to do something I'd always wanted to do in comics, which was to write a horror story. No, not a horrible story—I'd already written a batch of those. A horror story. Creepy, ooky, mysterious, spooky, that sort of thing. I also really needed the work.

I wanted to write a haunted-house story, but not along traditional lines. After a few false starts I hit on the idea of a haunted *doghouse*, which became my pitch for "Stray." Scott liked it and wanted me to draw it. I draw animals about as well as I break-dance, but Scott believed in me. Which was really nice. Luckily for us all, I convinced him to approach Jill Thompson instead.

I wrote "Stray" with Jill's art in mind, specifically the lovely watercolors she painted for her *Scary Godmother* books. I wanted "Stray" to have that storybook feel, and I knew Jill could render the animals beautifully and, perhaps more importantly, believably. I was thrilled—thrilled, I tell you—when Jill agreed to illustrate "Stray." She also asked that I put a Pug in the cast, something else I'm eternally grateful for. I can't picture this series without Jill—or Pugs, for that matter.

"Stray" was a single short story, only eight pages long. There were no further adventures planned for these characters. But the response to the story was very positive, and eventually our "Stray" gave birth to a litter of three more anthology stories, each one longer than the last, until "A Dog and His Boy" came in at twenty pages, practically a complete comic. While working on that story, Scott, Jill, and I started talking about doing a dedicated series with the characters. That's when we realized we didn't actually have a name for our series. Up to that point we generally referred to it as "those dog and cat stories Jill and Evan are doing." We considered several titles, some seriously (*Animal Rites, Animal Tales*—both problematic), some not so seriously (*Power Dogs, Animal Investigation Team Fight! Fight! Fight!* And, courtesy of Sarah, *Pugs and His Pals*). *Beasts of Burden* was the best I could come up with, which is why I named the town Burden Hill in the last short story. We're all used to it now, and only a few people have groaned out loud because of it.

So, that's how we got here. I still can't believe it's been seven years since we started, that Jill agreed to partner up with me on it, or that readers have taken to what we've been doing so enthusiastically. My sincere thanks to Scott Allie for making all this happen, for his support and guidance, and for his patience in putting up with me. Thanks also to Sierra Hahn and Freddye Lins for making things happen (and also for putting up with me), to Mike Richardson for his early and enthusiastic support of these stories, to Jason Arthur for his swell lettering work, and, of course, to Jill for her incredible work in bringing Burden Hill to life. Finally, I want to thank my wife, Sarah Dyer, who collaborated with me on the script for "A Dog and His Boy" and whose input helped immeasurably throughout the series. How she puts up with me, I do not know.

Well, that's it for now. I hope you've enjoyed your time in Burden Hill, and I hope you'll be back with us again sometime soon.

Evan Dorkin
Staten Island, New York
January 28, 2010

SKETCHBOOK

WITH NOTES BY JILL THOMPSON

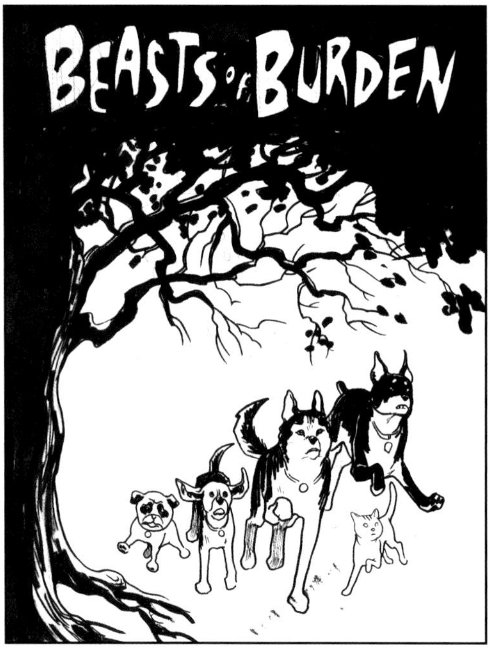
BEASTS of BURDEN

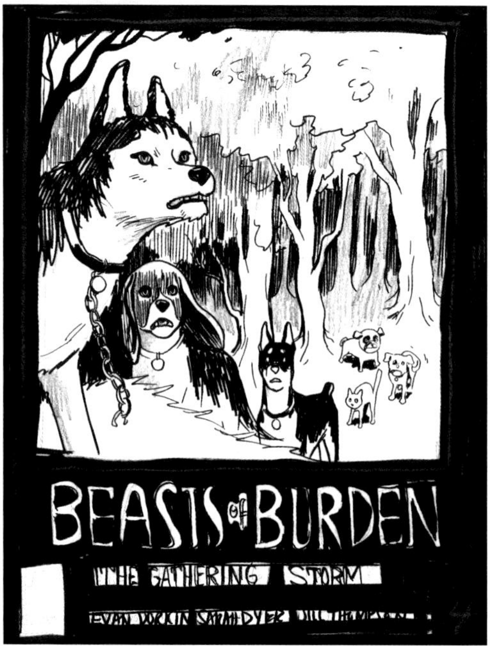
BEASTS of BURDEN
THE GATHERING STORM
EVAN DORKIN SARAH DYER

These are some of my cover sketches for *Beasts of Burden* #1 ("The Gathering Storm," the fifth story in this book). I usually don't do such detailed sketches, as it tends to take the wind out of my sails when I get to the painting part. The more finished the sketch, the more I feel like I've already finished the piece! Funny!

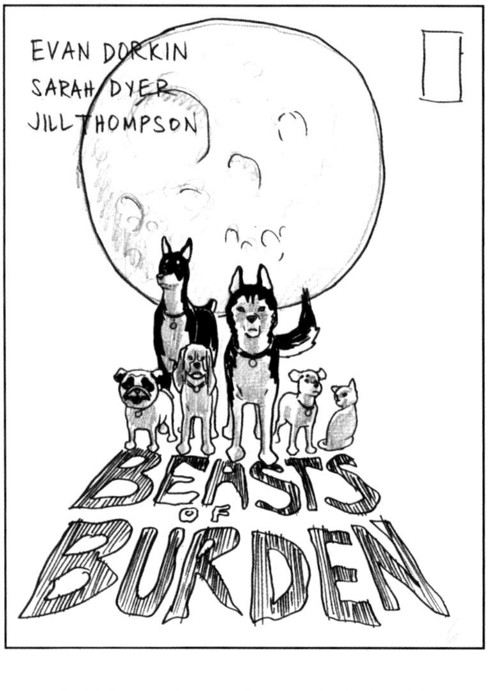
EVAN DORKIN
SARAH DYER
JILL THOMPSON
BEASTS of BURDEN

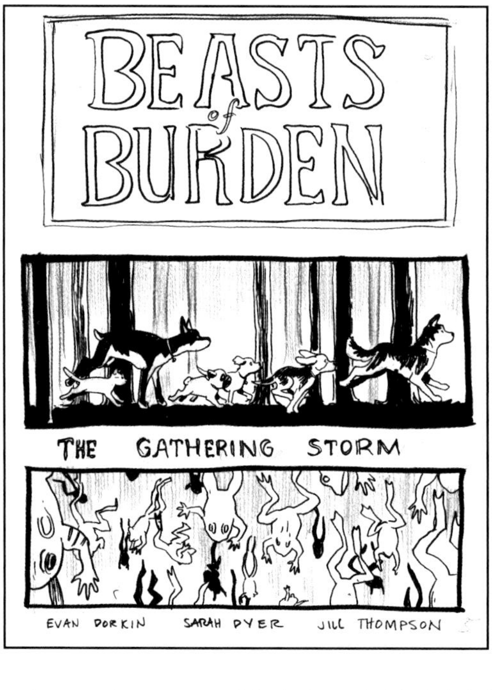
BEASTS of BURDEN
THE GATHERING STORM
EVAN DORKIN SARAH DYER JILL THOMPSON

I was inspired by old-fashioned "boys' adventure" books for all of my cover designs here—with the exception of the third one, which kinda looked like a *Dawn of the Dead* poster once I got done with it, and that's probably why it was not chosen by Scott or Evan! *Ha!* I am a huge fan of using the white of the paper as a design element, and sketches #1 and #3 would have had completely white backgrounds . . . The final cover to the first issue is on the facing page.

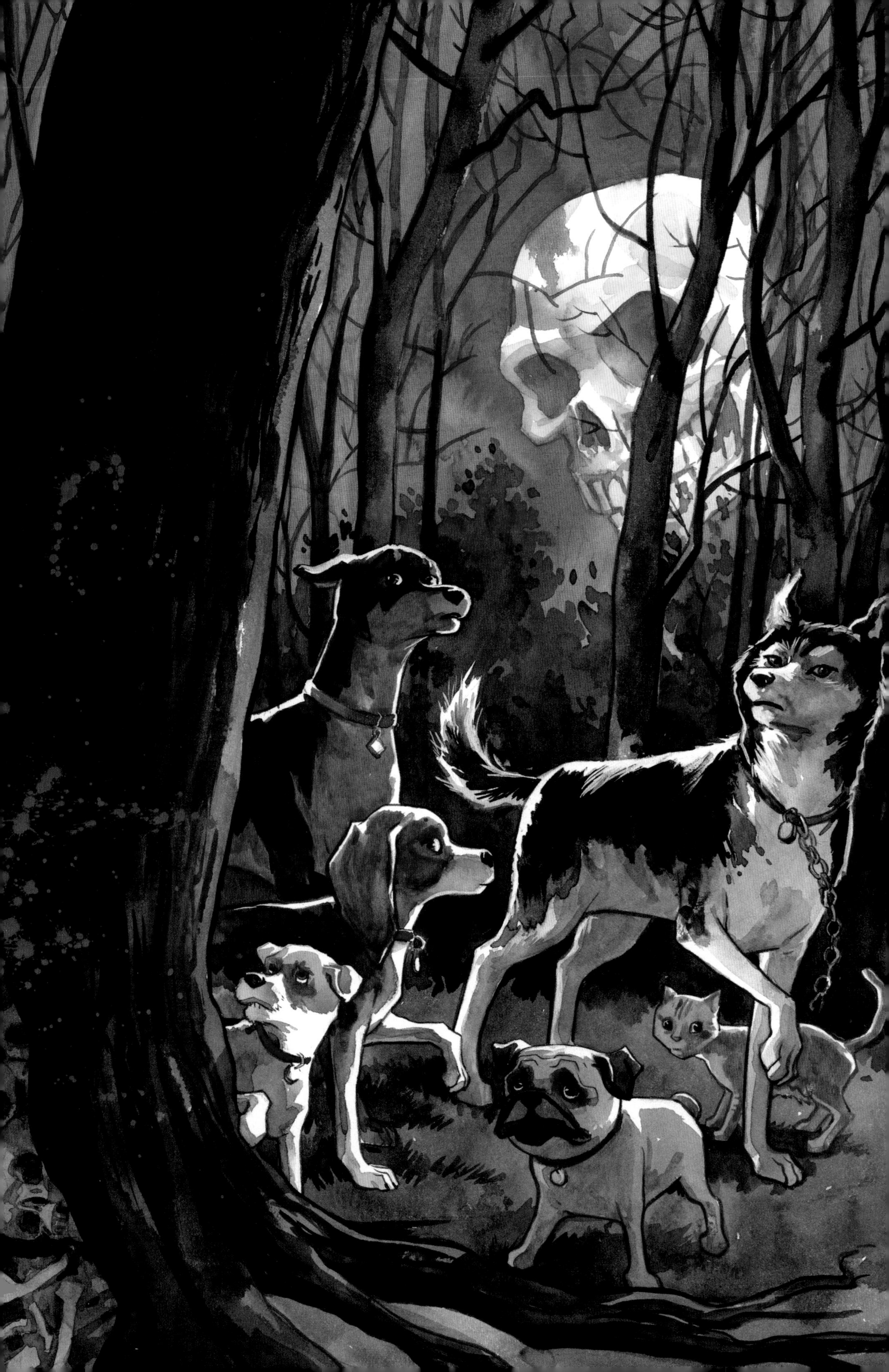

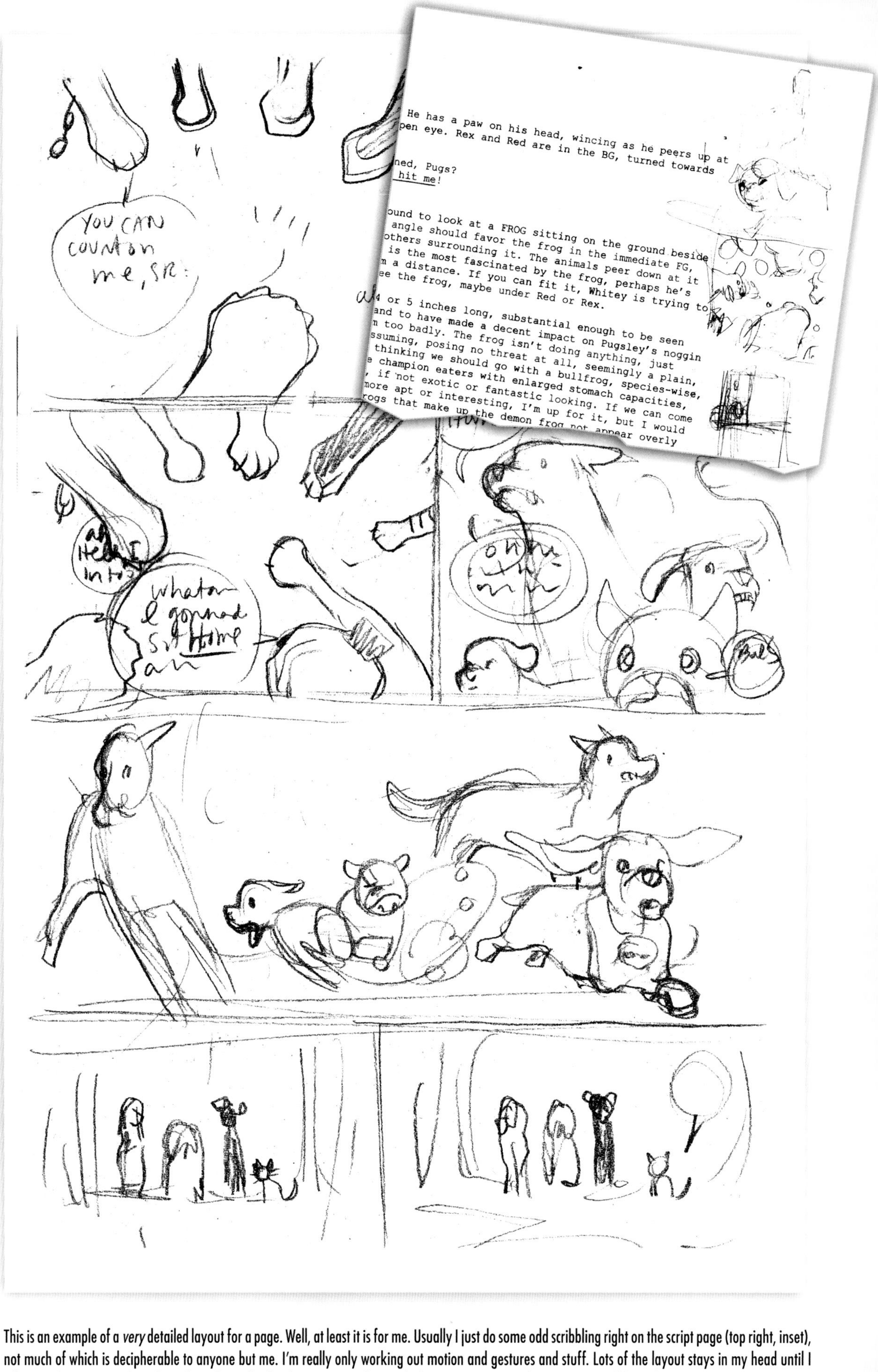
He has a paw on his head, wincing as he peers up at
pen eye. Rex and Red are in the BG, turned towards
ned, Pugs?
hit me!
ound to look at a FROG sitting on the ground beside
angle should favor the frog in the immediate FG,
others surrounding it. The animals peer down at it
is the most fascinated by the frog, perhaps he's
m a distance. If you can fit it, Whitey is trying to
ee the frog, maybe under Red or Rex.
4 or 5 inches long, substantial enough to be seen
and to have made a decent impact on Pugsley's noggin
n too badly. The frog isn't doing anything, just
ssuming, posing no threat at all, seemingly a plain,
thinking we should go with a bullfrog, species-wise,
e champion eaters with enlarged stomach capacities,
, if not exotic or fantastic looking. If we can come
more apt or interesting, I'm up for it, but I would
rogs that make up the demon frog not appear overly
YOU CAN COUNT ON ME, SR.

This is an example of a *very* detailed layout for a page. Well, at least it is for me. Usually I just do some odd scribbling right on the script page (top right, inset), not much of which is decipherable to anyone but me. I'm really only working out motion and gestures and stuff. Lots of the layout stays in my head until I take pencil to paper. And it's there that I do my final tinkering to see what works for me. Sometimes I have a great scribble and thumbnail only to abandon it because I could not make it work on the bigger paper. Crazy? Different? But it works when I'm creating! Not recommended for the fledgling comics artist.

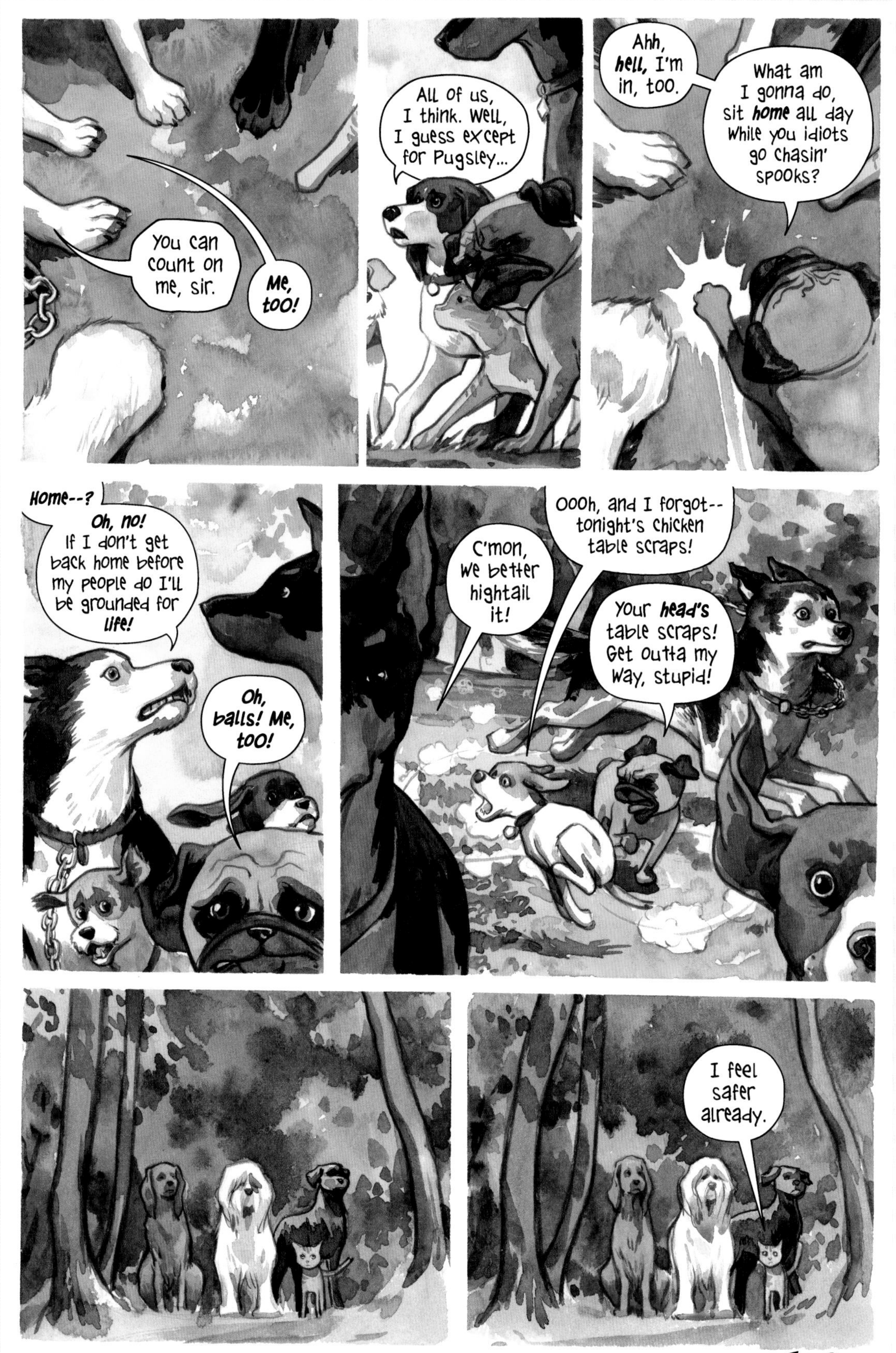
You can count on me, sir.
Me, too!
All of us, I think. Well, I guess except for Pugsley...
Ahh, hell, I'm in, too.
What am I gonna do, sit home all day while you idiots go chasin' spooks?
Home--?
Oh, no! If I don't get back home before my people do I'll be grounded for life!
Oh, balls! Me, too!
C'mon, we better hightail it!
Oooh, and I forgot-- tonight's chicken table scraps!
Your head's table scraps! Get outta my way, stupid!
I feel safer already.
The End

This is the finished page based on the thumbnail opposite. After some minor panel rearrangement and some tweaks to body language to keep the reader's eye moving where I wanted it, I was good to go!

Some more cover sketches, for the second issue ("Lost," the sixth chapter in this book). You can see that I got looser in my layout here, abandoning the inked step. I wanted to keep my energies inside and have them come out in the painting and not in the preliminary work. I'm an impatient person in certain respects. Mostly when I draw. Oh, okay— in much of everything! I like my gratification instantly! That's probably why watercolor is a perfect medium for my self-expression. You can't go back in and monkey around with it much after the fact. Boom—you put it down and it's there, with *just* a *liiiiitle* time to fool with it and make it do what you require, and then your window of opportunity is closed. Oils drive me crazy—I shmoosh them and smear them and they never dry—and acrylics? They dry fast like plastic, and I can't manipulate them as much as I like. And I want my results *right now*!! (Where's a smiley-face emoticon when you need it?)

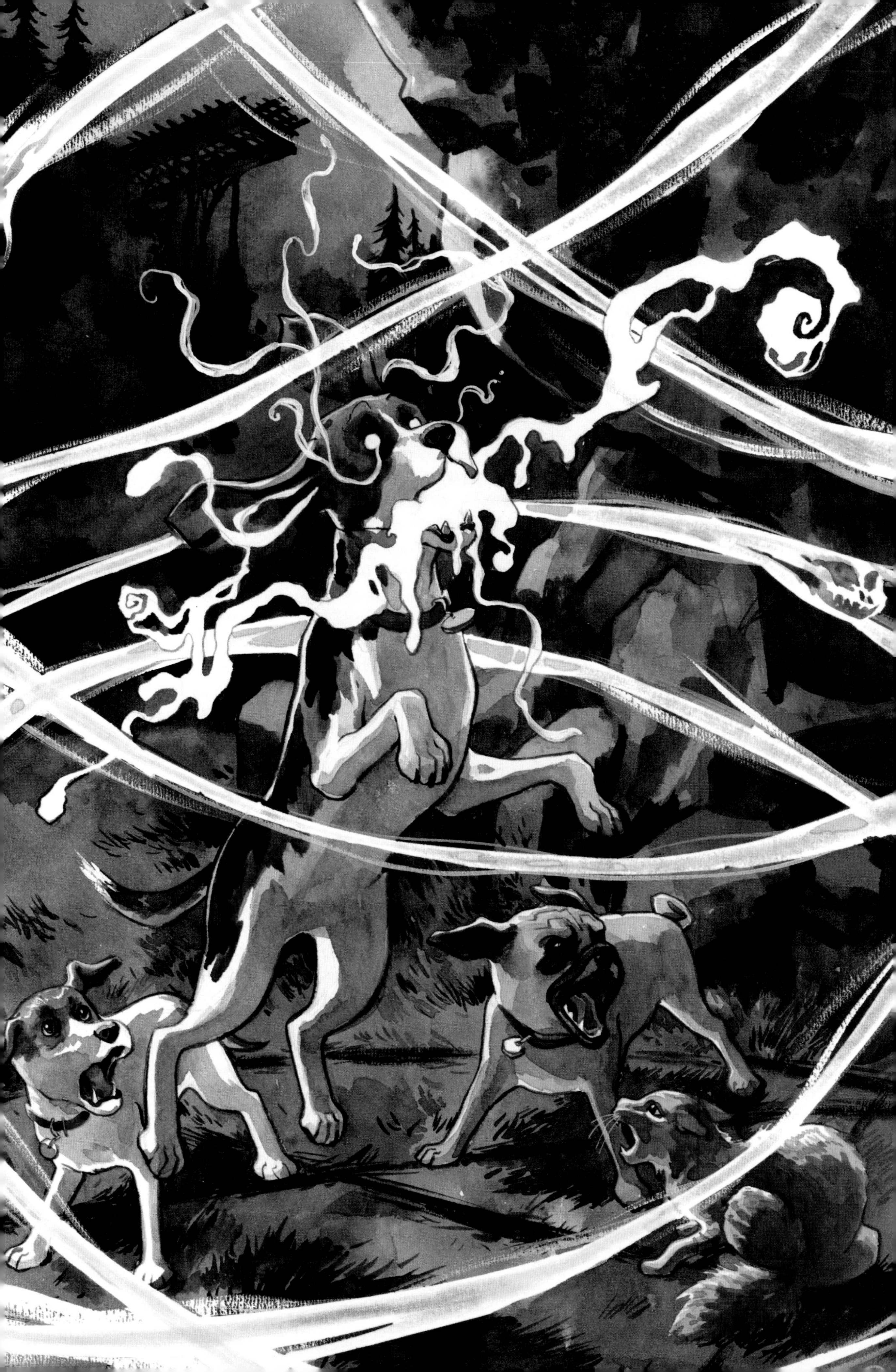

The Swifties cat gang. Even though we saw these guys for only two panels in "Something Whiskered This Way Comes," I knew we'd be seeing them again, so I wanted to draw some kit-kats that were differently patterned than the Orphan and Dymphna. And something that would not be too difficult to paint over and over again. Muggsy's and Johnny Whiskers's fur will probably have me cursing sometime in the future, but I rarely see a calico cat, and I wanted to include one of those. And Johnny Whiskers? He's based on dear, departed Lucien (or Lukey Lucan as I used to call him), one of the best felines to ever chirp and eat grasshoppers and walk the face of the earth.

The Orphan is based on Sammy, a spunky, rough 'n' tumble ginger cat who lives across the street. And the Getaway Kid is George, from a few doors down.

Below, pencil sketches for the cover of "Something Whiskered." Even though I liked all the designs, I really was pulling for the fourth one—the close-up of the cat's eye with the rats reflected in it . . .

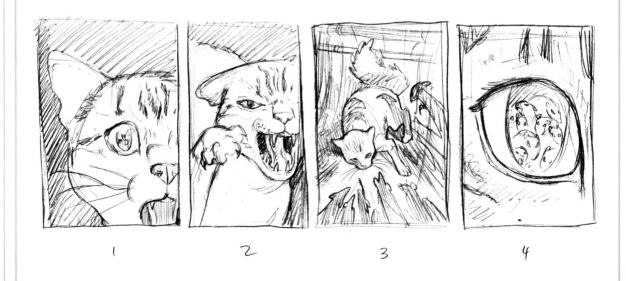

1   2   3   4

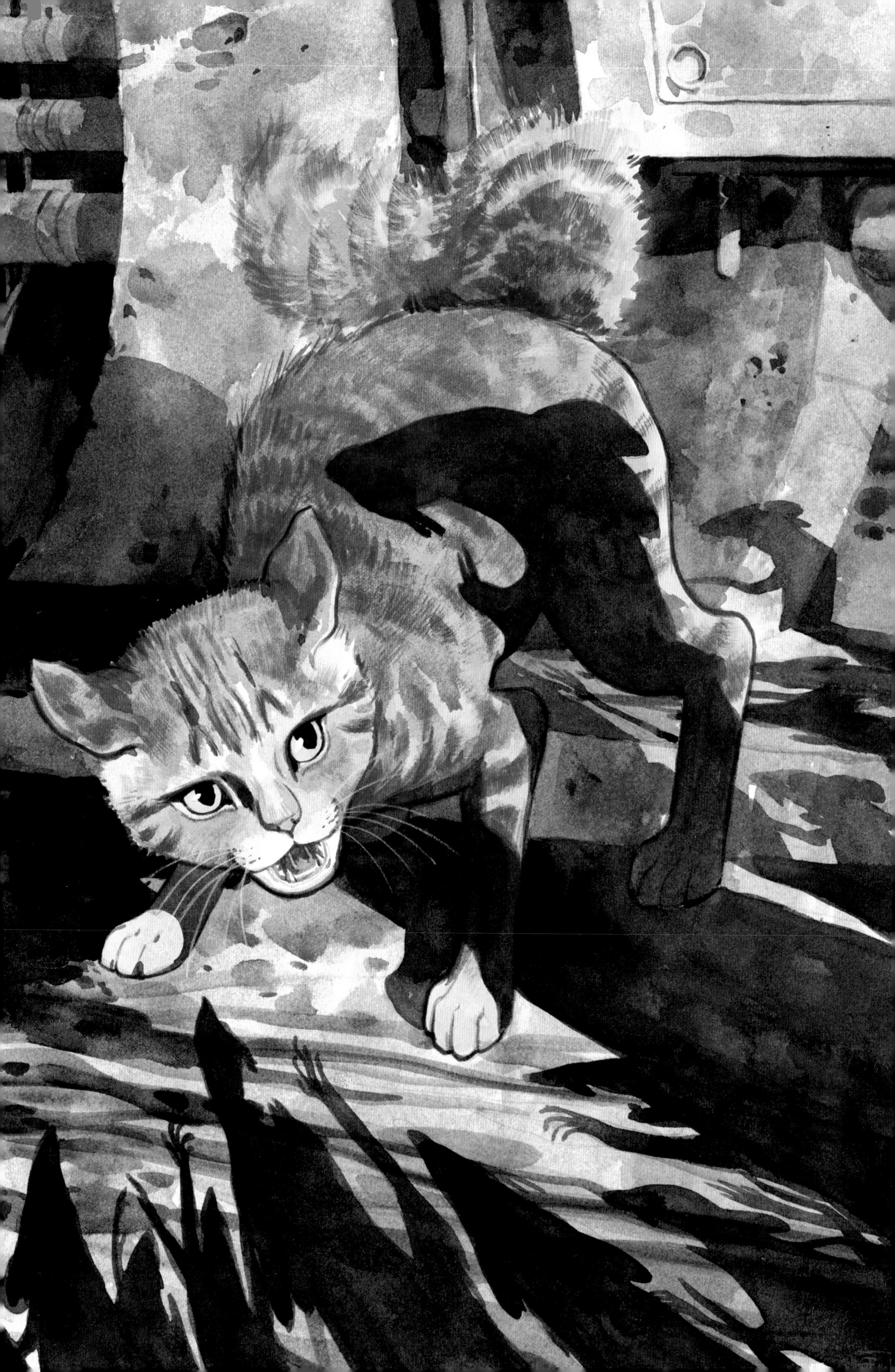

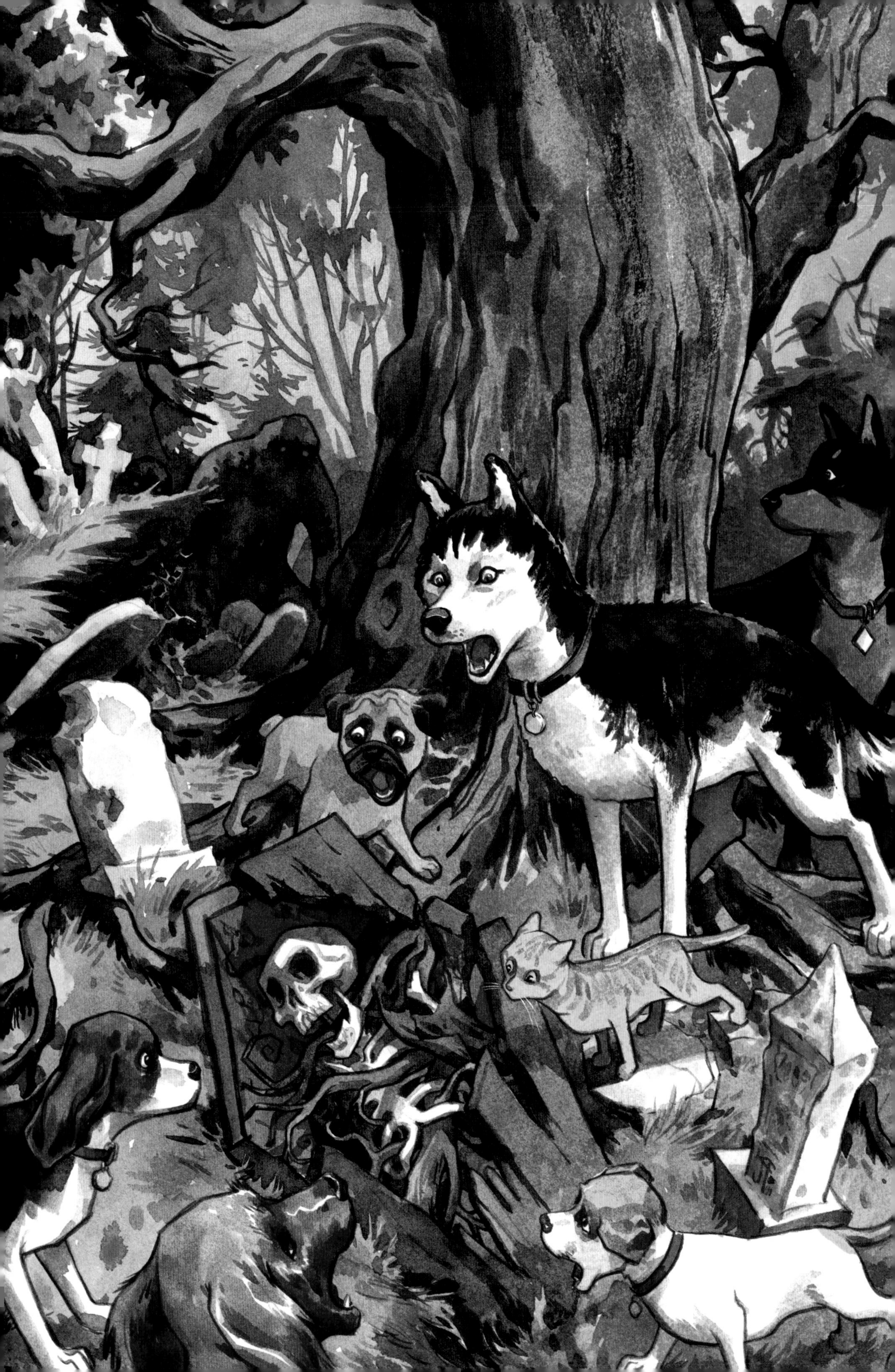

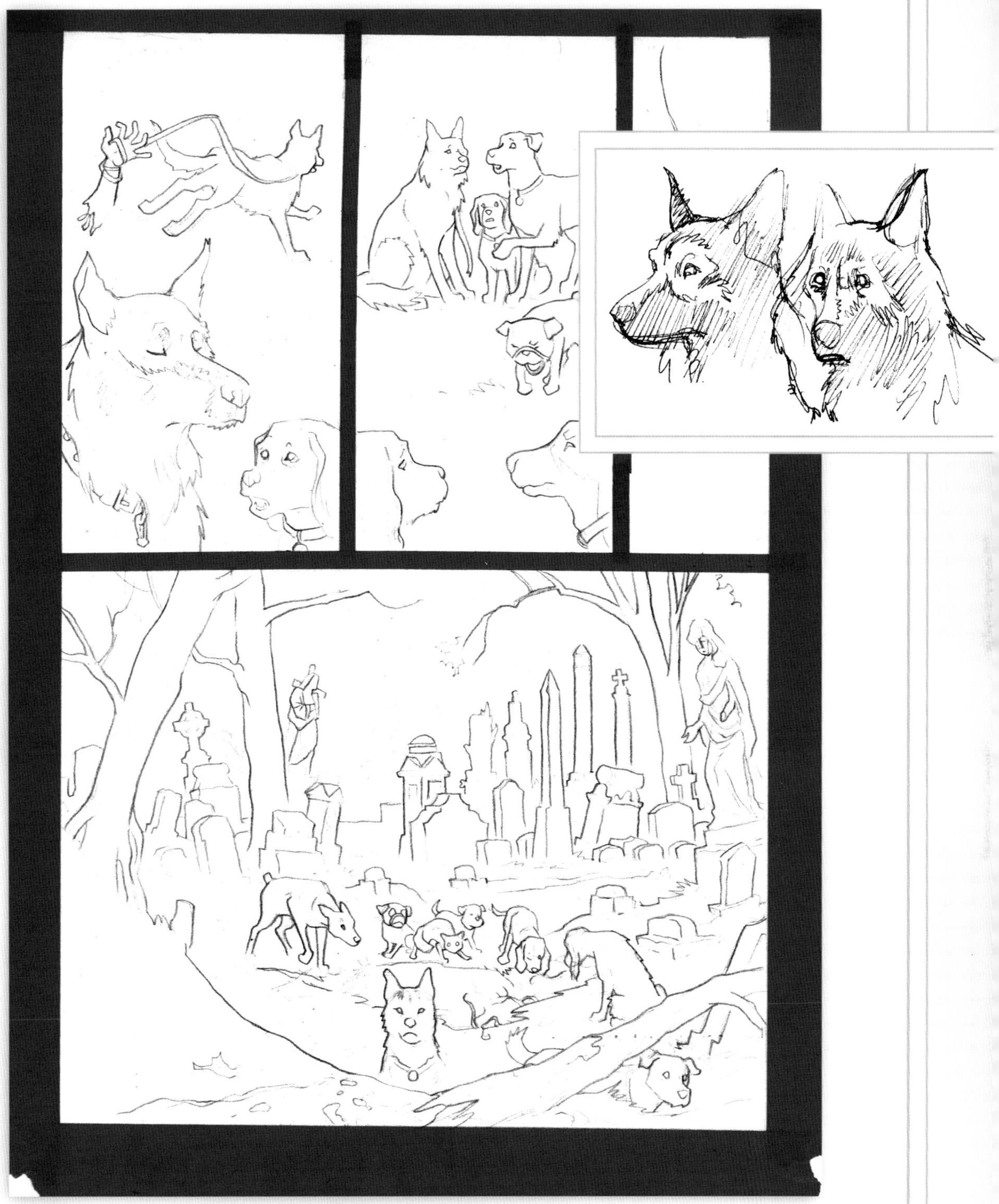

FACING: Cover to the fourth issue, "Grave Happenings."

INSET, TOP RIGHT: Ballpoint-pen doodle of Digger, the graveyard dog. That was skritched right on the top of the script.

ABOVE: This is a page ready to be painted. This is what I consider a tightly penciled page. The blue painter's tape keeps my edges and panel borders crisp. I don't really shade in any dark areas with pencil so much anymore. Maybe I should—it would force me to be bolder in value choices right off the bat . . . Must be gettin' lazy!

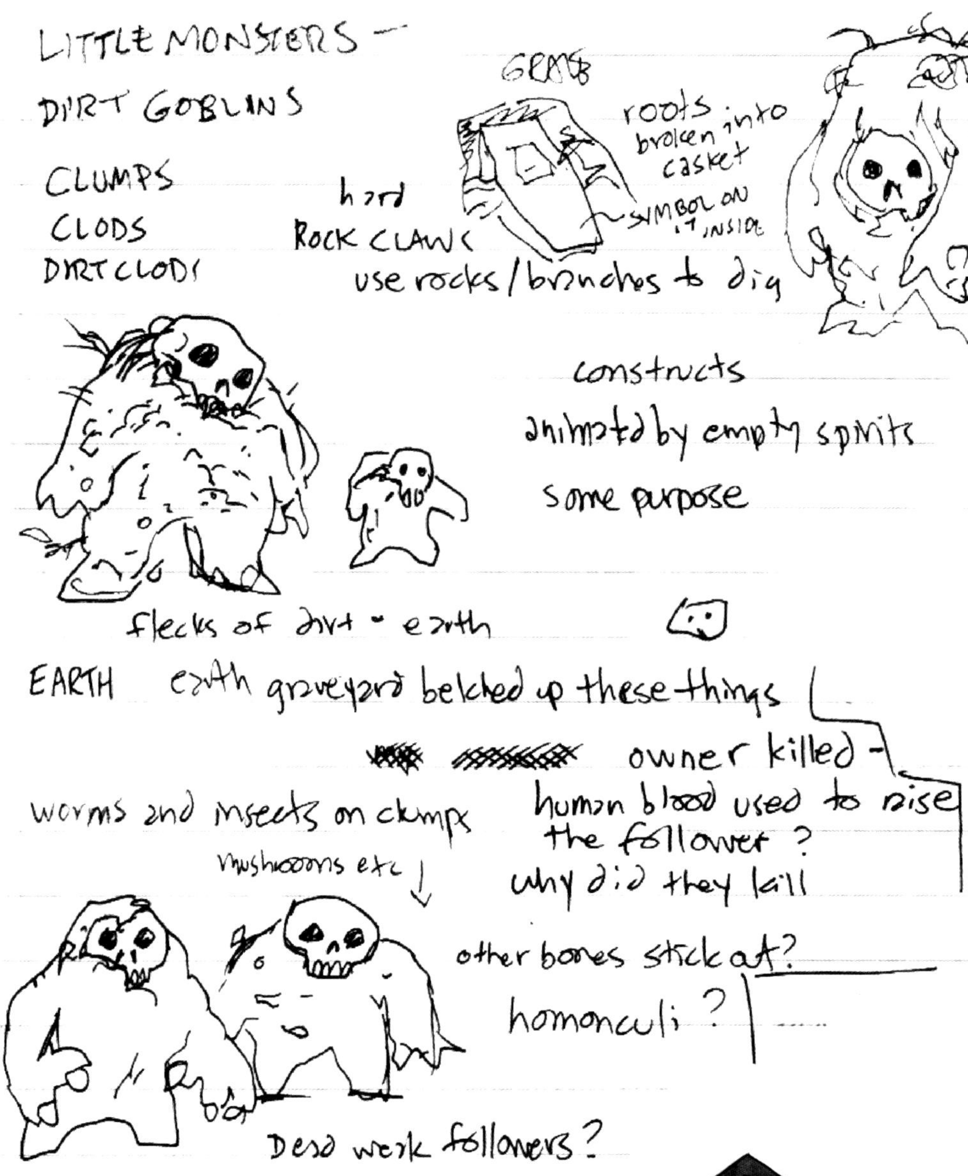
LITTLE MONSTERS —
DIRT GOBLINS
CLUMPS
CLODS
DIRT CLODS
GEMS
hard
ROCK CLAWS
roots broken into casket
SYMBOL ON IT, INSIDE
use rocks / branches to dig
constructs
animated by empty spirits
some purpose
flecks of dirt - earth
EARTH earth graveyard belched up these things
owner killed -
worms and insects on clumps
mushrooms etc
human blood used to rise the follower?
why did they kill
other bones stick out?
homonculi?
Dead work followers?

EVAN DORKIN: "Some very rough sketches of the skull golems I doodled in my notebook while plotting the fourth issue. Normally I don't send Jill any design ideas; if you look at her art, and look at mine, you'll understand why."

RIGHT: A little group shot I did of the gang that I ended up making into a print to give to fans at book signings. I think it conveys each character's personality pretty well. You get a sense of what each guy is all about.

FACING: *Hellboy* creator Mike Mignola graciously puts us over on the cover of the *Previews* catalog, she said using wrestling lingo . . .

FOLLOWING PAGE: An ad that ran in other Dark Horse books.

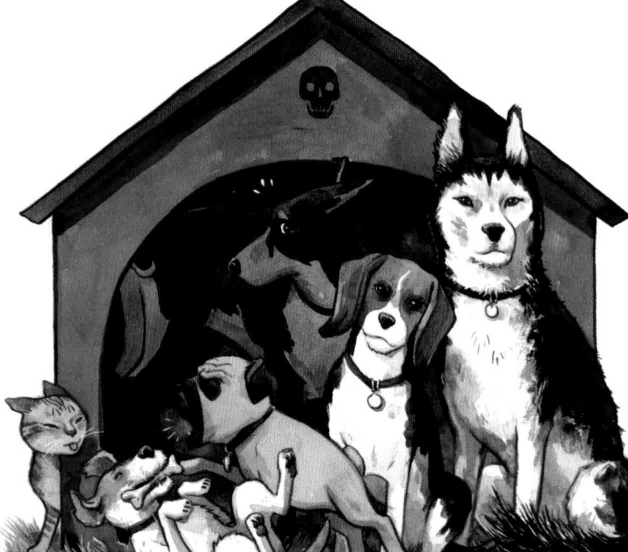

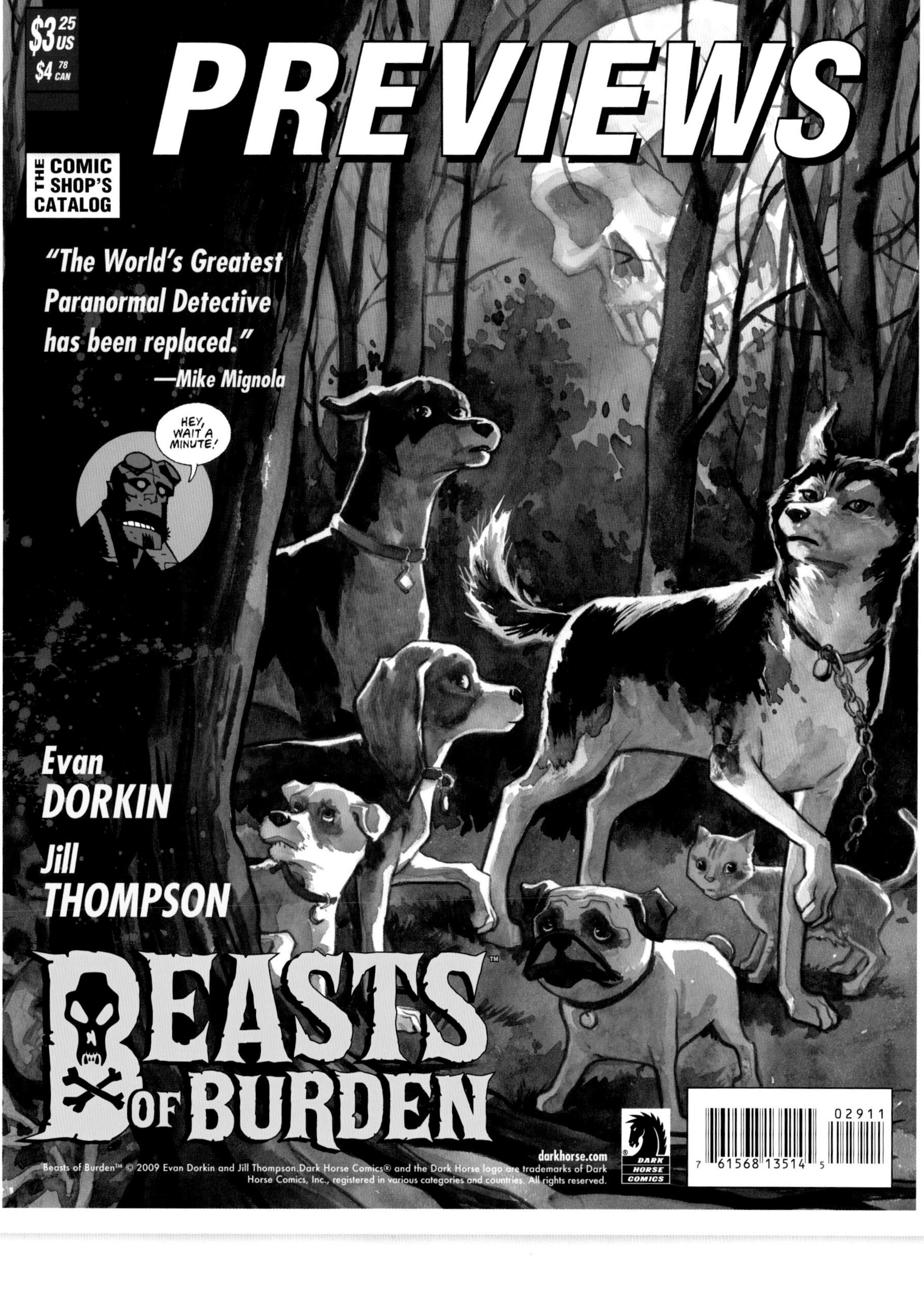
$3.25 US
$4.78 CAN
PREVIEWS
THE COMIC SHOP'S CATALOG
"The World's Greatest Paranormal Detective has been replaced."
—Mike Mignola
HEY, WAIT A MINUTE!
Evan DORKIN
Jill THOMPSON
BEASTS OF BURDEN™
darkhorse.com
Beasts of Burden™ © 2009 Evan Dorkin and Jill Thompson. Dark Horse Comics® and the Dark Horse logo are trademarks of Dark Horse Comics, Inc., registered in various categories and countries. All rights reserved.
DARK HORSE COMICS
02911
7 61568 13514 5

HAVE YOU SEEN THESE ANIMALS?

FIND THE *BEASTS OF BURDEN* AT YOUR LOCAL COMICS SHOP

 Discover the earliest *Beasts of Burden* stories for free at www.darkhorse.com/beastsofburden.

JILL THOMPSON   EVAN DORKIN

RECOMMENDED DARK HORSE READING

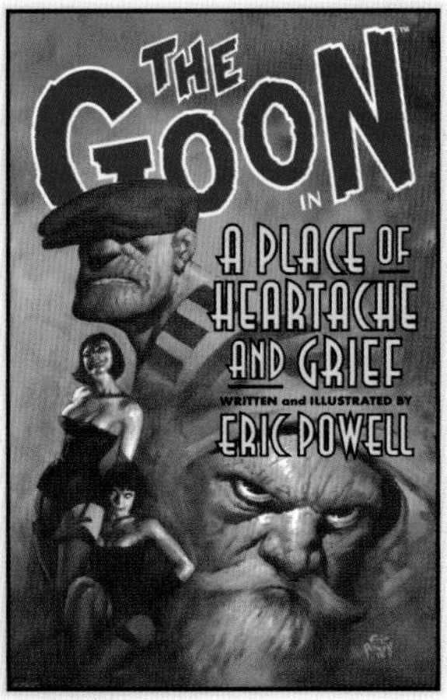
THE GOON
IN
A PLACE OF HEARTACHE AND GRIEF
WRITTEN and ILLUSTRATED BY
ERIC POWELL

THE GOON VOLUME 7: A PLACE OF HEARTACHE AND GRIEF

Eric Powell, Dave Stewart

An ancient curse spreads hatred, fear, and violence, drawing the most powerful and vile creatures to a town with only one hope for protection—the Goon. Even the Goon's lifelong deadly foe, the zombie priest, is running scared. But he has to remain to keep an eye on Goon and his violent sidekick, Franky. The death of one of the Goon's closest allies reveals an enemy thought long gone, returned to wreak havoc and destruction upon the Goon and those who stand by him. There's some funny stuff, too!

$15.99 ✠ ISBN 978-1-59582-311-3

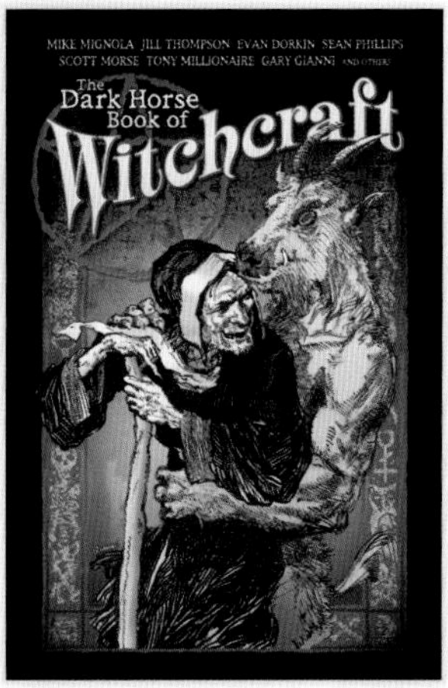
MIKE MIGNOLA JILL THOMPSON EVAN DORKIN SEAN PHILLIPS
SCOTT MORSE TONY MILLIONAIRE GARY GIANNI
The Dark Horse Book of Witchcraft

THE DARK HORSE BOOK OF WITCHCRAFT

Mike Mignola, Evan Dorkin, Jill Thompson, Scott Morse, and others

Dark Horse returns with another collection of bizarre tales by Eisner Award–winning artists Mike Mignola, Gary Gianni, Evan Dorkin, Jill Thompson, and Scott Morse. Mignola returns with another *Hellboy* story, and Thompson and Dorkin return to the characters in their stunning "Stray" story. Filled with other stellar comics offerings, including a classic witch tale by Clark Ashton Smith, and illustrated by cover artist Gianni, *The Dark Horse Book of Witchcraft* conjures up weird tales of horror and magic the likes of which one seldom sees in the comics medium.

$14.99 ✠ ISBN 978-1-59307-108-0

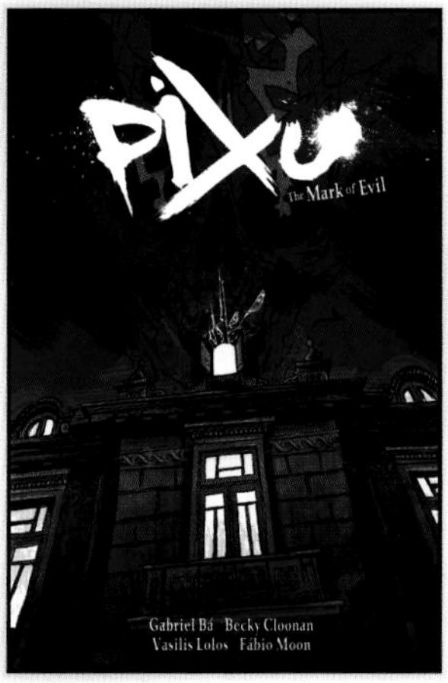
PIXU
The Mark of Evil
Gabriel Bá Becky Cloonan
Vasilis Lolos Fábio Moon

PIXU: THE MARK OF EVIL

Gabriel Bá, Becky Cloonan, Vasilis Lolos, and Fábio Moon

This gripping tale of urban horror follows the lives of five lonely tenants—strangers—whose lives become intertwined when they discover a dark mark scrawled on the walls of their building. The horror sprouts from a small seed and finds life as something other-worldly, damaged, full of love, hate, fear, and power. As the walls come alive, everyone is slowly driven mad—stripped of free will, leaving only confusion, chaos, and eventual death.

$17.99 ✠ ISBN 978-1-59582-340-3

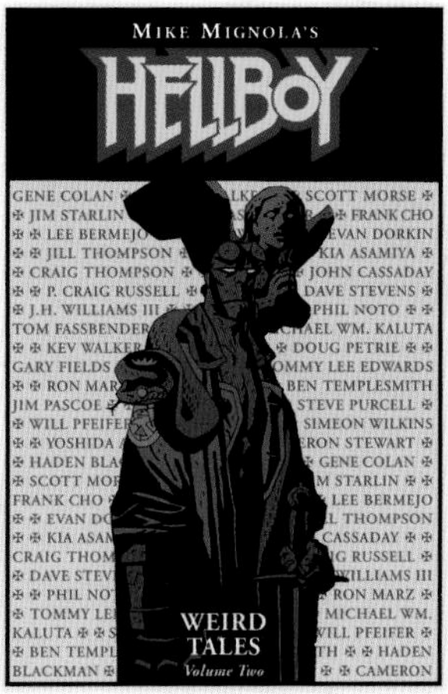
MIKE MIGNOLA'S
HELLBOY
WEIRD TALES
Volume Two

HELLBOY: WEIRD TALES VOLUME 2

Mike Mignola, Evan Dorkin, Jill Thompson, Gene Colan, and others

The second volume in the celebrated anthology series features more big names, including John Cassaday's complete *Lobster Johnson* serial. The award-winning *Hellboy* series has been lauded as much by other artists as it has by award ceremonies and fans. Dark Horse presents this lavish collection, complete with a behind-the-scenes look at the sketchbooks of the various artists. Collecting issues #5–#8 of the *Weird Tales* series.

$17.99 ✠ ISBN 978-1-56971-953-4

DARK HORSE BOOKS

AVAILABLE AT YOUR LOCAL COMICS SHOP OR BOOKSTORE! To find a comics shop in your area, call 1-888-266-4226.

For more information or to order direct, visit **darkhorse.com** or call 1-800-862-0052 Mon.–Fri. 9 AM to 5 PM Pacific Time. Prices and availability subject to change without notice.

RECOMMENDED DARK HORSE READING

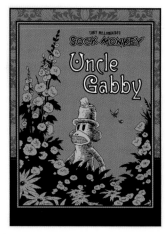

BUFFY THE VAMPIRE SLAYER SEASON EIGHT VOLUME 5: PREDATORS AND PREY

Joss Whedon, Jane Espenson, Georges Jeanty, and others

Buffy's world goes awry when former-classmate-turned-vampire Harmony Kendall lands her own reality TV show, *Harmony Bites*, bolstering bloodsucking fiends in the mainstream. Humans line up to have their blood consumed, and Slayers, through a series of missteps, misfortunes, and anti-Slayer propaganda driven by the mysterious Twilight, are forced into hiding.

$15.99 ✝ ISBN 978-1-59582-342-7

SOCK MONKEY: UNCLE GABBY

Tony Millionaire

The Sock Monkey returns home from the University where he has become a Master Poet dedicated to the Science of Un-naming Objects. He embarks on a journey of sentimentality as he rediscovers his childhood home. However, things are not as he remembers them, and he is subjected to an avalanche of heart-breaking realization.

$14.99 ✝ ISBN 978-1-59307-026-7

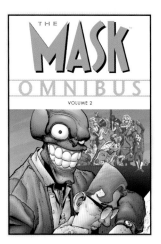

THE MASK OMNIBUS VOLUME 2

Evan Dorkin, Bob Fingerman, John Arcudi, and others

A mystical artifact from the ancient past, the relic known only as the Mask imbues its wearer with nearly limitless power . . . face-stretching, mallet-forming, clock-smashing power. Slap the Mask on your mug and nothing is beyond your reach—or the reach of a pie bomb—which is why every crook, grifter, creep, hood, miscreant, scofflaw, and other words in the thesaurus are out to get their mitts on it! Volume 2 collects over 350 maniacal story pages, never before collected, of the acclaimed comics series that inspired the megahit motion picture.

$24.99 ✝ ISBN 978-1-59307-937-6

MYSPACE DARK HORSE PRESENTS VOLUMES 1–5

Various

The online comics anthology *MySpace Dark Horse Presents* sees print in these four volumes—each collecting six issues of the ongoing series. Top talents from the industry like Mike Mignola, Joss Whedon, Eric Powell, Evan Dorkin (volume 2), Jill Thompson (volume 5), and many others bring new visions and stories. They are joined by some of the freshest new talent out there today—found on MySpace! These are premier comics unlike anything else! *myspace.com/darkhorsepresents*

$19.99 each ✝ Volume 1: ISBN 978-1-59307-998-7
Volume 2: ISBN 978-1-59582-248-2 ✝ Volume 3: ISBN 978-1-59582-327-4
Volume 4: ISBN 978-1-59582-405-9 ✝ Volume 5: ISBN 978-1-59582-570-4